GNVQ MEDIA: Communication and Production Advanced Textbook

Series Editor

Tricia Jenkins, Training and Education Manager, London Film and Video Development Agency, BTEC External Verifier and former Head of Media at Richmond upon Thames College

Contributors

Sam Bakhurst, freelance writer/researcher/projects manager, formerly GNVQ Coordinator at Quintin Kynaston School

Kathy Chater, freelance production researcher, consultant and trainer

Linda Hawkings, freelance marketing consultant and trainer

Paul Kaspar, Senior Lecturer in Media and Communications, Weymouth College

Jessica Pickard, freelance writer, former Head of Creative Studies Department, The College of North East London

John Turton, Edexcel BTEC's Lead Verifier for Media and Performing Arts

Helen Wright, freelance writer and media lecturer

Illustrator

Litza Jansz

Focal Press
An imprint of Butterworth-Heinemann
Linacre House, Jordan Hill, Oxford OX2 8DP
A division of Reed Educational and Professional Publishing Ltd

ℛ A member of the Reed Elsevier plc group

OXFORD   BOSTON   JOHANNESBURG
MELBOURNE   NEW DELHI   SINGAPORE

First Published 1997

British Library Cataloguing in Publication Data
A catalogue record for this book is available from the British Library

Library of Congress Cataloguing in Publication Data
A catalogue record for this book is available from the Library of
Congress

ISBN 0 240 51425 4

Typeset by Laser Words, Madras, India
Printed and bound in Great Britain

GNVQ
MEDIA:
Communication and Production
Advanced Textbook

Remember

To achieve a distinction grade, you need to have carried out a range of **complex tasks**. This means that you must be familiar with all of the activities associated with planning and producing a media artefact (a video, a radio programme, a magazine, etc.) and be able to **apply** them without expecting the teacher to break down all of the tasks for you. For this reason, the assignments in this book range from those which give you a reasonably detailed task guide through them, to simple scenarios which depend on you to draw up the necessary tasks.

Practise your skills

To become skilled and confident to an appropriate standard for assessment, **practise** is very important and you should take any opportunity you can to refine your skills and understanding of the processes associated with producing media products. This may be through presenting evidence for other units — for example, you might decide to present an article about film genre as though it were part of an established academic magazine, incorporating design and layout skills into your work.

CONTENTS

ACKNOWLEDGEMENTS

One of the central concerns we communicate to students undertaking the production of any media text is the importance of teamwork. This book has certainly been dependent on the collaboration not only of the writers and the illustrator, but also of friends, family and colleagues of myself, and of all of the contributors. Mark Hill embodies all three and provided ideas, informed critique and the necessary time and space in which to carry out the work.

The writers of this book had a difficult and time-strapped agenda. Without exception, every contributor has a more-than-full-time occupation within the media industries, within media education and sometimes both. Thank you for producing such quality material with such good spirit!

Thanks to the many teachers, colleagues and friends who helped to shape the thinking behind much of this book. In its various stages, discussions with Christine James at BFI Education, Jenny Grahame at the English and Media Centre, Joan Marshrons, formerly of Lambeth College and now of Wellbred Productions, Joan Leese of Video Engineering and Training and Graham de Smidt of Northbrook College have proved invaluable — and occasionally comforting! Andrea Robinson of LFVDA provided great support, especially when computer discs arrived scrambled and irretrievable. Maggie Ellis at the London Production Fund was enormously helpful in suggesting interviewees and finding interesting production material.

Special thanks are due to Eamonn McCabe and the staff of *The Guardian*; the staff of *Yes!* magazine; the staff of *More* magazine and Steve Taylor, former Head of Promotion at Virgin Radio.

Thanks are due to all those who provided illustrations for the book — picture credits are given for each figure, but in the case of Figure 3.2 we were unable to trace the copyright holder of the graphic novel *Malcolm X The Angriest Man in America* — and we would welcome contact details for Wayne Massop.

Special thanks are also due to Litza Jansz, whose witty cartoons greatly enhance the book.

Last, but not least, I would like to thank Steve McIntyre at the London Film and Video Development Agency for his support, encouragement and patience throughout the entire process.

Tricia Jenkins

For Mark, Jack and Emmie

INTRODUCTION

Media studies is the fastest-growing area in the curriculum. You might have a range of reasons for wanting to study the media and to learn the various skills required to produce a magazine, a video tape, a radio item or a CD-ROM. If you have chosen a GNVQ programme, the chances are that you see yourselves either working in the media, or using media skills in a working environment.

You are doubtless aware of the current debates concerning whether media courses will make you fit for jobs in the media. You are probably also aware of the countless inconsistencies and contradictions that surround the question of progression from a media course into work — for instance, the claims for 'a growing industry' against the backdrop of fewer long-term employment possibilities. As you will see in Unit 8, current and future models of work, particularly in the film and television worlds, are based on a freelance workforce in a fragmented industry of many small production companies. This means that it is unlikely that you can expect to leave college clutching your qualification and walk into a job. Indeed, research shows that many jobs in the media are 'graduate entry', so it is very likely that you will want to look towards higher education as your progression from the GNVQ.

Of course, you may decide to put your skills into use into other kinds of working environment — for instance, you might work in a video or press relations department of a large organisation which has nothing whatsoever to do with the media. As the world of multi-media explodes, you will find that the many skills you learn through studying on a GNVQ Media: Communication and Production programme can be combined through a computer platform to produce texts which combine words, images, sounds, moving images and graphics: you may even already have the technology at your school or college to generate CD-ROMs. The possibilities are endless, but the ways in which you might find jobs are not as straightforward as with industries which have clear progression routes between qualifications and employment.

That, in a sense, is one of the ways in which a GNVQ programme can help to prepare you for working in this kind of environment: you will need to build up your individual portfolio, to decide which aspects on the programme interests you and the aspects for which you show ability, and work to building your portfolio to demonstrate your commitment, interest and skill. It places much more responsibility on you than on your teacher. The 'no guarantees' in a sense exactly mirrors the world of work within these industries: you have to *want* to work in the media and want it bad. You will be unlikely to be nurtured — you're on your own to prove what you can do. You need to be self-sufficient, persistent, and yet someone who can adapt to being a good team player.

This book has been designed as a textbook to accompany the Advanced GNVQ in Media: Communication and Production. For that reason, the different sections of the book are presented in the order of the qualification. This does not mean that you necessarily have to use the book in that order. All of the units work together: theory and practice are cross-referred throughout and the techniques presented in every unit can be used in combination with other units. For instance, if you are asked to investigate current debates around censorship for work in Unit 8, there is nothing to stop you deciding to present that debate as a radio programme, an article, a video debate. That means that you research the topic, but keep practising your skills in the various media.

You will notice that in the evidence indicators in the qualification, a set number of pieces of work are required — usually no more than 2 for each unit. What you need to remember is that this does not mean two pieces of work that you have done altogether, but two pieces that will demonstrate that you can *meet the standards* identified in the unit: this should mean that you have had a fair amount of practice before you are assessed.

In this book we have flagged some of the possible cross-references between units. There will be more than we have identified. We have tried to mix 'hard fact' to help you meet the requirements of the qualification with interesting snippets, case studies, interviews, observations, with practical tasks which you can use in the building of your portfolios. We have cross-referenced throughout, so if you dip into the book and you need to be aware of information in another section, you can be directed there. We have used industry practitioners as contributors and as readers of this book before we went to press. This means that, within the constraints of a GNVQ programme, the information and guidance on practice in the book is as close to industry practice as possible. We have also endeavoured to make sure that the theory chapters both have a relationship to industry practices, and are on the same level as you might find on an A Level course.

The key for not only this programme, but for many media programmes is the degree to which theory and practice are integrated, the degree to which one is not the poor relation of the other. That is why that, despite the fact that we have organised this book to match with the structures of the GNVQ programme, the content will be of value to any student studying media — practice or theory. We hope you enjoy this book and find it useful in supporting your studies.

1 INVESTIGATING THE CONTENT OF MEDIA PRODUCTS

The GNVQ qualification in Media: Communication & Production has been influenced by both the industry and academics and media critics, whose job it is to consider the media from a more abstract and often more evaluative standpoint.

GNVQs nationally, and in all subjects, are specifically intended to bring these two perspectives together, and you will soon realise that each has its own strengths to offer. The academic approach can be very challenging and thought provoking, asking difficult questions about the way the media relates to our society like:

- What effects do the media have?
- How do people relate to them?
- Are they fair and accurate?
- How do they make meaning for us?

The industrial approach poses more nitty gritty, practical questions like:

- How are media products made?
- Who makes them?
- How are they distributed?
- How are they bought and sold?

Both aspects are necessary. In studying English, for example, we are asked both to write creatively ourselves *and* to analyse the work of other authors. In one activity, we take on the role of producer and originator, in the other, the role of critic and evaluator. Both are valid activities but they require different types of skill.

Unit 1 is, on the whole, theoretical and should therefore provide a useful context for the other units, introducing some of the discipline's key concepts like 'representation', 'genre', 'textual analysis', 'audience' and 'narrative'. You will also find that you can link these ideas to practical projects.

1.1 ANALYSE MEDIA TEXTS

'Critical' in Media Studies means evaluative, not necessarily negative.

This first part of the unit is about analysing and developing a critical language to describe what the media offers to us — its 'products'.

An underlying assumption which emerges is that analysing a piece of media can be compared to analysing a piece of literature. We can take a photo, a TV programme or an article and treat it as a 'text' that can be analysed as intently as you would a poem.

What is a 'reading'?

'Reading', for the media student, is not an activity restricted to written texts alone. The term is not one that has been selected casually. It derives from a particular school of thought and, in the comparison it implies between reading a book and 'reading' a piece of media (an advert, a pop song, etc.), it suggests certain things about the relationship between the object (the piece of media) and its consumer.

Fig 1.1 It is hard to imagine the term 'couch potato' being levelled at an avid reader of hardbacks, even though he or she may be as physically inactive as a soap-opera addict

Reading is an active process

There is a tendency in our culture to see reading a book as a reputable activity, improving the mind and so on, and to regard watching TV, for example, as a lazy form of relaxation (Fig 1.1). The term 'reading' tends to level out the value attributed to these two activities by suggesting that in both cases the mind can be positively engaged. (This is not to say that there are no examples of bad TV, just as you can find examples of bad books.)

Reading any text you are actively engaged in seeking out meanings and depending on a degree of learned skill. Just as you need to be literate to read words and sentences, so you need to be 'media literate' to make sense of the messages contained in comics, films, news broadcasts, etc. However, while we may remember our struggles to become *word* literate — reading tests at school, for example — we become media literate in a much less self-conscious way through exposure from an early age to the many media forms which surround us.

TASK

The following tasks are designed to encourage thought about the importance of media to members of our society.

■ In a classroom discussion, decide on all the activities that might be defined as reading the media, e.g., reading a newspaper, watching TV, glancing at an advert, seeing a poster from the bus. Make a list and use this as a basis for the following tasks.

■ Work out how many hours on average per week your class spends in contact with the media. What is the range?

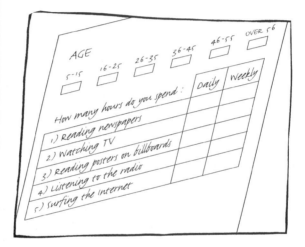

Fig 1.2 Example of a questionnaire layout

■ Design a questionnaire (Fig 1.2) that will make it easy to interview ten people each on the same topic. You will need also to record their ages. Remember, they will need a lot of prompting to remember all the media they consume.

■ Using your results, calculate the average weekly consumption time for different age groups on different types of media activity.

■ Write an individual report which specifies what you were trying to find out, why, your results and your interpretation of your results.

■ Present your findings using the following structure:

Introduction Describe what you were trying to find out, and the methodology.
Findings Describe the outcomes of the research in writing, and illustrate using graphs or pie charts as appropriate.
Conclusions Sum up the results to see how many hours of different reading activities are undertaken on average.

Media have their own languages and grammars

These terms are explained in more detail later (p. 13).

The term 'reading' implies an analogy (a sustained comparison) between a written text and a produced media product. This is an analogy that some media theorists, particularly those from a **semiotic** or **structuralist** background would like to press home.

THESE theorists would argue that, like our language, our mass media are structured by a 'hidden' grammar or set of rules. For example, you would never say: 'I did that tomorrow.' The words just do not go together, they break the rules of tense and time. In the same way, we would find it peculiar to be presented with a newspaper where the headlines were in smaller type than the stories. We expect news-readers to sit down as they speak and be replaced on screen sporadically by images, and we expect weather forecasters to stand up and point to pictures behind them. (Why the difference?) We also accept that in a romantic film, a conversation between two people may be accompanied by a sudden swelling of violins, even though this does not happen in real life, and it would be 'wrong' to have an action replay in the middle of *EastEnders*, however crucial a scene it may be. This is because established conventions are being broken.

Tools for textual analysis

Analytical concepts: these are ideas that help us to get to grips with a particular topic or subject area. For example, 'social class' is a concept which helps sociologists understand society, 'plot' is a concept that helps English students analyse a novel. Each subject area has its own specific analytical concepts, and Media Studies is no exception. Think of them as useful tools for media analysis.

Media Studies as a discipline is less than 25 years old, but none the less in its brief life it has evolved its own set of **analytical concepts** and theoretical assumptions as well as borrowing and customising ideas drawn from other disciplines like sociology and English literature. These concepts, like many ideas in the arts and social science subjects, are not set in concrete. They are there both to focus your attention on particular aspects of the object under review and also to give you a language in which to communicate your observations.

The terms and concepts outlined below are drawn mainly from one approach to Media Studies — the **semiotic** approach — which is particularly helpful in providing methods for analysis.

Reading a media text

In Media Studies, 'a text' might be a whole TV series from beginning to end, it might be a half-page advert or one scene in a radio play. The word 'text' tells you more about the way you intend to study the piece of media than the object itself. It means you are going to look at it in depth, break it down into its parts and see how it works as a piece of communication, carry out a 'textual analysis'.

Remember: readings are not necessarily 'correct': they are interpretations with which you may agree or disagree.

In order to illustrate some of the ideas that follow on from here, here is a sample reading, taking as the text the Microsoft™ ad, 'Is this software brilliant?' This advertisement was produced by the London-based advertising agency EURO RSCG WNEK GOSPER. (Fig 1.3)

Fig 1.3   Microsoft advertising campaign poster courtesy of EURO RSCG, WNEK GOSPER

Rastafari is a religion originating in/expressing Christianity which forbids the cutting of hair and is the inspiration for a lot of reggae music.

It should not be surprising to see black models in adverts in a multi-ethnic society like the UK, but none the less it still is fairly unusual outside fashion, sports or music shots. Media critics and organisations like the Commission for Racial Equality have commented on this absence.

Red, green and gold are the colours of the Ethiopian flag and often worn by Afro-Caribbeans who want to emphasise their ethnic roots and connections with Africa, and especially by Rastafarians for whom Ethiopia has a special place in their religion.

Previous cultural knowledge is important for how we read media texts. We use the knowledge and experience we have gained during our upbringing within a particular culture to make sense of all our subsequent experience, including that with the media.

CASE STUDY
A sample reading: *The Happy Child* (Microsoft ad)

The first striking thing about the advert is its boldness. It comes at you BIG. It is also very bold in its colours (unfortunately unreproducible here). The background is a very solid block of deep pink/red and the lettering on the left of the child's head is in a pale yellow and that on the right is in shiny green and gold. The block of copy — written advertising text — on the right is in black.

The child's locks flying across the page highlight the sense of vivacity, movement and excitement. The picture has been cropped wide, in other words it has had its edges cut off away from the boy's head so you can see almost all his hair. The effect is almost to suggest he is energised to the point where his hair is standing on end. (I see this child as a boy — do you?)

The sense of the child's excitement is underlined by what happens to the lettering that almost literally appears to be passing through his mind: 'Is this software brilliant' ('brilliant' is quite a childlike word) 'or is it just my imagination?' At this latter point, the lettering becomes quite literally brilliant — shining as it picks up the light and taking on a deep chunky three-dimensional effect. The lettering also changes colour, from pale yellow into vivid green and gold, and becomes less like written text and more like a series of solid objects. The question mark is nearest to us. This is not the only question that the copy asks in this advertisement, nor is it unusual for adverts to use questions as a way of drawing the viewer in.

The child is black, which is unusual in mainstream ads, and he also has Rastafarian locks.

This child is good-looking and neatly, casually dressed. His expression suggests the kind of intelligent, excited engagement that the parent of any 'bored kid' would find gratifying. Good software, his expression suggests, can engage childrens' interest and reintroduce a joy in learning and discovering for yourself. The change in the lettering as it appears to pass through his mind/imagination emphasises this sense of engagement. It is as if the letters themselves have moved from the abstraction of flat representational writing into something more solid and real — the 'awesome imagination' described in the (written) text of the advert attaches itself both to the software and to the power of a child's mind to convert the abstract into the alive and kicking. The letters now look as if you could pick them up one by one. They have developed a tactile quality, like the blocks smaller children use to learn how to spell. So all in all, the impression so far from this advert is of a cheerful child's world, but one which is designed mainly to appeal to adults/parents — who are, of course, the likely potential purchasers.

The bulk of the written copy in the ad seems at first quite surprising. Someone is speaking ('I'd like to thank') but it doesn't sound like the voice of the child depicted. There is a spoof on 'smarminess' — thanking everyone in sight — and the reference to 'luvviedom' — which evokes an echo of pretentious Oscar winners' speeches. This mildly satirical take on Hollywood is more likely to be accessible to parents than to children of the model's age.

The advert is persuasive, both visually through the layout and in the copy, convincing us that the software can work to make ideas seen in the 'mind's eye' of a child come alive. The ad has succeeded in evoking the child's world but within a mode of address that appears to be designed for adults.

connotation: what meanings are suggested by the text. Connotative meanings are more abstract, in that the 'reader' will interpret meaning subjectively.
denotation: what the text (i.e. image, page, shot etc.) actually shows

Media texts are made up of signifying elements

signifying elements: include not just the content of the photo or copy, but also the way in which that content is presented (e.g. writing style, lighting camera angle etc)

A piece of media can be broken down into the parts (elements) which signify (mean something to the audience). With *The Happy Child* advert, for example, we picked out the **signifying elements** of face, hair, expression, layout, lighting, framing, cropping, clothes, writing style, mode of verbal address, etc.

Elements in association

Elements in a text do not just signify alone, they signify in relation to each other (see Fig 1.4). An object that means one thing in one context can mean something quite different when it is transposed into a new context because it is put into a new relationship with its surrounding elements.

It is not unusual, for example, for words and images to lead us in one direction, only to pull us back in another through contradicting our first thoughts. This was the kind of tease structure of a particular TV ad, which aimed to encourage young people to give up smoking. In a sociable-looking pub, an attractive young woman is seen in close-up, drawing lasciviously on a cigarette. The camera lingers on her lips in a shot that would conventionally mean 'sexy'. Nearby two young men are watching. One asks the other if he 'fancies' the girl. 'No,' his friend replies, 'it would be like kissing an ashtray.' In this advert, a 'first impression' reading is set up in your mind by using standard codes (very recognisable patterns). Then these expectations are undermined by another element in the advert. Something that seemed on the surface to be attractive (the young woman) turned out to be 'bad'. The **preferred reading** — the one most obviously suggested by the text — was originally that the girl was sexy, but the latter part of the text offers a different new

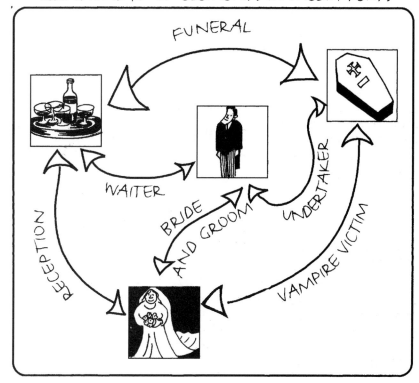

THE PRODUCTION OF MEANING BY THE RELATIONSHIP OF ELEMENTS IN MEDIA TEXTS

Fig 1.4 Four elements are represented here: a man in a formal suit, a bride, a coffin, and a tray of drinks. If you link the man with the bride, the meaning produced is 'bride and groom'. If you link the man with the drinks, however, you read 'waiter', or with the coffin 'undertaker'. The bride linked with the coffin, however, suggests the conventions of the horror genre, so she can be read as 'vampire victim'

preferred reading which is **oppositional** to the first and suggests the girl would smell of smoke.

Sometimes the same contradictory technique will be used, only the other way round — something that is bad is demonstrated to be good. It is worth thinking why advertisers often adopt 'paradox' (using apparently contradictory meanings) in their sales strategy.

TASK

See if you can find an advertisement that seems to work in a similar paradoxical way to those described above. In about a page, explain how it makes its appeal. You may find it easier to make your points if you cut out particular elements of the advertisement to discuss separately, before analysing the whole effect. If you do this you will need to photocopy the whole advertisement first.

It is perhaps surprising we are not offended by paradox advertising. But advertising is part of our culture. Indeed, a well-designed advert can offer one of life's little pleasures. We enjoy trying to solve the puzzles and enigmas it creates. That is one reason why advertising copy is so fond of questions and question

Fig 1.5   Objects take on new meanings in a new context Photomontage by Peter Kennard, "Haywain with Cruise Missiles" (1980), from the Greater London Council Peace Poster portfolio (based on Constable's "Haywain")

marks. Once we have started to turn our thoughts to the questions they provoke, however momentarily, then the advert has started to work because we are also applying our minds to the product being advertised.

Anchorage

The term '**anchorage**' to describe the signifying relationship between elements was first coined by the French theorist **Roland Barthes**. It is a clever analogy: if he had said that meaning was 'tied down' or 'nailed down', we would have a much more static idea about how the process worked. But an anchor at sea works by allowing a range of movement as the sea rolls and so, in using this term, Barthes was implying a certain fluidity in interpreting '**signs**' as he called (roughly) what we have called 'elements'. In media texts, an anchor can limit the range of possible interpretations but meaning is too subtle and too interactively produced between reader and text to be nailed into one place.

Note. Roland Barthes was interested in the relationship between the media and other aspects of society. Much of his theoretical work was an attempt to define the link between texts, signifying processes and the ideas that are circulating in society at a given time. He believed the media to be powerful contributors to what he called our myths '(a society's ideology). See page 15 for more on Barthes.

Polysemy: open to a number of potential meanings, particularly true of images

Barthes used the term 'anchor' to describe the relationship between words and image. In his opinion, the words provided the anchor to limit the '**polysemy**' of the text.

The power of the anchor to shape our responses should not be underestimated. It can tell us whether to view a particular event as the work of 'freedom fighters' or 'rioters'. Graffiti writers sometimes play with this power: 'If this car was a lady, she'd get her bottom pinched,' ran the caption under a billboard poster under the image of a gleaming new hatchback. Someone had added in white paint: 'If this lady was a car, she'd run you down.'

There is no reason why the term 'anchorage' should be restricted to describing the functions of words: Images can work with other images just as powerfully. In films, the music often tells you what to think and feel about what you are seeing. The film *Jaws*, for example, would have been virtually incomprehensible without the pounding music to tell you the shark was nearby, the rhythm and volume telling you just how near. The music, 'anchored' the narrative so we knew what was happening under the waves.

TASK 1

In small groups, cut out newspaper articles and paste them on to white paper. Keep the original caption. Exchange your articles with another group and then invent new, but plausible headlines for the images. Compare the new headlines with the original.

TASK 2

Collect some clips of video which include sound effects and music. Play the videos to your group with the sound turned right down and ask them to describe the sound-track. How accurate are they in their predictions? Play back the tapes, this time with sound. What does the sound add or change to the interpretation of the visual text?

Note: This experiment works best with clips where there is not too much dialogue, for example, the establishing on opening scenes of some films.

TASK 3

Reverse the experiment with some clips and play just the sound (if necessary, the monitor can be turned to face the wall). Ask the group to predict the images they will see. How accurate were they compared to Task 2?

Note: This experiment is also worth doing with a pop video where the visuals are often tied to the sound in a less obvious (Barthes would say less 'motivated') way.

TASK 4

Tasks 1—3 were all experiments in how meaning is produced. Write up all three experiments using the following terms: elements, text, visual, audio, anchor (anchorage). Using examples from your experiments, draw conclusions from your results about how meaning is made.

TASK 5

Look out for and copy down examples of graffiti where the graffitiists appear to have used the principles of (re)anchorage.

TASK 6

Write an essay illustrated by pieces of media (and/or your experiment results) which explains the following statement: 'media texts signify through the relationship between their elements.'

Codes

Definition

A **code** is a system of special symbols for transmitting messages. The word 'code' can be used in a number of different contexts like 'Morse code', 'dress code', but in Media Studies we are interested in representational codes — the ones which work to represent our world through the mass media.

Codes exist by agreement. We know in a film, for example, that if we see a shot of someone looking, then the next shot is likely to indicate what they are looking at, even though they are no longer visible. We know this because this particular piece of (narrative) coding is an accepted convention of film. We can *decode* it without stopping to think.

In Morse code, the dots and dashes on their own mean nothing, but when you combine them in particular patterns, they can spell out words and whole sentences. This is a useful comparison for the way media codes work. To make sense, a code relies on two things.

- The relationships between different elements of the text.
- Previous knowledge and experience in decoding.

To help with media analysis, these elements can be described in terms of the different codes at work in them. The **technical code** refers to the effects which are introduced (usually deliberately) during the technical process of production such as lighting, camera angle, focus, cropping, etc. The **written code** refers to the writing style as well (often) as the visual style of the lettering in graphics, captions, typefaces. We can also talk about **cultural codes**. For example, the fact that a boy is wearing jeans, trainers and a loose checked shirt suggests a kind of casualness but also a hint of 'street-wise' kid.

It is also important to grasp that, although we have subdivided codes here into different types, in any one media text, these codes are likely to be working together. For example, the technical code of soft lighting, with the cultural code of holding hands, the non-verbal codes of lingering looks and the aesthetic codes in soft violin music, all work together to suggest the genre of (film/TV) romance. As media *consumers*, we are interested in the whole effect; as media *analysts* we want to focus more scientifically on the parts.

Textual analysis: not the only way

There are other approaches to Media Studies which put less emphasis on the activity of textual analysis. Some media theorists think we should spend more time thinking about who makes the media and how it is made. Others are more concerned about their social **effects** on the audience's attitudes and behaviour. For example, they might ask the question: should there be limits on what children are allowed to watch and hear? Or, do violent videos lead to a more violent society? These are not questions that can be answered just by looking carefully at the content of films, newspapers, radio, advertisements. They would need to be studied in a more sociological or psychological way.

Although textual analysis is the dominant activity in this unit, there are two points worth making. First it could be rather limiting to restrict enquiry solely to textual analysis: that is why in the GNVQ, there are whole units dedicated to issues like 'audience' and 'industry' where the spotlight is moved away from analysing media texts.

Note: these ideas are not fixed — it is always worth asking 'where do these ideas come from and whose interests do they serve?'

Secondly, it is worth noting that, like all academic disciplines, the practice of textual analysis has its own background and history. It is strongly linked with two schools of thought: and **semiotics structuralism**.

Semiotics and structuralism

'**Semiotic analysis**' means analysing what something *means* and how it makes that meaning.

Semiotics is a fairly recent school of thought which came to prominence in the 1960s and 1970s. A 'typical' **semiotic analysis** would look in detail at the constituent parts of the text and how they work together to 'signify'. It is typical of semiotics that the objects being analysed in such fine detail should be a part of everyday life: an advert. This was one of the achievements of semiotics as an approach. It offered a method, a way of looking at things, that did not need to distinguish between 'high' and 'mass culture'. It was equally at home analysing an opera or a pop song. Before the 1960s, you could find serious, thoughtful analyses of how,

Fig 1.6 Biff cartoon courtesy of Biff Products

for example, a Shakespeare play was structured or how narrative worked in a classic novel but you would be unlikely to find a similar approach to the cover of a magazine or an article on cookery. (Roland Barthes has a study of both of these.) Traditionally analysis of our cultural products began with the question: what does it mean and how good is it (as art, as writing, etc.)? Semiotic analysis begins with the question: what does it mean and *how* is it doing it?

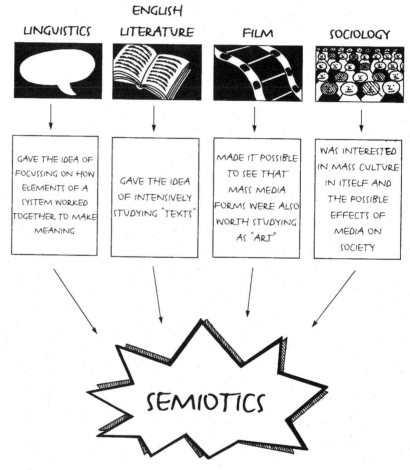

Fig 1.7 Semiotics family tree
Media Studies, which developed in the 1960s and 1970s, was largely based on two parent areas: structural linguistics, which examines the way parts of language fit together to make meaning provided a model and a method from which to work. English literature provided concepts such as characterisation, narrative and so on. Concepts were also borrowed from the then new subject of film studies and sociology

The origins of semiotics

Why, you may ask, use the term signify and signification if you can also always just say 'meaning'? The term 'signification', emphasises that all the time the text is working to make its effects: it makes you think about the process. The word 'meaning' puts less emphasis on the process and more on the results. A Semiotics approch would argue that both issues are equally important.

Definition

Popular and mass culture: popular culture refers to those forms and patterns in behaviour, taste, media use, dress and life-style which apply to a large percentage of the population. So soap operas, football, tabloid newspapers and pop music are part of popular culture whereas opera, classical music, croquet and most poetry are not. It is clear just from this rather crude definition that there can be value judgements implied here between 'good', artistic, upper-middle-class culture (high culture) and the 'bad' taste of the masses (popular culture). The point being made here is that semiotics, because of its particular approach, was able to avoid these pitfalls of value judgement. However, the debate about the validity of the distinction between the two kinds of culture goes on. It was influential, for example, in deciding the content of the national curriculum.

Note: Many students are drawn to Media Studies because they are interested in these other relationships. For example, they want to look at whether our media represent issues and groups in society fairly. This takes us outside the study of the text itself and into the question of **representation**. Others might be interested in the social effects of the media, for instance, do violent films increase real violence in society? These questions take us outside the text into questions about **audience**.

Problems with semiotics

Semiotics was a radical approach because it was new and it over-turned a number of traditional assumptions about what was worth studying. However it suffered from two serious weaknesses:

■ It was not very good for looking at the relationships between texts and the real world. Suppose you wanted to find out if a news report represented an event accurately, all the sophistica-tions of textual analysis could not prove the case one way or the other. Only if you could compare the news text to the real event could you come up with an answer (and this is notoriously diffi-cult since which version of the real event do you trust?). These points are discussed in depth later, but certainly semiotics as a discipline is not strong on answering these kinds of questions.

■ For similar reasons it was not very good at looking at the rela-tionship between texts and their audiences. If you look at the reading of *The Happy Child* ad, for example, the implication was that the meaning of the advert lay in the image and copy itself. In fact the meaning of that ad may depend as forcefully on *who* is doing the reading. A non-parent, for example, might engage with the text in a very different ways from a parent.

Readings and Society — a Famous Barthesian Analysis

The following analysis of a magazine advertisement for a range of Italian pasta products, demonstrates Barthes' 'two level' approach.

At the end of this section, there is a number of tasks which ask you to carry out a similar kind of two-level analysis. However, as you carry out these tasks you will undoubtedly find that the two levels of analysis are harder to keep apart than you would suspect. What usually happens is that Level two keeps sliding into Level one! It is hard, if not impossible, to perceive media texts, or indeed any aspect of life, without bringing in our associations and previous ideas with us. Barthes and other theorists recognise that the idea of denotation and connotation should not be taken too literally — they are just methods for being more searching in our analyses. Like the concepts introduced earlier they provide techniques or 'tools' for the student of media.

CASE STUDY
The Panzani Advertisement

In the image, there is a packet of pasta, a tin of pasta sauce, fresh tomatoes, Parmesan cheese, onions and peppers. All these objects appear to be tumbling out of a string bag and on to a kitchen table. The colours of the produce are mainly green and white, and the table is red. Barthes' analysis of the image then proceeds along two levels. First he describes in considerable detail what the ad *shows* and then he considers what the advert *suggests*. This distinction between **depictions** and **implications** is an important one for media theory so it will be pursued in some detail both here and in later units.

Barthes analysis was written in 1964 so both it and the advert it refers to are now rather old. However, it is a famous essay still well worth studying because it introduced a certain way of looking at texts, through the concepts of **denotation** and **connotation** which was both influential and controversial.

(the controversy angle is taken up in Unit 6).

He begins by looking at the brand name of the product, Panzani. This name, he says, fulfils two functions. First it simply tells you (it **denotes**) the name of the company. Secondly, however, because of its sound and associations, it also suggests (it **connotes**) the impression of Italy, or some sort of intrinsic 'Italianness'. Panzani is, in fact, a Paris-based, French company and this pasta is advertised and sold in France. For French people, Barthes argues, the name is much more likely to denote 'Italianness' than for Italians for whom this name would have no 'foreign' associations. He concludes that the message (the words) are therefore working on two levels:

"The linguistic message is thus twofold: denotational and connotational."

He continues his reading of the picture itself along the same lines. The scene in the pasta ad, he says, implies that someone has just returned from the market (has come in from outdoors) where he or she has bought fresh vegetables and this quality of freshness is also intended to transfer itself to the pre-packaged products. The can of sauce is literally surrounded by fresh ingredients suggesting that the shopper (despite having bought pre-packaged sauce) has shopped around rather than stocked up at the supermarket. However, because the goods are on the kitchen table, there is also the suggestion of indoors, of domesticity and the preparation of meals. So the image tells a story: the 'before' of the shopping, the 'after' of the meal all implied by the 'now' of the image. He also notes that the colours evoke the colours of the Italian flag (green, white and red) and hence reinforce the product's origins. As well as this, he suggests the composition of the shots and the lighting effects combine to produce the aesthetic qualities (the artistic, beautiful feel) of a still-life oil painting where it is not at all unusual to have fruit, vegetables, etc., tumbling beautifully out of baskets. In using this effect, Barthes argues, the image is engaging our 'heavily cultural' previous knowledge. In this (very summarised and simplified) analysis we can see that meaning is operating at two levels.

Fig 1.8 Roland Barthes, *Image-Music-Text*. Essays selected and translated by Stephen Heath (1977), Fontana. Essay entitled 'Rhetoric of the image'

| Level one | what is *shown* in the ad | can, packet of pasta, table, etc. |
| Level two | what is *suggested* in ad | freshness, 'Italianness', domesticity, before and after, classiness, artiness |

Denotation and connotation: a way out of the box?

The ideas of denotation and connotation are useful in another way because they begin to get us out of the closed 'box' created by using textual analysis alone. If the text can connote meanings, then, by definition, there must be some activity going on outside the text. The idea of connotation implies that, as readers of media, we must be bringing our prior cultural knowledge into the frame in order to create these secondary meanings (of freshness, 'Italianness', etc.) because, as we have seen, they are not there literally denoted in the text.

EVIDENCE COLLECTION POINT

Analyse the image below in two separate ways. First describe what is **denoted** in the image (being careful to avoid any of your own associations, stick to what you can see). Then consider what is **connoted:** what qualities, ideas, feelings, sensations are suggested by the image. During your analysis try to apply the following concepts: codes (technical, cultural), anchorage, the relationship between elements (in this case in the image), previous cultural knowledge.

Fig 1.9 Photographer: Peter Osborne

1.2 INVESTIGATE REPRESENTATION IN THE MEDIA

Apocryphal: of doubtful authenticity

There is a story, possibly **apocryphal**, which is told among Media Studies teachers, about a radical approach taken by a young teacher who was introducing the subject to children at primary school.

> 'What's this?' he asked, holding up a painting of a horse.
> 'A horse,' the children all shouted.
> 'No.' Long pause.
> 'A horse in a field?' asks one child.
> 'No.' Longer pause.
> 'A white horse in a field? ... A white horse in a green field?'
> 'No.'
> By now, the children were becoming frustrated and shouting out more and more answers. 'A farm horse?' 'A big horse in a field?' 'The farmer's horse?'
> 'No. No. No'.
> 'Is it', asked one child who hadn't spoken yet, 'a *picture* of a horse?'

Harsh though the teaching method might seem, this child had now hit upon the idea the teacher was trying to communicate — the principle of representation. She had grasped the difference between the real live animal running around in a field and the frozen after-image shown in the painting. This distinction between reality and its 'representation' provides the underlying theme for Element 1.2. It is probably the most important concept to grasp in media theory: that our media, by definition, cannot present reality to us, they can only represent it through the means at their disposal: images, sound and words.

The concept of representation is not as simple as just looking for bias in the media. Rather it describes the very nature of the media, because they have to 'mediate', that is operate as 'second-hand' sources of information.

It is true that it is possible to see systematic and sometimes unwelcome patterns in the way the media present certain groups or issues (like women, black people, youth, gayness, etc.) and you could choose an area where you feel this happens for your own particular case studies.

Representation: introducing the concept

The example of the picture of the horse introduces a kind of double-level way of thinking about the media. At first, this idea is deceptively simple. Of course, it is obvious that, if we hear the Queen speaking on our radios or see Michael Jackson on the television, they are not 'really' about to appear in our front rooms and say hello. However, the distance between the real and its media presentation becomes much harder to hold in our minds if, for example, we see news footage of a bombing in London or a military coup in another country or hear a report of a horrifying rape in another part of the British Isles. In situations where we feel very involved, the coverage is of real and important news events or where we were not there and are entirely dependent on the media for our knowledge, then the line between the two zones becomes harder to maintain, and we can all slip into talking as if there was no distinction to draw.

Studying representation, these are some of the issues that often come up:

- Do the media represent all groups in society fairly? Are they systematically 'biased' against or towards some people, some countries, some issues?
- If so, why does this happen?
- Are they over-dependent on **stereotypes**?
- Are some issues over-reported at the expense of others?
- Can audiences see through representations that are unjust or inaccurate?
- What ethical issues (moral questions) face those who make media representations, for example journalists, and do they take them seriously?
- Most difficult of all, if the media (and our language) continuously represent the world, how can we ever know it first hand? Are we always trapped in an 'at one remove' relationship with life, trapped in representation?

TASK

In small groups, take each of the questions above as a basis for discussion. After each question has been discussed, have one group member note down a summary of the main points that came up and what kinds of examples were used to support people's opinions. These summaries should be fed back by the note-taker to the rest of the class at the end of the small group discussions either verbally or with the help of an overhead projector or flip chart.

Definition

' Representation' refers to both the processes and the results when something is presented, portrayed, described or shown in the media. The *processes* are the ways through which the subject matter entered the media. These include why it was selected, how information was gathered and how it was packaged or constructed ready for presentation. The *results* are the words, images, sounds, etc., that appear in the media during the presenting of the topic.

TASK

Write a paragraph on what kinds of aspects you would expect to find discussed in one of the following (imaginary) projects:

- The representation of farmers.

- The representation of Europe.

- The representation of football fans.

- The representation of Los Angeles.

- The representation of pensioners.

- The representation of supermodels.

Video Nation is a TV programme on BBC2 which allows 'ordinary' people the chance to show aspects of their lives or to talk about issues that are important to them.

Many analyses of media representations concentrate on **pictures** and **words** because these seem the most obvious areas where 'reality' is presented. However, sound, as much as any other media technique, plays its part in representation. Some of the ways in which sound is constructed to conjure up and present **people**, **places** and **ideas** are revealed in the following interview with Mandy Rose, who is the Producer of *Video Nation* on BBC2. She reached that position through an earlier career as a sound recordist and freelance director.

TASK

Read the following case study, then provide short but clear written answers to the following questions:

1. Paying special attention to the terms 'wild track' and 'buzz track', summarise the sound recordist's role.

2. What does Mandy Rose mean when she says:
   a) you can use sound to make a 'socio-economic space'?
   b) the sound recordist's job is 'to record the sound that no one really notices'?
   c) 'the microphone can't do the same work as the brain'?

CASE STUDY
Representing with sound: part of an interview with Mandy Rose, Producer, *Video Nation* on BBC2

JP: As a sound recordist, what do you actually *do*?

MR: On a documentary the sound person's job is to gather the sound that matches the pictures as 'cleanly' as possible, in other words as uninterrupted by background noise as possible — not even by a humming fridge. In real life, there are lots of interruptions that need taking out for a film. In a way our job is to record the sound that no one really notices because it's unobtrusive. Sometimes that would just mean me saying: 'we can't run now, there's a heavy lorry coming.' Or, if there are intermittent sounds, like buses going past, then after the filming was over, I'd record some more of the sound so it can be added later to fill in so the intermittent sound is less intrusive.

JP: So sometimes you add *extra* sound even to an interview? So you're representing the interview not exactly as it happened? It's not just natural sound?

MR: Yes, that's true. That 'extra' sound is called a *wild track* like a ticking clock or a cuckoo calling, and it's necessary because there's a real difference in how you hear sound in the everyday and how you feel about watching pictures with sound. In everyday life, we are surrounded by sounds but we focus on what we want to hear. You blot out the rest. But the microphone can't do the same work as the brain in discriminating between the two. If you had these 'unnecessary' sounds on the film they'd be really bothersome: you'd feel the director was trying to tell you something with them.

JP: I noticed once when I saw you record an interview in someone's house you recorded 'silent noise' in the same room for a minute or two. Why was that?

MR: That's called a *buzz track* or an atmosphere track and it's used to fill in those little spaces in the editing. Every room has its own sound atmosphere, so you can't just cut from a person talking to silence. It would sound peculiar. Again it's the business of smoothing everything out by creating a sound environment that seems realistic. It's not that it is realistic — it's just that it seems to approximate to how things are in the everyday.

JP: Do you feel that working with sound is a creative job?

MR: I guess the creative part of the job tends to happen more in the editing room, especially with fiction. What comes out of the shooting is the dialogue, recording the talking as clearly as possible, but in the editing you can add things. There's a process known as *track-laying*, building up a sound environment, so you can add a series of new tracks alongside the voice track which can be mixed together in the dub.

JP: Is that when you'd add the music?

MR: Yes. Or — it's a bit corny this one — if you had a suspense story, you might add a ticking clock, or if it was a story set in a pokey little house, you might make the listener aware of the neighbours — or add traffic or sirens — so you're making a *socio-economic space*. The sound is helping with the drama. I used to spend ages running around looking for wild-track material.

JP: Are you aware of the sound-track?

MR: No! Never! it's interesting that even when I was working with sound every day, I wouldn't notice it in films unless I really made an effort. You don't notice sound unless it's wrong.

TASK

Try these tasks at home and keep a log of your observations on each task to be shared in class discussion.

■ Sit quietly in your home for a few minutes and listen. If you were going to be interviewed there, what factors would the sound recordist need to take into account?

■ In one evening, make a note of five sound effects on TV or radio that seem to you to have been added afterwards for effect. What effect was aimed at and did it work?

■ During a fiction programme on TV, turn your back to the television for about ten minutes and try to imagine the environments being created in the sound. Did you hear things you wouldn't normally have noticed consciously? What was it like listening to TV in this unusual way?

Representation as re-presentation

The interview with Mandy Rose highlighted the contribution of just one type of media professional in representation. But what does this term actually mean? At its most basic, it suggests that things are coming to us *second hand*. Let us take the imaginary example of a fairly straightforward news event like bad weather. Suppose that the event was the following:

> An unexpected gale force wind blew across an English seaside town and swept away fences, garages, the town's Christmas tree. As well as this, a number of small fishing boats were dragged out to sea from the harbour.

The first thing to say about this story is that it is already **re-presented** here. You did not see the gale or its effects: as with most media stories you were not there at the time. You have therefore to rely on this version of what happened. On your behalf so to speak, certain features of the story have already been selected. It is set in England, the story concentrates on damage to work-related and domestic property (as opposed to damage to the beaches, cliffs, environment, etc.), the detail of the Christmas tree has been selected for its human interest, and so on. In other words, although this story is a very legitimate one to broadcasters, it has already been structured for you in this account. Let us now suppose that a TV news crew arrives to record an item on the event. They cannot record the storm itself because it has already been and gone. They are limited then to **re-presenting** it: through images of torn fences, interviews with upset fishermen, shots of the upturned Christmas tree. They will select those images and sounds which according to their 'news sense' best typify the event. So, for example, the Christmas tree is shown but not the missing roof tiles on 23 Main Street. They may also select appropriate people to interview: the local Environmental Health Officer and a fisherman but not the old lady who, because of high winds, could not go to get her pension (but who remembers, and has told neighbours, how in 1944 the wind was much worse and a number of people drowned). So by the time the footage arrives at the editing room, it is already taking a certain shape. In the news room; the story may be accepted or, because of the number of other newsworthy events on that day, it may never be broadcast. It may be shown on a local channel but not on the national news. It will be edited and certain features will be lost (the Environmental Health Officer wasn't very interesting: let's lose him). Someone will write a script to introduce the item. Particular words will be used to describe the event: 'gale', 'freak winds', 'gusts of up to 90 miles an hour'. It may be presented as an example of the continuing bad weather hitting the country, as a freak event or as 'the town that lost its Christmas Tree'.

In this imaginary example, nobody has behaved dishonestly, sought to hide the truth or to bias the information coming forward. However, by the time the story reached its audience, it has travelled quite a long way. It has been reconstructed, manufactured, selected, packaged: the original event has been **re-presented**.

TASK

Read the following news story, then complete the tasks below.

An investigation has been launched by the Prison Service after a woman prisoner was kept handcuffed during the funeral service of her ten-day old baby. During the brief life of the baby, its mother (identified only as Mrs P.) was able to visit it every day in an intensive-care ward. On these visits, her handcuffs were removed so she could help care for her daughter. However, when the service was held in the hospital chapel after the death of the baby, two prison guards refused to remove the handcuffs despite being requested to do so by the chaplain. Observers commented that the chapel had only one exit and the prisoner seemed overcome with distress and unlikely to attempt to escape.

A letter of complaint signed by the chaplain and the senior nursing sister at the hospital which cared for the baby has been sent to the prison governor.

The controversy follows on from previous complaints about the handcuffing of pregnant prisoners last January when Jack Straw, Shadow Home Secretary, wrote to the Prisons Minister, Ann Widdecombe, asking about this practice and expressing his view that it was unacceptable.

TASK

In your class, divide up the following tasks to individuals and groups. The task is to take on different roles in representing or narrating the basic storyline above:

Tell the story from the following points of view and for the following media.

Points of view:

- A friend of the mother.
- A campaigner for the rights of prisoners in a letter to the governor of the prison.

Media:

- An article in the monthly newsletter for prison officers.
- A national newspaper like the *Sun*.
- A national newspaper like the *Guardian*.
- The local newspaper for the area in which the prison is located.
- The BBC *Nine o'Clock News*.
- The lunchtime radio news.

Pay particular attention that your language is appropriate to the medium and role that you are adopting. Think hard about the angle the piece would take and the tone in which you will present it. The newspaper and TV articles will also need you to think about what images you would seek to accompany the piece. Think also about how you would get extra information and who, if anyone, you might seek to interview and/or quote.

When the pieces have been written, read them aloud in class. (TV pieces might be presented to camera, radio pieces might be recorded.) After you have heard them all, write a two-page summary of the accounts stressing the following features: what were the differences between the way these accounts represented this piece of news? Things to consider include:

- The way the pieces were structured.
- The type of language used.
- The angle taken in the piece.
- Images, interviews, etc., proposed.
- What was the cause of these differences (e.g., personality of the people writing the piece, the nature of the medium, the nature of the audience, etc.)?

The whole truth and nothing but the truth?

In both the story of the gale at the seaside town and the handcuffed mother, it is clear that representations of events are heavily recast and restructured before they reach their audience. This is hardly surprising. If your friend asked you what you did at the weekend you would not relate everything starting from what you had for breakfast on Saturday morning. Instead you would select what are for you the most interesting parts, the highlights, and you would recount them in a way that gave the story some entertainment value: "guess who was there as well on Saturday?" Without necessarily lying, you would select and reassemble the events of the weekend in order to re-present them to your friend. So the fact that the media re-present our world to us is not surprising or suspicious. It is a normal aspect of human **discourse** (the ways in which we talk to each other) that this should be the case. Critics who accuse the media of not telling us the 'whole truth' are, in some ways, being naive because the whole truth would be untellable. However, in another way, these critics do have a point because what we do and do not learn from media representations is not haphazardly random, instead it is structured according to certain **rules**, **conventions** and **values.**

Note: discourse theory explores the use of language and its relationship to power

TASK

In class, debate the two statements:

■ Critics who accuse the media of not telling the whole truth are in some ways being naive.

■ The media can only ever **re-present** events to us.

Do you agree with these statements? What are they implying?

During the debate, take notes of the points of view that are expressed and the reasons given for them. Use these notes to help you either structure a written essay or present a recorded (video or radio) debate evaluating these two statements. You are welcome to agree with them, disagree with them or take a more neutral line. Your presentation should

■ make it clear that you have understood what the statements are getting at (in other words that you have understood the **concept of re-presentation** as it has been outlined in this element).

■ use examples and justifications in support of your views. Give reasons for the case you put. Examples taken directly from the media (e.g. a newspaper article) may also help back up your views.

Note: You should keep ALL your research notes

What is Represented in the media?

Events

Things that happen in the world are represented to us particularly through news formats. It is the reporting of events with political implications (like strikes or street disturbances) that cause some of

Tory tabloids and spin doctors to smear leader's wife as 'Britain's would-be Hillary Clinton'

Knives out for 'scheming' Cherie Blair

Anthony Bevins
Political Editor

HER CLOTHES have been criticised as too flash and too dowdy. The doe-eyed look she bestows on her husband has been laughed at as cloying. Now, as the pre-election dirty war intensifies, Cherie Blair is being portrayed as an ambitious schemer — the power behind the Labour throne.

The Tories are stalking the Labour leader's wife as part of an exercise to smear her as 'Britain's would-be Hillary Clinton', senior Labour sources have told the Observer.

Over the past week, both the Daily Express and Daily Mail have gone out of their way to produce reports about the power, influence and strong views of Mrs Blair, a leading QC, even though she has scrupulously sought to avoid the political limelight.

One Labour spokesman said: 'Every time she appears in court, there are reporters from the Tory papers stalking her and looking for suggestions of political inconsistency in the cases she is defending.'

Another Labour source said: 'We see this as the first sign of the return of Maurice Saatchi and Sir Tim Bell; the Tories have reverted to type.'

The attacks follow the same pattern as those on Mrs Clinton, whose legs and political views have all been regarded as

fair game. Glenys Kinnock was also singled out for similar treatment during the last election.

'We let it ride then,' a Labour leadership spokesman said. 'This time, we are confident that we can make it blow up in their faces. It will backfire.'

Nevertheless, last Tuesday's Daily Express piece was a classic of the genre. Taking up the whole of page three, it featured a large photograph of Mrs Blair, flanked by Tony Benn in the foreground and Tony Booth, her father, under the headline: 'Two Tonys who taught Cherie about socialism . . . and neither was her husband.'

Taken when she was the Labour candidate in the safe Tory seat of Thanet North during the 1983 general election, the picture shows her standing at a microphone.

According to the Express, 'Cherie, hand melodramatically on hip beside the slumped figure of her famous actor father, is urging a packed hall to support Michael Foot's anti-nuclear, anti-Europe, pro-union Labour Party . . .'

'It is one of the very few occasions in the life of Britain's would-be Hillary Clinton when she went out on her own, without minders to protect her and loyal friends to guard her reputation.'

Friday's Daily Mail carried a page two news report under the headline, 'Cabinet-maker

Cherie drops a Labour name', stating: 'Cherie Blair has raised political eyebrows by publicly nominating a close family friend to her husband's first Cabinet.

Leaving herself open to charges that she is behaving like Hillary Clinton as an unelected power behind the throne, Mrs Blair has singled

out Lord Irvine of Lairg to head the legal system.' It does not say that Lord Irvine, a friend of the Blairs, was first appointed shadow Lord Chancellor by Neil Kinnock in 1987, and was re-appointed by John Smith.

A Labour spokeswoman said the most forced example of 'Cherie-stalking' was a piece in the London Evening Standard

on 26 January, when it was alleged that the 'charming' Tony Blair had agreed to show his wife's American half-sister around the Commons. 'According to a friend, Mrs Blair gave her very short shrift indeed, saying she wanted no contact whatsoever with any siblings from Mr [Tony] Booth's other union.' The

spokeswoman said: 'They never bothered to check it with us. It is all a complete lie.'

Another source said: 'They know they can't penetrate Tony's popularity, so they are trying to get at him through her.'

Today's Mail on Sunday continues the campaign with a full-page feature, headlined:

'Will Cherie be Britain's Hillary?' Explaining 'how Labour's spin doctors may try to make Blair's wife a powerful first lady — without the sleaze', the article says: 'If you think Tony Blair will ignore her political views if he wins the next general election, you don't know much about such yuppie couples.'

Pick your Cherie: politician's wife, left, lawyer, right, and the harder image that the Tories would like to promote. Photomontage: Steve Salmon

Fig 1.10 Anthony Bevins "Knives out for 'scheming' Cherie Blair" article from *The Guardian* (4 February 1996)

the most vehement criticism of the media. Some politicians believe the media are over-sympathetic to strikers or rioters, while a number of political activists believe the media have a strong influence in supporting the controlling power of the status quo like the police.

Individuals

In our society, a small percentage of people are famous and live their lives in the public eye. The advantages to them in terms of wealth, influence, etc., are obvious but on the other hand many famous individuals complain about their treatment in the hands of the media.

TASK

Analyse the GUARDIAN article about the representation of Cherie Blair during the period before a UK election and write answers to the following questions:

- Explain the meaning of 'Cherie-stalking' as used in the article.

- Sum up all the different ways that Cherie Blair has been presented recently in the press according to the article.

- What are the views expressed by the various Labour Party representatives in this article about this media coverage?

- In general the article seems to condemn the smear tactics it describes as 'a dirty war'. Some people believe that this kind of behaviour on the part of the press is unethical (morally wrong), while others would argue that information about the lives of political figures is produced *in the public interest* because we need this information to form our political opinions, to decide how to vote, etc. Where do you stand in this debate? How much personal detail do we have the right to know about our political leaders and their families?

Social groups

'The main way in which black people are treated in newspapers is as a social problem.'
P. Gordan and D. Rosenberg, (1989) *Daily Racism*, Runnymede Trust, quoted in T. O'Sullivan *et al.* (1994), *Studying the Media*, Edward Arnold, p. 42.

Women, people from ethnic minorities, people whose origins lie overseas, people with specific accents, lesbian women and gay men, older and younger people, disabled people, larger people and so on, have all asserted at different times that the media represent them in ways that they find unacceptable. Several women's organisations, for example, complain about the 'page 3' syndrome whereby the image of a young, almost always white woman's body is used to signify beauty, availability and, in many of the accompanying captions, a degree of stupidity. Black groups have objected to many representations of black people, particularly the tendency to associate blackness with 'exoticness' or, in the case of young Afro-Caribbean men, with criminality, drugs, street disturbances and issues of 'law and order'.

Spokespersons from Asian cultures have complained that Asian characters are virtually non-existent in mainstream fictional media despite their significant presence in UK society. Several media critics have pointed out that the official voices in our media, presenters, newscasters, spokespersons, experts, etc., are, more often than not, white, male and middle class. Working class or regional accents are still relatively rare in our aural media outside fiction.

See later points about **media access**.

J. Galtang and M. Ruge (1965), The Structure of Foreign News, Journal of International Peace Research, **1**. Reprinted in J. Tunstall (ed.) (1970), Media Sociology: A Reader, Constable.

There have been some attempts to overcome these tendencies. Over recent years there has been a conspicuous attempt to employ more women newscasters and non-white journalists. Newspapers like the *Voice* and *Asian Leader* exist to report the week's news from black and Asian perspectives. The news reporter Trevor MacDonald has become a familiar figure on ITV's *News at Ten*. However many critics argue that it is still much harder for people who are not middle class, white and male to make progress behind the scenes into positions where they might have real influence over media content and representation.

Places

Our media are global. They present information to us which is drawn from all over the world and even from space. UK TV and radio have traditionally held a high reputation for much of their overseas documentary coverage. However, it is also true that not all places in the world are perceived as equally relevant to a UK audience. Media analysts Galtang and Ruge have argued that the media show a significant leaning towards the selection of news from countries that are either physically close or culturally similar.

In the UK therefore we are more likely to hear stories from countries like the United States and western Europe where the language, culture or religion is closer to that of most of the audience than from, for example, the countries in South America or from the Arabic-speaking states. Tendencies like this one which shape our news are referred to as 'news values' (what makes particular events or story angles valued as news).

Within the UK itself, there has been persistent criticism that the large media corporations, who tend to be based in London, favour news from the South of England and report events from an unconscious 'southerner' slant. However, the repeated promotion the South as 'the norm' also creates the impression that other lives are less relevant or less interesting. In this example we have encountered two important ideas in representation:

■ It is often the case that what is *not* depicted is as important in communicating a message as what is said or shown.

■ In studying representation, it is important to look for the **accumulation** of effects across a range of media and across a period of time.

Issues

One interesting angle on representation in the media is to focus on particular issues. Topics like HIV, single parents, the environment, the state of the Health Service, the state of education, the influence of violent videos, etc., are perennial media topics.

The issues surrounding HIV and AIDS have found a number of representational slots in the media. There are adverts to encourage AIDS awareness and safe sex in teenage magazines, scientific articles in the press about medical research, documentaries about HIV among prisoners, news reports (e.g. Princess Diana shaking hands with AIDS sufferers). There was considerable controversy when a photo of an AIDS patient near the end of his life surrounded by his suffering family was used to advertise Benetton clothes. However, it is interesting that it is in fiction that this topic has managed to escape from its 'scientific' or spectacular overtones and into a more humane environment — for example, the touching depiction in *EastEnders* of the struggle of Mark and Ruth to deal with issues like HIV couples wanting to have a child.

Processes in Representation

T. O'Sullivan *et al.* (1983), *Key Concepts in Communication*, Methuen.

We have already seen that the relationship between reality and its representation is a complex one. When that reality is an event, perhaps there is some justification for saying: 'well, this happened and then that happened and so basically if our media is truthful it should represent these events as they happened'. Many theorists would disagree even here and argue that there can only ever be *versions* of the event — 'remember that news values are about news stories and not events themselves'.

However, if we look at the example of **issues** like HIV, there is no apparent 'real story'. There are just many stories, many people's accounts, many angles, many fragments.

In this kind of example it becomes important to study the **processes** through which these representations appear.

Who is making the representation

Recently the Terrence Higgins Trust, which campaigns on behalf of HIV-related issues, sent to the people on its mailing list a small packet of postcard-sized images. On the cover of the envelope, there was a warning that inside you would find pictures of people with AIDS. When the packet was opened there were a number of images of people doing everyday things. The point the organisers were trying to make was that they were tired of the victim status afforded to people with AIDS. Although many of the previous appeals had been well intended, the continuous representation of very sick people has had the side effect of implying that these people were by definition helplessly subjugated by their illness rather than fighting hard for health. While trying to appeal for human sympathy, the previous campaigners had ironically succeeded in dehumanising the people they were trying to help. The Terrence Higgins campaign was a deliberate attempt by an organisation to redefine the content of a particular pattern of representations by calling this campaign 'positive lives'.

Fig 1.11
Photographs from a recent 'Positive Lives' postal campaign courtesy of the Terrence Higgins Trust and Network Photographers

The power of images

In media with a visual dimension (magazines, newspapers, TV, etc.) a story with strong visual potential or easily accessible images will be selected over an equally important issue which is visually unpromising. Some issues are hard to make visual and extra efforts need to be made. For example, a story about the ups and downs of the UK economy may well create work for the resident graphic artist in drawing graphs and bar charts. Equally an excellent photo can carry an item up the story rank order.

TASK
Taking a national daily paper, cut out five examples where 'extra' visual material has been added to make the story more interesting. For each example, suggest an alternative image or graphic that could have been used.

TASK
In two groups, cut out stories from the day's papers without their accompanying photos and exchange them with the other group. With the new stories you now have, agree as a team a suitable image for each and how you would brief a photographer or designer to go about taking or making it. At the end of this discussion, present your ideas to the other group and ask them to show you the original image. Write up this experiment indicating the similarities or differences in the visual representations you added and the ones from the original newspaper.

Bad News is Good news

Disruption, conflict and controversy can provide good copy. However, the organisers of the Notting Hill Carnival, for example, have often complained that the event has more publicity in the years when it has been associated with trouble between youths and police than in those years when it has passed peacefully, and also that relatively minor incidents of conflict at the festival are overblown at the expense of the bigger, more peaceful picture. In this instance an over-emphasis on disruption contributes to a **stereotype** — that Afro-Caribbean cultural events mean trouble. Certainly a story like 'bomb hits West End' is more likely to find media space than 'uninterrupted peace now passes the six months mark'.

CASE STUDY

GNVQ student Eamon McGinty from the North West Institute Further and Higher Education interviewed media professionals from Northern Ireland about the impact of the peace process in Northern Ireland on their working lives (The interviews were carried out before this process appeared to be threatened by bombs in London in the early months of 1996.) His conclusion was that, because of the 'bad news is good news' syndrome, peace 'paradoxically ... may make the journalists' job harder'. Selected moments from the interviews, which were edited into a three-minute feature and played on Radio Foyle, are presented here:

EM: Given that 25 years of war has supplied journalists with a constant source of headlines and drama, what impact has peace had on the media? Keiran Torish is a reporter with BBC Radio Foyle in Derry and he acknowledges that many aspects of community life have been neglected [in the media].

KT: We perhaps didn't devote as much time as we would have liked to stories about health and the environment and education, stories that research tells us people are very interested in.... One good thing about the troubles ending is that broadcasters and people in journalism can now devote more time to issues that are of concern to people.

EM: Like the print journalists, life is very different now for people like Cecil McGill, photographer on the *Derry Journal*.

CM: [Describes some of the terrible photos he's had to take, but also says the troubles] were a photographer's dream — there were pictures printed every day of the week in the height of the riots and bomb campaign. Now hard news is at a premium for a change and people are going to have to go out and work for news and *make* news and try to get an angle on everyday stories. Going way back before the troubles it was very quiet and you had to make your news, you know? ... Once the troubles came along, the news was there day in day out on a weekly basis. But nowadays you have to keep a sharp eye out for something different.

EM: It will never be the same again, at least that is what we all hope. But paradoxically it may make journalists' jobs harder. Pat McGart [editor of the *Derry Journal*] seems acutely aware of the need to change.

PM: We've had to change our approach to news. For years we had stories literally walking in on legs ... but in the last month you'll see there's been a 50–70% increase in human interest features, but that's all part of the new process of creating news rather than reporting news.

Source: Eamon McGinty (1996) GNVQ MCP, North West Institute of Further and Higher Education, Londonderry.

TASK

Write brief answers to the following questions:

■ In what ways does the feature by Eamon McGinty illustrate the expression that 'bad news is good news'?

■ In what ways can media workers now 'work for news'?

■ In 50–100 words, summarise Eamon's **angle** in this radio feature.

Star Quality

Quite mundane events can be made newsworthy by the presence of a 'personality'. TV actors, politicians, pop stars, the Gladiators, royalty, sports champions are in constant demand to lend their glitter and offer a photo opportunity at the opening of a swimming pool or the launch a new campaign. The non-fiction media have also been accused of **personifying** issues, in other words turning issues that are of general significance into stories about individuals to make the accounts more simple and more palatable. An example might be the recent merger of the two big media companies MIA and United. This is a significant event in the media world because it creates a new UK-owned media corporation which would be the seventeenth largest in the world and therefore able to compete with the large US-owned companies. However, the merger was reported, even in the broadsheet papers, as a story about how the two previous owners (both Lords but one a Labour supporter and the other a Tory) would get on with each other and who would come out as boss after the first couple of years. It is not that this is not an *interesting* question but, it could be argued, this focuses on personalities and leads to a loss of focus on some of the more important economic issues implied by this merger.

Is it narrativised?

Our mass media are more likely to represent an item or an issue if it has the potential to be presented as, or turned into, a traditional story format. This may mean, for example, casting some characters as 'bad' and others as 'good', even though the real picture may be much more complex. It is also worth looking at the way the stories are developed over time. Some items may only occur because they have been pulled into the limelight by other bigger stories. For example, a feature about the funding of breast cancer screening clinics is more likely to appear after a government report on women's health or a news story about someone who is suing the National Health Service for failing to diagnose this condition, than it is to appear spontaneously on its own. The original story in this example has set a context in which certain issues become sensitised. An organisation which campaigns for women's health might use this opportunity to offer a story on underfunding, or media professionals might follow up on the original item by contacting a clinic for a story. Sellers of private health insurance might react by placing more ads because this is a time when people will be more responsive. So although there is nothing at this moment new about cancer screening and funding, the issue has been made newsworthy as part of a larger story or narrative. It has been 'narrativised' — turned into a chapter of another, larger story.

How has it been constructed?

Once an item has passed through the net for selection, it will need shaping before it can be presented to the public. The majority of media workers are employed not in the **discovery** of items (in discovering news items or originating fiction scripts, for example) but in the second level activity of **constructing** items for **presentation** (reporting, editing, shooting, writing, laying out, etc.). The story about cancer screening clinics will need writing up; if it is for a newspaper, it will need laying out, with headlines and subheadings. Before that, perhaps, someone will commission a satirical cartoon, or maybe it will be felt that to be more balanced the report needs a quote from the Minister for Health or a spokesperson, so someone needs to chase this up. Maybe the story needs to be set in a particular context (previous funding levels, for example) so someone needs to check the archive material for earlier stories. This might give rise to a graph showing the average level of funding available to screening clinics over the last four years and its fluctuations. Perhaps now it will be decided that this subject is worth editorial space so someone needs to write an editorial comment. So, just as a factory produces a saucepan, through a series of processes of heating, bending, rinsing, cooling, packing, labelling, so a media industry processes the raw material it uses and often in very elaborate ways.

Constructing reality

Generally it is worth thinking about the *construction* process in two ways: **ideological construction** and **technical construction**, although in fact it is hard to hold these two concepts apart. Ideological construction refers to the factors affecting representation which spring from people's (or society's) ideas — either conscious or unconscious ideas, and technical construction refers to the influences that come into play through the use of media equipment and media processes.

Ideological construction

Let us suppose that the Queen visits an African country. What are the images that are likely to appear as a result on our TV screens?

Manuel Alvarado *et al.* (1987),
Macmillan Education.

The first thing to say is that there are very likely to *be* images selected from this trip, so at the ideological level we can say already that the visit is judged as significant (as opposed say to the visit by the Head of State of another African country which may or may not be reported but which may be significant politically). So, which images will they be? The authors of *Learning the Media* suggest they may fall into one of a number of pre-determined categories. One is the category of the 'exotic'. For example, the selected images may be of the Queen greeted by dancers in traditional dress. There is nothing wrong with these images but their choice over others may give the impression that this particular country is over-rooted in the past and has not really developed in a modern way.

Or they might emphasise the sad side of the country — what these authors call 'the pitied' — and show how the Queen may be surrounded by poverty and suffering on her visit. Or the country may be seen as unstable and dangerous, and questions may be asked about the Queen's safety. If images in these categories are continuously selected over images of the second sort it is probably not because the selectors are overtly prejudiced or they want to present a bad image of the country. It is just that these are the pre-set media categories (**stereotypes**) for representing 'Africa'. However, their constant repetition, at the expense of more positive — or just different — images creates a particular impression in the minds of the public.

Stereotyping

Definition

A **stereotype** is a representation that is cliched or oversimple. It suggests that certain features are typical of every item in a particular category — for example, all Italians have black hair and are very romantic. Stereotypes are often (though not always) associated with negative or prejudiced perceptions and are at their most dangerous when one group has the power to label or pigeonhole another.

TASK

Using the Commission for Racial Equality poster below, provide brief written answers to the following questions:

- Describe the point the poster is making. The term 'anchors' may be useful here.

- How effective do you think this poster campaign is likely to be in combating the stereotypes that arise from racial prejudice? Justify your answer.

- Using simple sketches, can you design a similarly simple poster to combat a negative stereotype that you feel strongly about?

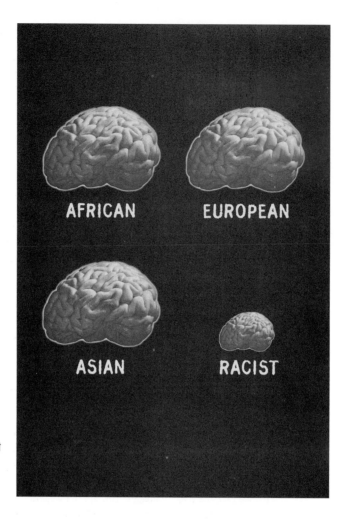

Fig 1.12 Poster from a recent European youth campaign against racism courtesy of the Commission for Racial Equality

The origins of stereotypes

Richard Dyer: The Dumb Blonde Stereotype, BFI 1979

It is often quite easy to see who benefits from a particular stereotype. It is much harder, however, to define how they come about. In his analysis of the 'dumb blonde', Dyer considers all the explanations of where the stereotype might have come from and why it came to the fore when it did. These explanations include one theory that the image might have arisen as a defence mechanism to assert the attractiveness of white people's physical characteristics at a time when black people in the United States were beginning to organise politically. As Dyer summarises: 'it is, to say the least, suggestive that at the very moment when fear of blacks was gaining a special intensity, Hollywood should come up with a supreme image of white beauty, the blonde.'

What are the effects of stereotyping?

It is important to remember that stereotypes are not just attitudes, ideas or things people say. Nor are they as apparently harmless as the UK examples given earlier. Many people's lives have been profoundly affected through the operation of stereotypes and this is particularly true when one social group has the political, military, economic or ideological power to exert control over the labelled group. During the Second World War, the Nazis were able to convince many ordinary Germans that the Jews were 'unpeople' and that their community leaders were involved in a plot to destabilise the Western economy in order to seize power. Cartoons appeared showing Jews as rats gnawing away at the roots of society. The German media were used for deliberate **propaganda** and no alternative representations were allowed.

Definition

Propaganda: the deliberate manipulation of people's thoughts and beliefs, and misleading publicity spread to control public opinion.

In a democratic society, representations are more likely to be contradictory since more opinions can be expressed. For example, in the UK, there is a lively black press producing papers like the *Voice* and *Ebony*. As well as informing their readers, these papers also take as part of their brief the need for positive representations. However, critics have questioned how powerful these kinds of representations can be compared to those found in the wide-selling mainstream newspapers is important therefore to look not just at what is represented and how, but also at how frequently certain types of images are presented.

The media are very powerful contributors to stereotypes in the following ways:

- **They contribute to the content of stereotypes**. Constantly repeated imagery helps build up a powerful picture of how the world is.
- **The media can appear to ratify stereotypes**. For example, the (male) TV commentators during a recent report on a women's rugby match laughed and made negative comments about what appeared on the screen to be a skilful and exciting game. The final remark was that one commentator 'wouldn't like to go out with' any of the woman players. The official position of these people as sports experts and media anchormen reinforced the message that tough sports are inappropriate for 'proper' women.
- **They stand in for first-hand information**. While our media is global, our personal experience is local. At most, we may know directly a handful of countries, a few groups of people etc. (e.g. many people have not been to Japan and may not

know any Japanese people, none the less they have an image of both the place and its citizens). Similarly, they have probably never met a major politician face to face, but would still vote in the next election. In both these instances, like everybody else in the technological world, one is dependent on the media, a second-hand (representational) channel for vital data. This is an inevitable fact of modern life.

Technological construction

Technological construction refers to the processes through which representations pass which derive from media technologies and production processes rather than from ideologies. For example, a decision in a newspaper office to run a photo small rather than large on a particular page may be taken because the photographed event is perceived as not very significant (ideological judgement) or because the photo is of poor quality (technical judgement) or because the photo needs to fit over two columns (production-process judgement).

Access and Representation

The question of access to the media can be understood in two ways. First, it implies that we should look at which individuals and groups in society are invited by the media to express their views, and secondly, it implies considering who gets access to *jobs* in the media where they can influence media content.

In terms of 'who gets to speak', most of this section suggests that the choice of stories reported and the selection of particular 'angles' can never be wholly inclusive. For instance, politicians, those with well-tuned publicity machines, academics, 'experts' and spokespeople who officially represent organisations are more likely to be in a position to express their points of view than people who do not belong to these categories.

In terms of 'who gets to work' in the media, as in many other areas of employment, like teaching, the police force, local councils,

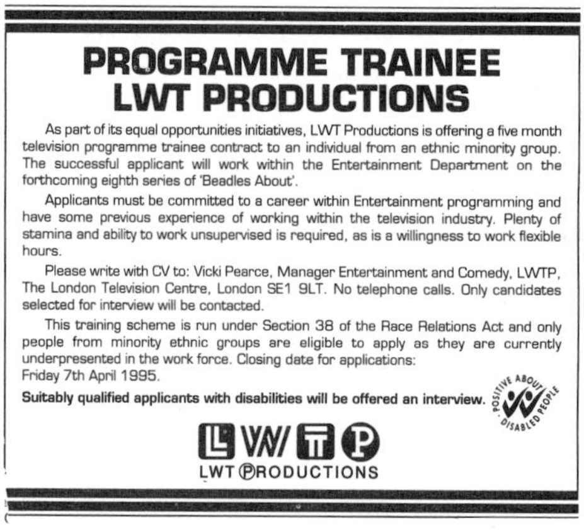

Fig 1.13 Broadcasters have made efforts on occasions to recruit people from a wider variety of backgrounds through targeted training schemes. Advertisement published in *Broadcast* March 1995

PROGRAMME TRAINEE LWT PRODUCTIONS

As part of its equal opportunities initiatives, LWT Productions is offering a five month television programme trainee contract to an individual from an ethnic minority group. The successful applicant will work within the Entertainment Department on the forthcoming eighth series of 'Beadles About'.

Applicants must be committed to a career within Entertainment programming and have some previous experience of working within the television industry. Plenty of stamina and ability to work unsupervised is required, as is a willingness to work flexible hours.

Please write with CV to: Vicki Pearce, Manager Entertainment and Comedy, LWTP, The London Television Centre, London SE1 9LT. No telephone calls. Only candidates selected for interview will be contacted.

This training scheme is run under Section 38 of the Race Relations Act and only people from minority ethnic groups are eligible to apply as they are currently underpresented in the work force. Closing date for applications: Friday 7th April 1995.

Suitably qualified applicants with disabilities will be offered an interview.

LWTP LWT PRODUCTIONS

etc., there have been efforts to recruit a wider variety of people, for instance, through targeted training schemes with broadcasters and through production schemes such as the Carlton Television/Arts Council of England initiative 'Synchro', which ran for three years working with new black directors producing short films on black arts, music and culture. The productions were supported with training and transmitted across the Carlton region. Although such schemes have undoubtedly provided valuable opportunities and have increased visibility for new black film-makers at least momentarily, many people are concerned that schemes can do little in isolation, and that there are dangers in segregating 'black programming' from the rest of the schedule. Carlton's current new directors scheme, '**Metroland**', attempts to open up access to new directors across the board, giving them their first opportunities to direct something for television. The 1996 series featured six documentaries, five of which were directed by women.

Emma Barker, Commissioning Editor at Carlton Television, says 'Metroland is one of the few series which gives directors new to television the opportunity and training to shoot a 30-minute documentary. The scheme is in its fourth year and the standard remains extremely high.'

However, as research undertaken by the Industry Training Organisation for Broadcast, Film and Video — Skillset — continues to confirm, there is still a long way to go.

Metroland is a Hawkshead Production for Carlton UK Productions.

Fig 1.14 **M**etroland's new director **J**acqui Timberlake's film *Breaking the Silence*, featured Kelly Turner (pictured) who in 1994, at the age of 14, reported her ex-boyfriend to the police for his part in a vicious racist attack. No other witnesses came forward. The film explores how Kelly and her family coped with the barrage of abuse she suffered for speaking out, and what she hopes for the future. Picture courtesy Carlton UK Television

This research focused on freelancers in skill areas and all those working in set crafts. Research shows that over 60% of the workforce in broadcast, film and video are freelance. Although the research was specifically to identify training needs within this sector, it also revealed the enormous imbalance in the workforce. Overall 63% of the freelancers surveyed were male, 37% female. The percentages vary markedly over the different skill groups, with men predominating in sound (94%), camera/lights (93%) and post-production (79%) and, to a lesser degree, among producers/directors (69%). Women form the majority of those in wardrobe/hair/makeup/costume (85%), production support (64%) and marginally among researchers/ writers (57%). Overwhelmingly the workforce is white (95%).

Fig 1.15 Skillset (1994) Employment Patterns and Training Needs, Freelance & Set Crafts Research pp 12—13 (Courtesy Skillset)

Practical studies in media representation: some hints

Element 1.2. requires an in-depth study in an area of representation. This can be a very enjoyable topic, not least because it gives a lot of leeway in choosing what area to study. However: a word of warning! Think hard before you commit yourself to a particular topic. Here are a few guidelines:

■ While virtually any subject can be studied in terms of its media representation, make sure that your study leads attention not just to the topic itself but to its presentation in the media. A particular kind of music, for example, may be very interesting in itself but is there a lot to say about how it is presented in the media? Ask yourself the question before you start.

■ Representation is a very big subject and it may be possible to work with other students on aspects of a particular topic.

■ Your understanding of representation will be richer if you consider a range of media (but be guided by the evidence indicators in producing your final projects). For example, a particular kind of martial art could be very fascinating to study, but is it ever presented in anything other than specialist magazines?

■ Remember the points made in this section about the media as a set of essentially representational channels. Feel free to criticise the way your topic is presented but not the fact that it is!

■ Remember: representation can be aural, verbal, visual, etc.

■ Remember the points from Element 1.1 where it was argued that the way something was presented (presentational style, lighting, framing, voice-over, etc.) is often as important in creating meaning as what is presented. Take these stylistic dimensions into account.

■ Remember the points made in this section, that what is *absent* from a representation can often be as important as what is shown.

■ Take note of the points made above about representational *processes* and do not limit your account just to representational content.

■ Try to remember the points made about how particular types of representations tend to accumulate to create a general impression or a stereotype. The logic of this for your projects is that a study will be stronger if it backs up its points with lots of examples.

EVIDENCE COLLECTION POINT

The evidence indicators require that you submit two case studies, each of which must include your understanding of the concept and your application of it.

The tasks throughout this section will make up a healthy dossier of material, some of which can be developed into more considered, detailed pieces of work. You may approach the case studies in a variety of ways, ranging from an academic essay, to an exhibition of photographs (you may wish to combine this element with option units), to a video, print or audio product.

Some of the assignments suggested at the end of Units 3, 4 and 5 also address these issues.

1.3 ANALYSE MEDIA GENRES

The concept of **genre** is relatively easy to understand. It refers to the way particular types of media products can be grouped into categories like: Western films, tabloid newspapers, documentaries. What is harder to grasp is why a concept about *categorising* media products should be important to media theory. This section looks both at definitions of the word 'genre' and how the idea helps us to understand how the media work in society.

This section considers genre from three basic angles:

- **What do particular genres consist of?** How do we recognise them?
- **Why do we have genres?** What are their functions for the audience and for those who make and sell media?
- **Why do we have the concept of genre?** How is it useful to students and other media theorists?

Questions of whether genres are a good thing, whether they encourage or restrict creativity, for example, are also raised. And some examples where media creators have tried to be experimental in their use of genre are also considered.

What does 'genre' mean?

> **Definition**
> ' **G**enre' is the French word for 'type' or 'kind'. The genre of rap is a particular type of music, the broadsheet is a particular genre of newspaper, *EastEnders* falls within the *soap-opera genre*, Dracula films are in the *horror genre*. Each genre has its own characteristic content, personalities, storyline, shape and way of addressing the reader. Genres are recognised by audiences extremely quickly and work with the individual text itself to shape audience response — e.g. we expect to laugh at stand-up comedy and prepare ourselves to do so.

The content of genres

The simplest way of defining a genre is to look at what it contains, although other, perhaps more challenging, definitions are offered later in this section. A tabloid newspaper, for example, as well as being a specific shape, is likely to contain the following elements: bold headlines, dramatic and dramatised storylines, relatively simple language and a high ratio of image to written text. A Western film is likely to contain: cowboys, horses, Western towns, shoot-outs, rustlers, gamblers, saloon girls, big hats, a sheriff. These generic features may not be evident in all texts. A Western can exist without a sheriff, a tabloid page can exist without a photo. But once a certain number of these features are present, we as an audience can recognise where we are and adjust our mental expectations accordingly. We can begin to anticipate particular developments and particular pleasures.

Genre iconography

Definition

Iconography: an icon is an object such as a statue or a painting which represents a larger concept. A statue of the Virgin Mary typifies Christianity, for example. Iconography in relation to genre means the typical 'icons', objects, things, motifs or signifiers associated with that genre — for example, the helicopter is an icon associated with films about Vietnam, the sheriff's badge is a typical icon for the Western film. The idea is particularly useful in describing visual-based media like TV, films and magazines.

TASK

Make a list of the typical objects/icons you would expect to see in the following genres:

■ A music magazine.

■ A fitness magazine.

■ A photography magazine.

■ A DIY magazine.

In a couple of sentences, describe the kind of language you would expect to find in each kind of magazine. (Some suggestions to start you off: descriptive, modern, evocative, precise, up-beat, detailed, technical, lyrical.)

Typical icons do not have to be individual objects. The Western movie is characterised by big hats and sheriffs' badges, but also by sweeping desert landscapes, dirt roads or dark wooden saloon interiors. The work of creating these backdrops in cinema is called **'mise-en-scène.'**

Definition

Mise-en-sc ène: literally 'putting it into the scene'. In film, it is the director's responsibility to create the visual environment through which objects or people are arranged, lit, etc. Some directors are particularly praised for their *mise-en-scène*.

Each genre evokes a typical setting. Soaps are very often set in the domestic environment with sofa, TV, coffee tables. These environments tend to be taken for granted yet they have actually been designed. Someone has had to think: 'would person X have a drinks cabinet?' or 'which pop stars would that teenager have on their wall?' The answers to these questions help tell the story, set the scene, establish character. The icons associated with *Coronation Street*, all the mantelpiece ornaments, personal possessions and photos are stored in well-labelled boxes between shoots at Granada TV so they can be replaced where they belong for the next episode.

Although iconography as a term usually applies to **objects**, it can also be extended to apply to all the typical visual content. Analysts may also use the term to describe typical types of shot, typical kinds of lighting or, in magazines, typical poses or typical layouts.

TASK

In groups of three, make a list of the words that describe the typical type of theme music you associate with the following genres within television: news programme, documentary, science programme, soap opera, comedy series, quiz shows, police series, romantic drama serial.

Choose one of the categories and write a letter to a musical composer commissioning a theme tune. Give the composer as clear an idea as you can about what you want from the theme tune.

OR

Choose one of the categories above and compose an appropriate theme tune either with notation or on tape. [You may wish to experiment with a sampling programme on computer.]

TASK

You have been asked to design the set and select the props for the main location to be used in a new TV sitcom which is to be set in either:

■ a travel agent's office, or

■ a school staff room.

Write a detailed (two pages approximately) description of what the viewer would see during the series.

It is worth noting that although genres demonstrate typical icons, this does not mean you can draw hard and fast boundaries between them. An office scene would not be 'wrong' in a sci-fi film, a dark damp street and a sense of impending threat would not necessarily be inappropriate in a soap. So the term 'genre' applies to particular typical **clusters** of icons rather than self-contained boxes of signifiers. Some icons, however, are so locked into their genres that it is hard to imagine them migrating elsewhere unless the original genre was being deliberately referenced. This 'quoting' is not unusual in adverts which borrow established generic elements intertextually — for example, the woman who picks up her cleaning spray and squints into the sun before going to 'rustle' the dirt out of the kitchen. Here the quality of toughness associated with cowboys and gun-fighting is transposed on to the nature of the cleaning product. Genres need to be thought about as fairly loose and fluid constructs.

Genre and narrative

> **Definition**
>
> **Narrative:** this usually means the story and the way it is told. However in Media Studies, it is useful to distinguish between *narrative* — *what* is told — and *narration* — *how* it is told, in what style, in what order, etc. For a fuller discussion see Element 1.4.

Narrative prediction

> **TASK**
>
> In groups of two, make notes about how the following stories might end. Make up two endings to each story: (a) one which fits the obvious genre, and (b) another which sends it off in an unusual direction.
>
> ■ *An army pilot has been sent out into the desert in his plane to investigate reports of unusual lights in the sky. As he approaches the scene of the reports, there are a number of bright flashes. A close-up of the plane's control panel tells us that a number of devices are out of control or showing strange readings.*
>
> ■ *Beth has recently arrived on an urban estate and is just getting to know her neighbours through meeting them at her daughter's school gate. She has told them that her husband works abroad. The episode this week ends on a close-up of a letter marked 'Her Majesty's Prison Services' on the doormat of her new home.*
>
> ■ *Two young men are helping police with their enquiries following the blaze at Wharton Warehouse earlier today.*

It is unlikely that you will find task (a) very difficult, while task (b) may produce some amusing or strange results. The fact that, with (a) these brief openings suggest other, not yet recounted, stories is not because you have personal experience with prisons or arson or deserts with strange lights. It is because you have well-developed knowledge of the relevant genres and their typical narrative patterns. As one critic has pointed out, the moments when a storyline unfolds in a way that feels wacky or strange (as perhaps with your task (b)?), it is more likely that it is breaking the rules of the genre than offending our common sense.

Note: 'Nathern Exposure' (Channel 4) is a good example of rule breaking

Narration

As the examples above demonstrate, particular genres tell particular kinds of story, particular narratives. But they also tell them/narrate them in specific kinds of ways. Both aspects of this definition of narrative are important to genre study.

The content of a tabloid lead story is likely to fulfil various criteria as a story — 'Di wants 20 million' — but what marks that particular example as (stereo)typically tabloid is more the language, the way it is told, than the content. The same story (narrative content) might well appear in the broadsheet press but it would feel different — 'Palace settles down for a long fight.'

Genre and themes

> **Definition**
>
> **A theme**: a topic or subject dealt with in a media product. Themes may be the overt content of the product, e.g., an article may tell us directly about the Royal Family or they may be implied in a more subtle way. The same article may suggest something about how we, as subjects of the Crown, should feel about the Royal Family. Genres often have an association with particular themes, e.g., the tabloid and the functioning of law and order, sci-fi and the shape of the future, etc.

Six Guns (1975) and Society

If Western films were really just about strangers riding into town they would soon become pretty dull. However, as with other genres, Westerns also refer to a number of more or less declared themes and part of our interest in them is to see how any particular individual text will deliver those themes. Typical ideas referred to in the classic Western include: justice and how it can be defined, civilisation versus savagery, the rule of law versus the rule of natural justice, property and boundaries, and the relationship of Native and later Americans with nature. Since genre is a dynamic, changeable force, each individual text may work these themes differently. None the less it may also be possible to perceive general thematic patterns over a period of time. Will Wright has argued, for example, that the position of the cowboy has altered significantly. In earlier cinema, the cowboy was often an alienated individual, to an extent socially maladjusted, and the work of the film was to draw him into society, perhaps through the love of a good woman, or perhaps because the presence of evil — like the rustler gang — forces him to adopt civic responsibility. More recently, however, Western heroes have been perceived as outside society but with good reason. Society may be seen as disgusting or corrupt, leaving the hero no existential choice but to remain separate. This was certainly the case in *The Unforgiven* (Clint Eastwood, USA, 1992), *The Wild Bunch* (Sam Peckinpah, USA, 1969) and *Dances With Wolves* (Kevin Costner, USA, 1990).

Genre and characters

The notion of 'typecasting' refers not just to the type of character played, but also the natural genre home for particular actors.

> **TASK**
>
> Write down the genres you associate with the following actors. Whenever you have difficulty, keep a note of what the difficulty was making sure you use the terms 'genre' and 'generic' when appropriate to analyse the problem:
>
> | | |
> |---|---|
> | Clint Eastwood | Harvey Keitel |
> | Julia Roberts | Uma Thurman |
> | Arnold Schwarzenegger | Susan Sarandon |
> | Sigourney Weaver | Keanu Reeves |
> | Kiefer Sutherland | Harrison Ford |
> | Tim Roth | John Travolta |
> | Madonna | Emma Thompson |

'I've been lucky. I've had a wonderful diversity in my career. I never got labelled the good lady or the bad lady.' Ex-MGM star, Janet Leigh, probably most famous for dying in the shower scene in *Psycho*. (USA, 1960), in an interview on the BBC's World Service 15 April 1996.

In the early days of cinema, studios tended to specialise in particular types of film; so too did their stars. Warner Brothers had both James Cagney and Humphrey Bogart signed up and used them in a series of gangster films until the name of the star and the name of the genre, especially for Cagney, became virtually synonymous. This allowed the studio to build up certain expectations in the audience: a 'Cagney' film from Warner promised specific box office attractions. It also fulfilled practical and financial considerations since this kind of film required a particular kind of set and particular kinds of prop which could be used over and over again.

Functions of genre

Genre is not simply a way of categorising types of media product for the purposes of study! It is valuable to the media **industries** in terms of identifying popular formats, marketing and packaging. Obviously, a successful formula will guarantee certain returns and minimise financial risk. For **audiences**, genre provides a framework for reading a text, and a degree of pleasure in the expectations the generic raises. How will the film or programme use — or play with — form, content, narrative, character. In television output, the 'flow' can be organised according to genre.

Genre and the media-producing industries

Genre fulfils very important functions — commercial, aesthetic and organisational — for media producers, allowing them, just as it allows the reader, to orient themselves to a particular product.

A journalist writing a piece for a tabloid newspaper, for example, will automatically adopt a different style than one writing a broadsheet article. So, in this example, genre is doing some of the work for that person, laying down possible pathways for production. No journalist expects to get up in the morning and reinvent the writing style of the newspaper for which they work. Nor does a typographer expect to start from scratch with the page layout.

Genres also allow for specialisation. It used to be that certain film studios, for example, specialised in particular kinds of films (e.g. Gainsborough-melodramas; Hammer-horrors; Ealing-comedies). It is still the case that particularly successful teams-writers, camera operators, lighting people, musical composers-will be reassembled to work on what they are good at. This is particularly true now with computer animators and special effects designers. With these relatively new skills, teams of creators tend to be selected because they gave a particular look to a previous work in the same genre. The likelihood is then that look will be recreated, if somewhat adapted, on the next project.

Genre can be very important when it comes to raising finance. A producer raising funds for a film is much more likely to receive backing if the financiers can get a firm image of what is proposed before they part with the cash.

Audience recognition

Turner, (1993) Film as a social practice, London. Routledge. p. 87.

'Audiences make genres as much as makers do.'

The result of genre recognition, is that the viewer/reader/critic will orient his or her reactions to what is there according to the expectations generated by recognising the genre in the first place, enabling more reasoned judgements to be made about the text (e.g., you would not judge a Western for not being musical enough, or a musical for not being horrific enough). Turner also suggests that genre makes the media more efficient. Because the rules are already known, a particular media product can deal with more material and at greater speed than if it had to keep going back and explaining itself. From the basis of this argument, it could be said that genre-based texts can be more, rather than less, demanding on their audience.

There is an illustrative moment in the film *Indiana Jones and the Temple of Doom* (Steven Spielberg, USA, 1984). 'Indi' (Harrison Ford) is about to be attacked by two heavily robed and turbanned desert soldiers each armed with a curved scimitar. As they advance towards him they cut ritualistic patterns above their heads with their swords. The sound of the blades swishing through the air is heavily amplified. They advance ominously towards Ford who looks aghast, but moments later they crumple to the ground when he takes out a gun and shoots them. The film at this moment often provokes a sustained laugh from the audience. One could analyse this in terms of **stereotypes**: canny American defeats simple Arabs.

But this is not what makes it funny. The humour comes from the way the text deflates audience expectations of genre. From Kung Fu movies, adventure stories, James Bond movies, such moments are usually resolved by a sudden display of exotic skill on the part of our hero. He too can box, kick, throw or whatever better than (several of) them! In the Harrison Ford movie, however, this narrative expectation is brutally punctured. What makes it original *is* precisely a knowledge of genre.

Is genre a good or a bad thing?

There are texts that use genre in exciting, challenging ways and there are also texts that lazily adopt the generic rules with the result that they feel tired and unstimulating. You might also want to distinguish between the different media. A critic who found TV over-formulaic might have a different view about film. An enormous amount also depends on the reader. Rap music, for example, has been called repetitive and tuneless, but its fans are sensitised to small nuances of expression which mean that, far from hearing sameness, they are experiencing difference with each new text.

TASK

While the TV schedules may appear to contain an enormously varied mix, the effect of studying TV output by genre is to reveal the restrictive and institutionalised formula of TV's dominant formats which underlie its surface diversity.

Take a number of coloured highlighters and use them to categorise the programmes advertised on the TV pages of a newspaper into different genres. Take your highlighted page and, in a written answer, use it to discuss the statement: 'is genre a good or bad thing?'

Were there programmes that did not seem to fit into any genre? What were these programmes and why did they not fit the mould?

When you look at your colour coding, do you find there are particular groups of TV programmes which you tend to watch? Analyse your own TV preferences *using the concept of genre as it has been discussed so far to help you express your views*. For example, perhaps you are drawn to programmes that feature particular kinds of characters or themes, or you like a particular kind of address to the audience, or you like to see particular kinds of narratives or settings or objects?

Is genre a channel for creativity?

See Element 1.2 Interview with Mandy Rose.

Returning to the programme *Video Nation*, Mandy Rose was asked whether this is a problem with the video-makers. After all, since the programme tries to encourage expression from people not in professional media roles, would it not be a shame if their originality was stifled by an instinct to copy mainstream TV?

'Everyone seems to have their own ways of saying things,' she says. The recent theme on food has been a bit of an exception though. Suddenly everybody's addressing the camera and whisking into bowls like Delia Smith!'

> **TASK**
>
> Identify a media product (a TV show, comic, newspaper, etc.) which in your view is made dull by its predictable adherence to genre rules. Write a review of the piece. You can be as scathing as you like but make sure your writing explains why the piece feels so genre-bound and what the conventions of this genre are.

Blade Runner — a case study in genre bending

Blade Runner is a film which was originally released in 1982, directed by the UK director Ridley Scott who also directed *Alien* (UK, 1979) and *Thelma and Louise* (USA, 1991). The story is set in the year 2019 and is based on a novel by the famous 'conceptual' sci-fi author Philip K. Dick called *Do Androids Dream of Electric Sheep?*. The storyline has all the hallmarks of classic science fiction, however, in its narration (the telling), Scott overlays a heavy element from a completely different genre: *film noir*. Film noir refers to the types of black-and-white suspense thriller associated with actors like Humphrey Bogart and Lauren Bacall. They are confusing, murky films usually set in a decaying urban landscape — towns where money talks — and peopled by shady and untrustworthy people. So atmospherically and visually, Ridley Scott has set his story worlds away from the usual *mise-en-scène* for sci-fi: spaceships and gleaming laboratories. Instead he has transposed the story into a future damp, dark and polluted Los Angeles.

Obviously the case study will make a lot more sense if you have seen the film! It is readily available on video but, because of its strong visual appeal, it is even better on film. At the end of the study, there are a number of tasks set on the case study. Only attempt these if you have seen the film/video.

If you want to enjoy the story of the film, you may find it wise to watch it before you read on.

You will also find this case study easier to follow if you have already viewed some examples of classic film noir. A few examples include: *The Postman Always Rings Twice* (Tay Garnett, USA, 1946), *The Big Sleep* (Howard Hawks, USA, 1946), *Farewell My Lovely* (Edward Dmytryk, USA, 1944).

> **TASK**
>
> Write down the objects, effects, types of story, types of character you associate with science fiction.

CASE STUDY
Blade Runner as science fiction — the narrative

The story of *Blade Runner* is relatively simple. In the year 2019 Deckard is rehired into his old job of 'blade runner' to hunt down the replicants who have escaped from an off-world colony and come back to try to 'meet their maker', the boss of the Tyrell Corporation. This company creates robots, using advanced techniques in genetic engineering, that are so lifelike that is hard to tell if they are human or not. This message is driven home to Deckard when he is invited to question the beautiful Rachel, one of Tyrell's assistants. After a long interview, he concludes that she too is a replicant, but one who believes she is human. The company has even implanted false memories of childhood to enhance her humanity. We learn that the off-world replicants have similar features. They also have a genetically based life span of only four years and they have returned to earth to discover if this term can be extended. Deckard hunts down the first three and 'retires' them with his gun. The fourth, the superhuman Roy Batty, could have killed his pursuer but, at the dying moments of his own life, reaches out instead over the edge of the building from which Deckard is hanging and, in a God-like gesture, lifts him to safety. The film, in the original 1982 cut, ends with Deckard and Rachael fleeing the city together, although, because of her genetic coding, they do not know how much time they will have together. In the later re-edit of the film, *The Director's Cut* (1991), the ending is more ambiguous.

Fig 1.16 Blade Runner (USA 1982, director Ridley Scott). The enormous, animated billboards, the futuristic vehicle, the decayed remnants of the past give Blade Runner its science-fiction backdrop (Courtesy the Kobal Collection and the Ladd Company/Warner Bros)

Note: Critic Pauline Kael describes the setting as "an electronic slum", "a medieval future".

Typical of science fiction, the film is set in the future but it bases the image of that future on aspects of the present. The society in *Blade Runner* seems to embody the worst aspects of our own. Big powerful corporations produce replicants who seem little more than slaves or prostitutes (one of the escapees is described in her file as 'the basic pleasure model'). Enormous animated billboards promote Coca-Cola across the sky while underneath, shady beings seem to eke out their existence by scavenging. There are remnants of recognisable sub-cultures, all unattractive. Alienated Hare Krishna lookalikes and half-human punks gather in threatening clusters on the streets. The buildings are a kind of 'futuristic 1930s' style but very run down and the streets are full of rubbish. The city feels dark, claustrophobic and polluted and it is continuously raining dark rain.

The human beings we meet seem devoid of affection, interested only in hustling, buying and selling. In this environment the humanoids often seem more human that the humans. Rachel is the only 'person' we see crying, for example; she also demonstrates that all-too-human foible of smoking cigarettes. All but Roy seem genuinely terrified of their human pursuer. The replicant Roy speculates philosophically on the nature of life and death and howls with grief when Deckard 'retires' his girlfriend. His final act of saving his partner's murderer is at one level a supreme act of forgiveness. So, if our sympathies are anywhere in this film, they are with the robots.

This is not untypical of the more thoughtful types of science fiction (and horror). While some monsters (the Alien, Dracula) are purely destructive, creations like Frankenstein often appear more sympathetic than their obsessed creators. The computer HAL in the film *2001: A Space Odyssey* (Stanley Kubrick, UK, 1968) is a great deal more personable than his uptight inventor who, in the sequel, abandons him to 'die' in the path of an exploding sun.

CASE STUDY
Blade Runner as film noir — the narration

Definition:
Film noir is a term which describes a particular kind of black-and-white thriller film produced by the Hollywood studios in the 1940s and early 1950s. The 'noir' refers both to the dark visual style of the films but also to their moody, suspenseful stories and the shady low-life characters who inhabit their world. At the height of the genre, many films were characterised by the presence of a *femme fatale*, a beautiful but dangerous and unethical woman who would tempt the main male figure to his destruction. The male character was often also the narrator in those films which adopted the voice-over as part of their narrative technique.

Film critics were quick to pick up the 'noir' references in *Blade Runner*, especially in its visual style. The film is very dark both literally and metaphorically. The sky is always dark either because of night, pollution or rain. As in film noir, interior shots are also dark, confusing and shadowy. The typical *mise-en-scene* in a noir film would be claustrophobic and oppressive. A little light slanting through half-closed venetian blinds (perhaps picking up a curl of cigarette smoke) or a pool of light from a desk lamp would make the rest of the shot hard to read. In *Blade Runner*, we find ourselves similarly disconcerted. Although we see both the city and a number of interiors — Deckard's flat, Tyrell's apartment block, the rooftop where he encounters the dying replicant — we never really know where we are in the city or the building. In terms of characters, the film is also noirish. There seems to be no one we can really trust and Deckard himself is hard, cynical and tight-lipped just like central male characters in film noir who were often private eyes, detectives or cops-who-had-seen-enough. The humans have few attractive characteristics yet the replicants are powerful, angry and legitimately vengeful. Rachel is one of the most sympathetic yet she too carries strong noir overtones — rolled hair in the 1940s style, lip-gloss and shoulder pads. She certainly looks the part of the *femme fatale*. However, her self-expression also gives nothing away. The part is acted in a flat, despairing, passive style which is also not easy to read in terms of character. Those who know the noir tradition would be tempted to read her as dangerous until proven otherwise.

Fig 1.17 Blade Runner (USA 1982, director Ridley Scott). Rachel looks like a 1940s femme fatale, from the styling of her hair to the lighting and poise of the cigarette (Courtesy The Kobal Collection and the Ladd Company/Warner Bros)

Perhaps the earliest indications of the noir references come in the introduction of Deckard's voice-over 'They don't advertise for killers in a newspaper' — very reminiscent of the hard-bitten wise-guy voice-overs that characterised noir (and are so often mimicked now for a humorous hard-man effect). 'I'd been trailing Vincetti for weeks and what I'd seen didn't make me like him. No. I didn't like him one little bit.' In fact in retrospect both Scott and Ford were unhappy with this narrative technique and it was removed from the re-edited *Director's Cut*.

Blade Runner was a box-office success. Viewers found its originality intriguing. The critics were divided in their opinion — some found the mix of film noir and sci-fi problematic. There was a feeling that the makers had become so entranced with the noirish ambiance that they had allowed the visual aspects of this style of narration to overcome the potential strengths of the sci-fi form of narrative. On the other hand, it could be argued that an audience's knowledge of the conventions of both genres can engage in a much richer, more complex reading of the film.

TASK

When you have seen the film, carry out the following tasks:

1. After watching *Blade Runner*, discuss in a small group all those aspects that seemed to come from the classic sci-fi genre and all those that seem to link with the film noir genre. Make your lists of ideas as long as possible and include issues of visual style, characterisation, plot, narration, narrator, props, iconography, setting, *mise-en-scene*, photography, camera movement, themes.
2. Using your notes, write an essay with the following title:
    'The narrative of *Blade Runner* belongs to the science fiction genre, the narration to the genre of film noir.' Discuss, indicating whether you agree or disagree with the statement.

Note: this piece of work could be a class debate, a radio piece for a film programme, a radio debate, a TV debate or an essay.

Genre and marketing

Media-producing industries usually find it easier to anticipate sales if one product is planned to 'hail' roughly similar markets to another. TV companies, for example, can anticipate what certain types of programmes will attract in the way of advertising revenue and this allows them to plan their projected (anticipated) income so that there will be enough money each year for making programmes and paying the staff. Advertisers also find genre a useful landmark for helping them 'position' their products.

Definition

Positioning a product: this refers to the deliberate image given to a product (like a particular brand of make-up or car) in relation to the image of other competitors in the market. So some perfumes are classy, some daring, some fresh and natural. These qualities often have more to do with the product's market position than with its intrinsic qualities.

An important part of positioning is the fact that product qualities can be created by juxtapositioning or putting the product next to something else. A perfume advertised in *Vogue*, for example, is likely to pick up that magazine's glossy overtones.

So it helps advertisers if they have a very clear sense of the genre profile of the space they are buying. Some advertising psychologists have gone as far as to suggest that the location of an ad is as important in selling as the advertisement says. Adverts for diet foods and make-up, for example, will be more effective interspersed into a fashion programme on TV than in the middle of a programme like *London's Burning* or *999*. The opposite would be true for smoke alarms or home insurance.

TASK

If you were placing advertisements, against which genres and in which media would you position the following products:

- A herbal washing-up liquid.

- Skiing holidays.

- Private health insurance.

- A car magazine.

- Bereavement counselling services.

- A new British cheese.

Write a paragraph on each product specifying the genre you would choose as a context. Give examples of particular media texts you would ideally choose, e.g., a specific TV show or a particular newspaper. In your paragraph, indicate what kinds of qualities you are hoping will transfer themselves to your product in the minds of your audience.

1.4 INVESTIGATE NARRATIVE STRUCTURES

Story telling is one of the media's foremost functions. We refer to newspaper 'stories', TV news 'stories' ('and for a round-up of today's main stories'). Advertisements often tell stories ('before I was like that, but now I am like this'), cartoons, comics and soap operas consist of a multiplicity of stories about different characters.

Even an apparently factual medium like sports coverage is often structured by story telling: 'last time these two boxers met, x happened. Will tonight's events tell the same story?' '... and after all the training, all the build-up, it was silver only at the Olympics for the British number one. But what a prize to take back to her club in Bolton.'

In the second example, the central sporting event event (race/contest) has been elaborated with both a past — training — and a future — the triumphant return to the club.

So endemic is story telling to our culture that its presence passes largely without comment. Why is narrative such a feature of our culture and of our media? What are its defining features? What kinds of narratives do we find in our media? And what effect does media 'narrativisation' (making events, etc., into stories) have on its receivers?

These terms 'narrative' and 'story' are often used interchangeably and they do indeed refer to the same phenomenon. However, as analytical terms, there is a useful distinction to make between them which can be drawn out by the use of three examples.

Three stories

How the earth was made (Fig. 1.18, p. 58)

This story is adapted from a legend of the Papago Indians in North America.

A joke in a pub

One day, this man goes to the doctor's and the doctor tells him he's ill and he's only got 12 hours to live. Horrified, he goes to tell his best friend. The two of them spend the evening discussing the terrible news.

But at about midnight the friend stands up and says he's going to bed.

'How can you do that?' says the sick man, 'I've only got a few more hours to go!'

Fig 1.18 The start of a comic book version of the Papago Indian story

'I don't know what you're going on about,' says his friend. 'At least you haven't got to go to work in the morning.'

Crane nap of boozer (*Sun*, 21 August 1995)

A drunk climbed a 160ft crane yesterday, walked the same distance along a 2ft wide jib then fell asleep on a 3ft square platform.

He was winched to safety by fireman at a building site in Swindon.

A police spokesman said 'Someone should sign him up for a circus.'

These three stories are each very different. They come from different sources, different parts of the world and have very different subject matter. Two are (presumably) fictitious and one is (presumably) true. However, they are all examples of narrative. Analysing what they have in common can lead closer to a definition of this key media term.

The defining features of narrative

Time

All the stories tell of events unfolding over **time**. These three accounts are narratives partly because they have the structure 'this happened and then that happened and then that happened.' However, this is not natural time, unfolding like day and night, 24 hours at a time. Notice how, for example, in the second story several hours pass (between 'afternoon' and 'midnight') in the space of a couple of sentences. Media narratives often use truncated time in the same way. In a film, for example, years may pass by, indicated by nothing more substantial than a dissolve shot or a caption '20 years later'. These are **conventional** ways of indicating the passage of time in film.

The three stories all make use of **linear time**. However shortened the time span, the events unfold in the same sequence as they would do if we were witnessing them in real life. However, many popular media fictional forms now cut up time in a less linear fashion.

Fig. 1.18 shows the Papago Indian story in comic book form. Here the convention of the 'wiggly' lines indicates dreaminess or memory, something being imagined or recalled. A radio play might indicate a similar passage of time either forward or backwards with a dreamlike/dissolve sort of sound effect. These are conventional ways of indicating the passage of time: they seem natural. Yet in fact there is nothing natural about them. The earliest fiction films of the 1920s and 1930s, for example, depicted events, if not exactly in real time, at least in a structure of time closer to that experienced when watching a play on stage. The camera would be set up in the approximate position of a viewer in the theatre and events would unfold in front of it as characters walked on and off the set. During subsequent years with the development of the cinematic medium, film-makers invented — and viewers became accustomed to — many of the conventions now taken for granted. Another way of describing this process is to say that cinema invented a **language** for itself. Just as verbal grammar structures spoken and written language, so filmic conventions unconsciously structure audience response to cinema stories. As 'media literate' consumers, this grammar is learned very early on in our lives, so we are rarely conscious of its rules.

Artists and story-tellers continue to experiment with the cutting up of time. The film *Pulp Fiction* (Quentin Tarrantino, USA, 1994) pushed this movement one step forward when one of its main gangster characters (played by John Travolta) is shot and killed and yet is seen in many later scenes ('later' in the film, not later in the film's imagined sequence of events) alive and well. In this case the film-makers dispensed with the usual conventions indicating shifts in time-frame and relied instead on the modern audience's ability to reconstruct cut-up narratives in their heads.

As **G**oddard, the experimental film-maker of the 1960s and 1970s, said: 'a film should have a beginning, a middle and an end — but not necessarily in that order.'
Quoted in Collins **G**em quotations. Harper Collins. 1985.

Problem solving

Each of the three stories above begins by implying a problem or **enigma** (puzzle) which the subsequent story then goes on to unravel: How was the earth made? What will happen to the man with only a few hours to live? What happened to the man who climbed the crane? In the first and third example, the question is answered by the time the narrative is ended, the problem is **resolved** in the reader's mind. In the second, the joke about the man with only hours to live, the resolution is less clear, but jokes work by defeating expectations — they are not funny if we can anticipate the punch-lines. This particular joke is playing with the linear narrative expectations of its audience by sending the story off into an unexpected direction at the end. In this way the joke is closer to experimental or **avant-garde** works which may deliberately defeat or deny the audience's expectation of a clear ending.

The popular film *Thelma and Louise* (Ridley Scott, USA, 1991) came close to doing the same thing. The film is essentially a road movie in which the two main characters are on the run from the law after Louise shoots and kills the man who is attempting to rape her friend. The women's action was justified but they do not believe that they will get a fair hearing from the law because Thelma had been dancing and flirting with the man earlier in a nearby bar. At the end of the film, they are finally cornered in a car chase. Rather than give themselves up, they drive off a cliff over an enormous canyon. This car shot is frozen in mid-air leaving the audience wondering if this is the 'real ending' (i.e., 'will they die?') or is this ending more symbolic of their search, throughout the film, for escape (from dull husbands, violent men, unfair laws, etc.). The ending is ambiguous in a way that is unusual in most 'realist' narratives (ones that try to convince you that they are really happening there in front of your eyes).

But *Thelma and Louise* is unusual. Most works of fiction in the media have 'tidier', more closed, **narrative resolutions**. Perhaps the man and woman finally get together, or revenge has finally been delivered where it was due, or the all-important bridge has been blown up. The central action has in some way been completed and the characters' lives have reached a point where we can leave them with most of our curiosity satisfied.

These last examples are stories with a classic **beginning, middle and end** and it is an interesting question to ask why they are

Ridley Scott (director of Thelma and Louise) on the ending:

'From the moment of reading the script I never had a second thought about the ending. It just seemed appropriate that they carry on their journey. It's a metaphorical continuation.'

Fig 1.19 Thelma and Louise (Director Ridley Scott, USA 1991) (Courtesy of the Kobal Collection and **MGM**/Pathe)

so popular in our culture. Research into the stories of Aboriginal people and with Navajo Indians (before they had had as much exposure to US electronic media forms) suggests that their traditional tales and myths are often structured differently from our classic story line which moves from an opening where **equilibrium** is unbalanced by some turn of the plot, to a closing where a balance is returned. So why is this structure the norm for us? Even in more open-ended forms like soap opera where the story never ends completely but runs on from week to week, we still expect elements of the story line to reach completion. If a character steals something, for example, or starts a new relationship, we expect to find out at some stage what happened to them next, how things went. Indeed that expectation, the anticipated pleasure of finding out, may be what makes us switch on our televisions for the next episode. Good scriptwriters know this and take efforts to ensure that episodes end with an appropriate cliff-hanger.

TASK

Discuss in class: Is it true that most of our media fiction has neat endings? If so, why should this be? Take notes during discussion and see how far they fit with the theories discussed later in the unit and with the material in Unit 6 on audiences.

Narration and narrative

The terms 'narrative' and 'narration' are often used interchangeably, however, there is a useful distinction to draw between them. The word 'narrative' means simply 'story', the sequence of events in the account as if they had happened chronologically. The word 'narrative' puts more stress on the way in which the story was told. The first indicates *what* is told, the second *how* it is told.

Characters and motivation, cause and effect

Two of the three stories at the beginning of this section feature characters with motives. The dying man is seeking company, the crane climber does what he does because he is drunk and the 'firemen' rescue him because it is their job. Another way of thinking about characters and motivations is to think in terms of **cause and effect**: *because* the man was drunk, he climbed the crane, *because* the man was frightened, he went to see his friend. This kind of causality, where things happen because of a character's inner state, is very common in popular media narration, particularly in fiction. Indeed it is one of the most effective ways of moving the story forward. Characters initiate actions because they are jealous, or seeking revenge, or they are in love or they are embittered by past experiences. The story is fuelled by the character's psychological state. One of the most important tasks facing a writer of fiction is the need to 'characterise', to give the characters person-alities, so that we can begin to engage with them, to empathise, to understand their motives and so (important to the movement of narrative) begin to anticipate how they will behave next.

A study of selected advertisements can provide a quick study in characterisation. Adverts also often tell stories but they cannot afford the leisurely pace awarded to a full-length feature film to establish the personality of the main characters. There are two ways round this. One is to employ established actors who bring with them, in the public mind, certain qualities. Perhaps actor 'x' plays a character in a series who is always reliable while person 'y' is associated with meanness or snobbery. Advertisers can use these associations to shorthand the narrative and save time and therefore money. The resulting advert is operating '**intertextually**'.

Intertextuality: the meanings produced in one media text are transposed to enrich the meanings produced in another.

See p. 35.

See p. 44.

A second way of establishing character at speed is to make use of stereotypes. It can take just a few seconds of loving looks to establish that this person is, for example a 'good mother'. The right *mise-en-scène* and a harassed looking young woman in a suit can provoke the idea of 'overworked secretary'. Once the person-alities are established, the advert can operate, in miniature, the same narrative codes as the 'realist' fiction film. An enigma or problem is established, a character is motivated to do something and the problem is resolved, for example: harassed secretary can't cope. Resolution? A nice cup of tea or a new photocopier. Good mother upset at roughness of towels. Resolution? Fabric softener. And so on. Experienced advertisers are careful about the timing of their narration. If you watch attentively, you will notice that the moment that the problem is solved is also often the moment when the product itself or the product name appears on the screen. The theory is that the brief moment of warmth released in the viewer by the end of the enigma (however minimal) will transfer itself into affection for the product (called in the trade 'product warmth').

TASK

Script and/or storyboard a 30-second narrative advertisement for a product or service of your choice (e.g., a particular brand of trainers, courses at a local college). The advert should incorporate the features of enigma/problem, resolution, stereotype and 'product warmth'.

Realist and anti-realist narratives

However 'naturally' a film or radio story appears to unravel, anyone who has visited a film set or a radio station can testify to the massive levels of work and artifice which goes on behind the scenes to create this 'realistic' effect. Behind the recording of even the most simple scene in a sound studio, for example, lies a work-force of sound recordists, sound effects people, script writers, sound editors, etc. On a film set, the labour that goes into creating the feel of reality is even more elaborate. A veritable army of professionals is involved in this process: hairdressers, costume designers, camera operators, lighting technicians, script writers, script editors, etc. Of particular interest in this context is the work of the continuity person whose job it is to ensure the seamless joining of scene to scene. His or her role is to make sure, for example, that if a person was seen removing their hat in Scene 1, it has not magically appeared on their head again by Scene 2.

This *appearance* of reality is a very important element in our pleasure in watching a film or listening to a radio play. However, this pleasure, and this tendency for producers of media fiction to opt for 'realist' narratives (i.e., to construct their stories in ways which make them seem as if they are really happening as we watch/listen), has attracted some negative comment from some media theorists and from artists who want to work in a more challenging way.

The arguments against 'realism' are complicated and different critics adopt different positions in the debate. When popular narrative forms open with an enigma or problem, already the audience is hooked because solving the enigma is the prime motivation for continuing to watch. What happens next, how it will be resolved, how **equilibrium** will be restored to the situation becomes the driving force. Take as an example a classic Western where the story may begin with an otherwise contented community experiencing some form of disruption — perhaps cattle rustlers are about or the sheriff has been killed or there is a new guy in the saloon making trouble. Continuing to engage with this story (rather than turning off or tuning to a new channel) will be for a number of reasons:

■ Desire to know what is going to happen (a narrative interest).
■ Enjoyment of identifying with the situation (an engagement with the realism of the film).
■ Enjoyment or being carried along by a fast-moving story (compressed narrative time).
■ Pleasurable anticipation of the moment when the problems get sorted out (narrative closure).

Perhaps this example makes clear the power of narrative and realism working together to engage an audience in a fictional world — in any medium. Once hooked, the 'classic realist' narrative (the typical narrative pattern described here) will carry an audience or reader along a fairly predictable route. The equilibrium at the beginning of the story will become further disturbed. Characters will be motivated to do things and the forces in the story will finally come to some sort of conflict or crisis, the plot will reach a **climax** which will lead to a resolution of the problem and a return to a (new) equilibrium. There are many variations on this theme, the forces in the narrative may be love, hate, revenge; the characters may be more or less subtly depicted; the climax may be a gunfight,

Dziga Vertov, a Russian radical film-maker of the 1920s condemned popular 'realist' cinema, saying that escapism into the world of narrative fiction works 'like a mawkish spider's web, like drunkenness, religion, or hypnosis, to stuff such and such conception into the subconscious':

He also claimed that the ruling classes:

used this new toy to entertain the working masses or more accurately, to distract workers' attention from their fundamental objective, the struggle against their masters..

See C. MacCabe (1976), *Screen*.

a battle in outer space or a courtroom scene but none the less the basic **structure** described here can be found in a large percentage of our fiction media, and, as has already been discussed, rarely corresponds to our experience of shape or structure or time in our own lives.

One criticism of the predominance of this structure is that it is too reassuring, while real life may be full of troubles and difficulties that deserve attention (e.g., hunger in parts of the world, unemployment or even our own personal problems). Escaping to a fictional world, where everything is resolved in a happy ending, it has been argued, distracts people from engaging in asking questions about their own social predicament. Marxist media critics, and others from a socialist, left-wing or Communist background are keen to point out that in reality, life is full of contradictions — between rich and poor for example, or between the interests of different social classes.

Another criticism of the 'classic realist text' is that it engrosses the audience in stories which, although they may present serious issues like crime, abuse, sexual harassment, will close down any debate by resolution of the story rather than confrontation of the issue.

To take one example, in the film *Fatal Attraction* (Adrian Lyne, USA, 1987) the character played by Michael Douglas has a brief, extramarital affair with the character played by Glenn Close. When he discovers that she is both psychologically unbalanced and, possibly, pregnant, he takes what steps he can to rid himself of her including offering her money for an abortion (before even asking what she wants to do about her situation). She continues to threaten both himself and his family and is eventually shot by the Douglas character's wife. The film was well made, very tense and the Glenn Close character appeared unstable and frightening. When she was finally killed, there is a tremendous sense of relief and indeed, in many cinemas people cheered. We are glad to see this woman, who has killed no one, be killed. Yet if this situation was to be described in a court case or in a newspaper, a number of us might find ourselves feeling some sympathy for an unstable, rejected woman who feels she has been dumped after a short affair. In other words the forward thrust, narrative tension and convincing

Fig 1.20 'Camera Shy'
Cartoon courtesy of David Shenton

realism of this film has engineered us into a position where we are thinking and feeling things that may not be consistent with our own personal sense of morality. The form has the power to suspend our judgement. (Interestingly this particular film ends with a very classic moment of re-established normality/narrative closure — a long shot of a photo of Douglas' family together smiling.)

In order to defy some of this power of the **classic realist text** a number of artists, directors, etc., have chosen to continue to work within a fictional framework but in a way which breaks the illusion of reality — in an 'anti-realist' way. For example, a character in a film may turn round and address the viewer directly face to face and in this way destroy the impression created in most narrative films that the audiences can see the characters but they are unaware of our presence. Alternatively the story itself may be structured in a way that varies from the 'classic' structure defined above. Perhaps, for example, the ending refuses to give us that expected moment of closure. Perhaps there are two or three possible endings available or we are left not knowing what happened to some of the main characters. Sometimes a narrative may be recounted by a number of different characters all with their own version and style. Here the viewer is offered a choice between accounts.

The three examples of anti-realist techniques given above have the following aims in common:

- To break, to a greater or lesser degree, the illusion of reality.
- To make the audience work harder and be more thoughtful about what they see and hear.

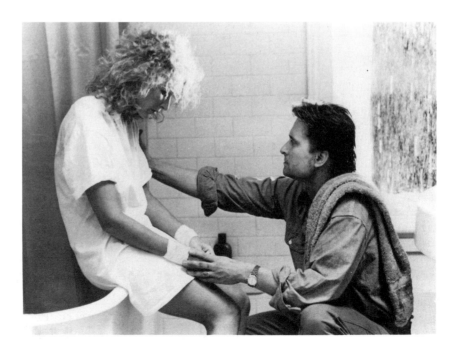

Fig 1.21   Fatal Attraction, Director Adrian Lyne, USA 1987, courtesy The Kobal Collection and Paramount Pictures Corporation

■ To increase the sense in the audience that they are an audience, to make them less absorbed in the story.

Other views on realism

The following selection of quotations from film-makers and theorists, and thoughts collected from a range of sources, give some parameters for the eternal debate concerned with the definition of realism, and the techniques that would best allow film-makers to achieve it. Is realism about using real people instead of actors in a film about a real situation? It is about creating a totally transparent fictional world, which is so convincing that it is felt to be realistic? Is realism entertaining? Is real-life entertaining? Can entertainment provide an accurate and truthful representation of reality? Is it more real, more truthful, to emphasise the fact that a film or video or television programme is constructed to make the viewer more aware of the presence of cameras, editing, all the constituent elements of film-making?

■ Lenin says of Hollywood, studio-based fiction in the 1920s and 1930s: '[it] hands out ready-made all the conclusions of a known theory, so that the reader [audience] does not even have to chew, but merely swallows what he is given.'

■ Documentary film was described by John Grierson (1932), the 'father' of the British Documentary Movement, as 'the creative treatment of actuality'.

■ Italian neorealism sought to use dramatic scripts to convey 'real' stories. The movement, which is identified as beginning with Rossellini's 1945 film, *Rome, Open City*, identifies as its central concerns and elements: realistic, authentic settings; ordinary people played by both professional and non-professional performers; everyday social problems; episodic plots which convey the rhythm of everyday life; and unobtrusive camera and editing techniques. Rossellini's realism was aided by the film stock he had to use, which gave his images a grainy, unembellished and documentary quality.

■ The argument for **cinéma-vérité**, otherwise known as 'direct cinema', was that narrative, narrator, etc., are too interventionist and distract us from the 'real' events taking place. The idea was, then, to record events 'as they happen', without worrying about, for example, concealing the film crew, or constructing a sequence of shots. This technique is often known as 'fly-on-the-wall'. The question to ask of this approach is: who is telling the story, to whom and for what purpose?

■ Paul Seban dismisses the realism of television news and documentary as superficial, indeed condemning it for offering spectacle, making tragedy part of entertainment:

■ Brecht argues that the spectator must be aware of all the contradictions within society and that in order to do this,

On Literature and Art, Progress Publishers.

The basic deception of 'direct cinema' is really its claim to transcribe truly the truth so that the film simply records objects and events mechanically. In reality the very fact of filming is of course already a productive intervention which modifies and transforms the material recorded. From the moment the camera intervenes, a form of manipulation begins.
Jean-Louis Comolli (1969), Cahiers du Cinema, **209**.

Television always stops at the moment when things are becoming interesting . . . It is terrible to think that finally, in television, misery and struggle are presented as spectacle. They show the rats, and the children who are going to eat them, the sordid picturesque, but they never say anything about the imperialism which is the cause of it.
'Entretien avec Paul Seban' (1969), Cinetique, **5** September, p. 10.
Brecht on Theatre.

the means of production of the artefact, whether it is film, television or a piece of theatre, must be made to participate in making meanings from that story. 'Realism does not consist of reproducing reality, but in showing things as they really are.'

■ Drama documentary has been the subject of many contentious issues. The fusing of two seemingly contradictory forms — 'fact' and 'fiction' — has caused media scandal after media scandal (Peter Watkins' *The War Game* was banned in 1968 and not shown until 1980). The debate about fact and fiction is the most prominent and visible aspect and consists of two approaches: one, a concern that the programme might be 'biased' and not in accordance with standards of 'impartiality' and 'balance'. Second, there is potential confusion for the audience. Broadcasting executives have expressed concern that viewers might be misled into believing that they are watching 'fact' when in fact they are watching 'fiction'. However, the programmes that have featured most prominently in the drama documentary debate are very often those that have been marked out for special attention, not because of their mixing of fact and fiction, but for their political content.

Note: be careful not to retell the story. Concentrate on the way it is put across and the kind of relationship which is established as a result between text and audience.

TASK

Chose three pieces of fiction media which seem different to you in their approach to narrative (i.e., different from the classic realist text). What are the differences in the way the story is told?

The following terms may be useful: realist, alternative, narrative structure, opening, closing, plot, mode of address, entertainment value, handling of time, enigma, equilibrium, climax, cause and effect, audience involvement, empathy, narrator(s).

Where is meaning made?

The degree to which you are convinced by the arguments in favour of anti-realism will partly depend on the answer to a deceptively simple question: where, in the relationship between text and audience, is meaning actually produced? Or, to put it more directly: who decides what a media text means? There are at least three possible answers to this question.

1. Meaning is produced by the people who make the media. For example, a journalist who is writing an article can decide what goes into it and what interpretation to offer the reader.
2. The traditions and conventions of the media **form** itself (film, radio, etc.) determine its meaning. This argument is particularly powerful in relation to the classic realist narrative form where, as we have seen, the power of narrative expectations and the conviction that we are there alongside the actors can sweep us along.

These three positions are elaborated more fully in Unit 6.

3. Meaning is made by the audience. The life experiences they bring with them decide the reading they extract from a text.

Non-fictional narratives and 'narrativisation'

So far, the arguments in this section have been supported by examples drawn from fictional media forms, and in particular from the Hollywood style 'classic realist text'. However, it is also worth considering the power of narrative in non-fiction contexts like TV news, adverts, newspapers, sports coverage, TV and radio documentary, etc. In general non-fiction media goes to less trouble to hide the means by which it has been produced. For example, it would not seem out of place in a sports programme to see another camera in shot during the broadcasting of a match. Yet it would seem very out of place in a work of fiction. News genres will often refer to their own work-force — 'convicted bank robber Walter Kidd told journalists today'. In some television programmes (crime documentaries/charity shows) it is not unusual to see the researchers, typists and administrative staff at work behind the shot.

However, in many instances of non-fictional media, the forces of narrative are still present and, some critics would say, much too present. The temptation to **narrativise** (make stories about) events that do not naturally fall into a story-telling format is partly a commercial one. We all love stories and stories sell goods. The media consultants to Jimmy White, the British snooker player, considered when he was an emerging young star, whether to give him a media image as a punk with a rebellious and anti-social personality. Such a character they felt would allow the media the chance to make many stories and hence Jimmy would get more publicity and be able to charge higher fees for his appearances (fortunately for us all, he refused to accept this image!).

News broadcasts often also follow the classic story-telling device of whetting the audience's appetite by hinting at future events as the story proceeds. They often end on an amusing note of human interest sometimes referred to as "the fluffy dog story", bringing the narrative a close with a happy to ending.

The making of media narratives

'Neutral' language is often used to describe the work of the professionals in non-fiction media: presenters 'present' a documentary, journalists 'cover' a story. This language gives the impression that the relationship between the real world and the world presented in the media is a straightforward and transparent one: stories are out there in the world waiting to be 'uncovered' and 'presented'. However, both this section and Element 1.2 on representation demonstrate that media workers are responsible also for **making** stories, **constructing** representations, **shaping** narratives. This is true even of the most unbiased reporting and there is nothing wrong or dishonest about this process. However, the instinct for narrativisation (entertaining) could override the need for detailed factual reporting. An example might be the way in which a complex difference of political opinions becomes reduced to 'a clash' between two MPs, an issue not of policy but of personality because this makes a better story.

EVIDENCE COLLECTION POINT

The lottery results present journalists with a paradoxical opportunity. On the one hand, these stories hold tremendous public interest. Many people buy lottery tickets and everyone would like to imagine what they would do if they won all that money. On the other hand, these stories have an in-built tendency to become dull and repetitive: Jack won £3 million, a week later Jill won £4 million, etc. So an issue for the news media is how to make each week's story more individual. It is a tempting opportunity to 'narrativise'. Find examples of how lottery wins have been narrativised in recent newspapers.

From now on and for always I cast off human immobility, I move constantly, I approach and pull away from objects. I creep under them, I leap onto them, I move alongside the mouth of a galloping horse, I cut into a crowd, I run before charging troops, I turn on my back, I take off with an air plane. . . Early Russian film maker, Dziga Vertov, quoted in Learning the Media, *Manuel Alvarado et al. (1987) Macmillan Education.*

The future of narrative?

Each change in media technology brings with it a change in the potentials of narrative and the relationship between stories and their audiences. The development of the printing press meant that stories (and practical information and social debate) could be shared among many more people and is seen by many historians for this reason as a key moment in the creation of modern democracies. The development of film technology allowed a whole new engagement between audience and text: one that brought the viewer much more 'inside' the action.

The introduction of interactive computer technology brings huge change in both the media and, as a result, social relations.

Potentially the most significant impact could be the involvement of the audience in shaping the path of the story. So far this has been relatively crude: while you are busy at your desk saving lemmings or killing aliens you are also to some extent 'writing' the story of the game. However, as interactive multi-media-based technology develops, it is possible to envisage a situation in which *you* could be the one to decide whether the wolf eats Little Red Riding Hood, if the Godfather dies or who wins World War Three. With the development of virtual reality, you could go even further and 'become' the agent of these happenings.

Interactivity certainly increases the involvement of the spectator in terms of their active participation, but is it possible that, at the same time, it disrupts one of the major pleasures of narrative: the experience of being swept along on a tide of events somewhat out of control? Charles Platt, writing in the influential international magazine, 'Wired' is one of the warning voices:

Wired, Summer 1995.

Consider the origins of storytelling. Besides a crackling fire Og the barbarian mesmerises his people with a gripping narrative. It begins: 'Once there was a warrior who lived far away in a tribe that cast him out into the wilderness . . .

A little kid pipes up: 'How far away did they live? Was it the other side of the mountains?'

The child's mother shushes him. 'Be quiet. Og's telling a story! Don't spoil it!'

And this is the point. As soon as you let the audience interrupt it can spoil that strange state of belief — that magical feeling of immersion — that a great story-teller creates.

2 PLANNING AND RESEARCH FOR MEDIA PRODUCTIONS

This unit will concentrate on researching material for media products. Audience research is also vital to the media industries. Although this is not carried out by the people who write the articles or make the programmes, it is important for them to know what audiences want to read, listen to or view in order to decide which subjects are of interest and how to present their ideas. This aspect of research is covered in depth in Unit 6, as well as the study of the effects of the media on audiences.

You will be introduced to a variety of research methods and their applications to any kind of media production you might undertake. It will be able to try out the various approaches to research for content and planning of media productions on manageable items that might later be included in a larger project. For example, you will produce a print item that might be a feature article in the quality press; you might then take the same research and adapt it to produce a feature within a radio or television programme. You might decide to expand the items you produce while practising your research skills and take them through to the production required by Units 3, 4 and 5.

2.1 INVESTIGATE RESEARCH METHODS

What is research?

Research is the process of finding information. What is done with that information afterwards and how it is presented depends on a number of factors. The information can be used to:

- write an essay;
- write a letter to an organisation;
- decide which course to do at university or college;
- find out how to do something.

Every day, everyone is likely to be engaged in some kind of research, and the process is no different if it is to be used for personal interest or to write an article in a newspaper or magazine, or to make a programme for television or radio.

Before you start, you need to decide what you will research and what you anticipate to be the *end result*. Is it an article, programme or advertisement? The different purposes will affect the kind of information you collect, the amount, the depth and how you use it.

Finding an idea

We would all like to think that ideas just arrive out of the blue. Without a brief to start off your thinking, you can spend hours searching for inspiration that never seems to come. Ideas do not generally come from the air — they are often based on or adapted from different sources. There is a great demand for ideas with the increase in the number of magazines, broadcasting (and narrowcasting) channels and radio stations. There is also a large market for training, promotional and corporate videos, most of which are commissioned and, therefore, have a specific subject, aim and audience in mind. Organisations that produce corporate videos, however, may be open to suggestions if a gap in the market can be identified.

Fig 2.1 Ideas are often based on or adapted from different sources

Sources of ideas

Ideas can come from:

- Printed material, such as newspapers, magazines, books, trade papers.

- Press releases.

- Conferences and trade fairs.

- Experts and specialists (e.g., a journalist might give you an idea for a factual article or programme; a police officer or doctor might tell you a story that you can use for a drama).

- Personal contacts — these may be friends or people you overhear in bus queues or shops. If you are working for an existing programme, members of the audience ring or send letters about subjects they think you should write or make a programme about.

- Previous articles in newspapers and periodicals or programmes, both radio and television.

These sources of ideas can apply to print, drama and factual programmes, in fact any media. You could write a factual article about homelessness for a newspaper or magazine, make a broadcast documentary about the same subject or write a play. You could also be commissioned to design an advertisement for a charity working with the homeless.

Finding an angle

Any idea can be explored from different views or 'angles'.

TASK

Take a subject, such as Christmas, unemployment or old age, and think of five different angles on it for a printed article or a broadcast programme. You might, if you choose Christmas, come up with:

- what do people eat and drink?

- how is the festival celebrated in different countries?

- what midwinter festivals do other religions have — what do they have in common with Christmas and where do they differ?

- what party games are there to play?

- what do people wear for Christmas parties?

Choose another subject and find five different angles.

To sell an idea to a commissioner in the media, you need to find something that will interest the reader or audience. In the advertising world, this is called the '**unique selling point**' or **USP**.

USP

What is it that this programme or article has that is different? Ask yourself these questions:

■ has it been done before?
■ has it been done in this way before?
■ why should it be done?

Do you have access to a particular place or event? Does your article or programme include people of particular interest, either because they are celebrities or because they have something of great interest to say? Have you found information that changes the accepted view of a situation?

Ideas also need a 'peg' on which to hang — why should this particular idea be developed now? Is it the anniversary of the birth or death of a famous person, or of an event? Has a book or survey been published?

Another consideration concerns the **purpose** of your idea. Does it fit into an easily recognised 'slot' on TV or radio? Is it suitable for commercial purposes? Is it your intent to make something for a completely different context?

Ideas do not necessarily have to target or fit an industrial or commercial model. The root of your idea may be driven by artistic, creative or political concerns, for instance, if you are making an experimental film or video, or a moving image installation piece for a gallery. If this is the case, you are more likely to be dealing with a public body when selling your idea, such as the Arts Council or a Regional Arts Board (more on this in Unit 8).

Readers and audiences

Having originated an idea, you need to know who it will interest. Who is the reader or audience? How are you going to present or package the idea? It is possible to take the same idea and work it in different ways for different kinds of media product.

Readership or audience research is not carried out by those who write articles or make productions (including advertisements). Specialist audience research companies are hired to find out what kind of people read particular newspapers or magazines, who the audience is for particular TV or radio programmes. Market research may also be used to determine whether an advertising campaign is likely to be successful, whether to launch a new product, or whether to commission a series of programmes after one pilot. Film distributors may require the ending of a film to change in response to previews shown to selected audiences.

The Shining has been dwindling fast since it was released in the US earlier this year. A two minute sequence was deleted from the end of the film in the first weeks of its run. After playing to generally bad reviews and erratic box office in America, the film was pre-tested before its opening in London and a further 25 minutes were cut.'
'Shine On And Out', Monthly Film Bulletin, November (1980).
The Shining (Stanley Kubrick USA, 1980)

As an individual or group originating an idea, there are two stages of marketing that idea: firstly, to the production company, producer or commissioning editor of a media company; and, secondly, the audience for which the product is intended.

TASK

Stage 1. Finding someone to buy and develop your idea

■ After you have chosen an idea, look at articles, programmes and films which are similar to your idea. Find out who wrote them, who commissioned them, who made them and where they appeared (channel, publication, etc.).

■ Look in the trade press to find out who is commissioning what. By reading *Broadcast*, for instance, over a period of time you will see the personalities with the purse-strings, and begin to notice what is in fashion.

■ Look at the ratings or circulation figures and see if you can begin to connect how audience research: affects who is likely to commission what; and what is to be expected of your product.

Polling organisations are also used to conduct surveys into, for instance, how people intend to vote at an election, or whether they think there is too much violence on television. Again, this kind of research is not carried out by the people who write the articles or make the programmes. For broadcasters, impartiality is obligatory by law and data collected by independent companies, such as MORI, is used. Newspapers do not have to be impartial (note the tabloids during the last general election in 1992), but figures from independent organisations are often used to lend authority to an article.

Note: See Unit 6 for quantitative, qualitative psychographic and lifestyle grouping research methods.

Developing the idea

Once you have your idea, you need to begin to develop it by finding out and organising the information you need. Sometimes it is clear who your readers or audience will be, for instance, if you have been commissioned to write for a particular publication or your programme is for a specific 'slot' in the TV or radio schedule. **Target audience** will be your primary concern if you are producing an advertisement or promotional material. Sometimes you will not decide on audience first and will decide in the course of the research period where the best appeal of your product lies.

There are a number of investigative methods that can be used in researching the content of a print article or programme. **Primary sources** include people, your own observation (perhaps backed up by photographs or video records) or specially commissioned surveys. **Secondary sources** include previously published material, broadcast programmes, archive material of information in databases, CD-ROM or on the Internet.

Fig 2.2a Front pages from the *Daily Mirror* and the *Sun* on 9 April 1992

Fig 2.2b Front pages from the *Daily Mirror* and the *Sun* on 1 May 1997

TASK

Primary and secondary research sources

There is a major pile-up due to icy conditions on a motorway in the UK and many people are seriously injured. Who will the primary sources be? Who will the secondary sources be?

TASK

Which of the following are primary and secondary sources?

- a diary;
- a biography;
- a police report from the scene of an accident;
- a letter;
- an expert who is hypothesising about possible reasons for a disaster;
- an expert who has conducted research and talks about that research;
- an autobiography;

Fig 2.3 Facts must be separated from opinions

Finding information

A well-known journalistic dictum goes: 'Never underestimate the audience's intelligence, never overestimate its knowledge.'

Information can be simply classified into two forms: facts and opinions. A fact is something that can be confirmed by *evidence* (although, remember 'facts' are not necessarily, unquestionably, 'the truth'). An opinion is how people interpret facts: what they *think* they mean. For instance, a pint glass may contain half a pint of beer. The amount of liquid can be measured — a *fact* — but some people will say the glass is *half full* and some will say it is *half empty*. That is an *opinion*.

Articles in newspapers and magazines or television and radio programmes can be made either summarising the accepted facts of a situation or disputing them.

There are three stages to finding the information. The first (and cheapest) is to *read* press cuttings, pamphlets, books — everything you can as background to the subject. This will help you to get a broad idea of the story and some idea of possible angles.

For instance, if you wanted to find out how many copies of a particular book were sold last year, you would not call a bookshop, which would tell you how many were sold in that particular shop. You would call the book's publisher.

You will then need to decide what *further information* you require, and how to track it down. If you need to speak to someone by phone to find more specialist or indepth information, you should prepare a list of questions to ensure that the call is most productive. You should also check that you are calling the appropriate place.

Lastly, when you are fairly clear about what the story will entail, you may have to go out and *experience* something, for example, interview someone in more depth than a telephone can achieve, or visit a location.

Recording information

You must always keep good records of the information you have found and where you found it. Make sure that all press cuttings and photocopies from books have the name of the publication, the publisher, the author and *the date* written on them. Keep a notebook and write down the organisations you called and the names and positions of people you spoke to, as well as the information they gave you. This both helps you to put information into context and makes sure that you do not call the same people twice.

See p. 506
'If you steal from one, it's plagiarism, if you steal from many it's research!'
Wilson Mizner

If you copy information from printed sources, note the title of the publication and its author, along with any other details, like its reference number if it is from an archive or specialist library. Using this sort of information can present **copyright** problems so you must devise a system which tells you which passages are copied out exactly and which ones are paraphrased. You could use quotation marks, underlining or different coloured ink to show which words or diagrams are taken from someone else's original work.

As well as a notebook, some people find index cards useful, especially when taking information from books or archives. The advantage is that you can shuffle cards around to sort out the best order in which to put information, for instance, putting two cards with similar or opposing information together.

Sources of information

Sources of information can be divided broadly into three sections: libraries and databases, official sources and individuals.

Libraries and databases

These include the following:

■ General libraries, such as a local public library, which will have a reference section and perhaps a local history section.

■ Specialist libraries which concentrate on a particular subject, for instance: the Fawcett Library collects material on women's history; the British Library Newspaper Library holds newspapers and magazines published in this country for the last few hundred years as well as some from abroad: The British Film Institute Library holds the largest collection of publications about film and television. You should always call in advance to find out whether the information you need is actually there, when the library is open and whether you will need to obtain a reader's ticket or pay a fee to use it. Increasingly, specialist libraries will put their data 'on-line'. Some libraries, such as the BFI, can tell you if the information you require can be found locally, for instance, in a university library.

■ Databases are usually held in libraries and can be held on microfilm, microfiche or CD-ROM. Information on computer may be linked to a central database holding details about local events. Newspapers, both national and local, are often found in libraries, either on film or CD-ROM. Some libraries also have encyclopaedias and other specialist information on CD-ROM.

JANET, the Joint Academic Network is useful for academic research. REUTERS, the worldwide news agency, has news story outlines on-line.

■ The Internet can also be used to obtain information, but you need to be careful here: some sources are more reliable than others. You need to be clear about what you want and where to find it before you start to avoid huge telephone bills.

Using a library

When using information from libraries, always check when it was published. It takes time to prepare and print a publication so by the time a book gets to a library, the information in it may be out of date. If you need up-to-date information, books are not necessarily the ideal source.

Official sources

Quangos: Quasi-Autonomous
Non-Governmental
Organisations

- Government departments.
- **Quangos** which have government funding to carry out public work, e.g., Arts Council of England, National Health Trust.
- Universities and academic schools.
- Trades unions, professional associations and clubs, for example, the National Union of Journalists, the Police Federation of England & Wales or a football team's supporters' club.
- Charities, like the Royal Society for the Prevention of Cruelty to Animals (RSPCA).
- **Self-help groups** and lobbying groups. Some groups, such as the Association for the Victims of Medical Accidents, help their members and lobby for changes in the law. The Electoral Reform Society is a **lobbying group** which campaigns for proportional representation. Greenpeace campaigns for the protection of the environment and has a high media profile.

Self-help groups are
organisations to support and
advise people with a particular
problem, for example, a
medical condition.
Lobbying groups concentrate
on trying to get changes in the
law in a particular area.

All of these organisations are very good sources of information and statistics, however, most will supply information with a bias towards their own interests and you need to take this into account when doing research. Addresses and phone numbers for these kinds of organisation will be found in the reference section of libraries.

Telephone enquiries

Finding the telephone number is the first and easiest step. When you ring up, you must have a clear idea of the information you need so the switchboard can put you through to the right section. Most organisations have someone who can answer general questions, so ask for the information office. Large organisations have press offices which can usually answer questions from the media or put you through to the right person.

Some organisations will ask you to write to or fax them, either because they want to check that you are from a reputable organisation or because they need to do some work to find the information you need.

When you ring government departments about something you are doing for the media, you must *always* go through the press office.

Find the name and address or fax number of the person you wish to contact. Explain what you need and give some idea of when you need it by. You will get a better response if you write on headed paper.

Letter writing guidelines
Remember:

■   Make sure you know the name and correct title of the person to whom you are writing, and his or her correct address or fax number.

■   When using someone's name, as in "Dear Ms Singh", you should finish your letter "Yours sincerely".

■   If you do not know the person's name and are using "Dear Sir/Madam", you should finish your letter "Yours faithfully".

■   You should enclose a self-addressed, stamped envelope.

Fig 2.4   Sample letter

Name of College
Address
Telephone number
(You may be able to have this printed out on official headed paper.)

1 Nov. 1996
Ms J Singh
Education Officer
The Museum of National Costume
Castle Gate
Donchester
DC3 3DC

Dear Ms Singh,

Following our telephone conversation this morning, I am writing to confirm that I would like information about visitors to your museum in the last 12 months for a programme/article about tourism in this area that I am preparing as part of my GNVQ. Can you tell me:

1)   How many people visited the museum in the last year?
2)   How many were adults, how many were children and how many were OAPs or received concessionary tickets?
3)   Which were the most popular and least popular months?
4)   What were the favourite exhibits?

I would also be very grateful for the results of any visitor surveys you may have carried out.
I have to complete the article/programme by the end of the month so I will need this information by 21 November. If you have any queries or want to discuss this further with me, you can leave a message with [name] at the above number and I will call you back. Thank you for your help.
I look forward to hearing from you.

Yours sincerely
Jack Jenkins
Student, GNVQ Media: Communication & Production

Individuals

People who have a particular area of expertise may not be attached to an organisation. They may be freelance journalists specialising in a subject or people whose lifelong interest or experience has made them experts in a particular field. You may find out about them either through something they have written, a book or a magazine article, or something that has been written about them. Because they do not always work for an organisation, they can be hard to track down. If they have written something, you may be able to contact them by writing to the publisher.

TASK

Choose one of the ideas from the task in Element 2.1 — finding an angle (e.g. Christmas, old age, etc.), or use the subjects of the productions you are developing for Units 3, 4 or 5. What sort of information must you find: facts, opinions? Where are you going to get this information? Make lists of the books you will need to consult and which organisations you could ring.

Fig 2.5   Choosing interviewees

Interviewees and contributors

You will often need to interview people to find more information (both facts and opinions) or to include what they say in your article or programme. This adds authenticity and human interest to your story. The kinds of contribution you want, whether you are writing an article or making a factual programme are:

- **Authority:** a person may be an expert because of his or her knowledge or job, e.g., a spokesperson for an organisation. He or she will offer *opinions*. An expert on the life of Sir Francis Drake cannot have experience of what it was like to be an Elizabethan sailor so can only give opinions. The manager of a group can talk about what will probably happen next if a member of the band decides to leave but cannot talk about what makes the band so popular. You would need to find a fan to talk about that.
- **Experience:** a person who has a first-hand knowledge of a subject or an event. He or she will relate *anecdotes* about what happened or express *emotion*.
- **Ability:** someone with a *skill to demonstrate*. Although this is mainly used in radio and moving-picture productions, you could use a series of photographs of a person doing something, e.g., cooking, mending an engine, running, in a print article.

Although, in general, you should mainly use the kind of people with whom your readers or audience can identify, it is a good idea to vary this occasionally, especially when choosing interviewees. Look for a range of backgrounds: age, social, ethnic and educational. It is tempting, especially when you are pushed for time, to use stereotypes, but it is more interesting (and responsible) not to.

Using the press to find interviewees

The programme or article might also want to find people to illustrate particular situations. As well as contacting likely clubs and self-help groups, this can be done by putting an advertisement into a newspaper or magazine, selecting the one to use by the kind of people sought. If you want to talk to young, single mothers, you might try baby magazines or the kind of publications they will read, as well as going to a local clinic.

■YOUR 15 MINUTES... Janet productions are seeking women who have had life-changing experiences with tarot, astrology or mediums.
TV researcher would like to hear from children of single mothers with positive stories to tell.
Call Janet on...

Fig 2.6   *The Guardian,*
1 July 1996

Contestants for quiz and game shows, although very different from this kind of interviewee, are often found by advertisement, especially in the programme listings magazines. They will be used for their ability, rather than their opinions or experiences, so the next section on interview techniques does not apply to them.

Interviews

The first contact that people usually have with a publication or a production is a **telephone call**. Their initial impression of the organisation you work for will come from you, especially if you do not represent a long-established company or programme strand. It is therefore a good idea to prepare what you want to say, even perhaps writing down all the key points you want to cover.

Introduce yourself by name and explain why you are calling. Give as much information as you can so you are put through to the right person. Unless you are doing investigative journalism, which requires considerable experience, always describe accurately who you are, and the purpose to which the research will be put.

You need help and co-operation, and the people you want this from need to trust you. Think about it from the person you are calling's point of view. He or she was probably not expecting this call and suddenly, out of the blue, a person wanting information suddenly rings. You will probably have to explain more than once who you are and what you are doing.

Sometimes you simply want information or, especially if you are writing an article for a publication, an opinion on something or an account of an experience. You can just write this down, but check that you have done it accurately (shorthand is a useful skill for anyone doing research in the media), perhaps by reading back your notes or sending the person a typed copy of the information you want to use. You can record the conversation on some models of answering machine but, as a matter of ethics, you should always inform the caller this is what you are doing: some broadcasters, like the BBC, require their staff to do this, even if the recording is for reference only.

Face-to-face interviews

After the initial conversation, you may decide to meet the person. This might be to conduct a longer interview. In television, it is usual to meet contributors before they are filmed except if they are already experienced in appearing on screen or in current affairs programmes with a very short timescale, where there may only be a telephone call to decide how well they will come across either in a recording or a studio appearance.

See Unit 1

In print and radio, you do not really need to see potential interviewees as you have already heard them on the telephone and what you hear is what you get. As tape is much cheaper than a full film crew, radio interviews are usually recorded at the first meeting and then edited. With the right equipment, you can also record an interview on the phone.

There are advantages to both methods. A filmed interview will give the potential contributor time to think over what to say but the freshness and immediacy of recording first thoughts may be lost.

You need to arrange a time, date and place. Give some indication of how long you expect the interview to take. If the interviewees are not used to dealing with the media, write to confirm the arrangements and why you are meeting.

Remember the reasons for including interviewees:
   opinion,
   anecdote,
   emotion,
   demonstration.

Preparing for the interview

Think of questions that will get useful responses. Instead of just asking interviewee for facts, you could ask them what they think of the situation, or make them relate an experience that will illustrate the situation.

Methods of recording interviews

Method	Advantages	Disadvantages
TAPE RECORDER		
Use where the subject is complicated or where accurate quotations are needed	Accurate record of what was said	Technically more complicated
		Interviewee may be self-conscious or unwilling to go on the record
NOTEBOOK		
Use where only a few things need to be recorded	Unobtrusive	Contact between interviewer and interviewee is broken while writing
CAMCORDER		
Use where the interviewee's appearance is a vital consideration or where a performance needs to be evaluated	Can see what the interviewee looks like and how he or she comes across	Interviewee may be self-conscious and unwilling to be frank
OWN MEMORY		
Use where detail is not important or where the subject is delicate	Enables a good rapport to be made between interviewer and interviewee	Important information may be forgotten. No proof of what was said

---

Using a tape recorder

Before the interview:

* Make sure you know how to use it.

* Test that it is working.

* Have spare batteries and tapes.

During the interview:

* Put an ident on the recording, e.g., say who you are, who the interviewee is and the date at the beginning of the recording. Mark this on the tape as well. This will also check that it is working before you do the interview.

* Do not fiddle with the equipment while the interview is in progress: set it up and ignore it.

* Ensure the tape does not finish unnoticed.

After the interview:

* Check that the interview was recorded before you leave.

Self-presentation

The research meeting has two purposes: the first is, effectively, to audition potential contributors, but the second is to gain their confidence. Dress, posture and manner will all contribute to the impression created so you must consider these as part of the preparation for the interview. .

Appearances are important. You need to look professional but not intimidating. The idea should be to show the interviewees that they have been considered and for some people casual clothes will be appropriate. Not too casual, however. When in doubt, dress up slightly to show an effort has been made.

Do you need to take anything else with you for the interview, photographs, for example, or copies of anything from which you might want to quote. If you are also considering locations, should

Most people form their views on those they meet within the first 15 seconds

YOU DON'T MIND US CHATTING WHILE I JOG ?!

Fig 2.7 There is a danger in overpreparing for interviews

you take a camera? There is a danger in over-preparing: taking everything you think you might ever need, it may look as if you are about to climb Everest!

Lastly, ensure that you know how to get there. Arriving late and flustered looks unprofessional and wastes the interviewee's time.

Conducting the interview

Calming nerves and getting off to a good start

Whatever the kind of interview, a few minutes' small talk is essential to ease both parties into the interview. Ask the questions you have already prepared but do not work rigidly down the list. Pursue interesting sidelines without losing sight of all the points to be covered.

Factual answers are easier for interviewees, so start off with them, both to check the research you have already done (an article or piece in a book is not guaranteed always to be correct), and to give them time to get used to you. When they have gained confidence and trust, you can go on to areas that are harder to answer, perhaps because they are things they will find hard to talk about or because they have to give an opinion that might seem controversial or ridiculous.

Which questions to ask

Any sentence starting how? who? what? why? when? and where? will lead to an open reply, giving more than a one-word answer. If what you want is a story about their experiences from the interviewee, "Tell me what happened ...?" should produce what is needed. Consider also how different phrasing will affect the answer:

- "What do you think will happen?"
- "What do you feel will happen?"
- "How do you see the situation developing?"

The reply will be slightly different to each of these. The first invites a reasoned analysis, the second a gut reaction and the third a speculative forecast. The interviewer can then follow up what the contributor says by asking closed questions requiring a more precise answer, perhaps by offering alternatives: "Does this mean X or Y?" or by asking the interviewee to confirm information with a simple 'yes' or 'no'.

Although the aim is to hold a conversation, the interviewee is the most important factor. Your views and experiences are, generally, not of interest and you may alienate the interviewee too if you express them. There are exceptions to this. If you are working on a personal subject, interviewees may talk more freely if they know you share or can understand their experiences.

Do not argue with interviewees, however misguided, repulsive or just plain wrong you consider their views! You might need to suggest that there are opposing views to elicit responses but this must be phrased impartially. Consider carefully which sources of opposing information or views you choose to quote.

On the other hand, be careful about expressing agreement: if both sides of an argument are to be included in the final article or programme contributors may be angry and feel betrayed if they were led to believe only their views would be represented. This might not have repercussions for you the first time you do it, but you may need their co-operation in the future.

Body language

Body language and posture are also important when you meet the interviewee. Hunching yourself defensively with crossed arms does not promote an atmosphere of trust. Sprawling backwards with your arms and legs spread out does not, however, suggest ease but superiority. Wriggling and fiddling with your hair or clothes is irritating and distracting.

Active listening means thinking about what the interviewee is saying, not what question you are going to ask next. It makes sure that you are getting what they say right. Check that you have understood by repeating what you think they have said in slightly different words.

Fig 2.8 Hunching yourself defensively does not promote an atmosphere of trust

Fig 2.9 Sprawling backwards does not suggest ease, but superiority

TASK

In groups of three, role play what you expect to happen during an interview that you are preparing. Record the interview on tape. Using the third person as an observer, ask him or her to note your approach to the following:

Questions:

■ Did you ask the right questions to get the information opinions and experiences you wanted?

■ Did the interviewee understand you?

■ Where the questions asked in the right order?

■ Did you try to make them say what you wanted to hear rather than what they wanted to say?

Behaviour:

■ Did you manage to make the person feel relaxed and forthcoming? (You can tell this partly by what they said and partly by how they were sitting — body language applies to interviewees as well as interviewers.)

■ What did your body language signal?

■ Did you ask questions politely or argue with the person?

   Ask the observer to feed back.
   The group should then listen back to the interview, considering the following:

■ in what way did you conduct the interview?

■ Were there any irritating mannerisms, for example, saying "like" every few words? (You will hate your own voice but you might as well get used to it now!)

   Each member of the group should carry out and review an interview.

Illustrating Your production

Finding information and interviewees are the major factors in most research. You may also need to illustrate the story, using one or more of the following methods:

■ still pictures;
■ moving pictures;
■ graphics, diagrams or drawings;
■ sound;
■ props and models (i.e. real objects).

Some of these, like graphics, you can prepare specifically but others will come from archive sources. This is where choices have to be made, especially in moving-picture productions where there are more options than in print or audio. You could, for example, find a still picture and moving pictures of the object or you might decide to get the object itself to use in the production. Do you just need the sound of music being played or will you need to see the people playing it?

Archives

All media use material from archive sources. Print journalism uses picture libraries, radio sound archives, television; video use both these and film archives too. Sometimes this is because it is too difficult or expensive to take a photograph or record sound or pictures because what you want is too far away or the event took place a long time ago.

Reproduction fees will depend on the use to which the picture is being put (print journalism, broadcast or non-broadcast programmes) and how big the readership or audience is going to be. Some libraries also have a special rate for educational use. They produce what are called **rate cards**, lists of how much the material they hold costs to use, but this only gives a basic idea. If you are using a lot of pictures from the same library, you can usually strike a deal. These may include fees for research, as well as using the material.

Note: Although it is unlikely that you will have a cash budget as a college production, you should be aware that rights of material to be used do belong to someone.

Still Pictures

Pictures libraries hold both colour and black and white photographs, or transparencies. Archives libraries can hold both prints and negatives, from which a print will have to be made and paid for, whether it is used or not in the final production. The use of the images then has to be cleared with the copyright holder, who charges an additional (often very high) fee.

Newspapers and broadcasters have their own stills libraries but also use material taken from commercial libraries. In newspapers or magazines, the name of the library or photographer will appear in small print by the side of the photograph: if there is no name, it will probably have been taken by a staff photographer and will belong to the publication itself. Moving image productions will not, however, put the source on the photograph but will list the names of the libraries used in the credits. Few will use specially taken photographs, as it is almost as easy to have a crew record moving pictures as to commission a photographer.

There are a number of specialist libraries which concentrate on one subject, such as the Environmental Picture Library or the Science Photo Library

Using still pictures

See p. 506

The photograph, painting or artwork you want to use may still be in copyright. There may also be reproduction rights in transparencies

DACS Designers & Artists Copyright Society

or copies of a picture owned by a gallery, even if the artist has been dead for more than 70 years and whose work is thus out of copyright. Many artists are members of **DACS**, the Designers & Artists Copyright Society, and they will help in obtaining permission to use their members' work. Not all artists, though, are members of this society. You will have to track them down and negotiate with them yourself. Increasingly the Internet is being used as a way of making collections available more widely.

Pictures or artwork taken from books can also be used for media products. The publisher of the book will be able to tell you who owns the copyright and so whose permission needs to be obtained.

CASE STUDY
Finding Moving pictures

Jane Mercer, film researcher, describes her experience:

My job is to find the footage requirements for any kind of moving-picture production. It might be a television programme, multi-media publishing, a corporate video or whatever.

I use a list of requirements that's either given to me or worked out in conjunction with the producer, director or writer of the project. The footage comes mainly from established libraries or archives but might also involve a great deal of lateral thinking about less obvious sources. Once I've located, selected and made sure the film is available for use (these are done at the same time), I have to agree charges. Ensuring the footage is available involves copyright and third-party clearance as well as other contractual constraints. The price will include royalty rates for the particular territories (worldwide, Europe, etc.) and use, like broadcasting or educational video. If I'm getting a lot of footage from the same source, I can usually negotiate a deal.

Having sorted all this out, I get the material on master so it can be transferred on to the chosen medium for when the editing starts. I also have to be ready for last-minute editing needs — holes often appear in the fabric at this stage.

Finally, when the project is finished or transmitted, I get together with the production assistant to draw up a detailed schedule of the footage used for production as broadcast. A return is made to the supplier as soon as possible so they can invoice us and be paid.

Viewing cassettes and master material have to be properly labelled and stored. All the paperwork involved at every stage has to be filed so it's available if there are any queries. I also make sure that anyone who's entitled to a copy of the programme, like a supplier, gets a copy.

Archive footage

Archive footage is used for three main reasons:

■ authenticity;
■ convenience;
■ expense.

The decision whether to use archive footage or shoot it yourself is taken for a combination of these reasons. Authenticity means that the audience needs to see the real thing. This might be a historical event or a clip from a film or programme being discussed. They might also need to see a place, e.g., South America where convenience and expense are the major considerations.

Film and video libraries

There are large, general archives, both national and regional, as well as commercial libraries. Some specialise in what is called **stock footage/library footage:** general shots of subjects like aeroplanes, animals or countries, often taken from out-takes or trims. These are useful when specially shot footage is either too expensive or too inconvenient to obtain.

Others are specialist libraries, like the film section of the Imperial War Museum which has footage from the two World Wars and all military matters involving British and Commonwealth troops.

(Before the advent of television, the cinema was where audience went to see the news both in this country and abroad.)

Other film libraries, like Pathe and British Movietone, are the archives of newsreel companies which used to make the short news packages that formed a standard part of cinema programmes until the 1970s.

Television companies also have archives of regional and network programmes.

TASK

Spot the library footage

Among your class, tape the evening's output from two or more television channels. Using a television listing guide, make a chart and record where stock or archive footage has been used. Do not ignore the adverts — they sometimes use archive material as well.

Compare the results across all channels. Present the findings visually (i.e., using graphs or pie charts) demonstrating.

■ percentage of stock footage for each genre of programme (including adverts);

■ reasons for use (geographic/historical/personalities, etc.).

Obtaining archive footage

Footage is usually costed by the minute. When the programme has been made, the programme makers tell the library how much footage has been used and the library then invoices for the amount. Music in a clip may require separate clearance.

Obviously, as students, the cost of locating material from major archives is prohibitive; however, if you have recorded material off-air and write to the broadcaster explaining that you want the clip for educational purposes, you may be lucky and have permission granted, assuming that the broadcaster holds the rights for the material.

Sound

There are three kinds of recorded sound:

■ **Music:** commercial discs and library/mood music can be used as background to enhance pictures and create an atmosphere, for example, of menace in a thriller. It can also be used to indicate where something is taking place, e.g., indigenous music over footage of a foreign country.

- **The spoken word:** used mainly for radio programmes but might also be used on the soundtrack of a drama to indicate the date when the action is taking place, e.g., a wartime broadcast. Recordings will mainly be found in sound archives but a number of local history projects have an oral history group who can record the memories of people in their area.
- **Sound effects:** these add to the action you can see. Using them to make real footage more impressive is ethically undesirable, if not forbidden, by broadcasters. In drama, however, they can be used to draw attention to particular action, e.g., opening a drawer to take out a knife. Like music, they can add to the creation of an atmosphere. No horror film is complete without the creaking of a door.

Using sound

Commercial discs present copyright problems when you want to use them in a production, which is why many dramas prefer to commission music specially or to hire musicians to record a particular piece of music. The main problems are as follows:

- Permission to use commercial recordings must be obtained in advance from the recording company, the publishers of the music and the performers. They will want to know how you are going to use it, how much you will need and what rights you want. Any of them can refuse permission.
- The rights to commercial recordings are usually owned by different companies in different countries. If the production is being sold abroad, permission to use the music has to be obtained from all the companies in all the **territories**.

Territories — 'Geographical areas for which the right to a media product acre bought and sold' Branston/Stafford, 1996

As well as getting the permission of those involved in the disc itself, there are two other rights involved in using already-recorded music: the right to record (i.e., to copy a disc or tape in order to dub it on to a programme) and the right to broadcast music. The first is administered by the Mechanical Copyright Protection Society (MCPS) the second by the Performing Right Society (PRS). The PRS not only issues licences to broadcasters, but places such as shops and hotels which play "musak" must also hold a licence. Inspectors check on this. Your college or school should have one so that it can hold concerts or play music at discos.

A third organisation, British Phonographic Performance (BPP), controls payments made for the use of recorded music which is broadcast. For non-broadcast videos, the organisations are the MCPS and Video Performance Ltd (VPL).

Mood music

Also called library or production music, this is subject to copyright but can usually be cleared worldwide relatively simply without the complications involved in selling a production containing commercially recorded music abroad.

If you use mood music in your production, you do not have to get permission in advance and there is a standard rate of charges. You send a music cue sheet listing which music was used and how many minutes and seconds to the MCPS, which then issue a synchronisation licence according to the rate card.

Sound effects

These are readily available on records and CDs but, although they are copyrighted, they are cleared like mood music. If the effect you want is unusual or highly specialised, you should think about doing it yourself.

Graphics

Graphics can be pie charts, bar charts or graphs to illustrate statistics or animated drawings. Graphics are not confined to

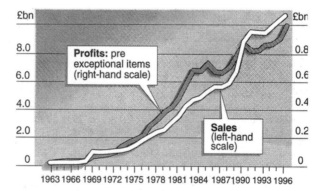

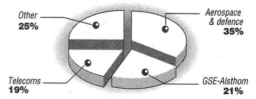

Fig 2.10 Taken from *The Guardian*, 4 July 1996

figures, they can be used for a variety of purposes, like headlines or credit sequences, and are produced in two ways:

- **Computer-generated:** this is the usual method. There are a variety of machines and the limits to what can be produced are mainly those of time and money.
- **Drawn:** although rarer, it is still a technique that can be considered. Because cameras are not allowed in court, special artists are often employed to sketch the people involved in trials. You might also want to use a cartoon or the kind of drawings and logos in this book to illustrate points.

When using graphics on television, remember that the screen is very small and the monitors in people's homes may not be of such high quality as those used professionally. In newspapers, too, the article in which the charts or drawings will appear has limited space. Keep it simple and include only the essential information.

Finding props

There are firms that hire props and costumes for productions, which are listed in directories of production services, and things like furniture for a set might also be hired from an antique shop.

People who have been approached for information or to appear in a programme might also have things that can be used. If you are doing an item about an invention, the company that is making it will gladly lend you one. For your own productions, ask friends and relatives but make sure, if the objects have any value at all, that they are covered by insurance, either your school/college's policy or the owners.

Locations

See p. 228 Unit 4 and p. 281 Unit 5

Middlemarch, recently adapted by the BBC from the novel by George Eliot, was based on Coventry in the 1830s. This town, however, was bombed during the Second World War and very little remains of the original buildings. In fact, Stamford in East Anglia was chosen as the setting because it still has many streets dating from that period.

Before going off to record a moving picture production, various members of the team do a *recce*. This is not always possible for a news story but is essential for a drama. How many and which people go depends on how complicated the production will be but the list will include the director, the production assistant and the cameraman/woman, the designer on a drama and possibly the sound recordist and a safety officer.

Finding locations

For a factual production, the story usually dictates which location to use. If you are doing an item about, for example, some aspect of education, you can choose between a number of establishments. The choice will depend on which people you are going to interview and which places best illustrate the points you are covering in the story.

Finding locations for drama productions is a trickier process. There are specialist companies, listed in production directories, which will check out places but usually the chief designer will spend time looking through files prepared for previous films and guidebooks and just driving round the country looking for the right

Stanley Kubrick's film *Full Metal Jacket* (1987, UK) about the Vietnam War was shot at a gasworks in Beckton on London's Isle of Dogs, using hundreds of imported palm trees.

Many local film commissions publish a code of practice which will help you organise more professionally your location shoots.

Eg:

The London Film Commission
c/o Carnival Films
12 Raddington Road
Ladbroke Grove
LONDON W10 5TG

Note: All of these factors apply to industry practices. You need to be aware of them although for your own productions a simple dialogue with the local police may be all that is necessary

place. Obviously, the nature of the drama will dictate the kind of location.

The British Film Commission was set up a few years ago, mainly to encourage foreign productions to make films in Britain by offering advice on locations and facilities. There are now a number of regional film commissions which can offer help in finding just the right place. Many local authorities in large cities also have film offices to assist location shooting in the area, and to promote the area to film companies.

Permission to use the site must also be obtained. Finding out who owns land can be difficult (sometimes it is an official secret). Houses and other buildings are usually easy, except if they are not occupied. If you cannot find out any other way, the local council can usually help because they will collect community charges or business rates.

Recording on location is a disruptive process. The police need to be informed of any filming and what type it is. If the production is reconstructing something like a robbery, a whole set of complications arise. It does not matter how obvious the film crew is, there will always be a good citizen who alerts the police to what appears to be a crime and there are things that cannot be done in a public place, especially where guns or replica guns are involved. Taking photos or recording for radio is less of a problem, unless you are going to be obstructing people or traffic.

Streets might need to be closed off for a period (this is where the police co-operation is essential) and people other than those being filmed can be inconvenienced. Make sure that everyone is informed and warned of the ways in which they might be affected. Consider

Fig 2.11 There will always be a good citizen to intervene in a shoot

whether you will need extra people to deal with the public to make sure they do not interrupt the recording.

Health and safety

You must also consider the health and safety of crew, contributors and the general public. Hazards can be either those that exist on site, such as:

- Electricity.
- Gas or other hazardous substances.
- Obstructions to exits.
- Heights.
- Water.
- Weather and environment: on location, weather conditions may have made the ground difficult to walk on; high winds may present problems and strong sunlight can dazzle.
- Night shoots.
- The general public: the crew is used to taking action to avoid hazards; the contributors will not be. There are wires to trip over, pieces of equipment to avoid and, in the event of any emergency, people must be escorted to safety. Check that you know where the fire exits are.

Hazards can also be caused by production requirements:

- Action (including stunts). What are crew and contributors required to do? Will the demands of filming add hazards to carrying out an action, even if it is something they do all the time?
- Noise.
- Weapons.
- Equipment.

If you are working with someone who has any kind of impairment such as short-sightedness, deafness, mobility problems or inability to read, even more care must be taken and potential dangers anticipated.

The process of deciding what problems may arise and how likely they are is called a **risk assessment**. Once the risks have been identified, a note of what actions to take to prevent incidents can be made. This can include:

- taking preventative action, e.g., moving obstructions where possible, putting up signs or stationing people at particular points both for safety and security;
- noting fire exits, escape routes and contact numbers for emergency services.

TASK

Risk Assessment Exercise

You have been sent to recce two locations for a drama production, one indoors, one outdoors. Go to the location and do the following.

■ Make a note of how suitable it will be for shooting in terms of potential shots.

■ List the problems involved in setting up the shoot (permissions, transport, noise, etc.) and how you will solve them.

■ Complete a risk assessment using the form in Fig. 2.12.

EVIDENCE COLLECTION POINT

The evidence required for this part of the unit is a production research handbook, containing information on sources, contacts, key approaches to research and main legal issues to be aware of at the research stage of a project. It is meant to represent an on-going process throughout the course of study. Each time you research a project, you will be able to look back at sources of information and ways of gathering information, using and adapting what you have done before and adding new contacts, new information as your experience increases.

You could, during the second year of your course, produce a student guide to research particular to your own locality and your own experience of the kinds of project undertaken on your GNVQ course, presenting it as a well-designed, published pamphlet and providing you with evidence for Unit 3.

PRODUCTION HAZARD ASSESSMENT

WORKING TITLE

Filming Date

Location Address

hedgehog productions ltd

Producer   Production Manager

Director   Designer

HAZARD ASSESSMENT CHECKLIST

Areas of Hazard	Rules/Regulations	
Access	GSR	
Animals - Wild/dangerous	TPR	
Audience/public	GSR/TPR	
Derelict buildings/dangerous structures	GSR	
Fire/flammable materials	TPR	
Inexperiened, child or disabled performer	TPR	
Manual lifting/handling	GSR	
Vehicles	GSR, TPR	
Violence/civil unrest	GSR	
Water/proximity to water	TPR	
Working at heights	GSR, TPR	
Other (please specify)		

GSR - General Safety Regulations (e.g. fire escapes, extinguishers, crowds. etc.)

TPR - Television Production Rules (e.g. securing cables, clearing streets, etc)
Usually these rules would be numbered in a handbook or manual. Go through the health and safety sections and list the main health and safety considerations, giving each a TPR or GSR number.

Details of activity and hazards identified: (please include a sketch where this would be helpful)

Precautions proposed: Details of crew/experts with responsibility for implementation of precautions:

Secondary precautions (back up for main precautions in case of failure):   Emergency arrangements (e.g. fire extinguishers, first aid):

Signature of Producer _____   Date _____

Fig 2.12 A production hazard assessment form

2.2 PLAN AND CARRY OUT RESEARCH FOR PRINT ITEMS

Who are you writing for?

Ideas for print items come from three sources:

- A journalist puts forward an idea to a commissioning editor who pays him or her to go off and write it.
- The editor asks the journalist to write a particular item that he or she requires for a publication.
- A 'think-tank' of those working on the title may put their heads together to come up with a range of suitable ideas and allocate the writing between themselves. This method of approach will usually only be found when a group decides to set a new title and are developing 'the look' of the product, or on collectively produced publications. Usually journalist and editors are very possessive about their ideas and are careful not to have them stolen.

Fig 2.13 A magazine's audience is not always obvious. Think about who reads what in your home regardless of who buys it. Your mum may buy *Take A Break,* but can you resist reading the 'true life stories'?

Every print item starts with the writer researching the publication for which they have been asked to write.

This will help you choose your angle on the content, determine your writing style and affect the kind of photograph or graphics used. If you are researching a fashion article for *Vogue*, you will be concerned with setting trends. You would have a long research period, use glossy colour photographs taken by a well-known fashion photographer and, perhaps, look specifically at *haute couture*. If you are researching a fashion article for your local newspaper, on the other hand, you are more likely to be concerned with following fashion. Your article would be written in a few days, produced in black and white, and is more likely to be concerned with high-street fashion.

Many publications have a statement of their aims. *The Face*, for example, aims for a particular style: to be a 'visual-oriented youth culture magazine'. If you decide to produce a print item for *The Face*, this would give you a good clue as to the content and final look of your print item. *The Big Issue*, on the other hand, aims: to campaign on behalf of the homeless and give a voice to their views and opinions; to highlight social issues; and to give homeless people an opportunity to work by selling the magazine.

TASK

If you had two print ideas, one about a new fashion on university campuses, the other on keeping warm outside in the winter, and you were given these two aim statements, where would you decide to place your print items?

Consider the conventions, content, audience and style of existing publications. (See Units 1.1 and 1.2 for approaches to analysis)

TASK

Choose two very different publications and compare and contrast two similar items from each, for example, a feature and an opinion column from a national daily newspaper and your local free newspaper. Look at the form and content of the items, the printed text, photographs, graphics and layout. Ask yourself:

- Do the publications print any kind of mission statement or aims, and do you think they fulfil them?
- What sort of language is used and is this appropriate to the audience?
- Is there a definable 'house style' for photographs and graphics?
- How are photographs anchored?
- How are issues and people represented?
- How many words and column inches are allocated to each item?
- Look at the adverts placed in your two publications. What do they say about the audience?

This task may also provide you with evidence towards Unit 1. Use the answers to these questions to write a description of the publications.

Genre

There is a range of genre for print items, each with its own stars and generic conventions. When you look through the contents page of any newspaper or magazine, you already have a certain amount of expectation about the type of material you will find in a feature as opposed to, say, the horoscope. Like the use of genre in other media, it has the purpose of determining whether work will be commissioned in the first place as the commissioning editor has to ensure a balance of different articles falling in with the style of the publication.

Range of Copy Produced

For example, many publications ran features on rave culture after the death of Leah Betts early in 1996.

■ **Features** are articles written about a person, issue or event, usually when it has some topical relevance. Features also include interviews and profiles of a topical nature.

■ An **interview** is an edited transcript of the interview itself with additional comment from the interviewer and usually includes at least one photograph.

■ A **profile** covers the career of a celebrity to date and may also include interview material, although this might not necessarily have been collected by the writer themselves.

■ **News** covers recent national and international events. The depth of reporting depends upon the publication. A broadsheet may devote many column inches, editorials and comment pages to an item which would barely get a mention in the 'Panorama' section of *Hello*!

■ **Fiction** may be commissioned specially for a particular publication, or be an adaptation of a recent short story or novel. The audience and style of the publication will determine the type of fiction published.

■ **Gossip** (sometimes called diary) columns chart the activities of the rich and famous. Magazines such as ***Hello***! take this genre as the bulk of their copy. While ***Hello***'s style is deferential and non-critical, some gossip columnists specialise in vicious criticism of those in the public eye.

Fig 2.14 Gary Larson's *The Far Side* cartoons appear daily in the London Evening Standard and have also found their way on to birthday cards, T-shirts & other merchandise

■ **Multiple interview** is where a set of standard questions are asked of a different celebrity each week, usually with a theme such as 'My room' or "A day in the life of".

■ **Comment, editorial** and **opinion** articles are similar in that they do not pretend to be 'objective journalism', but instead are a recognised authority's opinion of a person, issue or event.

■ **Previews** and **reviews**, where a film, book, television programme or event is commented on either before (preview) or after (review) it takes place, can either appear as 'objective' writing or the opinion of the reviewer. Similarly **horoscopes** may rely on a personality to interpret the stars or simply be a write up of the celestial picture with no reference to who may be interpreting it.

■ **Cartoons** are usually strongly identified with a particular publication (for, example, Gary Larson's cartoons in the *London Evening Standard*, Steve Bell's cartoons in the *Guardian*. They will usually be found on the same page and form part of the identity of the publication itself.

Other items include **letters pages, quizzes, competitions, make-overs**, and information on what is on in the **next issue**.

Finding Non-fiction Ideas

If you would like to write for a particular publication, ask yourself, who is the audience for that publication? Be aware of who your target audience is in terms of age, gender, race and social class. What are their interests? Is there an issue not covered in recent publications? Do you have a new or topical angle on the issues and concerns that tend to be covered by that publication? Do you have any special interests or knowledge which you could exploit? Do you know anyone you could interview who might fit in with the image of that publication and its readership? Do you have a strong opinion on a particular topical issue that effects the audience of a particular magazine?

What issues and people interest you? The art of good journalism is covering facts and telling an entertaining story.

TASK

A young man has saved a woman from the path of an on-coming bus. Someone telephones the newspaper and you are passed the information.

■ What interviews are you going to try to chase up?

■ What background material are you going to look for before the interviews?

■ What will you do for photographic coverage of the story?

■ Simulating the situation and with gathered reports and image/s, write a 400-word article for the local newspaper.

News reporting

To structure news articles, practise following some of these hints:

- Keep your opening sentence short, clear, to the point and accurate. Use active verbs rather than passive wherever possible but especially in your opening sentence:

  NOT: "It was decided by council officials yesterday ..."
  BUT: "Yesterday, council officials decided ..."

- For a news report rather than a feature, make sure that you do not stray from the essential information. This may be illustrated by interviews or supporting surveys or reports but only if it adds substantially to the reporting of facts.
- Sentences should be short but not to the point of avoiding important information. Precision is just as important. Again, paragraphs should be short (in general no more than five sentences) but again, precision should come first, readability second.
- Each paragraph should have a point — you should be able to write two or three words which summarise the content in each paragraph and the flow of the narrative should be logical.
- Be urgent but not dramatic — the facts should speak for themselves. Readers often become alienated by high drama. (Use words like "tragedy" and "massacre" with care.)
- Organise the flow of the article's narrative with care.
- It may be necessary to provide a context/history/background to a story for the implications to be obvious. Do this as unobtrusively as possible. ('Mr Close, who suffered his own personal tragedy last year when his dog died, was unable to ...')
- Introduce quotations via direct speech (Ms Breedon said: "I'm very happy to ...") or indirect speech (Ms Breedon said that she was very happy to ...). These make the text more engaging (and believable).
- Use facts and figures to back up information or do not use the information. There is nothing more off-putting for a reader than vagueness ("Ms O'Donnell dazzled the lecture hall with witty lines and some interesting ideas.")
- Try to avoid slang but if a word is appropriate for the style and context of the article, then use it with pride — do not use inverted commas to excuse it.

TASK

Choose an article from the news section of the newspaper. Find an example of as many of the elements listed above as you can. Does the journalist follow all of the conventions? If not, why not and what difference does it make? Write a short report, using extracts from the article to illustrate your points. Rewrite the article using *all* or *none* of the above elements. How does this alter the shape and organisation of the article?

Structuring an article

Your story may well follow a format which will go along these lines:

- *The lead* — opens the article.
- *The bridge* — situates or explains what you will be writing about.
- *The development* — the flow of the article through a logical sequence.
- *The ending* — a strong finish which is worthy of all the hard work which has gone into the article and kept a reader interested until the end.

Developing Ideas for Fiction

TASK

Research a variety of magazines (either mainstream or alternative) which publish fiction and comment on the length, style and content of creative writing you find. A broadsheet Sunday supplement may publish a lengthy section of a new book, and commission a critique of the new book for its arts section, whereas a locally produced fanzine may want a snappy, wacky tale with a local interest.

TASK

Choose one title and produce ideas for a piece of creative writing to be included in that publication. You may want to submit work you have written yourself, or select a section of a book. Remember to be aware of the length and style of work usually included in that publication.

TASK

Write the first two pages of your piece of creative writing or section of already published text and present to industry standards (see below). Indicate the length and content of the rest of your fictional piece and suggest why it would be suitable for the publication of your choice.

Now you have chosen the area you would like to research and have been commissioned to write it, you would be given a brief by the commissioning editor. A brief is the contract between you and the publication for the work you will produce. It is specific as to length, deadline, fee, expenses authorised and would carry a declaration of copyright declaring that the publishers own the copyright.

Whether you have originated the idea for your print product, or whether it was set by your teacher, now you must develop the idea. You should start with **secondary** research (see p. 76) to get as much background as possible, then more as to **Primary research**.

TASK

You are required to keep a record of the research you have carried out to develop an idea. Noting down all source material researched for an item will form an important part of this evidence and will also indicate the different research methods used. You will need a book or a folder that you can carry round with you so that you can enter information as and when you find it. If you scribble references on the back of a bus ticket it is unlikely that they will ever make it into your research notebook. When you have completed the project, you can transfer the most useful sources into your production research handbook (Element 2.1).

Fig 2.15 It helps to keep information in one place

Using interviews

Remember, there are two reasons you may need to interview someone. First, to get information or a quote on an issue. This type of interview can be done on the telephone where you will have to cultivate a good telephone manner, easy but not over-friendly, persistent but not bullying.

Read the section on preparing for an interview.

If your article is the interview itself, this will be better carried out face to face at a place which will reflect some thing of the interviewee, his or her home is ideal, a work area will do. Try to avoid meeting over a meal as your tape recorder will only pick up the clatter of cutlery and it is impossible to eat and take notes at the same time.

Be realistic about the resources you have available to you in terms of material, time and finances. You do not have to get a star name to have an interesting article, it is the quality of the writing itself, the approach and the suitability for its publication and audience that counts. If you do not have personal contact with a person in the public eye, they may be contacted through a press officer or other contact. Sometimes you will have to track down people by following one lead to another. This requires persistence and determination.

NWR Publications

Freelance Writer's Agreement

Between (the writer)
Address
Daytime Tel:

And
NWR Publications, PO Box 1, GUILDFORD GU2

1	Provisional title of article.	'ICE MEN'
2	Provisional publication date.	26 May 1997
3	Deadline for submission of manuscript	1 January 1997
4	Commissioned length	1700 words
5	Writer credit to read	NORRIS RILEY

6   Rights licensed for publication:
First UK right (NWR Publications)
Wordage rate @ £100 per 1000 words commissioned (plus leaflets/pamphlets/collected articles at a rate to be negotiated).

7   Payment within 28 days of publication

Signed (NWR Publications) ....
Date

Signed (Writer) ....
Date

Please sign both copies and return one to NWR Publications.

Fig 2.16   An example of a freelance writer's agreement

TASK

Keep a careful note of all the contacts you make during research. This may include home and office telephone numbers of all notable people and helpful agents, publicists and others with whom they may be in touch. You never know when you might need to phone them again to clarify a point or whether they may be useful when researching another item. Remember to keep your information up to date and change contact names when a new person moves into the post. This directory of contacts can be added to your production research handbook.

Know Your Deadline

(See p. 358)

Make sure you use investigative methods that fit into your deadline for delivery. There is no point undertaking detailed **qualitative** work for an article that has to be submitted within a few hours as you simply will not have time to carry out that sort of research. Referring to research already carried out or expert opinions may be another way of covering the topic. A feature can be short or in depth. A short feature will have to be produced swiftly and there is no time to search for indepth research on the topic.

For example, for a short feature on a subject such as stress, you could look at recent press cuttings (these give the most up-to-date details on a person or issue), telephone spokespersons for stress clinics and well-known stress cures.

A longer feature will require a more in-depth approach including some primary research, but you will have more time to produce your item. You may interview several different people who have suffered from stress and get a detailed picture of their lives. Possibly the interviewees have overcome stress using different methods. You will look at these different methods, visit centres where they are being carried out (photo opportunities), as well as talking to manufacturers of recent stress cures and alternative approaches to overcoming stress.

WRITING TECHNIQUES CHECKLIST

■ Use plain words instead of clever ones.

■ Use nouns and verbs more often than adjectives and adverbs.

■ Never use a long word when a short one will do as well.

■ Use a simple sentence rather than a complicated one.

■ Vary sentence length.

■ Put words you want to emphasise at the beginning or the end of a sentence.

■ Find a "voice" for your writing.

■ Write in as natural a style as possible (conversational if possible).

■ Write clearly.

TASK

You are a journalist for your local paper. Local bus routes are threatened with closure and you have been asked to produce an article on the service they provide to the community. Your article should be no longer than 300 words and must be delivered within two hours.

If you see an interesting angle as a result of your research for this exercise, you may want to develop it with interviews and further research for a longer feature.

Content Considerations

There are various legal and professional considerations you should look out for before producing copy. The **National Union of**

Anthony Davis (1988),
Magazine Journalism Today,
p. 191.

See Unit 8 (and p. 191) for
legal and ethical considerations
of primary concern to the print
industry:

■ The Press Complaints
   Commission (p. 506)
■ Libel (p. 505)
■ Official Secrets Act (p. 505)

Journalists Equity Council campaigns against thoughtless or stereotypical representations of people and social groups. You must take care with your use of language and choice of photographs and graphics to portray different social groups and types of people fairly. Use your knowledge of representation and stereotypes from Element 1.2 to inform your print product. For example, avoid writing 'policemen' which genders the police as male where 'police officers' serves the same purpose without assuming that all police are male. Some publications take stereotypes to the extreme such as a motor column declaring "The ladies will find this little car a joy with its easy-to-use controls and pastel colours."

Obviously, the same attention to legal and ethical issues must be observed as for the production of any media product.

Using Photographs

Photographs have the function of breaking up large sections of text to make the page more visually exciting and add to the information contained in the copy. Some articles rely on images more than copy. Any supporting photographs or cartoons must conform to the parameters of style set by the publication, e.g., glossy art photographs for glossy art publications, and black and white stark photographs for social comment. You must also consider what you are trying to do with your article. Do you intend to inform, persuade or entertain? The style of your text informs the reading of your photographs and visa versa.

If you are taking studio photographs to support your print item, using models or asking to photograph an interviewee, you must make sure that they sign a release form. This is a legal document ensuring that the magazine or newspaper owns the rights to that picture and is important in a dispute, and can also help the publication make money if that person becomes famous and the picture is often used in association with them.

There is an increasing trend in newspapers and their supplements to have photographs of the journalists themselves at the head of their article such as John Lyttle pictured at the head of his weekly column in *the Independent*.

John Lyttle

Fig 2.17 Journalists as
'stars' — **J**ohn Lyttle's weekly
column in *The Independent*

Photographs in features have the power to demonstrate, to show and to create an identity with a particular thing or person. A film star can say any number of things in an interview, but it is the quality and appeal of the photograph of him or her that accompanies the article that defines sex appeal!

Almost any type of article (except letters) benefits from a visual back-up. Where would travel writing be without exotic pictures to help transport your to another location? Cookery and fashion, consumer and gardening, news and diaries, they all use visuals to authenticate and enrich the text.

TASK

You have been asked to prepare a major feature for the consumer pages of a 'glossy' magazine of your choice. The feature will outline some of the products you can purchase to prepare you for the next season including fashion and accessories, home, car and garden goods and unusual gift ideas. Your feature will include words and photographs, but will be biased towards the visual. Choose your magazine and research the items that will be included in your article. You may take photographs of these or sketch your ideas for how the photographs would be taken. Produce copy which supports the visuals and suggest how you would arrange the layout.

TASK

Research a text-based feature idea for a specific publication of your choice. Justify your submission by outlining how your idea conforms in its style, content, subject matter and length with other feature ideas for that publication. Write your feature idea and submit it to industry standards (see below). Make sure that you keep careful records of all research carried out and note down all contacts made.

Purpose

You have carried out your research and have photograph opportunities planned or found library stills. Before you write your print item, you must decide on its purpose, that is, why are you writing it? Do you wish to inform, entertain or persuade your audience? The tone, language and style of your article will depend upon this aim. An informative article will include facts and figures and present new information in a clear and easy to understand style. The photographs chosen to support your article will give new insight and information on the subject.

An item designed to entertain will be witty and may have an amusing photograph, or more likely a cartoon or graphic to accompany it. An article written to persuade will use strong and emotive language and have a powerful and convincing through-line of argument which will have to be well planned and researched. The supporting photographs or graphics will strongly support your side of the argument. For example you would not write an article titled 'GNVQ — Hard Work For You' about the gruelling number of hours you have to work each week and support it with pictures of students sunbathing, lounging in the canteen and playing cards.

The language you use, the construction of your argument, the photographs and graphics that support your writing determine your item's power to persuade, entertain and inform.

Delivering Your Copy

Your chosen publication will have a book outlining the house style, that is the rules on spelling (whether to use organise or organize, jail or gaol) and punctuation, use of exclamation marks and quotation marks. Copy should be submitted typed or word processed on one side only. Arrange your layout with wide margins (around 66 characters per line) with generous space at the top and bottom of each page and double or triple spaced lines.

You will find more detail in this in Unit 3.

At the foot of first and subsequent pages, type 'mf' for 'more follows'. This is because the final page may fall off and might not be missed and your feature would go to print without an ending. At the head of second and subsequent pages, type your name and catch line, and at the end of the article type 'end'. Alternatively you may be able to access the editor electronically and deliver copy by direct input for on-screen subbing.

Headlines do not have to be included at this stage as it is impossible to know how many characters you can use, but editors usually welcome it if you include a few suggestions. When you write headlines do not use the past tense: make them sound very 'now' active and vigorous. A headline is more than just a label. It should be suggestive, exotic and sell the promise of what the reader will find if they read on.

Advertising

Advertising is an important source of income for newspapers and magazines. The quality of adverts published, what they advertise and how they are reproduced reflects the 'look' of the publication. For example the black and white roughly-reproduced adverts for *Viz* t-shirts in the back pages of **Viz** fits perfectly with the feel and image of that publication. Would it work just as well inserted into the Paris Fashion Week pages of *Vogue*?

There are several elements that you must consider to make a successful advertising campaign:

- The target audience: what section of the market are you trying to attract with your advertising campaign? The more specific you are, the more effective your campaign is likely to be.
- Specific quality of your product: what is special about your product that you can promote? what sets it apart from other similar products on the market?
- Slogan/copy and writing: you will only have a limited number of words that you can use for an advert yet the words used have to persuade the audience to buy a particular product. What words are particularly appealing to your audience? Are there words with a special significance for a particular group. How do the words interact with the supporting visuals?

TASK

Design a print advert for a mainstream magazine of your choice

Working in small groups, you are a copy-writing and production team in an advertising agency. You have been given two products to promote. One is a new 'wacky' sparkling fruit drink, the other is a boxed set of six hours of classic second World War Two and war-theme music.

■   Use market research techniques to research the potential buyers for these two products. This may take the form of a questionnaire.

■   Use audience research techniques to match the demographics of the potential buyers to the magazine of your choice. You may have to write to the magazine itself to research the demographic breakdown of its readership.

■   Produce copy for each of your adverts and a 'mock-up' (or rough version) of how the words and visual would work together. You may want to produce a few different versions of the same advert.

■   Investigate the costs of advertising space.

■   Where would your advert be placed in your *flat plan*?

See Units 6 and 7.

See Units 6 and 7.

See Unit 3.

Evaluating print ideas

During Element 2.2 you will have originated and researched a number of print items some of which will be print based, others image based. These will be recorded in your research notebook. Evaluating the success of the articles you have researched so far will help you decide which print items you may wish to produce for Unit 3. Reviewing will help you to recognise where your research may have been weak so that you can improve on that aspect of technique for next time. For example, maybe you found it difficult to use a telephone to get information. Before attempting Unit 3, it will be worthwhile to observe other people's telephone technique. Maybe script your conversations beforehand, and return to practising your technique with role-play situations.

Reviewing also helps you recognise your strengths so that you can repeat success. Maybe you found that you had a very relaxed but thorough interview technique and that you really could get interesting information out of people. This is an important skill to recognise and to use again in future.

TASK

Evaluate your process

How well did you go about researching your print items? Did you complete your research to deadline? Did you use a variety of sources, both primary and secondary to gather information? Did you note down source material in a methodical way? How effectively did you deal with people in interview situations? Did you make sure you fully understood your brief and were you aware of the type of publication you were researching for?

TASK

Evaluate your result

Review your aims for your article. In what sense were those aims achieved? Where did your piece succeed and where could it be improved? Did you demonstrate an awareness of the understanding of genre and style? How does it compare to existing publications in terms of style, format, content, use of visual back-up material? Analyse your work in terms of representation and use of language. How well do your photographs, cartoons and graphics support your copy? Did you submit your work to industry requirements? Are your photographs reproducible in print form?

2.3 PLAN AND CARRY OUT RESEARCH FOR AUDIO ITEMS

Radio is probably the first thing that springs to mind when you are considering producing an audio product. However, audio production can include an enormous range of forms from music recording to theatre sound-effects tapes, audio 'books', children's story and music tapes, multimedia CD-ROM audio tracks and the audio track of a tape slide show. Fine art 'installations', where the experience of viewing as well as the art works themselves is of importance, may also use sound to create an atmosphere in the gallery space.

Sound is a direct route to emotions and a major element in creating atmosphere. Watch a key segment of any horror film with the sound turned down and you may see a frightening scene, maybe a lone man being apprehended by something sinister in the middle of the night. But when you can hear everyday life going on around you, the birds outside, cars on the road, you feel safe. Now watch the segment with the sound turned up and notice the difference: the low rumbling sound, threatening music, sharp panting breathing as the victim tries to catch his breath. The soundtrack creates atmosphere, tone and mood, it creates the horror and informs our reading of the visuals. The soundtrack may also have a physical effect on us, it may give us goose bumps, or a silly sound effect will make us laugh. Radio has both a cerebral and psychological function. The restrained voices of a Radio 4 debate programme may seem to be dealing with ideas, but they also offer the comfort of another voice, companionship and human contact to their audience.

Range of audio items

You can choose any audio item to research and develop for Element 2.3 but although the audio items you eventually decide to produce for Unit 4 may be for radio, it is worth considering other uses of audio production. The most obvious is music production which will not be dealt with here. Other items might be atmospheric tapes to accompany an art exhibition or performance art, soundtracks for CD-ROM, audio books and sound effects tapes. Sound is a versatile and exciting medium. It is cheap and easy to operate and allows you to experiment. Creating sound is not a literal process. If you want to create the atmosphere for a ruined castle for a CD-ROM, for example, you might not get the best results from recording an atmosphere track in a real ruined castle (if you can find one!). You may have to record and use other sounds,

See also Unit 1 where
producer/sound recordist
Mandy Rose describes
constructing 'reality' through
sound.

maybe speed them up or slow them down, amplify or distort them until you have created a sound which says 'ruined castle' to you. In this sense you are the most important resource for your audio item. Your time and imagination, your willingness to try different approaches will pay off in a richer and more exciting audio track.

Sound tells a story

Just as pictures verify for a news audience that the events reported actually did happen, so sound authenticates the story told in an audio item. Sound will back up the words, add to the atmosphere and help create a more vivid picture in the audience's mind.

> **TASK**
> Using nothing but sound (i.e., no words or dialogue), devise a short story that can be told in exactly 60 seconds. Now record the sounds and dub edit them.
>   (See Unit 4, p. 235 on recording techniques)

Sound as atmosphere

Interpreting ideas in sound may lead you to use layering of different 'found' sounds, creating evocative atmospheres. You can pull sound from any source and mix it like a painter does paint until you have the 'feel' that suits you.

> **TASK**
> Your college is mounting an exhibition of a variety of fine art items created around the theme of power. Research and produce an audio track reflecting this theme which will be played in the gallery on continuous loop. Your eventual tape will be 15 minutes long, but for research purposes you must produce a five-minute sample of sound. Your research notes, with reasons for your choices, should also be presented.

Sound for CD-ROM

Many large publishing houses are presently busy recreating their series of factual books as CD-ROMs. Encyclopaedias, science, nature and school textbooks are just some of the sorts of titles being adapted to the new media. Part of the adaptation process includes creating sounds that support visuals and add extra information to the text. Voice-overs which speak text are also recorded. The discipline of this process ranges from the recording of exact commentary with tight time limits, to the imaginative freedom of creating new sounds. The aim of the soundtrack is more than merely a spoken book, it has to make the CD-ROM 'come alive'.

Note: You may want to develop this idea to use as Evidence for Unit 4.

TASK

You are a creative sound engineer working for a publishing company. Your company is converting some of its information books to CD-ROM. You have been asked to create sound and commentary for a new CD-ROM in the children's science series. Choose two pages from a children's book about dinosaurs taking care to select pages covering very different subjects (i.e., a mother tending her nest and a dinosaur fight).

Design a sound-track to add to the information found on the page. This will include scripting the spoken text to deliver the information included on the page in an interesting way. The words must be married to the appropriate visuals to enhance the learning experience. You will also need sound to create an atmosphere and inform on current ideas on what sorts of sounds dinosaurs made.

Keep records of research you have carried out, books used for reference and contacts made. You might also compile a record of useful ways of making sound effects for future reference.

Radio

Radio is perhaps the most versatile and accessible media in which to work. Equipment is relatively cheap and straightforward to learn to use, and programmes can be produced to industry standards on fairly inexpensive equipment.

Radio forms benefit from there being no visual boundaries to the medium, instead they use imagination and draw pictures in the audience's mind. A radio drama can take you into the future or back to ancient Egypt, anything is possible with the use of appropriate sound effects.

Although radio is global, it is also immediate. Millions of people may be listening to the same station as you, but as a listener you are by your set with the presenter seemingly talking just to you. Radio speaks to the individual and offers the warm sound of a human voice.

At the same time, radio is a transient, ephemeral medium. Once broadcast, the programmes disappear into nothingness. Radio also only occupies your mind and ears leaving your other senses free to do other things at the same time. Radio cannot demonstrate, it cannot show a graph or a map, or teach a surgeon how to carry out an operation. This is not to say that radio is not a visual form: Writing for radio requires you to draw on your visual imagination so that sounds and words suggest a picture.

Writing for radio

Radio has its own forms and conventions and the style of writing must reflect these. You could not simply record the dialogue of a television drama script to adapt it for radio, or produce a straight reading of a novel as the best way of presenting the work on radio.

The audience has to be entertained by sound alone and its imagination will have to be stimulated to fill in its own pictures. The easiest way for you to become familiar with this style is to listen to the radio. Not just to one programme, but to a number of different programmes on different stations. Think particularly about how it is written, and what sort of sound supports the text.

A radio script must sound as if the narrator or character (in a drama) is talking and not reading (unless it is fictional diary entries or letters). Similarly, dialogue must sound genuine and not 'bookish'. The only way to ensure this is to read aloud as you write, delivering the words as conversation. You should also be prepared to adjust dialogue if, in production, the actors find it difficult to deliver your wording or phrasing naturally. Remember that dialogue might also have to carry extra visual information to help the story, as well as a more frequent mention of characters' names to help the audience in establishing different identities.

There are some general points to consider when writing for radio which you can use across a variety of genres.

- Decide what you want to say.
- List your points in logical order.
- Make sure that the opening is interesting and informative.
- Write for the individual listener — visualise him or her while you write (do not think of the audience as a faceless 'mass').
- Speak out loud what you want to say and then write it down.
- Use 'signposts' to explain the structure where appropriate.
- Paint pictures, tell stories and appeal to all the senses.
- Use ordinary, conversational language and write in short sentences or phrases.
- Use punctuation to aid clarity for the reader.
- Type the script, double spaced, wide margins with clear paragraphs.
- When in doubt, keep it simple — remember, the idea is to express, not impress.
- Ensure that you finish with a clear 'rounding off' or résumé.

Source: R. McLeish (1994),
Radio Production, Focal Press.

Radio genre

Some stations may use only a few different types of programmes to build up their schedules, whereas others use a broad spectrum. Specialist music stations transmit a series of music shows punctuated by news (such as Radio 3 or JFM). Whereas Radio 4's schedule includes news, magazine, discussion, interview and fiction genres, to list but a few.

See Unit 1.

See Unit 1.

TASK

Identifying Radio Genres and Station Style

Record three programmes of a day's schedule from a station of your choice. Identify the different genres. What forms and conventions do you recognise which make you decide a certain programme belongs to a particular genre? In what ways do the productions convert the understood genre conventions to their own station style? What is different about a local radio news item from, say, a World Service news item that shows the style of the respective stations?

Radio music programmes

Music programming is a popular use of radio air time because record tracks provide a wide range of cheap, high quality and enjoyable sounds to a specific audience. Creating a successful music programme means that you have to be specific about the audience you wish to attract. A useful rule of thumb to go by is that most people form their musical taste in their teens. If you want to reach an audience of 50-year-olds, then you might tend to play music from the 1960s, and contemporary music which has been influenced by that era.

R. McLeish 1994, *Radio Production*, Focal Press.

The persona of the DJ is also important in creating a music programme. DJs tend to fall into three categories: the *low-profile* DJ who merely links the music drawing as little attention to him or herself as possible. The *speciality* DJ who knows a lot about the type of music being played and punctuates the show with interesting anecdotes and information about the music and performers, and the *personality* DJ who is the centre of the show and whose personality alone draws in the audience.

See Unit 2.1 and Unit 8

When researching for a music show, you have to be very aware of the rights of performers and record companies.

News

R. McLeish (1994), *Radio Production*, Focal Press. Example: Native South Americans had news of the destruction of the rain forest long before it became vogue for this to be news in the western world.

News is defined as 'that which is new, interesting and true'. In this respect it is culturally specific, as what is 'new, interesting and true' for one group of people may not be so for another. News organisations in democratic countries strive for a sense of objectivity to give credence to their 'balanced' point of view on world events, whereas news organisations in non-democratic countries may highly censor and distort news for propaganda purposes so that items may be neither 'new' or 'true'. In this country, the rules governing censorship and self-censorship of news items that apply to print also apply to audio and TV news items.

See Element 2.2, and Unit 8.

Speech radio stations tend to have longer news bulletins than music stations, and local radio stations have local news in addition to national and international news. News items may themselves be divided into two parts: news, that is the reporting of events, and current affairs, which is the discussion of events and issues in the news.

As a producer, the order of news programmes is of key importance. **Primacy** and recency affect the listener's understanding of news so that an item covered first will be best remembered and considered more important. The final statement will also affect the total impact of a news broadcast.

When reporting news stories it is important to give as much information as accurately as possible.

Primacy: being first in order of importance

source: R. McLeish (1994), *Radio Production,* Focal Press.

Researching news stories — the five Ws:

Who?
What?
Where?
When?
Why?

The script for your news item will answer as many of the 'five ws' as possible. All information included must be from reliable sources and it is *not* the journalist's job to conjecture.

TASK
Record the midday news of Radio 4 and your local radio station. Analyse, compare and contrast the two station's news output. Include content analysis (counting the seconds given to each item), the language and delivery of the announcer, the sequence of news items, the amount of discussion about items and any interesting omissions.

Using the newspapers from the next day's news, choose a single news item which would appear on both radio stations. Write a script for the news item for a Radio 4 newscaster and a script for your local radio newscaster taking into account the contrast in conventions and styles that you have already noted. Comment on how you would expect the script to be delivered.

Discussion programmes

In a discussion programme (for example, *The Moral Maze* on Radio 4), a chairperson oversees the discussion of a topical issue by a number of experts and interested parties. A discussion programme will not normally include all points of view as this tends to be confusing and inconclusive. Remembering that the audience cannot see the panel members, and so similar sounding voices may be confused by the listener, the producer will try and select panel members with different sounding voices. For example, trying to select a male and female representative for the two opposing points of view on a topic. A representative and an interested party may also be included on the panel.

TASK

As small production teams, you have been asked to produce a discussion programme for a radio station of your choice concerning a topical issue affecting students at your college (for example, parking, transport, IT support, leisure facilities at college). Appoint a member of your group as chairperson and devise a central question for the discussion (e.g., does the cafeteria provide an adequate service to students?). Research a panel of experts and interested parties to discuss the issue (the manager of the cafeteria, site manager and a vegan student might be obvious choices for this example). Note down the parameters of their arguments about the issue so that you have a rough idea of the sorts of things they are likely to say.

As a group, help the chairperson devise a list of questions to prompt the discussion. The chairperson should have a clear idea of the type of issues they want to cover to help them keep the discussion 'on course' and move it on if the opposing sides keep repeating themselves.

You must keep a record of all research carried out and contacts made as evidence that you have planned your discussion programme.

You may decide to produce your discussion programme for Unit 4.

Sports

Radio sports programmes offer live and pre-recorded coverage of sports events, and discussion by specialists about the play, current form of sports personalities and implications of results. Input originates from a combination of studio and outside broadcasts.

Sports presenters are skilled at delivering visually descriptive commentary to help the listener visualise the event. The sound of atmosphere at an event will add to the picture created in the listener's mind. Before coverage, presenters have to carry out a considerable amount of research to inform their commentary. They must be prepared with an official programme of events with timings of when play will start and finish; names and histories of key teams and players, and have an understanding of the importance of the sporting event and the implications of the possible results. It is also useful to know a bit of history about the ground and be able to refer to the smell and 'feeling' of the venue.

Sports commentators tend to be characters with an intense, if not pathological, love of sport. One could not draft a news reporter in to cover a sports event as a one-off unless that person was passionate about that particular sport. Sports commentators have detailed knowledge coupled with a precise control of English which creates almost a poetic and mythical feel to an event. We do not just tune in to the cricket at Edgbaston, it is 'the splendid grounds at Edgbaston where men have been made and broken'. And, if you have never visited Edgbaston, the commentator will describe the

Fig 2.18 Sports commentators tend to be characters with an intense love of sport

grounds, stands, the scent and the bustle of the place, the flower pots and even the seasonal flowers.

For this reason it is wise to choose a piece of sports commentary as your audio item only if you are a committed fan of the sport. You are more likely to be covering local sporting events which, in themselves, have their own sense of history and importance, with major characters and reputations at stake. The task of research will be must easier if you are already familiar with the rules of the sport.

You may wish to perfect your technique and produce a live commentary for Unit 4.

TASK

Write a script introducing a local sporting event including who is playing, the importance of the match, information on key players and everything of interest to the listener that you can include before the actual event.

Record your commentary on location before the event itself adding your comments on the weather, the mood and expectations of the crowd, up-to-date information on the form of the players and a description of the ground. If you are simulating a live broadcast, you will present your audio item uncut.

Listen to your recorded introduction and compare it to a sports commentary from broadcast radio. How could you improve your use of English, the detail of your description, the order of information and how you conveyed atmosphere and a sense of occasion?

Magazine programmes

Magazine programmes consist of a series of short items including interviews, discussion, features, music, current affairs, serialised adaptations, original fiction and competitions. Although there is a

Note: Interestingly 'Womans Hour' has shifted its image of knitting and jam-making and now attracts a significant male audience.

large range of items, they are designed to be of special interest to a specific audience. For example, *Woman's Hour on* Radio 4 consists of articles aimed specifically at women, while *The Locker Room* (also Radio 4) looks at items affecting men. Magazine programmes have a fairly constant format and structure, a regular transmission time and regular presenters so that the various items hold together under the programme's strong identity.

TASK

Choose and record two hour-long magazine programmes. Time and describe each of the items and links which constitute the programme. Present your findings in the form of a pie chart with each degree representing a minute of time and colour code the different items. Analyse what it is that makes the programme 'stick together'. Is it the presenter's links? Is there a theme to the choice of items? Is it the signature tune music used?

Research ideas for a five-minute feature for a specific magazine programme, remembering to keep a record of all primary and secondary research. Produce a script for your feature indicating supporting sound which will be used.

"As with all forms of story telling that are composed in words, not in visual images, radio always leaves that magical and enigmatic margin, that space of the invisible, which must be filled in by the imagination of the listener".

Angela Carter (1985), 'Preface', *The Collected Plays.*

Radio drama

Writing radio drama allows you almost boundless possibilities as a writer.

Your selection and development of possible story ideas is not restricted by feasibility in the same way as it is for video. In the listener's mind, sounds can recreate distant locations, mass crowd scenes and historical period, so these kind of considerations cease to become a limitation. However, where the television director, to create mood and meaning, has the help of all the visual codes of *mise en scene*, sound and the actor's body language, the radio producer (there are no directors in radio production) must purely evoke through words and sound.

Creating characters

Dialogue and the characters speaking that dialogue are the backbone of radio drama. Characters have to be well researched and defined before they can live and breath as believable people. Whether you are creating comic or tragic scenes, characters need to come across as real to your audience, and it is your powers of invention that makes them real. When creating characters you have to describe them in as much detail as possible. It is your job as a writer to know them inside out. What are their ages, height, weight and appearance? Are they good looking, clean, unpleasant? Is there anything unusual about the character, a birthmark or a mannerism that is unusual? What class and race do they belong to, where did they go to school and did they enjoy it? What prejudices do they have and what are their hobbies. What is their attitude to religion and politics. What are their likes and dislikes, taste in clothes, music and food. Would they choose a vindaloo or a safe biriani?

TASK

Based on your own experience and observation, write a profile for a fictional character, either for a drama or comedy.

When the characters are fully rounded and believable, you create the plot. For some writers, the plot is of key importance and the characters are designed to serve the needs of the plot. Plots tend to follow a familiar pattern starting with an equilibrium, the equilibrium is upset and, at the end, order is restored. When constructing your plot, ask yourself: is it believable? Is the story told through drama (conflict and danger)? Does each new plot movement have a conclusion or a pay-off or are there strands that do not go anywhere? Are your characters pushed to the limits by the plot? Does the plot move forward with each scene? Does it follow your characters through from equilibrium, to disruption to restoration of order at the end?

TASK

Briefly outline a plot for a ten-minute radio drama based around the title line of a song. The title of the song must be included in your drama. Produce a step-by-step outline of the plot charting each new scene and describing what happens in it. Make sure that each scene moves the action forward and that it is your main character who takes part in the action. Plan where your story is going to end and this will you give you an idea of where you are travelling to as you write.

- scripts should be presented in double or treble spacing to allow for notes or adjustments;
- dialogue should be in lower case;
- character names, directions and sound effects should be in upper case;
- number each piece of dialogue or sound effect and underline them or use bold typeface;
- mixing/editing indications should be included (e.g., fade down, fade under, cross fade, etc.).

The script extract here shows some of the conventions of script layout. As with television scripts, dialogue is in lower case; character names, directions and sound effects in upper case. Each piece of dialogue or sound effect is numbered for quick reference when producing in the studio.

Layout points to note:

- Sound effects and directions are underlined or in bold.

- Mixing/editing indications are given: eg., fade down, fade under, cross fade, etc.

- Lines are double- or triple-spaced to allow for notes and corrections.

Rockall—Drama script excerpt

1) **FX:** _____ **SOUND OF RADIO SET**

SEARCHING FOR A STATION

2) **RADIO ANNOUNCER:** `...Rockall, Bailey, Fisher, Dogger, Bite ....
(FADE UNDER DIALOGUE)

3) **GEORGE:** Damn! Missed it again!

4) **FX:** _____ **TAPPING AT WINDOW**

PANE

5) **FIRST INTRUDER: (OFF)** 'You'll be needing these, George. You left them on the rocks last night.'

6) **FX:** _____ **WINDOW LATCH UNDONE**
—CREAKS OPEN

WIND AND WAVES FADE UP.

7) **GEORGE:** **(FURIOUS)** Who the hell are you?

8) **FIRST INTRUDER:** 'Lord of the Gulf Stream ...but you can call me Jim.'
ETC...

Fig 2.19 Radio Drama Script Excerpt P. A. Kaspar (1996)

TASK

Write your radio drama staying true to the characters you have developed and keeping to your story outline. Submit your script to industry standards.

TASK

Record *The Archers* omnibus edition (Sunday morning), and listen carefully to work out the interweaving storylines. Choose one of these storylines and script the next episode for that particular subplot using the layout indicated above.

Radio advertising

Advertising can be found on commercial radio stations and provides a large proportion of the income for those stations. On BBC stations, advertising is limited to trailers for future programmes which employs some of the techniques of commercial advertising.

TASK

In groups of three or four, as a copy writing and production team in a large advertising agency, you have been given two products to promote. One is a new 'wacky' sparkling fruit drink the other is a boxed set of six hours of classic Second World War music and war-theme music. You have already researched the audience for these products. Now you have to produce a script for each product which could be produced as an audio item for Unit 4.

■ Use audience research techniques (See Units 6 and 7) to match the demographics of the potential buyers to that of a commercial radio station (either local or national). You may have to write to various radio stations that you feel would match the potential buyers.

■ Produce copy for each of your adverts and submit it to industry standards.

■ Investigate the costs of advertising space. Suggest potential broadcast times for your adverts and give reasons for your choices.

Compare your approach for radio with what you produced as ideas for print star ads.

Start by considering the key features of the product you are promoting and then match these key features to what you know about the target audience. Out of this list, choose a single memorable feature of the product and develop a short statement which connects the product's intention with a desirable effect. This is called the 'consumer benefit' or 'consumer premise'. These may be statements such as:

- A fizzy drink makes you more attractive to the opposite sex.
- Driving a certain car makes you a successful family man.
- Whiter washing makes you a better mother.
- Visiting the January sales will save you money.

You can test this premise by asking a selection of people if they believe it.

As you write copy from this premise, remember that radio is a visual as well as an aural form, indeed, as many of the senses should be appealed to as is possible. A Miller Genuine Draft lager advert for Virgin radio starts with the sound effects of a bottle opening:

The sound effect creates a picture of a well-chilled bottle of lager which tempts the taste buds to react and interests the listener in the copy.

MILLER GENUINE DRAFT

PRE-RECORDED TRAIL

Music

SFX: Bottle opening

VO: FM 105.8 / 1215 Virgin and Miller Genuine Draft are taking the lid off America's greatest cities

We have secured four unique tours of New York, LA, Chicago and San Francisco - and we're giving you the chance to go Underground.

This weekend - trip number one Chicago. See the very best the windy city has to offer..... then

SFX: Lift - "going down"

VO: Take a walk on the wild side, an underground tour of the most happening restaurants and latest clubs.

Listen all weekend, plus look out for more chances to win at your nearest Miller Genuine Draft Pub.

Underground America this weekend on Virgin

Script format: Copy is presented with extra sound effects clearly identified

Fig 2.20 Miller Genuine Draft pre-recorded trail. (source: Virgin Radio)

Another way to attract the audience's attention is to parody a known radio form. The Carling Black Label advert uses the form of a radio sports commentary to create humour. The sound effects of a roaring crowd also implicate the listener in the euphoric prospect of winning the competition on offer.

CARLING BLACK LABEL
YOU'RE THE REF SCRIPT

(FX = FOOTBALL COMMENTATOR)

IT'S VIEWED BY OVER 8 MILLION PEOPLE EVERY WEEK...

(FX)

IT CAN PULL A NATION TOGETHER...OR TEAR IT APART.

(FX)

AND ALL NEXT/THIS WEEK ITS YOUR TICKET TO WIN...

(BED GRINDS TO A HALT)

VIRGIN AND CARLING BLACK LABEL PRESENTS YOU'RE THE REF

(SFX WHISTLE AND CROWD ROARS...MUSIC ROCKS UP)

ITS YOUR CHANCE TO "TAKE A SHOT" AT 1000'S OF POUNDS IN PRIZES
INCLUDING BRITISH MIDLANDS HOLIDAYS, A YEARS SUPPLY OF CARLING
BLACK LABEL, MATCH TICKETS OR CD PACKS.

(FX)

YOU'RE THE REF, AT PARTICIPATING PUBS...AND ALL THIS/NEXT WEEK WITH
NICKY HORNE...ONLY ON FM 105.8 VIRGIN
                    1215 AM VIRGIN.

Fig 2.21   Script for You're the Ref (source: Virgin Radio)

2.4 PLAN AND CARRY OUT RESEARCH FOR MOVING IMAGE ITEMS

Fig 2.22 You need to make the most of equipment when it is available to you

Making moving image items is expensive and time consuming. Planning and research are vital to develop ideas to a stage where they can be written up into a proposal to be submitted to a production company to be commissioned. After commissioning, further research and planning are necessary for the smooth running of your production. In the production of film and television, where personnel and equipment are hired by the day and sometimes even by the hour, good planning is essential to make the most of expensive services. If you are a director of a television drama, it is no good hiring a crane for a key shot without first checking that the machinery can gain access to your location, that the camera operator can work on the equipment, that you have planned the shot itself, and that the actors know their parts. With planning, you get your shot. Without planning, you waste time and money, not to mention the good will and respect of work colleagues. In most colleges, resources are in short supply and time restraints are strict so you will need to plan and prepare to make the most of equipment when it is available to you. Thorough research helps limit the time you waste in production.

There is a huge range of moving image products, and new systems, for creating moving images are launched all the time. You may be familiar with film and television products and these may be the first things that spring to mind when you think of moving images, but new multi-media technologies are utilising moving images in novel ways such as with CD-ROMs and interactive products for new markets. These new products will develop their own forms and conventions and you may be interested in researching some of the more recent forms of moving images. If your college or school has software packages such as 'Photoshop' and 'Macro Media Director', and the capability to write CDs, there is nothing to stop you producing an interactive CD-ROM sequence as one of your products (for any of the practical units).

Storyboarding see p. 137 and 283

Storyboarding see p. 137 and 283

TASK

CDRO**M** on dinosaurs for children

Take the scenario described in the audio section (p. 115) and analyse at least 3 CDROMs for their visual approach. Note the different visual approaches (eg computer-generated graphics, animation, line-action video etc)

Now use a storyboard to plan your visuals for the dinosaur project.

You can video your storyboard frame by frame and add a rough soundtrack to show how your CDRO**M** pages might look

---

Planning guide for Pre-Production

Inspiration and ideas — see p. 73 to remind yourself of techniques for generating ideas.

Once you have an idea for a production, you will begin to consider the form that would most suit your idea. You may be interested in adrenaline sports, say, but how best would you develop this idea? You could set a television drama; record a fly-on-the-wall documentary about the antics of a group of people who bungee jump and ski off piste; you might decide to include it as an element in a game show (like *The Krypton Factor*); or create a video game animation. Deciding what is the most appropriate genre for your idea may depend on the research possibilities open to you. If you have a contact who will help you film an adrenaline sport event, then it is more likely that you will have a documentary on your hands. If you want to explain the drama and grief of an accident in an adrenaline sport, you may want to adapt the book on this subject as a drama for film or television. You may not be able to decide how you will develop your idea until you have done some further research.

Primary and secondary research

Note: as with research for other media, begin with secondary research and follow up with any necessary primary research (see p. 76)

As with Elements 2.2 and 2.3, it is essential to keep records of all the research you have carried out whether you will end up using it in the final production or not. Your research notebooks form some of the evidence of work carried out for this unit, as well as providing you with material for inclusion in your production research handbook.

When you have decided on an idea, go to the library and look at every book which is referenced to the key words of your idea. To develop ideas about people lost on a desert island, for example, you would look up 'castaway'. You must also think around the idea to get additional information. After castaways look up 'desert island', 'Pacific Ocean', 'survival' and 'lost at sea'. Also dip into novels, either fiction or autobiography, that cover the subject. By doing this you may discover that someone has already made your idea in one shape or form, in which case you might want to use their experience. For example, if you are making a documentary about castaways, you might want to ask people who have written about their experience as a castaway to be interviewed for your programme. You might want to use fiction or sections of text spoken by an actor as an atmospheric element in a documentary. CD-ROMs and the Internet, newspapers and magazines may provide you with further information. Your research will give you key information about the experience of being a castaway — how to survive, building a shelter, gathering food, medical emergencies, keeping morale going and trying to be rescued. These may form key sections to the structure of your documentary, key elements of your drama or rounds of your game show idea — whatever genre you decide to use your idea in, research underpins the quality of product.

The proposal

When you have developed your idea and chosen its form, you will have to write a proposal in order to sell the idea to pay for production. It is the proposal you give to a producer or commissioning executive that will convince them to buy your product.

A proposal must persuade the producer or commissioner to choose your project among the many others they have to choose from. The document does not only sell your idea, it sells you. An executive is more likely to commission a project from someone who can prove they have carried out research and planning, structure their thoughts coherently and be able to present their work well than someone who presents their ideas in note form on a shabby piece of paper.

Your proposal should have a top sheet containing your vital details (name, address, etc.) and the title, genre and length of your project, e.g. 'Castaways', an original 4 × 60-minute comedy drama.

Introduce your proposal with an opening sentence that explains your idea in a nutshell, a short punchy sentence or few sentences that 'says it all' to make the commissioning executive sit up and take notice and make them ask questions. This writing style which sells, informs and intrigues is used all the time on the back of book covers to help the person browsing in a bookshop decide which title to buy.

TASK

Read some book jackets to form an idea of length and style of your introduction.

Follow up the introduction by a clear explanation of your idea which covers the salient points you may have had to omit from the opening sentence. This may include a synopsis of the story and the style in which it will be made (for a drama); how you intend to film a documentary and what evidence you will use to follow your argument; the rules and format of your game show. In short, you are describing how you are going to achieve the product you promised in the introduction and give a more detailed picture of what the finished product will look like.

See creating a character for radio drama, p. 123.

Next you must detail the key characters of your project. If it is a drama you will produce character outlines. For a documentary, you will give histories of the major contributors and their relevance to the subject of the documentary. A game show may rely on the particular skills and qualities of the game show host, a known comedian might be key to the success of a sit-com. The personalities that 'carry' any show, be it a cookery programme or a feature film, are important selling points that control the tone and feel of the project and their persona would have to compliment that of the project itself.

It is wise to indicate who the audience would be for your project, but you will have to do this in a subtle way as many commissioning executives do not like to be told the best slot for your item. Do not feel tempted to say that your item will appeal to everyone, it will only look as though you have not done your research. You can indicate your intended audience by quoting research carried out so far, e.g., 'In Britain, three-and-a-half million people take part in adrenaline sports every year, and organisers of the events are reporting a rapid increase in interest.' A phrase like this clearly says that there is an audience for your programme and also demonstrates that you are aware of the considerations of a film or television company on producing an idea, that is, they must have an audience for their product.

Another way to indicate audience, scheduling and the nature of your product itself is to say what kind of programme (or film) it is like, or if it is an adaptation, what angle are you taking with your adaptation.

Your proposal should be word-processed, double spaced on one side of the paper only.

TASK

Devise an original drama idea for film or television and present it as a proposal following the guidelines above. You are first time writer and will have to include the first five pages of script with your proposal to prove to the commissioning editors that you can write.

If your proposal is accepted and you are commissioned, you will then go on to develop and write the script.

Script writing

Writing drama

It is an often quoted fact that 95% of the work that goes into writing a script is in the planning, research and preparation of the script. You will already have read around your subject to develop your characters and create plot ideas. You will also have developed your ideas into a proposal which outlines the story and the major characters and how you intend to film your moving image idea.

The next step is to produce a scene-by-scene breakdown of your drama saying what happens in each scene. Some writers have a card system where each scene is written on a different card. This enables the writer to shift scenes around if he or she finds the scene is not working in a particular place. Once you have produced a breakdown go through each scene using this checklist:

Scene breakdown checklist

■ Do the characters develop through each scene so that they know more at the end of the scene than they did at the beginning?

■ Does the action move forward with each scene? If the scene is going nowhere, is it really necessary?

■ Is there more than one thing happening in each scene?

■ Is information given through conflict as opposed to exposition (where the character simply says what is going on or fills in back story). If you find that your characters are simply talking it will not sound true to life. Maybe the information is not necessary or it can simply be shown instead of told.

■ Do you say anything with words where you could say it with images? Images are more potent than dialogue and are an easier way to put across information and create meaning in the mind of the audience. Do not **say** it if you can **show** it.

'ROCKALL' (extract)

12. INT. NIGHT CLIFFTOP COTTAGE FRONT ROOM

> GABRIEL AND ANGELA SIT IN THE
> WINDOWSEAT, KEEPING VIGIL OVER
> GEORGE WHO LIES UNCONSCIOUS ON
> THE MADE-UP COUCH. THEIR CLOTHES
> AND THE BLANKET ARE GREEN. OUTSIDE,
> THE WAVES CAN BE HEARD BEATING ON
> THE CLIFFS BELOW.

> GEORGE
>
> I'm going now.....if I don't go now.......

> HE TRIES TO RISE, GRASPING THE
> TRANSISTOR RADIO. THEY RESTRAIN HIM
> AND FORCE HIM BACK INTO BED.

> GABRIEL
>
> You're going nowhere until you get your strength
> back. Here.....(GIVES HIM A FLASK) Drink
> this...it will calm you down.

> GEORGE
>
> But I've had no news for so long....just
> weather....no news.......

> FADE OUT

Fig 2.23 Sample script extract from 'Rockall'. P.A. Kaspar 1996

You can only start writing when all the research, characters, plot and structure are in place. There are published format books which tell you exactly how to format each genre for film and television. As a rule of thumb, the instructions for radio scripts apply.

Writing adaptations

Adapting a novel, short story, or even a poem for film or television is another possibility. Many great works of art are inspired by art of a different genre and debate always follows famous adaptations from one form to another. You must decide what it is about the book that you will take for your adaptation. Francis Coppola made the film *Apocalypse Now* (USA, 1979) as an adaptation of Joseph Conrad's novel *Heart of Darkness*. The elements Coppola used from the novel were the voice-over narration, the story of journeying along a river, and the theme of the horror of man's condition. He took those elements and mixed them with some journalistic writing about Vietnam, fiction and myth to create the film.

Make sure that character names stand apart from dialogue and that stage directions are clearly defined from character and dialogue. Start each scene with a heading and conclude each scene with an instruction to 'cut to' or 'fade out', etc.

```
13.  INT. DAY    SCENE AS ABOVE
                        BRIGHT  MORNING  SUNSHINE  STREAMS
                        THROUGH  THE  WINDOW. THE  STORM  HAS
                        PASSED. GEORGE  LIES  ASLEEP. GABRIEL
                        AND  ANGELA  EXCHANGE  GLANCES.


                                GABRIEL
                        Wake up now George. It's time..........


                        GEORGE  COMES  ROUND. THEY  HELP  HIM
                        OUT  OF  BED.
                                ANGELA
                        You've got to climb by yourself. Here's a
                        stick....prop you up! And wrap this around you.
                        (WRAPS  HIM  IN  THE  GREEN  BLANKET.)
                        And don't forget...(HANDS  HIM  A  VINTAGE
                        ROBERTS  RADIO)


                                        CUT  TO


14. EXT. DAY         THE  MOUNTAIN  ABOVE  THE  BAY
                        GEORGE  REACHES  THE  SUMMIT. HIS
                        FACE  IS  FLUSHED  AND  WILD. HE  PLACES
                        THE  RADIO  REVERENTIALLY  ON  A
                        CENTRAL  ROCK  AND  TUNES  IN.........


                                RADIO  ANNOUNCER
                        Rockall, Fisher, Dogger, Portland Bill etc. etc.


                        (Extract from 'Rockall'. P.A.Kaspar  1996)
```

Fig 2.23 (continued)

When you have decided what it is about the novel or short story that you want to keep, you can jettison the rest. Intricate and convoluted thoughts where whole sections of text are spoken by a character have no place in a film or television drama. If the element cannot be dramatised then it cannot be made into a drama. You might find that it is only the novel's theme, or a very small section of the story that interests you. If this is so, then just work with the small section. There is no clear line where a drama that is inspired by a novel becomes an adaptation, the most important thing is that it should appear as a complete work in its own right, regardless of it being an adaptation. For example, you can understand *Apocalypse Now* even if you are not familiar with *Heart of Darkness*.

TASK

■ Find a book or a short story that you feel would adapt well to a film or television drama. Comment on which particular elements of the novel interest you and which you intend developing for your project. You may decide to do a moving image adaptation of the novel you have looked at for radio drama. You must take care to picture scenes of your adaptation to make sure that you will utilise the visual quality of the medium to its full potential.

■ Write a proposal for your adaptation idea stating clearly what it is about the novel you intend to use and what new elements you will devise to make the drama work.

■ Write the first five pages of script for your adaptation idea.

■ Comment on the decisions you made in creating your adaptation script. Was it easy to have material already written for you in novel form or was it a problem trying to access the text for visual writing?

■ Choose a film or television adaptation that you have seen recently and comment on the differences between the novel and moving image texts.

Writing for documentary

Writing commentary for documentary follows its own set of rules. If your footage has already demonstrated information, resist the temptation to repeat what has already been said in your commentary. Use the commentary only to add to the images, to say what cannot be said by moving pictures alone. If your documentary relies heavily on facts, find a variety of ways of giving facts and figures such as using diagrams or visual motifs. Visual reinforcement of this kind makes information more memorable. You may write your documentary voice-over for two voices (or more, although this is unusual). This can give the documentary a rhythm and feeling of moving forward, and also imply a sense of balance.

Just as for radio, your voice-over writing should not sound as if it is being read, but should follow the natural rhythms of the spoken voice. You will have to write the commentary first and read it aloud to adjust the script to normal speech rhythms.

Having edited your video, you will have to time where the voice-overs are to be, what they are to say, and write them to fill that gap. This also means reading and timing your voice-over inserts.

Research for production

When you have completed the script and it has been accepted for production, you have to start carrying out your production research and planning.

Storyboarding

Storyboards are used in planning moving image products as a way of testing whether the script is going to work, planning camera angles and movements, and arranging for the shooting of sound. In the industrial process of film and video-making, detailed storyboards are drawn up by the director. Involving the camera operator, sound person and designer are a way of making sure that key personnel are all talking on the same wavelength and imagining the same things from the script. When you draw a storyboard, you sketch your moving images ideas on to a series of 'screens' in order to plan how you will shoot and edit them and the end result looks a little look like a cartoon version of your script.

Storyboards are usually used in the planning of drama and commercials, where each frame must be very precise. They are less likely to be used in planning documentaries. Detail on producing storyboards can be found on p. 283.

TASK

Produce a storyboard for the title sequence of your drama idea including notes on how the shots will be achieved.

When you have devised your storyboard, you will have reached the pre-production stage which requires a new wave of planning and organisation. You will have a list of things that you need to do in order to be able to shoot the images that your need for your item. You may have to obtain permission to film at a certain location, collect or borrow props, audition actors, rehearse, book equipment, buy stock and arrange catering and transport. Pre-production planning is a huge job which cannot be left to one person and cannot be done at the last minute. If you are arranging an interview, you would have to fix a time possibly weeks in advance, visit the location where you will carry out the interview, discuss technical details to plan the shots you are going to want, as well as preparing questions and researching the subject you will be discussing.

TASK

Draw up a pre-production schedule which allows time for planning well in advance of the shooting days themselves to allow time to make other arrangements if you find that you cannot do something that you have planned.

See Unit 5.

EVIDENCE COLLECTION POINT

Advertising

- Analyse three television adverts, commenting on structure, use of language and narrative, stereotype and representation.

- Produce a treatment and storyboard demonstrating your television advert ideas for the two products you have been selling in print and audio, the new wacky fizzy drink and boxed set of Second World War records. When devising your advert do not forget to aim it specifically at the target audience for the product.

EVIDENCE COLLECTION POINT

Planning a sequence for a Non-Fiction Item

- Develop an idea for a current affairs programme for a current television strand (such as *Panorama* or *QED*). Produce a treatment for the programme outlining:

- the topical issue you intend to cover;

- the experts and evidence you will use to develop your argument;

- supporting material that will authenticate your approach to the topic and add visual interest;

- the presenter and style of presenting;

- the length and cost of your programme.

- Write a two-minute introduction to your current affairs programme summarising the different angles on the topical subject and the representatives and their perspectives on the argument that you will use in your programme. The introduction will use a variety of ways to catch the audience's interest.

EVIDENCE COLLECTION POINT

Planning a fiction moving image item

- Analyse the trailer for a feature film. Note the forms and conventions used in feature film trailers.

- Storyboard a trailer for a feature film idea which may be an original idea or an adaptation. Bear in mind the target audience for your film and ensure they are addressed specifically in your advert. Be aware of the generic conventions of your film and how genre is suggested in film posters, as this is an important element in marketing the film to an audience.

EVIDENCE COLLECTION

This unit has contained a variety of tasks to help you practise and refine your research skills. Research is a time-consuming business and, given that as GNVQ students you are unlikely to have the luxury of enough time, one way of economising would be to research a particular area in depth and use the information in different ways, to produce different kinds of media products in different media. The following assignments should give you some ideas.

ASSIGNMENT 1

Adapting research ideas

Use the research methodologies introduced in this unit to provide you with material for adaptation into a number of formats using the same context, as described below.

Male body image is becoming increasingly important. Men's magazines (apart from special interest and sports publications) include fashion, health and fitness, even make-up and fragrances for men: the cult of the body beautiful is well and truly here.

Carry out research to establish what kinds of beauty treatment appeals to men (e.g., chest-waxing, facials) and why body image is important to them. Is there a difference in attitude between different socioeconomic cultural groups? You might look at men's magazines like *GQ* or *Loaded*; you might explore the impact of the increased media visibility of the gay scene. You might visit your local beauty parlour and health club.

Use this information to develop the following:

An advertisement promoting a beauty product or service for men

Produce:

■ an idea for a print advertisement, including copy;

■ a 20-second radio commercial script;

■ a 30-second TV commercial script and storyboard.

A factual article or programme

This could take a 'serious' approach — e.g., the obsessive approach to body-building, the adverse effects of hair-restoring products — or it could take a humorous approach, for instance, explaining why men go through the agony of having their backs and chests waxed.
Produce:

■ a feature article for a women's magazine of your choice;

■ the script for a five-minute radio feature, to be inserted into a weekly magazine programme

- the treatment for a 30-minute TV documentary.

Planning a fiction idea

- Develop a proposal for a short, romantic story set in a fitness club. It is to be serialised in a magazine of your choice over six weeks. (Remember, the style and audience of your magazine will affect your approach — is it for a *Woman's Own* readership or a teenage magazine? Is it new gay fiction, or aimed at 'Cosmo' woman?) Write the first part of the series — it should be no more than 500 words.

- Develop a proposal for a radio soap set in a men's boutique. Do not forget to develop your key characters. The soap will play 15 minutes per day. Script the first episode of the soap. Take each storyline and note where episode 2 would lead on each.

- Develop a proposal and treatment for a TV sitcom set in a beauty parlour in suburbia. Storyboard the opening sequence. Analyse the storyboard, explaining how each slot encapsulates a vital aspect of character, location, relationships and situation.

ASSIGNMENT 2

Adaptation from a literary source

Read the following extract from Sara Paretsky's *Guardian Angel*.

Sara Paretsky writes crime fiction, in which her central character, V. I. Warshawsky, is a tough-talking, female private detective. Adapt the extract (you can embellish, change or add to as much as you like) as:

- a 20-second radio/30-second TV advertisement for dogfood;

- a 20-second radio/30-second TV advertisement for Sleeptight beds;

- a radio script for *Book at Bedtime*;

- a pre-title sequence for a new cop serial called *V.I. Warshawsky*.

Sex and the Single Girl

"Hot kisses covered my face, dragging me from deep sleep to the rim of consciousness. I groaned and slid deeper under the covers, hoping to sink back into the well of dreams. My companion wasn't in the humor for rest; she burrowed under the blankets and continued to lavish urgent affection on me.

When I covered my head with a pillow she started to mewl piteously. Now thoroughly awake, I rolled over and glared at her. "It's not even five-thirty. You can't possibly want to get up."

She paid no attention, either to my words or my efforts to dislodge her from my chest, but looked at me intently, her brown eyes opened wide, her mouth parted slightly to show the tip of her pink tongue.

I bared my teeth at her. She licked my nose anxiously. I sat up, pushing her head away from my face. "It was this indiscriminate distribution of your kisses that got you into this fix to begin with."

Happy to see me awake, Peppy lumbered down from the bed and headed for the door. She turned to see if I was following, making little whimpering noises in her impatience. I pulled a sweatshirt and shorts from the heap of clothes near the bed and padded on sleep-thickened legs to the back door. I fumbled with the triple locks. By that time Peppy was whimpering in earnest, but she managed to control herself while I got the door open. Breeding shows, I guess.

I watched her down the three flights of stairs. Pregnancy had distended her sides and slowed her progress, but she made it to her spot by the back gate before relieving herself. When she was finished she didn't take her usual tour of the yard to drive away cats and other marauders. Instead she waddled back to the stairs. She stopped outside the ground-floor door and let out a sharp bark.

Fine. Let Mr. Contreras have her. He was my first-floor neighbor, part owner of the dog, and wholly responsible for her condition. Well, not wholly — that had been the work of a black Lab four doors up the street.

Fig 2.24 Extract from Sarah Paretsky *Guardian Angel*, Penguin, 1992

3 PRODUCING PRINT PRODUCTS

As with all of the production units (3, 4 and 5), you may already have begun the process of producing printed items. If you are following the GNVQ on a unit-by-unit basis, you will almost certainly have produced proposals and, possibly, articles. You may also have tried laying out your item on a page. These items may be used within or redeveloped for the print product required for this unit.

Print publishing is the oldest form of mass media, originating with the invention of the printing press in the fifteenth century. This made possible the mass production of printed materials for the first time. Compared with other media, print products are the most prolific and among the most wide ranging, from the humble parish newsletter to the best-selling national daily newspaper, from corporate brochures to glossy fashion magazines. Book publishing was revolutionised early in the twentieth century by the emergence of Penguin in 1935, which made available cheap, paperback copies of best-sellers and classics at affordable prices.

Print products can range from the involvement of just one author (e.g., a novel) to the work of entire teams of writers, photographers, editors, etc. (e.g., newspapers). Even the work of a single writer, however, needs an entire team of people to take it through the publishing process, from the point before the writing begins (commissioning), through the various stages of writing, editing, proofing, design and layout to printing, distribution and marketing.

This unit will help to guide you through that process, aiming to reflect real working practice as far as is possible. While this may not always be practical (in terms of available resources, time and expertise) or even desirable (in terms of aiming to experience as broad a skills training as is possible rather than specialising), you will be able to assess how the process of print production that you will be undertaking fits into the picture of professional working practice.

3.1 PLAN THE PRODUCTION PROCESS FOR PRINT PRODUCTS

Know Your Medium

Before you can begin to plan a print published product, you will need to establish whether you want to produce a 'replica' national or local newspaper, or whether you want to do something more specialised. Although it is good practice to undertake writing news and feature articles which emulate the style of the daily or weekly press, it is probably more practical, given the restraints of time and resources under which you are likely to be working, to aim to produce a college newspaper, a specialist fanzine or a magazine into which you can incorporate skills such as photography, which you may be studying as a GNVQ Optional Unit. If you have the opportunity to negotiate having articles printed in your local paper, this would be a better way for you to gain journalistic experience, not to mention a cuttings file for your portfolio.

Some schools and colleges have negotiated a regular one-page slot with their local papers on a monthly or bi-monthly basis — excellent experience if you are able to organise it.

Print products, however, can range from the above to a set of glossy brochures publicising a festival or event. A film festival programme, for instance, could provide you with the opportunity

THE PRODUCTION PROCESS

RESEARCH TARGET AUDIENCE
INVESTIGATE COMPETITION
CONSIDER ADVERTISING, COVER PRICE, DISTRIBUTION AND SALES
PLAN, SCHEDULE, BUDGET PRODUCTION
ASSIGN ROLES AND RESPONSIBILITIES
AGREE PRODUCT OUTLINE
PLAN DESIGN, STYLE, HOUSE STYLE, TITLE
PRODUCE MATERIAL IN ACCORDANCE WITH DECISIONS
LAYOUT, EDIT, SUB - EDIT
PRODUCTION
ADVERTISING OF PUBLICATION
DISTRIBUTION
SALES

Fig 3.1

both to compile a printed product, design visually stunning page layouts and write the kinds of film reviews which would enable you to produce evidence for Unit 1.

If you have particular graphics talent, you may wish to use them to produce a 'graphic novel' — you could do this either by using computer graphics, or the images could be hand-drawn and scanned in. Graphic novels tend to draw upon classic imagery from comics such as *Batman* or futuristic stories. You could use a graphic approach to tell quite different stories, rather than simply reproduce the genre's usual narrative line.

Planning Print Products

To justify the launch of a new print product, a proposal needs to convince those investing in it that the publication is viable, given the available resources and expertise. It is no good planning to produce a glossy magazine when available resources run to a photocopier and a few cups of tea. The proposal also needs to outline how the publication will compete on the open market with similar products, how it will target the audience and how it will make a profit despite competition.

Note: You may wish to build on something you have developed in Unit 2.

Originate, justify and agree proposals for print products

When planning your own printed products, ask yourself:

- What is the **purpose** of the publication?
- Who is it aimed at (the **target audience**)?
- What kind of publication will it be (newspaper, magazine, leaflet, etc.)?
- What will the **content** be?
- What are the **aesthetic** considerations (style, look, format, etc.)?
- What are the **resource requirements**? How much will the production cost; what staff and expertise will it require; what materials will it need — amount and quality of paper, photographs, paste-up or electronic layout of the product, time? Are these within your capabilities?
- What are the **technical requirements** of your product? Are they available to you and does your team have the skills to use them?

There is no one right way to make a proposal — it depends on the medium, the company, the nature of the product (is it 'serious', in which case a more formal approach would need to be adopted). This proposal for a new teenage magazine is one way in which you might present your ideas.

Fig 3.2   Graphic novel
Malcolm X The Angriest Man In America (© Wayne Massop)

I.R.C. plc

Proposal for a new teenage magazine

Concept: The idea behind the magazine is to produce something which is aimed at both boys and girls. It will be a 'youth' version of something like *Sky* magazine and will be heavy on visuals, glossy, a midway price so that it retains status but is affordable for those young people who want to buy it as a part of their lifestyle statement. The target audience will be 14 years upwards, go-get-'em, trendy youngsters with a bit of extra cash in their pockets. These people watch the *X-Files*, listen to Oasis and indie music, travel quite a bit, are interested in film, music, clothes, broad (although not boring) political issues. We'd like to see a perfect bound, glossy magazine with lots of two-tone, out-of-focus photography (especially shots by up-coming photographers) and plenty of images generally. The type of stories we'll cover will include interviews, days on film sets, a page which is written and produced by different young people each month with our assistance, reviews of music, films, theatre, books, etc. The magazine would like to see a non-judgemental ethical stance taken throughout. This way we will not alienate readers, especially over issues such as drugs, sexuality, etc.

Style: We're looking for a distinctive black-and-white style which uses colour minimally. A 'jazz, cool, sunny-day' feel needs to be created where jeans and caterpillar boots with T-shirts look OK anywhere throughout the magazine. We want a firm border to each page but an experimental feel, with mixed typography to give a subversive but safe feel.

Cost implications: These are difficult to assess at this stage but we are looking at an eight-strong team with emphasis on the camera skills for each journalist. There will be no separate sub-editor so the production team and the editor will have to take responsibility for ensuring copy is OK. We will need Macs with Photoshop on one, the usual repro facilities, overheads will be low and deadlines tight, especially if we are involving outside input. One of the biggest expenses will be the paper for reproduction, as the magazine must avoid a cheap, 'comicy' feel.

TASK

In a small group discuss the above proposal and agree the parts which you think are feasible in your own school/college. Are there ideas which you could not realise with your skill and financial resources, but which you think are effective nonetheless? Remember to justify your arguments by referring to *why* it will work (why the audience will buy it) and *how* it will work (given resource and time constraints). Sketch out a couple of ideas for how the magazine layout may look (including the front page). Keep all notes on justifications and suggestions for layout and design. You may wish to develop this proposal further in order to produce the magazine.

All of the considerations about how and why a new publication will work require research and when proposals are presented for agreement, they need solid evidence of that research to prove the need for the product. These are as much **marketing** considerations (see Unit 7), as a way in which to ensure that you think through the purpose, audience and style of your publication.

(see Unit 2 for content research, and Unit 6 for audience research)

Organising Your Team

see Element 3.1.

When organising a team, it is important that there is a consensus in your approach when generating proposals. You will then need to decide how to divide the workload. Will you each take responsibility for a page or section? This may be more appropriate for the developmental stage of the process. When it comes to production, it will be more appropriate for the team to allocate roles which reflect real practice, so that each member of the team concentrates on a particular skill area (say, design), perhaps trying a few others briefly along the way (for example editing, photography). This type of practice reflects a growing phenomenon, called "multi-skilling" whereby journalists are learning to originate, follow through, write up, edit, design initial layout and sub-edit for each piece to a greater or lesser extent.

If, however, your team is really well organised, you may decide to assign each team member to a particular area of focus even at the proposal stage. This will ensure that the proposal you make will be thorough and well thought out. Some of the team roles may include responsibility for the following:

- images, visuals, colour, artwork, design, layout;
- editorial content and how this addresses the needs of the audience;
- technical requirements;
- financial, human, time resources;
- administration, finalising agreements, overseeing meetings and putting forward the proposal;
- research, market — audience and competition.

A person responsible for an area above may then take this role forward into the logical team role for production. For example, the team member in charge of images may become picture editor or picture researcher, etc.

As individuals in the team suggest ideas for material for the proposals, each agreed article or page concept will need to be researched to see how it might be produced. Your research will have considered:

- the conventions of that particular print publishing product (what do these types of products often contain, look like, offer their readers?);
- the competition (what similar products are there?);

You may undertake this kind of exercise as part of requirements for Unit 1.

- the types of material which seem to be appropriate for the particular target audiences;
- contemporary styles and designs (in order to gather ideas or to strike out with something new and challenging).

Working Through Ideas

This would not happen in the publishing industry as specialisation of roles and useful experience is fed into the general discussion in preparation for a new publication.

To develop a sense of identity and consistency of style in a new publication, consider format, design, style and content ideas *before* embarking on further research. Ideas may change and develop but leaving these areas open to interpretation will invariably lead to each member of the team proceeding down different paths. These ideas should be discussed and agreed before any team roles have been decided. Make sure that you organise at least one formal meeting at the beginning of developing your proposal and one towards the end, keeping minutes at both.

TASK

Use the following agenda to structure an initial planning meeting to develop a new product or relaunch an existing product. Prior to the meeting, you should prepare some handwritten notes around target audience, product, format, design, text, images, structure, resources, income, content ideas (editorial position) for the teenage magazine proposal on p. 147

House style

Your discussions may need to take account of "house style", which is the style preferred by the publishing institution for the content and design of the product. This will include, for example, the choice of typeface and fonts in headings and sub-headings, and where those headings and sub-headings are situated on the page, the way borders, captions, mounts, etc., are used, what recurring designs appear on or around each page. It is these things which give a print product a sense of identity, an individual design concept which make it distinctive to the eye almost immediately. In the same way, 'house style' also refers to the way one particular print product uses language, tone and style of language in the way it addresses the readers. This emerges out of, or works alongside, the notion of editorial concept which gives a feeling of unity to the publication as a whole, despite the many different contributors involved. This is also the style in which the print product interacts with its reader.

I.R.C. plc

For the attention of New Product Development Team:

Initial planning meeting for product _____ (working title)

Date: _____

AGENDA

Here are some suggestions for areas which you will need to discuss in your initial meeting. You may have more to add:

Target audience
Who are they? What do we need to know about them? How will we test the potential for this type of publication? What kinds of research need to be undertaken?

The product
What is its main aim and purpose? How do we support this aim? For example, if it is to be educational, whose involvement might we need?

The format
What kind of publication will it be? How will the product be used? How does this affect the format?

The design
How will the target audience influence the design of the product? Can we create an original design idea to give the product a distinctiveness over the competition?

Text and images
What is the importance/ratio of text to image? What are the implications for the reproduction (printing process), the type of paper required and the price of the final product? Consider this against the preferred price range for the target audience.

The structure
How will the overall structure of the publication be organised? Will it be in sections? Will it follow the conventional narrative structures as its competitors?

Resources
What is possible given the resources available?

Income
Are advertisements necessary? If so, how will this affect the overall design of the product?

Content ideas
House style? Should the product lean, for example, towards a features style, a newsy style, a coffee-table style? How does this affect the content? How will all of the other key features affect the content? How can we create a formula which has been proven to work while creating a formula which is novel and exciting?

DID YOU KNOW

In order to maintain a consistent written fictional house style, many publishers produce guidelines for its authors. An obvious example is the publisher of romance novels, Harlequin, **M**ills & Boon Limited, which issues guidelines with advice on construction of the characters and story structure required by the publisher for each of their particular series:

> **Word Count:** *50,000.* **Tone:** *Category romance that is very contemporary, fast-paced, fun, flirtatious, entertaining, upbeat . . .* **Absolute no-no:** *Paranormal elements ("Yours Truly" novels are an entertaining reflection of real life).* **Absolute must:** *Hero and heroine meet, directly or indirectly, through the form of written communication.*

Extract reprinted with the permission of Harlequin, **M**ills & Boon Limited.

Fig 3.3 Some sample covers of **M**ills & Boon books

TASK

Choose a book of a genre which you have often read or know well (e.g., science fiction, horror, adventure, romance). Under the following headings, write a possible style sheet for that book (or series), defining the audience for it and, in a short report (oral or written), evaluate how the style and target audience are reflected in the style of the design of the front cover of the book.

- Word count.
- Tone.
- Absolute no-no.
- Absolute must.
- Description of target audience.
- How these other factors are reflected in the design and style of the front cover.

In the same way, newspapers and magazines develop a house style. This may be reflected in the type of language used, the type of design, use of colour, page layout, even the type of images used (for example, one tabloid newspaper will use more close-up images of people in the news, while another may aim for action shots and establishing shots). This sense of house style in newspapers is rarely printed in guidelines but evolves under a strong editorial team.

TASK

Gather together a selection of images and headlines from two tabloid newspapers. Evaluate and make notes on the differences in house style for each individual tabloid newspaper.

Agreeing the proposal

Note: Minutes in all practical teamwork are essential planning tools, enabling you to assign responsibilities and making team members accountable. They are also very useful 'evidence' in determining individuals' contributions to a project and in demonstrating the decision-making process.

Having held your meeting to discuss either the proposal supplied earlier in this unit, or your own proposal, you will need to **minute** your meeting, summarising your discussions, highlighting the decisions made and listing action points, with the name of the team member responsible for carrying them out.

Budgeting the project

Predicting costs is an extremely important job which requires a great deal of knowledge and experience to be accurate. However, even within a school or college situation, where you as an individual or team do not usually part with hard cash for the resources necessary to undertake your projects, it is important to understand the level of resources required to produce a magazine or newspaper, as you are likely to be restricted by budgets for materials and reproduction. Obviously, in a commercial situation, calculating the cost of producing a magazine, brochure, newspaper, etc., is an essential part of calculating the viability of the project in terms of covering costs and generating income.

In a school or college situation, you can ignore running costs such as lighting, heating, wages, etc. Therefore, it really is a question of resources and reproduction. You will need to do some research here to make sure that each individual article and section of the publication has been accounted for in your estimates. Therefore for each proposed page, you will need to calculate:

It is a useful exercise to plan out a budget as if you will have to pay for all of these aspects of production even if many of your overheads will be covered by the educational establishment in which you are studying.

- equipment (photographic film and, where relevant, developing material, printing, photocopying, audio tapes for interview, batteries etc);
- travel, food costs, copyright on found images or text;
- printing, reproduction, developing, binding, etc.

Once you have looked at money going out, you need to look at how you propose not only to recover your losses but also to make a profit. For this you will be considering the *cover price* and *advertising*.

In this way, you can develop a more realistic (although a limited) sense of how projected revenue needs to exceed expenditure in order to break even or make a profit.

TASK

Using the example of a content proposal for *IRC plc*, develop a proposal and budget for your own print product, in a format which can be presented to the client (or your tutor), and which can be agreed by the production team. As a team, you must be prepared to justify your decisions. Therefore it is helpful to draft a list of reasons for *how* and *why* for each aspect of the proposal, backed up by research wherever possible.

Fig 3.4 You need to be able to backup a magazine proposal

Scheduling the production process

The worst scenarios of print production include cases where all the material has been beautifully produced but the team has run out of finances or time when they reach the printing and production stage or the equipment needed has not been booked.

Scheduling involves working out how you can produce your product within given time and resource constraints. You have to deliver a product to specification, to a certain standard and by the deadline set — therefore you need to organise a plan for that process. As ideas are worked on and discussed in a more concrete way things will change and plans will alter as a consequence. This is quite usual; however, it is very important to devise a production schedule right at the beginning of the process. Everybody needs a deadline, and for this to be practical, all considerations must be anticipated as far as is possible.

Human resources — who does what

Decisions about who does what should be a balance between gaining experience and using experience for the good of the outcome of the product. Professionalism involves commitment, insight, experience and a balancing of creativity and dogged determination to do one's job properly.

Although the precise tasks may vary, the main roles in print publishing are:

Editorial department

Editor: The person in charge of the content and direction of the publication. Co-ordinates conferences/meetings where decisions about content are made. Takes full responsibility for everything that is printed.

Deputy editor: Takes control for the editor if he or she is unavailable. Supports and works with the editor.

Assistant editor: Liaises between the editor and the production and editorial departments, initiating ideas and deputising for departmental editors.

Sub-editor: The person (or people) in charge of the actual copy produced, ensuring it will fit on to the layout, that it is proofread, consistent in style and language to the section and the overall publication, that there are no glaring mistakes, may write captions for pictures. A copy taster is a sub-editor who, at page layout stage, decides what should and should not go in according to space restrictions.

Mac operators (in a newspaper): Layout and design.

Artists (in a newspaper): Layout and design of display and classified advertisements.

Designer (in a magazine or book publisher): The person (or people) who translates ideas into design ideas so that the printed page reflects the concept and appeals to the target audience in the clearest, most powerful (and often simplest) way.

Picture researcher or editor: The person in charge of images for the publication, whether they are found images (from other sources, for example, a picture library) or commissioned photographs.

Separate departments may exist within the editorial department (such as fashion, news, features, sport, etc.). They have:

Editor for a section (head of that department): Takes responsibility for their section and its contents, organises journalists, writers, photographers, writes or contributes copy, attends meeting with the editor and deputy editor.

Reporters, journalists, authors: Those who collect, research, write and type copy into the computer for publication content, either generated by themselves or with direction for the department (or book) editor.

Production department

With newspapers, the printing will take place in-house or will certainly be managed by the newspaper company. With magazines, books and advertising print products, the printing and reproduction will take place out-of-house.

Production manager/team: The person (or people) who forms the link between editors and designers and outside agencies who supply services (such as printing) and who ensures copy gets to the right place by the right time in order to be produced.

Where the printing takes place, there will be skilled print operators to reproduce the computerised copy into clear, readable print text ready for binding.

You may not be in a position, as a student, to undertake all or even more than a couple of roles throughout the production. However, it is very important that each person in a production team knows and understands where his or her responsibilities lie.

Scheduling considerations

Ask yourself these questions when scheduling your production:

- ■ **Production Methods**
  - — How will we organise the production process?

- ■ **Resource requirements**
  - — What equipment will we need, and when should it be booked?
  - — Who is responsible for what?

— Given time and finance constraints, can we produce the material to the appropriate standard?

■ **Deadlines**
— What is the deadline for *individual items* to be submitted?
— What is the overall deadline for the product?
— What contingency should we build in?

■ **Risk Assessment**
— Health and Safety issues should be accounted for at this stage (see Unit 2).

Meetings in the production schedule

Remember: For the sake of professionalism (and the portfolio!) it is important to have all meetings minuted of all matters discussed and decisions taken.

It is important to ensure that meetings are regularly scheduled, with clear agendas and minuted, with action points and agreed deadlines. If you are working towards a large production, in departments, you will find it useful to meet as separate departments as well as having full team meetings.

Agreeing outline and layout of product

Whilst you are considering your product proposal, bear in mind the following hints to help you to fine tune your ideas for page and article concepts:

■ Images draw the eye to the page. If you are to sell a product/article/page design within the first few seconds, powerful or interesting images will help.
■ People are interested in people. It is very difficult to write an interesting article on the effects of a war without homing in on how it affects a family or a person directly by telling their story. Similarly it can be more accessible for a reader to gauge what a record sounds like if at least one person is interviewed about what they think of a new album.
■ There is no point in writing about something if you do not have a particular angle on it. For example, a music festival is very enjoyable but can make dull reading if all you are doing is writing about which act followed which. What about the role of drugs or drink? Maybe follow two people, one of whom drinks, the other who does not, and assess their different responses to the festival. Or ask them to keep a diary of each day of the festival. Does the person not drinking feel pressured? You need to assist the reader by guiding them into the narrative or the meat of the article via an approach which is simple but interesting.
■ Make sure the concepts for your articles are appropriate for the target audience.

■ Make a decision about whether you think your concept is appropriate for a single/double/more page spread and why. Is it intended to be a regular feature or is it a stand-alone?

■ For each concept, sketch out ideas showing how the article or page concept might look on the printed page. This will bring the concept alive by giving it a "look" for the printed page, however rough the layout may be. When concepts are agreed, they are placed into a **flatplan** for the product.

Fig 3.5

Article concept: The article is called "The Hidden Me". It is a style feature on three people who are usually quite conservative in the way they dress. They are sponsored for the magazine to be styled in a way in which they fantasize or dream about but haven't dared to do. Now they can have the hidden 'them' brought out and the money raised goes to a charity of their choice.

Balance of Content

Does your publication have:

■ regular features;
■ long articles;
■ short articles;

- articles/pages which interact with the reader (letters or profiles);
- heavy subjects;
- lighter subjects.

TASK

When you have assigned tasks and agreed page and section concepts with the rest of your team, use the above headings to ensure that you have a balance of content.

Making a flatplan for your print product

Flatplan: a plan of each page of the publication which is laid out flat so as to provide an overview of the product in one glance.

All print products have what is called a **flatplan** during the production process. This can sometimes be pinned up on a board or written on a white board so that it is easy to make changes to it at any stage. It can also be printed out on one page and altered with the date of the alteration written in the top corner.

The flatplan emerges as a result of considering the style and content of the publication and economic decisions: how much space will need to be sold as advertising; how many pages the publication will be. When these decisions have been made, the pages to be sold are crossed out on the flatplan and the editor will then fix in the features that they either already have, or know are coming. As work begins, the position and size of different features may well alter. This can be a result of a variety of factors, for instance, an excellent interview which should be placed nearer the front, or a film release date which has been put back, etc. If the advertising team is not able to sell as much space as anticipated, the editor will need to decide to run with extra copy or reduce the folio (page) count. It is usually better financially to reduce the number of pages, keeping expenditure low whilst maintaining cover price. However, disappointing your readers is also a gamble.

Identify Material For Print Items

You may already have articles or features you have worked on for Unit 2. If you are following a photography option as part of your course, you may have an appropriate series of images to be incorporated.

You will need to reconsider these in the light of the type of publication you are producing.

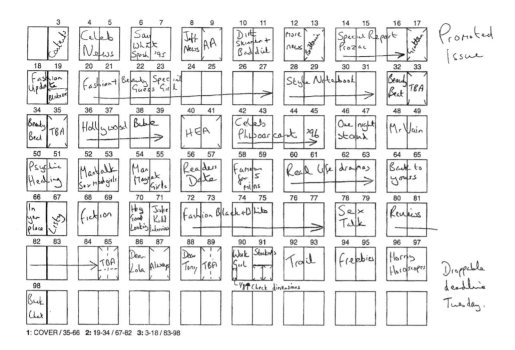

1: COVER / 35-66 **2:** 19-34 / 67-82 **3:** 3-18 / 83-98

Fig 3.6 Initial Flatplan

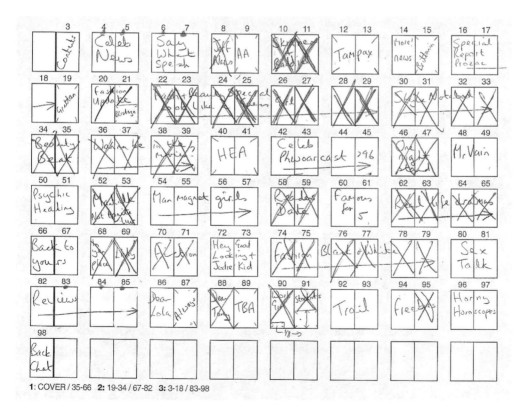

1: COVER / 35-66 **2:** 19-34 / 67-82 **3:** 3-18 / 83-98

Fig 3.7 Final Flatplan

TASK

For each agreed page/section concept, collect examples of and make notes on the type of material to be used and ideas or suggestions for researching or gathering further material.

Content Considerations

As part of the process of identifying material for inclusion, you will need to discuss the legal, ethical and representational issues that emerge, both as a result of the stylistic approach and tone you have adopted for the publication, and for each individual article.

If you find that there are problems with the material, ask yourself:

■ What are the constraints? Legal, ethical or representational? More specifically what are the potential problems?
■ How could the material be altered so that it is less open to criticism?
■ Is it worth taking the risk in going to print? How can this be justified in terms of the stated objectives of the print publishing product?
■ What are the possible solutions? Which is the most likely?

TASK

Identify the following pieces of legislation and make notes on how they might affect content choices on your intended product:

■ Defamation Act, 1952.
■ Copyright Patent Design Act, 1988.
■ Race Relations Act, 1976.
■ Equal Opportunities Acts.
■ Official Secrets Act, 1920/1939.
■ Sex Discrimination Act, 1976.

See Element 8.2, for detail of this legislation.

Checklist: Planning the production process

You should have:

■ A committed, organised team, the members of which are clear about their roles and responsibilities.

■ A proposal for a print product, identifying the medium, purpose, target audience, aesthetics, resource requirements, technical requirements.

Remember: the unit requires that you produce *two* print products as a minimum level of evidence.

■ A production schedule with deadlines, meetings and risk assessment.

■ Secured resources for the production of your product.

■ A clear flatplan for the product.

■ Page, section concepts.

■ Sample text, visual material and a series of sample sketches for possible layouts of material for the above.

■ Notes (possibly in the minutes of meetings) identifying potential content considerations for each item.

3.2 ORIGINATE AND EDIT PRINT MATERIAL

Print products rely on the energy, innovation, precision and hard work of journalists, writers and photographers to produce the actual body of material for a publication. Researching, investigating, following through and writing up material which began as an idea involves a range of skills which cannot be learned without hard work, experience and practice. This section aims to help you to develop some of those skills.

Having agreed and planned your product, the next stage is to produce the necessary material. Look back to Unit 2 for approaches to research, bearing in mind that you are now working towards a complete product, as opposed to individual items.

To give you a context in which you can develop your own products in ways which simulate real working environments as far as possible within your school or college, it is helpful to understand the way real newspapers, magazines etc. generate and organise their material.

Newspapers — An Industry Perspective

In order to taste some of that pressure — and the excitement — that faces news journalists, it is worth setting up links with a local newspaper. You can also work with your teacher to simulate a newsroom in your school or college.

In your newsroom, you could use the Internet to access some of this material. Alternatively you could use CEEFAX or TELETEXT to give some of the day's main headline stories.

Your news team could have reporters at several locations who will bring back stories to your newsroom for sorting. If you are 'on-line' at your school or college, one of your reporters could e-mail you information from their news 'hot spot'.

In the industry, the news desk on a daily national paper is on standby for up to 20 hours a day. Night news editors work late into the night in anticipation of last-minute news bulletins which can be squeezed into the next edition of the newspaper. The sense of pressure which builds up in the newsroom on a day-to-day basis is difficult to reproduce outside the context of a newspaper: there are tight deadlines, news stories breaking all the time, images arriving on-line, advertisements which have not been confirmed.

News Arriving

News agencies such as Reuters, Press Association, UPI and Associated Press send news, sports and financial stories into the news desk. They are sorted through by 'copy tasters' — people who have an eye for a good or important story.

News editors collect information from a variety of other sources — for example, researchers will be developing investigative stories, or journalists in news 'hot spots', where current events are in the news (e.g. at the House of Commons). On-going stories also develop over a number of days.

Once all available story outlines are in, the editors begin planning page layouts with their team. Sometimes one team will be responsible for one page; sometimes for a section of several pages,

The figure shows labels pointing to parts of the *Evening Standard* front page:
Masthead, Dateline, Headline (Splash), Sub-head, Byline, First paragraph (Intro), Copy, WOB rule (white out of black), Cover price, Promotional panel (Blurb), Headline, Byline, Photograph, Picture credit, Continuation line, Column, Headline, Extended picture caption, Column rule

Fig 3.8

If you are able to take a whole day to simulate this exercise, very strict deadlines on your reporters and photographers will need to be given. This presents a problem for photography in a school or college situation, where you are unlikely to have the resources to shoot, develop and print in one day. Alternatively, you could use instant film (although this is expensive), or a digital camera.

or even a full supplement. At this point, stories and photographs are commissioned. A team will run with this plan unless stories change, or the prioritisation of stories changes. The final layout may look quite different if news continues to come in, or a minor incident turns into a full scoop!

Whilst reporters are out writing the stories, the overall editor of the paper holds a conference or meeting to discuss the major stories of the day. Each editor will run through their intentions for their section. A dummy newspaper will be presented, with the space blocked out where the advertisement space has been sold. Often the number of ads. dictates the number of pages per edition, as adverts are the life-blood of newspaper production (income from cover price alone would produce a loss for the paper). After the conference, the editor will usually meet with leader writers to agree the subjects for the paper's leader or opinion column which reflects the newspaper's view on the major issues of the day.

The Journalist's Job

Some journalists are out covering stories; others remain at the office to chase up information. Sometimes a team of journalists

Newspaper offices have hard copy or electronic files of cuttings etc. which are available within moments — this is much more difficult to replicate in a school or college situation. However, your library should have available back issues of quality newspapers on CD-ROM.

could be contributing to one story — one gathering live to-the-moment interviews, the other digging up the necessary background information to provide the context for the story.

There are general reporters and specialist reporters who concentrate on their own areas of expertise. Freelance and foreign correspondents also supply copy. Columnists might write about news, or other issues, from a subjective point of view. This is where it is often easiest to locate the paper's political leanings and demonstrates the difference between news and views (facts and opinions).

The journalists must also **check their facts**, by constantly seeking information that will back up or confirm their reports.

Journalists produce their copy usually on computer at the newspaper office, where they are networked between the reporter and the various editors direct to the printing base. Under pressure, reporters might phone in reports, or key them into a lap-top and send them 'down the line'. When dictating, their stories are input into the editorial system by a copytaker (a high-speed typist).

Features

This may be where items you have prepared for Unit 2 may be useful.

Features pages usually fall in the middle section of the paper. Many broadsheets now publish 'tabloid sections', which are separate tabloid-sized newspapers featuring feature-style items, often with a daily focus on particular areas. For instance, *The Guardian* on a Monday has a particular emphasis on media. Features cover subjects in more in-depth ways and are often prepared in advance.

Pictures

A picture editor services news, features and sports. Tabloids have more photographs per story than broadsheets and therefore often have a larger team of photographers. Freelance photographers also supply or can be commissioned to cover a story. The use of freelancers is becoming more widespread, partly because it gives the possibility of a wider range of pictures to choose from, but more importantly because it is less of a financial commitment for the paper than having staff photographers. Selected images are electronically digitised by scanning and combined with text for output to film for platemaking.

Design

You will need to identify the people in the team who can best produce graphics, illustrations and cartoons to support the various stories.

The design department is responsible for the overall appearance of the newspaper, its typefaces, graphics, illustrations and cartoons, positioning of ads. etc.

The ABC circulation figures provide a benchmark in order to convince potential advertisers that they are reaching a credible circulation, so offering the advertisers a stable audience/buying market. See Unit 8.

Bromide: A Photo sensitive paper used in photo-typesetting on which an image is created. In a college/school environment, you could originate this on disc or as simple paste-up.

Advertising

Display advertising is sold by column centimetre and by the page. Display advertising is a promotional advert, usually a part of a wider advertising campaign which has mainly an image with accompanying text. The artwork is provided by the advertiser. The price of the advert will depend on where it is placed (if it is next to a particular feature or in a popular place then it will be more expensive). There are specialist departments who deal direct with display advertisers to arrange partnerships and deals which are profitable and acceptable to both sides. This is a crucial part of the newspaper's income.

Once a display advertisement has been booked into the newspaper, the copy department contacts the advertising agency responsible for the advertiser to obtain the material to be reproduced. This is supplied as **bromides** or camera-ready artwork.

The classifieds are usually written adverts which are quite short. Artwork may be supplied simply as a logo which can be faxed through and scanned into a computer. These are the adverts for holidays, cars, births, marriages and deaths.

Fig 3.9

As with any other product, sales are vital. Particularly with newspapers, this is important in order to attract and keep advertising revenue. Therefore all means of attracting readers is important for any editor to consider. This may include reducing the cover price, which is a gamble but it may at least increase readership in the short term and welcome some new loyal readers. Newspapers also offer free tickets, interesting serials from unpublished material as a preview, exclusive interviews, promotional material including bingo and advertising on television.

Regional press

When asked to name as many newspapers as they can think of, media students will usually come up with a vast variety of national newspapers titles and actually very few regional press titles. This

Fig 3.10

Local newspapers tend to have a loyal market and are an excellent place for students to gain access, insight and experience of newspaper production first hand. Some of the nation's best journalists work for local and regional newspapers.

situation is actually the reverse in terms of how many newspapers are produced across the country.

The regions across the country reflect communities as distinct from each other as they are from the national press to which we so often refer. In addition to being "British", the various parts of Scotland, Northern Ireland, Wales and England have their own identities. Similarly, the concerns which bind a particular part of those regions will differ within the very region itself. For example, Glasgow, Edinburgh and the Highlands have as much to separate them as they do to bind them together culturally. These differences are reflected in the local media from these regions.

In terms of status, the regional press has always been considered as being as worthy of as high class a journalism as the national press. Regional journalists are relatively low paid and the natural career progression for journalists is often to join national titles based in London.

Since the 1960s, the "paid for" local newspapers have been joined by the arrival of freesheet newspapers, distributed free to households in a given geographical area. These are entirely

You may wish to contact the local newspaper to propose your ideas and to create links.

dependent on advertising revenue. This, along with the attempts of the national press to regionalise sections of their papers have increased competition for the paid locals.

> **TASK**
> Your local newspaper is interested in attracting a younger audience. Investigate, originate ideas for, design and produce a double-page spread which is aimed at a local, young audience. You will need to conduct some market research to develop your proposal and ideas.

Producing images for a newspaper

On first glance at a news page, it is most likely that the first thing to which your eyes will be attracted will be the most dramatic or largest image on that page. Images are vital in newspapers as introductions to news stories, a pathway into the written text for the reader. It is also true in some cases that the image can tell a part of the story behind the news-focused text. Whether it reflects an extreme moment of sadness or distress or jubilation, images speak louder than words.

> **TASK**
> Look through several newspapers. See if you can find images which serve mainly as a support to the written text, and other images which add something of their own to the story behind the news. Put these in two separate piles. Are you able to work out what elements of the image give it this additional quality?

Organising the photographic content of a newspaper

In each edition of a national newspaper, there can be between 150 and 400 photographs. (This will differ enormously from newspaper to newspaper). With so many images to commission, organise and place, who makes the decisions about which photographs are used and how they are used? Eamonn McCabe, Group Picture Editor of *The Guardian* and *The Observer* talks about his experience of becoming a picture editor, and the process of picture editing within the context of producing a newspaper.

CASE STUDY
A profile of Eamonn McCabe

Eamonn McCabe started out photographing rock and roll bands as a fan and for his own interest. One day he went to photograph The Who. One of his images, of Pete Townsend leaping in the air with Keith Moon on drums, was very successful. This photo, as all the others, was taken using available light only, no flash or technical wizardry. From this moment, Eamonn was hooked. He went to the United States and started to take photographs for film storyboards (an excellent way to practise photographing skills). Returning to the UK, Eamonn took a job for about a year as a photography technician at Imperial College, London, to learn the chemistry of photography. During this time, at weekends he would go to rugby matches (another of his interests) and take photographs. Developing these at work, he began to sell the photographs to local newspapers. Through contacts in the local newspapers, he began to sell his photographs to the national press.

Becoming a freelance photographer is a slow business to start with, but Eamonn went on to become full-time sports photographer at *The Observer*, and then to Group Picture Editor at *The Guardian* and *Observer*. Not many picture editors are photographers. Most are from libraries or agencies and have a background in buying or selling photographs instead of taking them. Eamonn describes the different aspects of his job.

S.B.: **How do you commission a photograph?**

E.M.: Picture editing is very easy. Looking at a contact sheet, the right image leaps out and it doesn't take an expert to spot that. With a bit of training, most people could do it. The difficult part of the job is choosing the right photographer to cover the job. There's no point in sending somebody on a gay march if they think all gays should have been put down at birth. There's no point in sending somebody to a football match if they hate football. You learn to send the right person. Some stories are a lot harder to illustrate than others and you have to send someone who will at least try. Some are more comfortable with people and some are better at inanimate objects. We have specialists on the staff and we work with a few freelancers as well. The magazine has a different culture which is aimed at the pop star and the film star and we have to buy pictures in of those people. It tends to be more of a research job.

S.B.: **So how is your day organised?**

E.M.: I go to the meeting in the morning, get a feel for the mood of the day. Then there's a meeting at lunchtime which is more of a tightening up of what we definitely are going to be doing. Then there's a meeting at 6 o'clock which is far more of a sorting out, when we look at what we've done and see on what page each of them will be placed. I decide with different page editors which images will be used and where. We disagree at times. There are days when you fight for an image and other days when you compromise. I know when to attack and when to defend. Picture editing is a false title really. It's running a department and running a bunch of people to the best of their ability. It sounds like all you do is choose pictures, whereas in fact, with respect, most people could do it.

S.B.: How do you choose the right picture?

E.M.: You will choose a picture depending on the audience for a newspaper. In a tabloid newspaper, the image will be more newsy, more urgent in style. A newspaper like *The Guardian* is in some ways a newspaper only in name. It's really a feature paper. We're more interested in the issues behind the news. There are news stories which we run but we're really concerned with looking at where this is all going, how this will affect people's lives.

S.B.: What moral decisions do you have to face?

E.M.: I wouldn't condone somebody wanting to photograph a dead man's wife and child. So I wouldn't send my photographer out to hang on that type of grief. I would look for types of grief which are far less intrusive. I would hate the day when I told a photographer to hang outside and get a picture of a grieving widow. Whereas with a different sort of newspaper, they would see that as a part of their normal practice.

S.B.: How does payment of the photographer work?

E.M.: If a freelancer sells a photograph to a newspaper and it's used by another newspaper they will be paid again. However, if it was a member of staff then the image will be borrowed. We do swaps. Then when the picture has been chosen the contacts are put into the library. No photographer ever throws anything away.

S.B.: What percentage of a newspaper's photographs are taken on that day?

E.M.: In each edition of the newspaper, 30% of the pictures will be live, 30% from files and then 30% are foreign pictures which are sent in on the wires. These come mainly from photo-journalists. There are three major press agencies: European Photo Agency, Associated Press and Reuters. They have photographers all around the world. The digitally scanned images are much better quality than your ordinary prints. Some photographers now use a camera where the image is taken directly on to computer disc which can be entered straight onto the computer.

S.B.: What other changes have occurred with new technology?

E.M.: Using technology you can manipulate, enhance and distort images. If you take the premise that every picture is political, every photograph you take is political and every choice you make is a political act, enhancing (making something lighter or darker or if you take a tree out of the image) isn't as crucial as taking out people or things which changes the meaning of the image. **M**anipulation of images has always taken place but it has always involved using a specialist artist which would need a lot of preparation and time. The difference is now I can do it with a bit of training, you could with a couple of days' training. It is cheap and easy. History has been changed by this and now history can be changed very quickly. I feel very strongly about this. At the moment people believe what they see in an image. If we develop a name for altering images, people will never believe us again in the same way. Every use of an image is so powerful. I have to be reminded of that sometimes.

S.B.: Having chosen an image what happens then?

E.**M**.: Having chosen an image, the people involved in making decisions will be me and the overseeing editor for those few pages, for example, the foreign editor. My job is to deal with the page designers and sub-editors who say what they have been asked to cover and request images to go with those stories. I lay out images to go with those stories and try to get in what I think are the best images.

Regarding where they go on the page, the single most influential issue is the advertising. We have adverts which are 38 by 6 (38 inches and six columns) which is the bug-bear of my life. It feels like half the page has been taken up which leaves you half a page to deal with. There's only so many designs you can do to deal with that. The landscape five-column picture or the small three-column up-right. Size is therefore determined by the advert. A famous photographer, Bert Hardy, said 'photographs are in papers just to hold the advert up. But they keep us in business.'

S.B.: Who writes the captions?

E.**M**.: The captions are written by sub-editors. Captions are a real problem, I think. You used to have caption writers. You don't have that any more. The caption and indeed the whole context into which a picture goes is so important. It can alter the meaning of the image."

S.B.: Do you have any layout tips?

E.**M**.: Pictures have to work very quickly in papers. People have a small attention span so you can't have complicated, dense photographs. They have to be light and bright and easy to read visually. If you have portraits, the face should be looking into the text — it will make the portrait a conceptual part of the whole. The quality of the print is very important. I try to make the prints as clean as I can before they go in.

S.B.: Do you have any hints for photographers?

E.**M**.: Always get there early and leave late.

TASK

Looking at newspaper images

Spot the difference: Here is an example of how parts of an image may be cut out or enhanced using computer technology to manipulate the image. In this case we have made the changes as obvious as possible.

(a)

(b)

Fig 3.11

Comparing the two images, make a list of all the ways in which the two images are different. What difference does it make to the meaning of the photograph (if any) to have removed anything?

You are overall editor at a newspaper and a new picture editor is to start work there. Write a list of ten tips to help him/her in the new job.

TASK

Which image to use?

Here is an example of a set of contacts for a story on the England team's new hopefuls with Terry Venables.

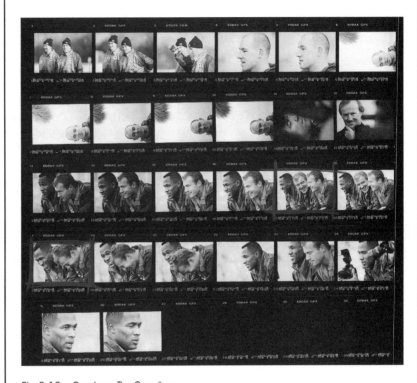

Fig 3.12   Courtesy *The Guardian*

The story is for the back page. Make your own choice for the right image and give reasons for your choice of picture.

TASK

A Sunday newspaper is running a series of articles about street fashions.

■ Plan and research a series of photographic sessions, making careful note of where to spot good street fashion and if there is any fashion event coming up to act as a contrast/comparison.

■ Carry out your commission and take the photographs, if possible using a selection of lenses and styles (you may be able to use some of these for other newspapers).

■ Select the best six images and supply the contact sheet (or negatives). Give one or two examples of images which have been blown up and provided with captions.

Note: If you are doing a photography option as part of your GNVQ, you will be able to undertake this task yourself. Otherwise, you could either use an automatic camera or you could commission a photography student to carry out the shoot under your instructions.

TASK

A tabloid newspaper is writing an article on falling standards in education. You have been asked to provide photographs which reflect this. At the same time, a local newspaper has asked you to provide some positive images of the local schools and/or colleges in the area.

■ Plan and take the photographs.

■ Supply the images for each newspaper. Write a report which explains why each image works for the intended angle of each newspaper.

Picture sources may include the following:

■ staff photographer;
■ freelance photographer;
■ picture agency;
■ picture library.

Images arrive 'over the wires' in newspaper offices and the picture editor has to make decisions about which images may be used.

TASK

Different images for different angles

The following two images on the wires cover the same story — demonstrations in Paris. What type of story might the different images be used for? What is the difference in the angle for each story?

AP/Leaf Picture Desk Proofing Printer

No.   Date   Time   C P Slug

A0397 12/12/95 15:05 J   COMP MRX REUTERS I FRANCE PAR04 EUROPE FRA ST GFO

PAR04:FRANCE CHIRAC:PARIS,19951212-
8 Pictures in queue
Link up at 14:26:22 on 05-12-95

CATEGORY: I SUPP CAT1: POL
OBJECT NAME: FRANCE CHIRAC
SOURCE: CREDIT: REUTERS
COUNTRY: FRANCE
STATE: CITY: PARIS URGENCY: 4
SPECIAL INSTRUC.: 0
CAPTION WRITER: CP/WS TRANS REF: PAR04
HEADLINE: CHIRAC AND DE CHARETTE

PAR04:FRANCE-CHIRAC;PARIS,12DEC95 - French President Jacques Chirac (C) talks
   with Foreign Minister Herve de Charette (R) after a meeting at the Elysee Pa
lace December 12. President Chirac welcomed the news of release of two pilots
   held by Bosnian Serbs since August "together with all French citizens'.   cp
/Photo by Charles Platiau REUTERS

(a)

AP/Leaf Picture Desk Proofing Printer

No.   Date   Time   C P Slug

A0838 12/12/95 15:16 J   COMP MRX REUTERS I FRANCE PAR05 EUROPE FRA ST GFO

PAR05:FRANCE STRIKE:PARIS,19951212-
8 Pictures in queue
Link up at 14:26:22 on 05-12-95

CATEGORY: I SUPP CAT1: POL
OBJECT NAME: FRANCE STRIKE
SOURCE: CREDIT: REUTERS
COUNTRY: FRANCE
STATE: CITY: PARIS URGENCY: 4
SPECIAL INSTRUC.: 0
CAPTION WRITER: JD/WS TRANS REF: PAR05
HEADLINE: DEMONSTRATORS CARRY FLARES BEHIND BANNER

PAR05:FRANCE STRIKE:PARIS,12DEC95- Demonstrators hold flares as they follow a
   procession of protesters through the streets of the French capital, December
12. Thousands of protesters took to the streets against Prime Minister Alain
   Juppe's reform plans.   jd/Photo by Jean-Christophe Kahn REUTERS

(b)

Fig 3.13

Consider these questions:

■ What information can you gather from them?

■ Which part of the paper might the images be assigned to in the first instance?

■ What do you think the stories might be about?

■ Would you choose them for your paper?

TASK

In your team, list the different departments and individual jobs which you will need to have in your newspaper team. This may include:

Editorial

■ Editor (and possible deputy and assistant editors).

■ Sub-editor.

■ Editors for sections of the newspaper (news, sport, features, political, fashion, etc.).

■ The journalists for each section.

■ Photographer/s.

■ Picture editor.

■ Artists.

■ Mac operators (or PC operators).

Production

■ Supervisor (who liaises with editorial) and ensures deadlines.

■ Advertising (and marketing, sales and distribution) team.

■ Technician — reproduction, printing, binding.

Make sure the team is large enough to ensure the successful production of the newspaper. Once you have identified the team, make a list of roles and responsibilities for *Each job* listed.

Fig 3.14 A Marked up magazine cover showing key features

Magazines

The make-up of a magazine office will depend on the focus for the magazine, the amount of funding available, the conditions in which the magazine has been established and the size of the readership.

Assuming we are looking at an average magazine which is largely supported by advertising revenue, serving a largely urban population with a mature readership, the outline of the office may look something like this:

Editorial

Editorial may have around five staff members.

- The **editor**, sometimes called the managing editor, supervises the columnists and the freelance contributors. The job involves managing the budget, being responsible for the editorial content of the magazine and the coverage the magazine gets in terms of advertising and representations in other media. The editor will meet with the art editor and the publisher to prepare a dummy for each issue, reviewing copy either pasted up on boards or on the computer. Before deadline, the editor will be checking copy, writing titles and teasers for columns and articles, checking layout and approving proofs. The editor is ultimately responsible for all content editing, deciding what should go where and organising for other members of his or her team to put it together.
- The **assistant editor** writes a couple of features possibly for each edition. In some instances the assistant editor would take some of the content editing firmly into his or her domain, and take full responsibility of a couple of particular areas of the production of the magazine, for example, the checking of quality of images. He or she will meet with the editor to develop ideas for future editions of the magazine.
- The **senior staff writer** will do some sub-editing and contribute to the features. He or she may be responsible for rewriting poor or clumsy copy.
- The **junior staff writer** will be a copy reader, checking information, correcting copy, and will sometimes write a feature.

Production

- The **production editor** will organise schedules for the editorial team to make sure the magazine is produced by the deadline set. The copy must be at the colour house and printers by a certain time and it is the responsibility of the production department to make sure it gets there. To do this, the production editor will chase all the departments for copy, doing the final proof reading, sending layouts to the colour house and checking the cromalins when they come in.

Pictures

- The **picture editor** will sort through the pictures which have been commissioned and choose the best images. This will then be negotiated with the editors from each individual section of the magazine.
- The **picture researcher** will be responsible for setting up photo-sessions, tracking down library shots and organising schedules and administration of the pictures department.

Art

- The **art director** will oversee several magazines and will be responsible for the overall ideas and design style of each magazine.
- The **art editor** is in charge of the designers, and advises on layouts and designs the more complicated layouts.

Depending on the magazine focus, there may be several more departments, including beauty, travel, fashion, music, etc.

Most magazines also rely on a pool of freelance writers to supply articles and features.

> **TASK**
>
> Organise your team into a magazine office production team. Assign roles for each member of your team as a part of that production. Make sure that you have chosen the roles necessary to produce a magazine successfully. When you have allotted roles, make a list of responsibilities for *Each job* on the team.

Magazines as a print and graphics product

Obviously magazines are run along similar lines to newspaper production but without the same pressure of daily deadlines. There is also much more scope for freelance contribution as there is more time to hand out stories for research and for writers with a special area of interest or specialism to produce stories.

Choices of magazine are usually determined by specialist interest, or 'lifestyle' considerations, where the notion of 'designer' print and graphics product plays a part in the marketing of the magazine.

Getting familiar with a publication and its readers.

When you begin to work on a magazine, it is vital to find out about the readership for that particular publication. (The same is obviously true of other print and graphics products although it will have less impact on the range of material covered.) To get an insight into the style of a magazine, you must read and study as many back issues as you can.

> Use the following checklist to help you get a feel for a particular magazine:
>
> - Read the main features and observe the type of language used: is it casual? How long are the paragraphs? The sentences?

- Look at what type of images are used. Who are they aimed at and how?

- What type of style is created in terms of paper, font, design, etc.?

- What kinds of issues are covered?

- What types of interviews are covered?

- What sort of advertising is featured?

Key elements in magazines to note

- **The list of the magazine's staff** — particularly important when considering approaching the magazine for work (freelance writing or other). If you are approaching the magazine for freelance writing this will be the managing editor. Some larger magazines will have an articles or features editor. If you are keen to offer freelance photographs, look for the picture editor.
- **The by-lines compared with the office staff** — if these are different, then the magazine buys in freelance work.
- **The types of stories/articles a magazine runs** — magazines run along formulae of different sorts. Some will never do personality profiles, some concentrate on this. Some never do long articles, some rarely short ones. This is key if offering stories or images to a magazine.
- **The overall appearance of the magazine** — what type of lifestyle is being appealed to with the cover? What type of reader?
- **The type of paper used in the production process** — is it slick and shiny, or dull and flimsy? This reflects the magazine's own financial situation and is also an indication of the target audience's financial situation as the smarter paper will be reflected in the cover price.
- **The use of colour** — is it used only with the adverts or also with the editorial pages? This too is a reflection of finances (unless a new magazine is overspending on production).

You can also write to the editor of a magazine to request writers' guidelines for freelance contributors (they are less likely to have the same for other types of freelance contribution). These can be very revealing.

Magazine content

When anticipating what might feature in a magazine, the projection will be at least four weeks ahead. Therefore, the magazine content has to reflect what will be topical when the magazine is published and not what is topical at the time of writing. For this purpose, the editor or the features editor will have a large diary, and information which may be relevant to future copies of a magazine will be listed there. The list will include festivals (such as the Henley regatta), interesting or important anniversaries (such as "100 years of cinema") and major events (such as a film's release, a sporting event, etc.). This type of information can come from libraries (books on important dates and historical references for anniversaries) or from press releases. A popular magazine approach is recording or remembering news events and returning to them some time later to see how lives or events have changed.

TASK

For your magazine, collect a diary of information which is relevant to the publication date of your magazine. Use this diary to direct your publication's content.

Book production

The production of books is significant when learning about print media production. This area is probably the least likely print product you can simulate in a school/college situation. However, the process is still worth studying, in that you may be in a position to publish a 'booklet'.

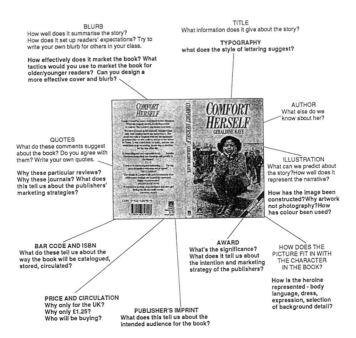

Fig 3.15 Marked up copy of book cover (courtesy The English and Media Centre)

The functions in a publishing house are:

- commissioning
- copy-editing
- design
- production
- publicity
- marketing
- distribution

Commissioning a book

Under the **editorial director** are **commissioning editors** who are responsible for finding interesting ideas which will be successful, and finding the right authors for these publications. The editor is the main contact between the publishers and the authors. Editors may specialise in one particular area of publication (adult fiction, children's educational, music, etc.), and similarly, publishing houses will usually specialise (educational, children's publishing, etc.).

Developing the book

Having decided on a publishing idea, the editor will seek out an author or authors. They will encourage and support the author during writing, providing constructive criticism. The editor needs to be aware of production methods, in terms of the financial limitations and also what is possible in terms of design and colour, within resources constraints.

Into production

Once the material arrives and has been edited to suit the style and aesthetic requirements of the editor and/or publishing house, the text will be **copy-edited.** This is also known as desk-editing. The desk-editor will supervise the progress of the material from manuscript to bound copy. Illustrations are produced in consultation with author and editor, 'prelims' are drafted, the cover copy (or book jacket) designed and produced, proofs (first typeset copy) of the manuscript are checked again and, if all is agreed, the book goes to print.

Book production design and support

Obviously it is difficult to simulate the process of selecting and rejecting manuscripts, editing and proofing, etc., because of the length of the process, complexity and time. It is important, however, and interesting to produce material which accompanies and supports book production.

The area of book production that is considered here on is the design and production of the **prelims, end matter** and **cover**.

Prelims

The matter appearing before the text which may include:

- title page;
- the back (or verso) of the title page containing a copyright notice, printer's imprint and bibliographical details and a list of contents;
- half-title;
- information about the book;
- contents list;
- foreword.

End matter

The matter which appears after the main body of text which may include:

- appendices;
- notes and references;
- bibliography;
- glossary;
- index;
- further information.

Cover

The marketable part of the book, that which will make the reader pick it up. It may include:

- a design/illustration;
- the title;
- the author's name;
- a piece of selling copy (the 'blurb')

- the International Standard Book Number (ISBN);
- a bar-code (which contains the price and ISBN number).

Principles of book design

- All text and images should enable the reader to follow through the flow of the book from start to finish with ease. Often this means simplicity and clarity with design ideas.
- Text and images should be designed with the genre, purpose and audience of the book in mind.
- The cover design is the first selling point of the book as product (after external marketing) and as such must work to reflect the contents and sell the product.
- Every single part of a page or cover is part of the design. Therefore, no background white should exist unless it is the designer's intention that it should do so.
- Pages in a book can either be conceived as being symmetrical (one which is centred in the middle of the page), or asymmetrical (focused off-centre of the page).
- The format (size) of the book, the size of margins around the edge of a page, the structure of page layout (how many columns a page will have, for example), typefaces and overall style are all design decisions which need to be considered as a part of the design process.

TASK

Produce the front cover, prelims and end matter for a horror novel.

- Research the horror book market, concentrating on how style, design, language attract readers to buy horror books.

- Write a report summarising your findings.

- Design, research, layout and produce the front cover, prelims and end matter for a horror book called *The Silent Hotel*.

- Design and make a scaled model of point-of-sale promotional displays.

- Evaluate your production.

Other print products

Comics and graphic novels provide an audience with image-led print products. These are constructed in a similar way to other print products but obviously rely on the input of artists to design the material and produce the narrative much more than any other publication.

Graphic novels use cartoon images in a series of boxes to tell the story. These novels are becoming more and more popular as they are accessible to a wide audience and can be a dynamic and interesting way to read a narrative.

In a similar way, video and CD covers also require graphic design appropriate for the product and are as important as book and magazine covers in terms of attracting an audience. Video covers will often make use of the posters used in marketing the film for theatrical release in the design, while CDs covers can be more abstract, often using graphics rather than photographic stills to provide the identify and 'flavour' of the contents or artist.

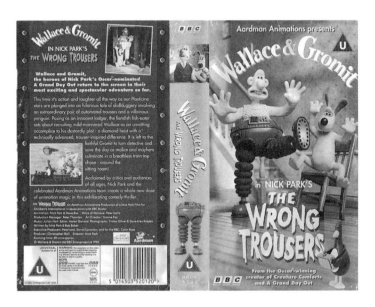

Fig 3.16 Wallace and Gromit video cover. Courtesy of BBC and Aardman Animations

Note: You may wish to investigate whether there is in fact a film festival or film series running locally at a cinema or educational establishment. In this case, gather all the necessary information, research the target audience, the purpose and style of the festival. It may be possible to negotiate a design contract with the organisers of the festival.

Leaflets, Booklets, Flyers

Designing and developing leaflets, booklets and flyers seem simple. They are, however, as much a challenge in terms of design and concept as any other print product. Creating and producing a professional product which works is, in some ways, more challenging with smaller print products than with publications such as books, magazines and newspapers. You have only a small space in which to produce a product which has style, design principles, is balanced, interesting and communicates the information necessary in a powerful way.

TASK

A new specialist film festival is starting up in your area and you have been commissioned to design a leaflet advertising it. It has been sponsored by three companies — make sure you include their logos and acknowledgements on the front of the leaflet. Research, design and produce the film festival leaflet.

Carry out research for material

Fig 3.17 A selection of
publishers' colophons

Unit 2 describes research methods which you may need to adapt to
suit your particular audience or house style. You may also need to
generate additional material, in which case you should again refer
back to Unit 2 for approaches to writing techniques.

You may have already prepared features or news items. This
being the case, you may need to adapt them to suit your particular audience or house style. You may also need to generate additional material, in which case you should refer back to Unit 2 for
approaches to research and writing techniques.

Style

The style of any print product is important in defining it as one
which is significantly different to its competitors so that an audience's eye will be caught and a potential customer attracted. This is
true, also, of such print products as books which develop styles of
presentation (a **colophon** or a spine design) which become immediately recognisable and synonymous with that publishing company's
style of literature.

TASK
Investigate the signifying emblems which mark out one publisher from another. Collect
a selection of colophons, designs and styles from different publishers. Is it possible
to work out what type of books each company publishes from the style of these?

Mathematical approach

■ To work out how deep a picture will be when altered to a certain width (for column width), multiply the required width by the actual depth and divide by the actual width.

■ To work out how wide a picture will be when altered, multiply the required depth by actual width and divide by the actual depth.

Practical approach

Place tracing paper over the image. Using a ruler, draw a diagonal line from the bottom left to the top right of the image. **J**oining up the vertical lines with the horizontal lines to this diagonal will provide you with many opportunities to alter the image Fig. 3.19.

Fig 3.18 Reducing or enlarging Photographs

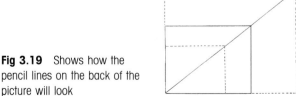

Fig 3.19 Shows how the pencil lines on the back of the picture will look

TASK

For a print 8 inches wide and 10 inches deep, to reduce it to be 4 inches wide, how deep will it be?

[Answer: 4 × 10 divided by 8 = 5 inches]

TASK

For a print 8 inches wide and 10 inches deep, to reduce it to be 100 mm deep, how wide will it be?

[Answer: 100 × 8 divided by 10 = 80 mm]

Picture cropping

The whole of an image is rarely used. An image may be cropped to make the essential feature of the image the prominent focus. It can be cropped either tall or wide.

Fig 3.20   Picture cropping

Writing headlines

A headline might be suggested by the journalist and is sometimes used. Sometimes, the sub-editor will write the headline and occasionally an assistant editor will suggest an alternative. The headline's positions, style of lettering, character count and size of type will have been indicated in sketched form by the artist sketching out the layout.

Headline Conventions

- Punctuation is avoided wherever possible as it looks messy.
- Names of places are avoided.
- Active words are better than passive.
- Present tense is preferred to past tense.
- House style must be considered.

Many feature headlines are a play on words, for example:

Do us a flavour!

Alliteration: each word begins with the same letter

about the use of chemical flavouring.
Other headlines use **alliteration:**

Studio Squirms as Sandy Squeals!

The challenge is to sum up the story in the few words for which you have space:

```
Rail Chief Ousted In Shock
Vote
```

TASK

Cut out headlines from a variety of magazines and newspapers. For each headline do the following:

- Write a short summary of what you expect the contents of the article to be.

- Identify the devices the journalist or sub-editor used in writing the headline.

- Assess the effectiveness of the headline, giving reasons for your answer.

- Cut out copy from one magazine and one newspaper. Bearing in mind the house style of each publication, write an appropriate headline for each article.

Follow safe working practices

Investigating stories and looking to capture exciting or interesting images means being on the front line in a variety of situations,

For example, the opening of a school fête or a celebrity interview prior to a concert. It could, however, also mean being in the middle of a violent demonstration or visiting an unknown person's apartment late at night. Therefore it is important to remember basic safety rules:

- avoid explosive situations — try to feel the atmosphere;
- make sure you can get away from a situation quickly if necessary;
- try to avoid meeting people in the dark;
- try to avoid visiting new people at their own house — aim to meet on neutral ground;
- make sure someone knows where you are and can contact you;
- take a colleague along if you are at all unsure of the situation;
- if you are carrying expensive equipment make sure it is insured and hidden wherever possible; take a colleague along to help you if at all possible.

If you are using expensive/dangerous/new equipment you must make sure:

- it has been properly serviced;
- you have been given adequate training;
- you are aware of any dangers and what to do if it goes wrong;
- you do not make yourself vulnerable by being out alone.

Checking accuracy and sourcing quotations

An extremely important job for any journalist or sub-editor (and, on occasions, editor) is to **check that information is accurately recorded and references and quotations are accurately attributed.** Information wrongly quoted in a published context can cause financial and personal damage to the misquoted party and has been known to lead to vicious law suits. Obviously, this will be less of an issue in your situation. Nevertheless it is important and professional for you to take responsibility for your work's accuracy.

Some tips:

- Using a tape recorder during interviews is a very good way to ensure that all information recorded is correct and accurate.
- Checking figures with other (probably secondary) sources is another way of reducing the chance of error.
- If you quote a person, make sure that the reader is clear as to who said what. If you quote from another printed

> source, you must always clearly identify the book or publication from which it came, the publisher and the date of the publication.

Checking for offence

See Unit 2.

Issues of representation

Like all other media, print publishing products represent reality through structured narratives. Choices are made about what to publish and what not to publish, about what image to choose and how to crop or manipulate it so that it means what the editor wants it to mean. The representation of facts is a responsibility. In making choices about what is to be represented, automatically there are choices being made about what is excluded.

Equal opportunities in published material

The National Union of Journalists (NUJ) has an Equality Council which works to ensure equality reporting. 'Those of us who earn our living in book publishing — whether by commissioning, designing, producing, presenting or selling books — have a professional and social obligation to use words, phrases and images that do not reinforce offensive or discriminatory attitudes.' Source: NUJ.

Some language is now recognised as being prejudiced in terms of sex, race, sexuality, age or disability. For instance, the simple assumption being made in this sentence — "the editor needs to know if he has to ..." — automatically excludes women editors.

Negative representations involve a moral responsibility — the printed word is powerful. Consider the following as a part of your print production (it may even be worth devoting a meeting to considering some of these issues when you come to produce printed material):

- a responsibility not to perpetuate stereotypes;
- a responsibility towards the subject/s;
- telling a story *simply* does not necessarily mean over-simplifying the issues;
- it *is* possible to resist easy answers to issues raised;
- does the house style conflict with personal beliefs?

Legal and ethical issues

See Unit 8.

Libel is probably the law most frequently applied to journalists.

It is the coverage of actions or comments attributed to a person which may be considered to carry with it "injury to reputation". This includes visual material (pictures of any sort including cartoons) and written text. Not mentioning someone's name does not necessarily protect the writer or publication, if the details are obvious. Quoting another's negative comments is not necessarily foolproof either.

Defences to libel action include the following:

- *Fair comment* — referring to a publication's statement of opinion rather than factual reporting. This statement needs to be proven to be a fair reflection of opinion and in the public's interest.

■ *Justification* — proving that what has been written was true.
■ *Privilege* — the defence of reporting from court cases, at parliament, council meetings, etc.
■ *Innocence* — whereby the publication offers innocence and lack of intention with offer of amends and public apology.

Proofreading the text

The first draft of an article is just that — a *first* draft. The initial stage of editing should be to do with the actual structuring and writing of the article. The next stage after completion is proofreading. Take time to look through the first draft yourself. It is useful to call on other people to do this for you (paid or unpaid!) as you will have spent so much time working on the copy that you will not always notice mistakes. Reading the work aloud is a good way to test appropriate use of language.

Proofreading checklist.

■ facts
■ spellings
■ sentence construction
■ typographical mistakes
■ the consistency of how things are written (numbers, dates, etc.)
■ it follows the publication's agreed house style
■ meaning is clear
■ the language does not sound too laboured
■ the punctuation

TASK
Design a "students only" version of your school or college prospectus.

TASK
Design and produce a flyer for a disco/rave/party which is balanced (in composition), and appropriate for the target audience, using visuals and text.

TASK
A local art gallery wishes to attract a wider audience with new leaflets/flyers. Investigate the market, design, develop and produce the appropriate material.

3.3 SUB-EDIT AND LAYOUT PRINT PRODUCTS

In a professional environment, all decisions are made for the ultimate good of the product. This means that even if you have produced an article, it may not ultimately be included or may be altered by the section/page editors and overall editor (in newspapers and magazines or section head (in other forms of publication).

Selecting Material For Inclusion

Newspapers may reject material if a story:

- is too far away geographically to be of interest to the readers
- is outside the target audience's range of interest
- does not add much more information to a story covered in an earlier edition
- is legally unsafe, in poor taste or morally questionable.

A copy-taster's job is to check incoming information for interesting material for a publication. In the same way, your team will be tasting copy to decide whether it has enough range and scope to work to your agreed brief.

Design page layout

Designing the page layout is important because:

- it creates a plan which maps all work on to the space available;
- it allows time to experiment with different designs, looks and concepts before the final copy.

Each publishing house will have its own version of a printed layout sheet. It is, in fact, possible to design your own, which may

Checklist: Layout

To design a page layout effectively and quickly, the processes which have led to this point must be completed efficiently and thoroughly:

■ Writers must have their work in on time.

■ Work must be proofread and been given an initial "once-over" by the sub-editor.

■ Photography must have been commissioned early, retrieved and decided upon.

■ All other artwork must have been designed and completed, checked for mistakes and submitted for inclusion.

■ Any adverts for inclusion must have been decided upon, artwork checked, size agreed upon and confirmed officially (including financial or other supporting transaction).

■ All work for submission should have been checked along the way for suitability and feasibility (sometimes stories have to be dropped because they do not deliver as much as they promised).

■ The overall editor should have a clear idea of all sections and spreads, all material (text and image) intended for inclusion.

■ Ideas for possible page designs should be tested, looked at and checked by the page/spread editor.

■ Headings, sub-headings, inserts, flashes and captions should be completed as far as possible.

■ Legal, moral and ethical issues must be checked and agreed.

be necessary if you have an unusual format. In this case, you need to map out the number of column spaces available within your chosen format. If relevant, you will need to decide how many columns your publication will have (you can check other similar publications for a rough idea). You will also need to work out how many inches up the page you have. You will then be able to measure space available in terms of column inches.

With any other sort of printed publication you will need to find a way to estimate the number of spaces available for words and images. This may be in terms of measurements or blocks. It is up to you, but you must be able to work out a way of mapping the text and images on to the page so that this is clear to you and to the sub-editor.

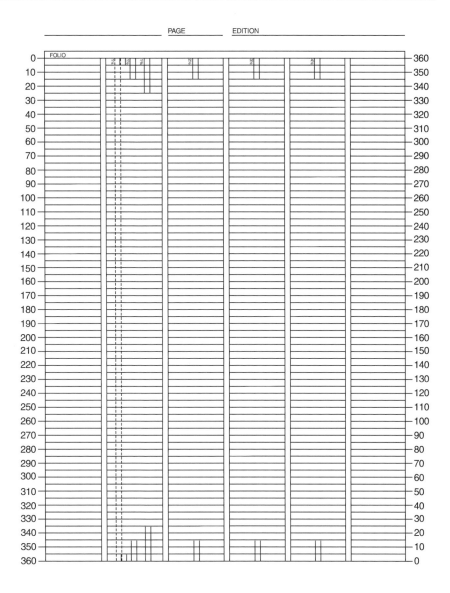

Fig 3.21   Layout sheet

Resources

How you use your layout sheet and how you eventually produce your publication will ultimately be dependent on the level of resources available to you. In any case, even if you are attempting to produce your work using simple cut-and-paste techniques, it is crucial that you plan the layout sheets with some awareness of the process used by a professional publishing company.

TASK

In preparation for the design and production of your publication, investigate the technology which is used professionally for similar publications. Concentrate on the following areas:

■ Computer technology — what programmes are commonly used to design the publication? What are the types of effects which are available with this programme?

■ Photographic technology — how are the images taken and reproduced for optimum quality?

TASK

In small groups, analyse the layout of one chosen publication. Identify and make comments on the effect of the use of the following:

■ the use of white space;

■ the use of special effects;

■ the way text and images have been combined;

■ the use of different fonts;

■ the use of flashes;

■ the use of inserts;

■ symmetrical and asymmetrical design;

■ the use of borders, margins, outlines;

■ stylistic features typical of that type of publication.

Good design techniques

The page design for any printed publication is a technique which is often forgotten about and underrated. If all else has been completed without fault and the material is wonderful, if it is badly laid out on the page then it may well end up unreadable and, indeed, unread.

Checklist: Basic design techniques

Combine text and image in a way which:

■ is easy on the eye, not too fussy;

■ encourages the reader to read on;

- makes sense (so that images match texts; there are no glaring errors such as the photograph of a children's party next to an obituary);

- works as part of the whole (the publication in its entirety) and within its section;

- is in keeping with the notion of the publication's house style, corporate or house design;

- balance them together.

Good design cannot be learned by reading alone. Practising and experimenting is how to learn both about the basic design principles and how they work and about one's own creative flair and individuality. So *do not* expect your first design to be the blue-print for the publication. There should be a series of sketches, different design ideas and several "good" design attempts before deciding on the final layout design.

Approaching the blank page

Begin by looking at the basic "grid" of a page and considering the following areas:

- format;
- margins;
- position, style and size of artwork;
- size of typefaces;
- estimated number of words per column-inch and therefore the total estimated number of words for the page;
- details — inserts, titles (size and positioning), captions, intros, flashes, bylines, etc.

Useful Layout Tips

Borders

Resource centres and libraries contain design books which provide the reader with sample border designs which add much to the design on the printed page.

Boxes

Putting information into a box makes the page much more accessible to the reader. Providing information which has been sectioned off into bite-size chunks makes a page more approachable from the reader's point of view. A list of opinions is much more likely to be read if they are boxed (preferably with images) rather than contained within a long paragraph.

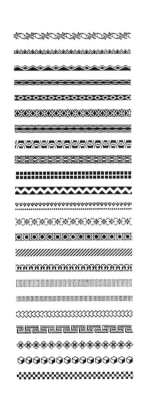

Fig 3.22 Some examples of border designs

Typebreakers

Printers hold a variety of typebreakers which may be used to divide sections of text. These are often used between paragraphs or chapters in books or at the beginning of paragraphs in magazines, with a drop capital.

You may wish to design a typebreaker which is specific to your publication.

Drop capitals

Using a drop capital at the beginning of a paragraph is common practice, particularly with magazine, book and advertising production.

Fig 3.23 Example of typebreakers

Simple Layout

A final layout should show the placing of body copy, pictures in their final size with caption, where they are placed on the page, headlines, borders, bars, boxes, tables, graphs, advertisements,

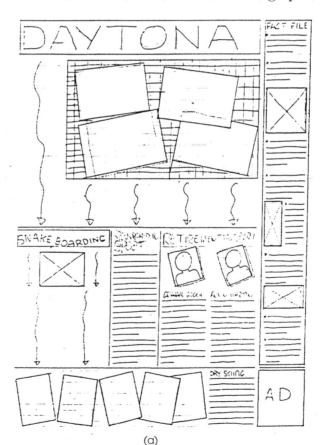

Fig 3.24(a) Layout from 'YES' magazine

(a)

page numbers and page information. The easiest thing to do is to draw a simple layout and put numbers on to the boxes which correspond to numbers placed on the back of the images, copy, etc. The headlines or any other small information should be sketched on to the layout, body copy should be indicated using squiggly lines. If you are not able to produce a computer-generated version of your printed product, then you should make a "dummy" of the product where everything should be produced exactly to size and in exactly the intended format for the final version.

Format

You will need to consider the following:

- page size;
- positioning (landscape/portrait);

Fig 3.24(b) (b)

Fig 3.24(c) The 'YES' layout
with the finished thing

(c)

- ■ what is possible given the availability of resources and in terms of reproduction processes;
- ■ type of paper to be used (again, resources and purpose of publication);
- ■ use of colour/black and white — balancing resources and the level of professionalism required, impact of the final product.

Margins and grids

Is the design for single pages or to be balanced across a double spread? Most professional publications use their own printed layout sheets for cut-and-paste or sketch design ('raw' copy) and a DTP programme for final layout (or 'good' copy).

The secret to using the grid on your page layout sheet is to consider it as a basic structure for the page for the main bodies of text, larger images and advertisements. Do not be afraid to break away from the static lines of the grid and be more imaginative.

TASK

Cut up two news pages from one issue of a tabloid newspaper.

- Draw a page outline of the same size, including vertical and horizontal lines. The vertical lines will reflect the column lines. The horizontal lines will reflect the line spacing.

- Place the adverts on the page. Put in the rest of the copy so that it not only fits (you can cut and trim to fit if necessary) but also so that the page works and is easy to read. Make sure that none of the copy clashes with other copy or the advertisements.

- Follow the same exercise, only this time cross out a greater amount of the page for a larger advert. (A half page if it was a quarter page, etc.). Replace copy, making decisions about cutting copy and images where necessary. The problem of competing with advertisements is common in newspaper design.

Typefaces

Note: choice of typeface or font is not arbitrary — typefaces are an essential part of a publication's design concept.

Type size is measured in 'ems' which is the square of any given body height of a letter. This refers to the height of an 'M'. Type size is measured in points and one point is defined as 0.13837 inches. This is relevant when designing page layouts where the grid is mathematically transferable directly to screen and can, therefore, be calculated almost exactly word for word. (You are unlikely to be in a position to be quite so precise when designing your own layout.)

Choosing typefaces

The first consideration needs to be which typeface looks best on the material on which the publication is to be printed. Put simply, some typefaces look better on some type of paper than others. Typefaces with contrasting thick and thin strokes are generally better on uncoated paper (non-glossy). It may be worth trying several different **styles of typeface** before making any decisions about which styles to use. This will also be relevant for how much space on the page the typeface will take up.

The simpler and more limited the variety of typefaces you choose, the more formal the publication page will appear.

The next step would be to add a variety of fonts (italic, bold and sizes) within one typeface (for example Roman or Univers). This would create a centred and simple but relaxed design style:

Flash script

ABCDE

Bragadoccio

ABC

Playbill

ABCDE

Fig 3.25 Some examples of different styles of typeface

If aiming for a dramatic and anarchic impression, then a variety of typefaces *and* a variety of fonts will give that effect:

Type size

Type is measured from the top of the tallest letter ("d" or "b") to the bottom of the lowest letter ("q" or "p") and these sizes are measured in points. There are 72 points to an inch. Therefore 36-point type is a half-inch deep. Most publications will obviously have a typesize in place. However, it is worth looking at the different effects of type size and the use of space between the lines the 'leading'.

Putting pen to paper

When roughing out your design plans, do not forget the following:

- make sure you have all (proofed) copy of texts and all artwork to be included;
- be aware of how much word space you have available to you (if the copy is to be processed through DTP);
- use the grid references carefully to balance work and have a page structure;
- experiment with different page designs;
- consult with your page editor and/or the overall editor;
- you can alter the size of images to be included.

When drawing the layout page for your publication, you should first choose its size and column format, then sketch in or make a dummy copy. For a magazine, this should include:

- the title or masthead;
- other details, including price, data, issue number, barcode, etc.;
- size, type, design, location of the main picture;
- inserts;
- strap;
- stand-alone quotes;
- flashes (in decks) with blurb.

Sub-editing the product

As well as acting as a second (or third) proofreader, the sub-editor in many instances will act as a kind of "text designer". They will be acting on behalf of the editor to arrange the articles or text and artwork in accordance with the wishes of the editor and the overall aims of the publication. The sub-editor has a responsibility to check the factual information provided, the readability and suitability of the work. They will make the first decisions about the length of articles suggesting to the page layout designer where the text images should be placed. This will be the rough outline to which the page layout designer works.

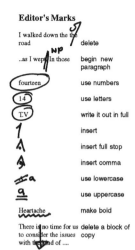

Editor's Marks

I walked down the the road — delete

..as I wep In those — begin new paragraph

fourteen — use numbers

14 — use letters

T.V — write it out in full

/ — insert

∧ — insert full stop

∧ — insert comma

a — use lowercase

a — use uppercase

Heartache — make bold

There is no time for us to consider the issues with the kind of .... — delete a block of copy

Fig 3.26

The sub-editor may also be required to change or write headings, sub-headings, captions and flashes.

To check for common mistakes and inconsistencies in the text, use the following checklist to guide you:

Checklist: Sub-editing

■ Capitals — check that those words which have taken a capital should have one and those which have not been given one do not need them. Common mistakes include the difference between a unique power such a 'Prime Minister' and generalising the term such as 'prime ministers' when referring to more than one.

■ Punctuation.

■ Numbers — check that numbers are consistently recorded either in words or in figures.

■ Abbreviations — common abbreviations need no full-stops (such as BBC) but make sure that the reader will always understand any abbreviations used.

■ Dates — check that the dates used are listed in the same way (25th December or December 25).

■ Titles — are these to be placed in italics or quotation marks? It is more common to use italics.

Layout and paste-up

You must ensure the following.

■ All material is straight
■ If you are to reproduce using photocopying, that your copy is positioned where it can be photocopied two-sided.
■ Place all copy "dry" in the position designed on the page layout grid to make sure that it actually works.
■ No marks are visible around the text, including the layout grids. This may mean tracing the grid references on to tracing paper so that you are able to place copy on to blank white, and test the grid references by placing the grid references carefully over (or under) the text.
■ All artwork is as clear and as clean as it can be. Any marks will reproduce badly.

Producing the final copy

It can be disheartening after a lot of hard work to discover that the outcome is not as glossy or impressive as you had wished. Recognising the limitations in which you work is important, as is acknowledging the ways in which the result could have been improved despite those circumstances: However, in the first instance you *must* investigate all possibilities for reproducing your printed publication. This may include judging whether realistically you may be able to sell the product and cover the costs of having the product printed professionally locally. If this is the case, you will need to consider how to market your product and how you might be able to convince local businesses to advertise in the publication.

See Unit 7.

Otherwise, you will need to take care that copy is as organised and as clean as possible before reproduction, as quality is lost very quickly through photocopying. This will require time and patience, and may possibly require you to enhance or even re-commission images or graphics which do not reproduce well.

Having the front cover made from a thicker type of paper or even in colour can make a lot of difference in terms of the professionalism of the publication's presentation. It may also encourage more people to buy the publication. Similarly having a more effective and attractive binding system helps to give the product credibility. Time should be spent investigating these alternatives early on in the production process.

Proofread the finished group product

Galleys: the plates on which the text has been produced

Proofs: the real page when typesetting has occurred and just before printing

Over-matter: words which, after setting, do not fit on the printed page

Casting off: writing words to fit the page exactly.
It is helpful to read the text line by line using a ruler.

In traditional printing, the first text proofs are **galleys**. These have the text in columns without being divided up into separate pages — this is why page proofs which normally emerge from desk-top published material are sometimes still referred to as galleys. These can now be proofread before paste-up rather than after it.

When **proofs** return from the printer, there may be some *over-matter*. The sub-editor will have to delete enough words for the text to fit completely on the page. Often, a sub-editor will delete an entire paragraph and rewrite the remaining words, **casting off** with exactly the right number of words.

The point of proofreading is to check errors which have emerged from the type being placed on to the page ready for printing. Figures and facts should be checked against the copy. Errors should be marked in the margin. There are British Standard proofing marks for professional proofreaders. You should avoid single words appearing at the foot or the head of a column (known as "widows and orphans"). When all material has been proofread and altered, the publication can go to print.

Did you meet your deadline?

Using your minutes from meetings, notes of alterations made and different flatplans you can begin to review the production process, especially while it is still fresh in your mind. Doing this will enable you to think through mistakes made during the process, consider the reasons for changes (in staff, material or resources) and plan your next production in the light of these experiences.

3.4 REVIEW AND EVALUATE PRINT PRODUCT

Distributing the product

Do not be under-ambitious with your publication! If local shops have advertised in it, they may be keen also to have it on sale locally. If you have managed to encourage a local newspaper to print the product alongside theirs, they may agree to distribute it also. You may, on the other hand, decide to limit marketing and distribution to your institution, that is fine, although it has its limits in terms of your experiences of professional processes.

Planning distribution you should consider:

- If you are aiming to sell the product, how you will organise this?
- If you need to generate revenue through selling advertising space, how you will approach this?
- How will you market your product for the intended audience?
- How will you distribute the product as widely as possible?

You need to show an awareness of how you have considered reaching your target audience through distribution and outlets. If, for example, your product is intended for children then it would be a shrewd move to advertise and set up a point-of-sale at a primary school, outside a children's clothing shop (for parents and guardians). To do this, you need to take into account the following:

- Do you have permission from the establishments in which you hope to establish a point of sale?
- How are you intending to package your product for transport?
- How are you intending to transport the packages?
- If you are handling sales, how will you collect the money and where is its destination? Will it be used to try to recover production costs according to budget?
- It may be useful to ask the vendors to keep a tab on how many sales they make and who the sales are for. This is a kind of controlled market research and sales technique. You sell the product and after sale you ask a few details about why the client bought the product and for whom.

Testing audience response

All publishing companies need to have a clear sense of audience interaction with their product both before and after publication. With organised and widespread distribution, the post-production assessment is often completed by analysing sales figures, critical responses or client feedback. For your purposes, the audience feedback you will be seeking should be critical, constructive and should feed directly into improving the next printed product you produce.

There are several ways in which you can gather responses from audiences for your product. You should probably work around one or both of these models:

- face-to-face interviews with readers;
- questionnaire response sheets.

The kinds of information an objective audience will be able to provide you with will involve the following areas:

- Why the client bought the product.
- Whether they thought it was professional or not, and why.
- Which parts of the product they thought worked well and which need to be improved.
- How suitable it was for them (if they could be considered a part of the target audience) or the person for whom they are purchasing it.
- Whether it was successful in its aims (of which they will obviously have to be informed).
- Whether it was easy to read.
- Whether it was well designed, organised and presented.
- What they would seek to change in the publication.
- Whether they found any of it offensive or off-putting and why.

Reading and representing the audience response

This exercise will also feed into work you may need to produce for Units 6 or 7, not to mention providing you with useful material to develop as evidence for all of the core units (i.e., the calculations required to generate the statistics for application of number; the presentation for communication and the production of charts or graphs could be done on computer).

What you do with the results of your audience responses is crucial. It is common within the industry for presentations to be made about the results of this type of audience survey. Making presentations is a key communication skill for any media industry.

Firstly, you need to feed back statistical responses to some of your key questions. For example,

"42% of those asked stated that they bought the magazine for this reason … " or

"Two-thirds of all respondents disliked the book cover and would not have picked it up in a bookshop."

To clarify these figures and make them speak for themselves, making large charts of certain essential results is useful. You may wish to put this type of information into the form of a bar chart or pie chart, perhaps using different colours to represent different responses or different age groups, etc. You could display this on a flip chart or on an overhead transparency. It may be that you made a video of the responses and wish to use parts of that to underline major issues.

Secondly, after having looked at the response statistics, you may wish to consider some points made by respondents which do not fit into any of the areas which you can cover using statistical data. This will, of course, be information which arose from discussion which is more personal or individual, perhaps quoting some interesting responses. (qualitative data — See p. 358)

Thirdly, as a result of the audience research you will then be able to make a brief evaluation of target customer response, what key issues have been raised and how the production team will consider these issues in light of future publications (useful even if you do not intend making another similar product).

When planning your audience surveys, you need to assess how many people to interview to form a meaningful sample of responses and how to present and record data.

Techniques for this kind of activity are covered in some detail in Unit 6.

Evaluating the success and quality of the product

Considering the print product to be a simulated professional exercise conducted within resource constraints, you need to try to reflect objectively on the standard of the outcome and how this measures up to your intentions, the purpose of the publication and the competition in the marketplace. If there is more than one group producing a print product, it may be useful to interview the other group with a series of questions about your product, directing them to provide clear, constructive critical responses. Another way to try to reflect objectively on the product, is to consider the various elements of the publication individually before considering it as a whole. You might wish to use the following model to record feedback data:

CASE STUDY
Further North Productions

Printed Product Evaluation Sheet

Circle the number which corresponds closest to your opinion:

1 = Very good
2 = **G**ood
3 = Satisfactory
4 = Not very professional
5 = Needs quite some improvement

(a) For the section of the publication _____, how well constructed are the articles?
1   2   3   4   5

(b) For the same section, how well researched are the articles?
1   2   3   4   5

(c) How clear and appropriate is the language used?
1   2   3   4   5

(d) How catchy are the headlines?
1   2   3   4   5

(e) How clear is the presentation?
1   2   3   4   5

Further North Productions is a simulated company set up by the North West Institute of Further and Higher Education in Londonderry, Northern Ireland. All **G**NVQ projects are commissioned by the company.

(f) How good is the readability?

1   2   3   4   5

(g) How distinct is the style?

1   2   3   4   5

(h) How closely does the page correspond to the purpose of the publication?

1   2   3   4   5

(i) How well does the content relate to the product's target audience?

1   2   3   4   5

(j) How clear and well organised is the layout?

1   2   3   4   5

(k) How professional is the outcome?

1   2   3   4   5

If you collect the results of your analysis and consider the product as a whole, its success in terms of your expectations, audience response and professional outcome, you will have a well-rounded evaluation of the publication.

TASK

Make a presentation to the group (as a team if you wish) evaluating your product and representing your findings on tested audience response to your publication.

Evaluating the process

Evaluating the process is probably the area where it is most important to make an objective view of your own as well as your team's performance. To undertake a useful **assessment** of **the effectiveness of the planning and production process**, you will need to follow certain stages of analysis. These are as follows:

■ The success and professional quality of the product (audience research and objective analysis).

■ The effectiveness of the planning and production processes (consideration of resources available; equipment used; effect of equipment; technology available and its effectiveness; technology which should be used; appropriateness of deadlines; organisation of teams; approaches to work which were and were not effective; decisions made regarding content; how, in comparison with intentions, the result was or was not effective; the quality of the outcome).

■ Individual and team roles in the planning and production process (personal assessment below; professional assessment of the input of team members in terms of effectiveness of contribution, commitment and the effects).

■ How well the production and planning methods used reflected professional practice (given the restrictions) and how effective these were. A useful way to do this is to consider what you felt did not go so well and why, and the effect this had on the quality of the product.

■ What you would do differently next time in order to make the production process more effective.

When assessing the performance of others, criticism should be constructive, not adversorial. Action plans will help you assess your intent against minutes, which record actual action lines. In terms of assessing your individual role, it is necessary for you to be completely familiar with what is expected of that role.

You may wish to ask yourself the following, when assessing your own performance:

■ Did you work hard?
■ Could you have worked harder?
■ Did you learn new skills?
■ Did you respond to instructions well?
■ Did you manage others well?
■ Did you work well with others?
■ Did you try to follow professional practice?
■ Did you limit yourself to what you know?
■ Were you well organised?
■ Were you pleased with the outcome of what you worked on?

EVIDENCE COLLECTION POINT
Checklist

The following can contribute to your portfolio of evidence required for this unit:

■ Research notes and materials.

■ Project proposals and product outlines.

■ Flatplans

■ Concepts (article/page/product).

■ Schedule.

■ Included and excluded material.

■ Budget/resource documentation.

■ Notes on content issues (e.g., copyright, representation, defamation, etc.).

■ Minutes from meetings at all stages of the project.

■ Proofread corrected text.

■ Notes on visual and textual material gathered.

■ Examples of drafts and rewrites.

■ Draft and final page layouts.

- Sub-edited material.

- Notes explaining reasons for selection (or exclusion) of material.

- Final, edited copy of the print product.

- Report evaluating individual and team roles.

- Report evaluating the product.

- Log of the production process including record of ideas generated in planning meetings, notes on discussions with team, details of role allocation and individual responsibilities, health and safety issues.

ASSIGNMENT 1

Planning and producing a local community newspaper

You are a member of the board of management of a local community centre. The centre runs a range of activities for all members of the locality, from playgroups to a lunch club for old-age pensioners. It runs classes in a variety of subjects, from photography for women to traditional dancing. All of the activities reflect the needs of the local community, which is culturally diverse. The centre has published a newsletter for some time, but the management committee has decided that it could involve local people in the production of a community newspaper which would be published monthly. Its purpose would be to publicise up-coming events, run reports on the centre's activities, articles on local 'personalities' and assist in fund-raising for the centre. As there is some design expertise on the committee, the aim is to produce, within the limited resources available, a publication which would look professional and attractive, and which could, potentially, attract some local advertising. The budget for the magazine is limited — no more than £60 per issue, with a circulation of 1000.

- Carry out research to establish the breadth of the target audience for this publication, and to establish the appropriate style and range of content for the newspaper — this will mean canvassing opinion as to what might be regular items, how much advertising you will carry, whether individual community groups will take a certain amount of space for each issue, etc.

- Look at comparable community newspapers.

- Investigate advertising possibilities, appropriate cover price, intended distribution and sales.

- Plan, schedule and budget your production.

- Assign roles and mark out responsibilities.

- Agree the outline of the product and generate material.

- Hold regular meetings.

- Plan design, style, house style, title appropriate to your target audience.

- Lay-out, edit and sub-edit to plans.

- Produce publication.
- Distribute (and sell) the product.
- Evaluate the product and production process.

ASSIGNMENT 2

Planning and producing an image-based print product

You are a small, independent publishing house producing image-based 'cult' books and magazines. Your audience is mainly aged 16–35. You are launching a new series of graphic novel publications based on cult movies such as *Reservoir Dogs* and *Pulp Fiction* (Quentin Tarantino USA, 1991 and 1994), or *The Adventures of Priscilla, Queen of the Desert* (Stephan Elliott AUS, 1994). You are to produce the cover (front and back) of the publication, plus a double-page sequence.

- Carry out research, comparing the content of other movie/fan publications and looking at styles of other graphic novels.
- Investigate your possible production methods.
- Prepare rough design ideas for cover and style of the publication.
- Decide on style and produce rough storyboards for the sequence.
- Produce the product, including prelims and end matter.

You may be able to make use of this product as evidence towards Unit 1.

ASSIGNMENT 3

Producing a children's book

You are working for a well-known children's publisher. You want to extend the range of audio/book publications to include short stories from a variety of cultures. The age range is 6–8 years old and the product is an audio cassette, which may include storytelling, dramatised sequences, music and sound effects, accompanied by an illustrated booklet with clear indications of when the text matches the audiotaped reading (these are marked on the audiotape by a sound cue — the book will have a visual cue). You have been commissioned to produce the booklet.

- Research audio/book publications for this age group and decide on possible styles and approaches for your publication. You will need to consider how much text to include, how the pictures will enhance the audio reading of the story, whether to draw the pictures, commission them or use photographs.
- Plan and produce the product, using the evidence checklist to guide you through the process.

You may wish to produce the audio cassette to accompany the booklet as evidence for Unit 4.

You may be able to form a relationship with your local newspaper to enable you to produce an item such as this on a regular (although weekly would not be sustainable) basis. This would provide you with excellent real product for your portfolio, as well as experience of working to real production schedules and budgets.

You may wish to undertake this as a whole class project, with each individual student producing one page. If you do approach the project in this way, you will need to decide exactly how the material from all of the contributors should be used (how many words, what are the main topics, how many pictures, etc.). You could also adapt this brief to address other interesting career areas, or perhaps unusual jobs.
You may also wish to use the brief as a basis for a video production or radio project.

ASSIGNMENT 4

Plan and produce a centre-page insert for your local paper

Your local newspaper has a circulation of around 10,000. The majority of readers are over 35, living and working locally. Increasingly, due to a decline in local employment opportunities, people commute to their workplace and, as a consequence, circulation figures are beginning to fall. The newspaper wishes to attract a younger readership to extend the audience profile and win lost readers back to the publication.

You have been commissioned to produce a four-page weekly insert which can be removed from the newspaper as a separate section. The audience you wish to attract is 16–25.

Using the evidence checklist to guide you through the process, plan, produce and evaluate the first four-page insert, testing the product on an appropriate audience sample both during the research and evaluation stages.

ASSIGNMENT 5

Plan and produce a careers booklet

You have been commissioned by a broadcaster to produce a careers booklet on jobs in the media to accompany a series transmitted weekly at 7pm entitled *Careers in the Media – A Rough Guide*. Each episode of the programme takes an aspect of the media, such as advertising or television production, and describes some of the key jobs. Interviews with individuals in these jobs form the basis for the programme, and this should be strongly reflected in the booklet. The presentation should be of very high quality, fairly glossy, and the cover should incorporate the broadcaster's logo, as well as that of the production company and any other relevant broadcast credits. You can often obtain examples of materials that accompany television programmes by contacting the information or education department of your regional broadcaster.

Using the evidence checklist on page 209 to guide you through the process, plan and produce this booklet.

ASSIGNMENT 6

Planning and producing printed marketing materials

A local band has just signed a record deal with a major recording company. Design and produce the covers for their cassette tape and CD.

4 PRODUCING AUDIO PRODUCTS

Although within the parameters of the GNVQ, any of the audio production forms is acceptable, provided that you cover the range of the unit, this book will concentrate on *producing for radio* — the most fertile and accessible area for developing multiskilled audio techniques and giving a more thorough understanding of the medium. In addition, some basic principles of multi-track music recording will be covered. However, it will not concentrate on the role of presenter or DJ in 'driving' the desk and broadcasting the 'output'. The focus here will be on planning and producing the input.

If you are producing moving image products on to film (rather than videotape) where sound is recorded on to a separate magnetic tape and then married with the picture later, you will find many of the techniques suggested in this unit invaluable. Many of the processes also apply to recording sound for video and relevant points are indicated throughout the unit.

As with all of the production units (3, 4 and 5), you may already have begun the process of thinking about producing audio products. If you are following the GNVQ on a unit-by-unit basis, you will have produced proposals and scripts for **audio items** which may form part of a larger production, you can develop as evidence for this unit.

You will see that the unit requires you in Element 4.1 to agree a programme brief, carry out necessary research and produce scripts for the production. Obviously, you will need to make use of the research methods and script presentation techniques you have developed, or are developing, if you are to make a good quality programme. However, this unit concentrates on pre-production, production and post-production, as well as introducing some of the technical principles of sound, which will help you to understand better the various processes you need to go through to make a successful recording.

4.1 PLAN THE PRODUCTION PROCESS

Radio genres

In Element 1.3, you will have explored the concept of genre. In element 2.3 you will have planned and researched items within radio genre.

You may be working from a brief set by your tutor, or from one devised either individually or in a team. Whatever the circumstances, once you begin to work on your idea, having decided the form and possibly the subject, you will no doubt begin to talk about the format or genre. Before working towards **agreeing the production brief**, it is worth exploring the main constituents of radio genre.

Radio genres include:

- News reports
- Documentaries
- Features
- Magazines
- Satirical reviews and sketches
- Commercials
- Drama
- Discussion programmes
- Phone-in programmes
- Music programmes
- Commentary

Fiction or non-fiction?

There are blurred distinctions between fiction and non-fiction as categories. News programmes obviously fall into the category of non-fiction, although where the listener, or sometimes the person being interviewed, feels that there is bias, the factual credibility of the programme can be questionable. There are deliberate blurrings of the boundaries in hybrid genres such as documentary features or drama documentaries.

See also Unit 5 on television documentary drama.

All GNVQ units describe the skills which you must be able to accomplish and the underpinning knowledge with which you should be familiar, not just a list of tasks you simply cover. This means that you need to find any opportunity you can, both within your course and independently, to **practise research skills** and to **practise with the technology**.

You may have prepared a news item as evidence for Unit 2

Radio genres are described in Unit 2.3. However it is worth making some additional points to enhance your understanding of working with genre on complete programmes.

Recorded news reports

Most radio stations have at least two news programmes per day. If you examine a news report, it is possible to work out the 'building blocks' that edit together to create the finished piece (typically under 3 minutes long), as well as the qualities that give it news value, eg immediate topicality and proximity to the audience. You also need to consider the radio station or programme in which it will be broadcast. This may well determine story selection and running order, and will certainly affect the way in which the bulletin is packaged (its delivery, the number and depth of stories, the music preceding the news, the style of presentation). Unlike newspapers, which can use different typeface sizes and styles, headlines and photographs, radio news can only emphasise the importance of a story by its placing and treatment. A typical news bulletin, lasting five minutes, may include eight or nine items, with the first two or three stories given one minute, the remainder decreasing to 30 seconds or less. Radio news coverage, then, unless in an extended speech station such as Radio 4, is much more limited than newspaper coverage.

Typical recorded news reports will tend to adopt the following conventions:

- A **scripted link** from the news-reader/presenter, contextualising the report and introducing the journalist.
- **Scripted narration** by the journalist also linking into key sections of the report which might include the following:
  - **Interviews** with main people/experts in the story, where possible providing a balance of opinion;
  - **Vox pops**, where the same questions are asked or a number of people to canvas a range of opinion about an issue, to give an impression of the thoughts, feelings and reactions to the story's focus. These are usually recorded on the spot, complete with background ambience;

Vox pop: 'Voice of the people', informed opinion from members of the public.

  - **Actuality**, recording the sounds of what is actually going on, that help to contextualise the story, e.g., factory, motorway, demonstration, pub noise, etc. This also serves as a form of proof that the journalist actually was there and that this was not all secondhand. In television reports, the 'piece to camera' (PTC) has a similar authenticating role.
  - The **hook**, where the report begins with a burst of actuality, which serves a double function, both setting the scene and providing a 'hook' to catch the audience's attention and interest. Another form of hook might be more scripted, beginning the report with an enigmatic or contentious statement that requires resolving.

Sequence: The difference between a magazine and a sequence is that a magazine usually has a specific audience in mind and is tightly structured around the various items; a sequence is generally longer (1–4 hours), with a broader audience appeal, usually focused on music and presentation.

How these elements are ordered at the editing stage may vary. However, narration might well begin and end the piece, while also providing links into interviews and vox pops. Remember there are no captions or subtitles in radio, so people's identity must be verbally introduced. In planning or designing a complete programme which has a number of elements, the *clock format* is often a useful way of looking at its overall pattern. This way, the producer can see the overall balance of the programme at a glance. In the case of a **sequence**, the clock format can help to ensure that format changes can be made, or repeat items can be scheduled in appropriately. This device is also very useful in planning music programmes.

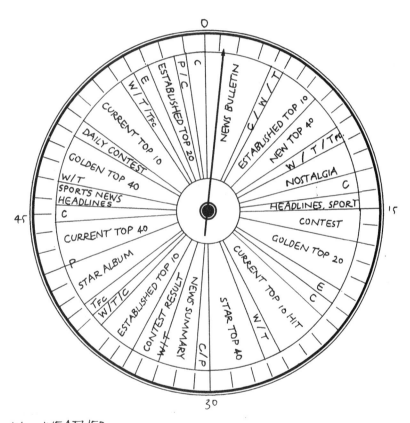

W   WEATHER

T   TEMPERATURE

Tfc   TRAFFIC

P   PROG. TRAILS PROMOS

E   EVENTS

C   COMMERCIALS

Fig 4.1   The Clock format

Documentaries and features

The distinctions between radio documentary and radio feature are frequently blurred, partly because the raw material in both genres may overlap considerably and partly because terms like 'documentary feature' are often used to describe a programme that employs a range of techniques. There are times when it is more appropriate to use a documentary approach, where only 'factual' material is used. There are other instances, for example, historical programmes, where there is no actual documented evidence, and where it may be necessary to produce material 'not based on fact'.

Documentary

Proactive: creating or controlling a situation of taking the initiative

The subject matter of documentaries is likely to be based on an ongoing contemporary issue which is explored and investigated in much greater depth than a news report would allow, while aiming to provide the listener with a real understanding of the human issues involved. Also, in a sense, because of the documentary's more investigative nature, the journalist's role is likely to be much more '**proactive**' rather than the news reports more 'reactive' role in responding to the day's news agenda.

The documentary's structure might echo many aspects of the shorter news report but with a greater reliance on the role of the interviewees and of recorded **actuality** rather than relying purely on the role of **scripted narration** (indeed, no narration might be used, e.g., fly-on-the-wall approaches or the interviewees are left to speak for themselves). This has the added effect of appearing less packaged and mediated than the news report, as the listener has a greater input in working out the possible connections, implications and significance of the actuality and interview material.

The feature

While the documentary is more within the stricter journalistic codes that should apply to news reporting (e.g., balance of opinion, lack of bias, integrity of sources, etc.) the feature invites a more personal, impressionistic look at a subject with a more creative treatment and entertainment value being perhaps more to the fore. Consequently, although it might contain 'documentary' material, like interviews, actuality and vox pops, the feature might also contain music, sound effects and fictional or re-enacted sequences, used in an imaginative, personalised way.

Magazine programmes

These are deliberately structured for a variety of style and content, and tend to be a composite of several separately produced shorter pieces. You will notice that many radio genres or formats draw on print terminology. There are useful comparisons to be made in terms of your approach to developing and producing a magazine programme. Magazine programmes, just like printed magazines, usually have a specific audience in mind, a regular structure and an overall sense of style. The *Today* programme, for example, on Radio 4 presents over two hours a day following a magazine format, made up of the following items:

- news headlines (live);
- expanded commentary (live);
- short and extended interviews in studio or down line (live);
- news reports (live and pre-recorded);
- short documentaries (pre-recorded);
- features (pre-recorded);
- personal comment (live);
- weather report (live).

You may have already scripted one or more items such as these which could be recorded and incorporated into a magazine programme.

Other non-news based magazines, like Radio 4's *Woman's Hour* or *Kaleidoscope*, would still retain a similar though more restricted mix, including scripted presentation, informal studio interviews and discussion and documentary or feature inserts.

Commercials

As with television, these have no specific generic similarities other than length (usually 20 or 30 seconds). In style they might follow the codes and conventions of other genres. (Anything from reportage to drama.) Again, as with television, a heavy reliance is placed on the role of music as an identifiable tag, sometimes echoing the DJs or station's 'jingles'. For example, Martini, advertising on Jazz FM (now known as JFM), made several advertisements which made use of recognisable jazz music styles.

A sharp example of this was *On the Hour*, (available on BBC cassette) wickedly satirising the conventions of radio news. Similarly, *Knowing me, Knowing You* with Alan Partridge, effectively lampooned crass, egotistical, sensationalist chatshow hosts (this show eventually found its way to television).

Satirical reviews and sketches

Here radio becomes very 'self-referential' in that the object of humour in satirical reviews is often the codes, conventions and cliches of radio itself.

Drama

See Unit 2 for approaches to constructing character and narrative

Radio drama has huge potential and can be a powerful release for the listener's imagination, because so much is *suggested* rather than fully realised. While sound effects can quickly and cheaply evoke foreign lands, wild storms or interplanetary travel, radio drama is at its most powerful with simple, well-scripted voices and, in particular, with a single voice reflecting and commenting on the world. At this point it becomes a very direct, personal link between speaker and listener — a relationship that no other medium can quite match, perhaps because at this level it becomes part of an almost ageless oral tradition of *storytelling*.

Soap

If you wish to study the basic codes and conventions of radio drama, listen no further than The Archers, the longest running radio soap, which has been on the air for over 40 years. As with television soaps, The Archers is set in a fixed location — in this case, a rural English village — with the same characters in each episode, multiple storylines and has an open-ended narrative structure. In terms of technique, where the 'fade to black' might be used in television to mark changes of time and place, in radio drama the sound fade is often used. Atmospheric **'ambient'** sounds, recreating outdoor or indoor locations help in the scene setting (sometimes a second or two of ambient sound before the dialogue begins functions in the same way as an *establishing shot* would in film or television). A sense of movement is also given by cast approaching or retreating from the microphones.

See Unit 1.
Ambient taken from the surrounding area

Adaptations

Taken from popular novels, short stories and theatrical plays, storyline, narration and dialogue are reworked so that it becomes effective as a story in sound. These are either dramatised with different actors and sound effects, or read aloud using 'voices'.

Discussion programmes

Broadcast discussion programmes are usually focused on current issues or topics about which there is genuine public concern. Usually the participants in the debate will express different views on the subject, with an 'impartial' chairperson to steer the discussion forward. When planning a discussion programme, selection of participants who will provide a balanced range of opinions is very important. It requires quick thinking on the part of the chairperson to steer the discussion and it is fairly easy to 'load' a discussion to take on a particular point of view, particularly if some of the participants, who may be the appropriate 'experts' in the field, are not experienced broadcasters. One way of planning a discussion programme is to produce a flowchart which begins at the pre-production stage and ends with follow-up and possible ideas for the next programme.

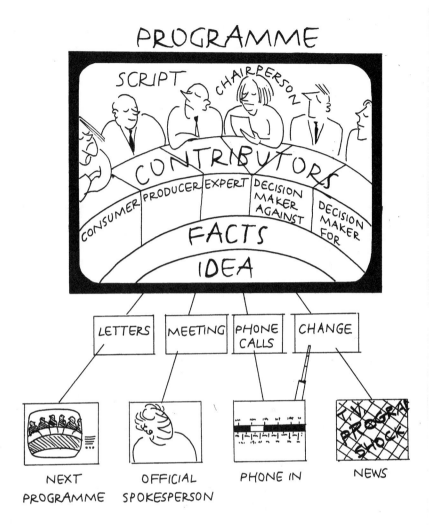

Fig 4.2 Discussion programme planner

Music programmes

Programmes which make use of pre-recorded music are characteristic of an enormous number of radio stations, with increasing specialisation in terms of dedication of programming to specific musical styles, e.g., Kiss FM (dance), JFM (jazz) and Classic FM (classical music), not to mention all of the local channels devoted to particular forms of 'indie' music. Formats vary, but music programmes could include dedications and requests, commentary on particular artists, tracks or music style, news bulletins, contests and their results, programme trails and run-downs of the 'top 20'. When planning music programmes, the 'clock format' is an excellent planning tool for achieving a balance and continuity.

Commentary

See Unit 2—on sports coverage

Radio can be extremely effective in bringing an event alive for the listener, be it a sporting event, a royal occasion, the scene of a disaster or war zone. The secret of good commentary is the ability to create 'pictures' in the listener's mind which not only communicate what the commentator can see, but will also give a sense of the atmosphere, of how people who are at the event itself are responding to it, even the smell of the air can add an extra dimension to the description, which can be more effective and powerful than television coverage.

Planning the production process for non-fiction

You will have researched and produced treatments and scripts for audio items in Unit 2 which you may wish to develop further and produce into complete programmes. On the other hand, you might decide to start afresh on a completely new project. The planning and scripting sections below should help you to shape your ideas, however, you should look back to Unit 2 to find the detailed techniques of research and script writing.

There are many procedures common to both radio and television in the researching, planning and interviewing stages. Indeed, BBC correspondents are now 'bi-media' trained, often producing reports for both radio and television on the same event, to the point where the audio from a television interview is frequently edited into a radio report.

The programme brief

This is simply a description of the features of the programme. The term 'programme' is used here to cover all audio products you might make. The brief is more or less interchangeable with the term 'proposal': in a sense, the proposal becomes a brief once it has been agreed to pursue the idea. It should contain the aim of the programme, a summary of the content, the key features of the programme as agreed by the production team, the medium to be used (e.g., cassette, reel-to-reel, DAT), the target audience and a summary of resource requirements.

Planning news

Compare this with the newsroom at a newspaper — Unit 3.

In local and national radio stations, items for news reports are normally agreed on a daily, early morning basis by news editors and allocated to journalists with a very quick turnaround envisaged. (e.g., 1 o'clock or 6 o'clock news). It could take considerable time and practice for you to get up to this sort of professional running speed, as it condenses the entire production process into a few hours. While this could be undertaken as a production exercise towards completion of a training course, a more realistic timescale might suggest treating an ongoing local issue that would allow time for research and scheduling of key interviews, without risk of the story becoming yesterday's news.

The planning of news programmes usually involves deciding a running order of items, followed by completing **cue sheets**, which provide a standard layout for the organisation of the information necessary. It must contain information about the proposed date and time of transmission, a suggested on-air **intro**, the 'in' and 'out' cues of the programme, precise duration of the material and suggested on-air 'back announcement' or 'outro'.

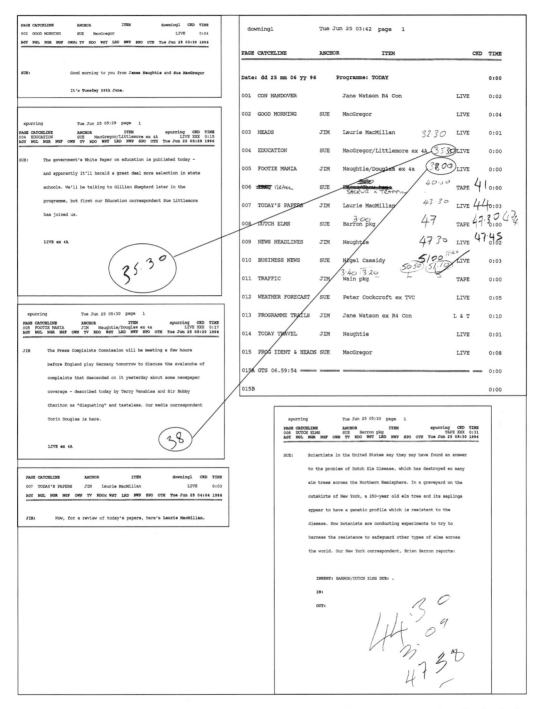

Fig 4.3 The running order of items for the first half hour of Radio 4's Today programme. Each item is clearly numbered, the presenter is identified and whether the source is live or a taped package. Timings are also indicated. The handwritten markings indicate revised items and timings. The cue sheets start with item 002 — Sue MacGregor's opening to the programme. If you match the page numbers on the running order and cue sheets, you will see where changes have been made to each

---

Interview questions — a reminder

Having researched your story from primary and secondary sources, a critical part of your planning is to frame the questions you are going to ask your interviewees. The essential skill is in framing open questions that do not simply result in a blunt 'yes' or 'no', but which are still sufficiently 'guided' to lead your interviewee to expand on the issues relevant to your programme.

Planning an extended documentary or feature

Often, radio producers work single-handedly on the planning stage of a documentary programme. There are decisions to be made regarding style and treatment of issues as well as the topics within the chosen subject area of the programme. The title is often the last thing to be decided, and can be, perhaps, taken from a significant statement made within the programme. *Working titles* are therefore used to identify projects in the planning stage. Broad headings might resemble those of a television proposal, though there is no strict format.

Features follow a similar process with additional planning for reconstructions, dramatisations or music if required.

Checklist: Programme proposal or programme brief

These headings are broadly what you would expect to find in a project brief:

■ Working title.

■ Aim.

■ Duration.

■ Intended audience/programme slot.

■ Synopsis, including indication of key questions and what actuality is required.

■ Contacts, sources (primary and secondary), access.

■ Budget.

■ Deadline.

Towards a script

As with television documentary, much of the detailed scripting for non-fiction programmes occurs *after* production, when you have recorded your interviews and actuality, and can select and shape your material into an effective story.

Transcripts

Transcribe: write up as text

The shaping process can be helped if you **transcribe** your interviews , so that notes and selection ideas can be added with a marker pen, indicating what is to be kept and where it might feature in the programme's structure.

Scripted narration

Note: Though your narrative script will be *read*, it should come across as though the narrator is *talking* to the audience, so it needs to be written in a conversational style. As you write your narration, 'talk' it out loud, and if it does not come across as normal speech, change it. You should also try to make your language as *visual* as possible in your descriptions.

As with television, there are different styles and approaches to radio documentary; a major factor being whether scripted narration is used. In many ways, it is much easier to use narration, as this can provide straightforward links from one element into another and also fill in any information not provided by interviewees. However, the pure interview/actuality programme has the potential for a more powerful audience involvement, as there is no journalist presence acting as intermediary or 'mediator', packaging information and drawing conclusions on your behalf.

Production script with running order

On paper you can now assemble all the elements of your programme, and also **mark up** your script with the timings of each insert as well as the transitions: cuts, fades, cross fádes, fades under, etc. You are now ready to 'produce' your programme.

Whether you will be mixing sounds together on to one mono recording, or keeping sounds separate on to two (or more) tracks through 'multi-tracking' do not forget to set out a clear production script in advance that separates out the different programme elements into two channels or sources, written against approximate timings.

Intros and outros

A good opening is vital to ensure that the listener will continue to listen! The start of a factual programme might make use of a scripted narration which frames broad questions to be addressed in the programme; a more dramatic **intro** might involve using a controversial statement or making use of sound effects. When a programme ends, it must leave a lasting impression with the listener, so a considered **outro** might involve the narrator summing up the key issues, for instance, or speculating on the future consequences of the subject matter.

Magazine programmes

The planning for a magazine programme involves co-ordinating a team to produce the different elements. The various inserts then involve a separate planning, researching, scripting and production process. However, it is in the scripted links to both pre-recorded inserts and to live studio interviews and discussions that considerable preparation is required.

Links

These can tax the imagination and sometimes lead to very clichéd results, whether pre-scripted or 'busked' live, e.g. after a fractious debate: 'Well, after that stormy outburst, let's go over and hear what the weather's doing ... Bill?'

While avoiding forced links like this, your programme will still require some kind of thematic linkage if possible, to avoid the impression of a 'bitty' sequence of disconnected items. Often, an established presenter will rewrite much of the script so that the linking material has its own consistent, personal style. The links also have to take account of the station style, for instance, whether it is appropriate to inject a note of humour or personalised comment.

Planning the production process for fiction

Scripting for drama and commercials

Because drama and commercials (which often take the form of 'mini-dramas'), are totally 'constructed' in the studio, a highly detailed script, with exact dialogue, sound effects and intended music is required in advance. When producing your script, you should use the conventions of script layout as used by the industry to ensure utmost clarity.

See Unit 2.3

While commercials might share some of the codes and conventions of other genres, there is a different planning procedure involving the establishing of agreement with the client.

Production Resources

Part of the planning process will involve you in **securing resources** for your production. You will either be working to a fixed budget or be required to produce one for your production. This may change the way in which you decide to treat the subject, as might availability of equipment and studio time. If your school or college has not already done so, it is a good idea to devise a 'rate card' for equipment hire, studio time, etc. Selection of appropriate equipment for the job will be informed by the nature of the environment in which you will need to record. You could base the rates on those of a local station. You should also not forget to cost in the time spent on research, the crew and cast time and any clearances for pre-recorded material if it is copyright.

Technical requirements

The budget will also have some effect on what technology you decide to use (although in an education situation, the likelihood is that you will have little choice about what is available to you). However, you will need to take account of the situations in which you will need to record and how you need your source material organised so that you can edit it appropriately. In a large station, you would put together a requisition list, identifying precisely *what* pieces of equipment you require, *when* and for *how long*. For instance, you might need a range of microphones for recording in different locations.

Selecting interviewees and casting drama

During the planning and research stage of a drama production, it is likely that you will have had key cast members in mind already. With a non-fiction programme, you may have already identified the presenter or narrator. Before the production can be scheduled, the personnel who will be in the programme obviously have to be identified and contracted to undertake the work.

The selection of participants, whether for a discussion programme or a documentary or news programme, is very important in terms of achieving balance. You need to consider balance in different ways, to take account of expertise, opinion and whether the participants are representative of a cross-section of society (you may well want to ensure that a discussion programme is not dominated by white, male upper middle-class voices).

Unit 2 goes into some detail on identifying interviewees for factual programming. With drama, you would need to find actors. This can be problematic in a college or school situation, particularly if you need a variety of age ranges. You might think about speaking to the drama or performing arts department to try and find actors with some training. In the industry, a producer might try casting directories or, failing that, putting out an open 'casting call' to a number of agents.

Once you have set a time and place for your casting session, you will need to hear your prospective actors read. It is useful for you to have prepared a list of aspects that you need to consider when conducting the casting session. You should prepare a separate sheet for each actor, with room for you to write notes, ensuring that you take account of his or her acting skill, suitability for the character, voice, etc.

Production roles

Of course, there can be no production without a crew. The **producer** will have been involved from the first ideas stage of the project. It is the producer's role to oversee the entire production process and achieve a programme that fulfils the requirements of the brief, and does not run over time or over budget. The producer co-ordinates all stages of production.

If the programme is a magazine, news, phone-in, discussion or music format, a **presenter** (or presenters) is needed to steer the discussion or form the links between each item. The presenter can be a very important factor in terms of establishing and maintaining a consistent style.

The **studio engineer** is responsible for the operation of the recording equipment and mixing desk in the studio, as well as for sound mixing and editing at the post-production stage.

Journalists are the greatest source of news, providing items for a station's news bulletins. Investigative journalists are likely to be used more in documentary items, in that they are charged with exposing 'truths' or scandals.

Often, journalists also do their own **research**, although other fiction and non-fiction programmes require researchers.

The recce

Wild-track: Sounds recorded at random for use at a later date.

See Unit 2.

If you're covering events 'on the spot', it will not necessarily be possible for you to conduct a 'recce' (or reconnaissance) before you begin. If you are planning to record on location to construct documentary or feature items, however, you should be in a position to check out the location first in terms of determining its suitability for recording and making the necessary judgements about the most appropriate equipment to ensure a good result. Drama is usually studio-based, although you may decide to collect 'authentic' atmospheric sounds, or **wild-tracks**, for use later at the post-production stage.

If you are recording in a public or private place, just as in planning for film, video or television production you will need to seek permission.

In terms of assessing **audio characteristics**, any location is likely to have much poorer acoustics than a studio. If you are recording outdoors on a busy road, for instance, it is better to avoid standing near traffic lights, where the traffic sound is likely to vary between 'idling' and pulling away.

If you are recording indoors, you should try and avoid spaces that are too 'lively', i.e., where you are surrounded by many hard, smooth surfaces like windows, marble or stone floors, high ceilings. If you can find a carpeted room, with curtains or other soft furnishings, this will improve the quality of your recording (unless you are specifically seeking an echoey environment).

You will also need to consider **health and safety** requirements, as well as determining if there are sources of power at the location, should you require them.

Scheduling a production

Whether managing the production process for fiction or non-fiction productions, it is essential for all concerned to construct a detailed plan of action or **production schedule**. In scheduling your production, it helps if you work backwards from your deadline, as this is the most 'immovable' of your dates.

Checklist: Production Schedule

■ **Key dates**: for pre-production (planning, scripting), production (recording) and post-production (editing).

■ **Recording schedules/callsheets**: giving times, places, personnel, contact numbers, transport details, as applicable.

■ **Resources**: involving equipment, tapes, studio space, etc, all of which needs booking well in advance.

■ **Recce notes**: where applicable, concerning location detail, potential sound problems or access problems and risk assessment notes concerning hazards and how the potential risk factor can be minimized/avoided.

4.2 RECORD AUDIO MATERIAL FOR PROGRAMMES

About sound

As a medium for communication, sound is perhaps the most powerful in its ability to **suggest** ideas and **evoke** moods and images, whether through music, dialogue or ambience, precisely because it leaves all the imagining to the mind. Consequently we, the audience, contribute much more to the 'storytelling' (whether fictional or non-fictional) than with film or television, being more involved and engaged rather than 'spectators' (although of course, the notion that film or television viewing is 'passive' is highly debatable).

Ironically, audio production is actually *less* demanding of a concentrated, static audience. We listen to radio, cassettes and CDs in cars, on Walkmans in the underground, the kitchen and the bath, and it has become a very individual, almost private relationship, where once listening to music and radio were very public events, with the coming together of family and extended community.

Hearing sounds

Normally, our hearing is far more sensitive than our vision. Firstly, it covers 360 degrees horizontally and vertically. (Compare this with a much more restricted field of vision.) Secondly, in terms of 'pick-up' sensitivity, crossing over senses, if our ears were eyes, we could see a small candle flame ten miles away. Thirdly, our hearing has *directional* properties, telling us from what spatial position sounds are coming. (Our response to stereo recordings relies on this.) This ability links back to our natural need for self-preservation, knowing where danger might spring from. Fourthly, our hearing can focus or 'tune in' on particular frequencies and 'lock on' to them. For instance, at a crowded, loud party, we can follow a conversation with relative ease by selecting the sounds of the voice we are listening to from the cacophony of background noise. This quality of our hearing is sometimes referred to as the 'cocktail party effect'.

Physical characteristics of sound

Soundwaves

Sound does not move in a stream like a current of water, but more like the ripples on the surface of the water. The splash of a stone is like the sound *source*, and the ripples radiating out in all directions carry the message from the splash, gradually becoming weaker and less clearly defined. Although invisible, the same effect is happening in air as sound travels from a source. Air is 'elastic', and stretches and compresses around a vibrating object, (the sound source), and the resulting pressure rise or *compression* and pressure drop or *rarefaction* are passed on to the surrounding air, rippling out at a speed of 1,120 feet per second! The length from one ripple or wave peak to the next is known as the *wavelength*, measured in meters, and the number of these waves occurring per second is known as the *frequency*, measured in Hertz (Hz).

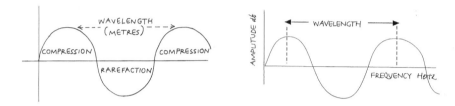

Fig 4.4

Our ears pick up the sounds through tiny bones that are oscillated by the soundwaves, recreating the sound vibrations in our heads. Our ears are sensitive across a very wide frequency range, from low frequency bass sounds of 30 Hz (like the low rumble of a passing lorry heard indoors), to the highest treble violin 'screech', within which there might be frequencies or *overtones* well above 15 kHz (15,000 Hz). The full range of young ears is from about 20 Hz to 20 kHz, but the spread drops off dramatically as people grow older. The human voice, more than any musical instrument, has the potential to cover the widest frequency range, a mixed choir ranging from about 100 Hz to 10 kHz.

Measuring loudness (amplitude)

The measurement of loudness relates not simply to some abstract numerical figure, but to what we can actually hear. The smallest *recognisable* change in loudness is measured as a decibel (dB). Different frequencies have relative amounts of audio 'power', with the mid range (500 Hz to 3 kHz) holding most power. (This also covers the main musical scale for many instruments.) The higher frequencies are vital for giving the instruments their particular 'timbre', as this is where the 'harmonics' and 'overtones' are found.

Reflected sound

Sounds from a source do not simply come straight to our ears or to the microphone, they also arrive having bounced off every available hard or 'reflective' surface and, in so doing, change considerably the nature of the sound. This is known as *reverberation*, creating a

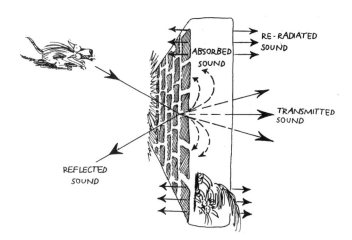

Fig 4.5   Reverberation

lengthening 'decay' to the sound. A variety of reverberation effects can now be produced artificially with digital 'reverb units'.

Choosing the right equipment for the job

Microphones

Just as the charge-coupled device (CCD) chip in a video camera converts light energy into electrical signals so the microphone converts acoustic energy into an equivalent fluctuating electrical response. The better the microphone, the more accurate is this conversion.

A measure of the quality of a microphone is how *evenly* it responds across a wide frequency range. For instance, if it creates a strong electrical signal only across the mid range, it will miss out the finer detail timbre of sounds and would not be suited for musical recordings, though as a 'dictaphone' microphone it might suffice.

Directional characteristics

It is the directional 'pick-up' properties of different microphones (the area of sound to which they best respond), that most influence their selection for specific recording tasks. Here are the main types of microphone and their uses:

Omnidirectional microphones

PICK UP OMNIDIRECTIONAL
RESPONSE

Fig 4.6

Properties: Responds equally to sound coming from *all* directions.

Recommended for: Recording situations where overall mixed sound is required, e.g., ambience, choirs, discussions where only one microphone is available. Useful for **studio** presentation and interview recording when there are no other sounds to be excluded.

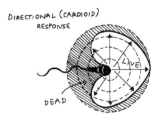

DIRECTIONAL (CARDIOID) RESPONSE

LIVE

DEAD

Fig 4.7

Directional (cardioid) microphones

Properties: Called 'cardioid' because its pick-up pattern is heart-shaped, from the front end of the microphone, hence it is possible to 'direct' or point it at a specific sound source (e.g., mouth, guitar sound hole).

Recommended for: Recording in situations where you need to isolate one sound from others, or at least 'favour' it. This could involve interviewing in noisy environments such as factories, high streets or war zones **location/exterior/interior.** They are also used throughout the music industry for live and recorded performance. Standard PA (public address) systems also use them, as an omni-directional microphone is more likely to pick up its own amplified signal from the loudspeaker and create 'feedback' or 'howl-around'.

Highly directional microphones

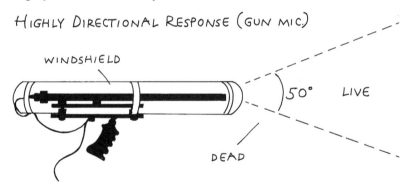

HIGHLY DIRECTIONAL RESPONSE (GUN MIC)

WINDSHIELD

50°   LIVE

DEAD

Fig 4.8

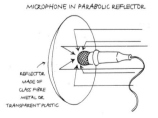

MICROPHONE IN PARABOLIC REFLECTOR

REFLECTOR MADE OF GLASS FIBRE METAL OR TRANSPARENT PLASTIC

Properties: The exaggeratedly directional properties of these microphones can 'focus' on a particular sound source in an environment within a narrow pick-up field.

Recommended for: Film and video work where the microphone needs to be out of shot, but must pick up specific sounds. Even more extreme directivity can be achieved by '*parabolic reflector*'

Fig 4.9

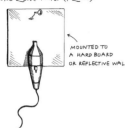

Pressure Zone Mic. (PZM)

MOUNTED TO
A HARD BOARD
OR REFLECTIVE WALL

Fig 4.10

Bi-Directional Response

Fig 4.11

microphones, used for wildlife recordings (e.g., birdsong), and for surveillance work.

Pressure zone microphones (PZM)

Properties: Similar to omnidirectional microphones. These need to be attached to a hard, reflective board placed strategically in the room or studio. Both direct and reflected soundwaves striking the board are picked up through the microphone placed close to the board's surface.

Recommended for: Interview and discussion group where a permanently placed, inconspicuous microphone can pick up the general sounds within a room. (Used as standard in police interview rooms, the PZM can be seen mounted above the cassette recorder in *The Bill*.

Bi-directional microphone.

Properties: A figure of eight pick-up zone.

Recommended for: Recording two sources placed opposite each other, e.g., table-mounted for one-to-one radio interviews.

Recording Sound

Tape formats

Essentially, there are two means of recording sound, *analogue* and *digital*.

Analogue

Audio tape is essentially a strip of thin plastic coated with minute metal oxide particles, the most common being *ferric oxide* (Fe_2O_3), and *chrome dioxide*, (CrO_2). CrO_2 has the potential to record higher frequencies more responsively, but can cause more wear on the tape heads over a long period of time. The finer the particles and the more saturated the tape surface with them, the greater the tape's capacity to record high resolution sound.

Sound is recorded by the tape first passing over an *erase* head, wiping away any previous recording, then passing over a *record* head, where electromagnetic induction *aligns* the polarity of the particles according to the fluctuating signal. A *playback* head reads the alignments as current which is then translated back into sound via amplifier and speakers.

BASIC TAPE RECORDING LAYOUT

E — ERASE HEAD

R — RECORD HEAD

P — PLAYBACK HEAD

Fig 4.12

Tape speed

The speed at which the tape runs past the recording head has a major influence on the quality of the recording. The principal reason for this is that the more tape surface available to record individual sounds, the more particles are available, which means the higher the fidelity of the recording. Professional reel-to-reel recorders have a choice of speeds, from $3\frac{3}{4}$, $7\frac{1}{2}$ to 15 IPS. For musical recordings, where clarity and wide frequency response are demanded, 15 IPS is recommended, though this will eat up your tape at an alarming rate (you should first calculate the running time of your tape at the chosen speed). $7\frac{1}{2}$ IPS, will record speech clearly and accurately, but $3\frac{3}{4}$ IPS ideally should be used where the concern is content information rather than quality of recording.

Compact cassette recorders tend to play at one speed only, though some multi-track cassette, 'porta-studios', have a choice between the standard 4.5 cm/s and 9 cm/s which, with a CrO_2 tape, can provide very good results.

IPS: (inches per second).

cm/s: centimeter per second

Tape width

The other major factor affecting tape's recording quality is its width. On cassettes, this is standard, but reel-to-reel recorders come in different widths, the standard domestic and radio production width being a $\frac{1}{4}$ inch, while professional studios tend to use formats of $\frac{1}{2}$ or 1 inch.

Compact cassettes are only half the standard tape width, and are 'quarter-track' formats in that it is intended for *two* separate stereo recordings, each with left and right tracks, making four altogether.

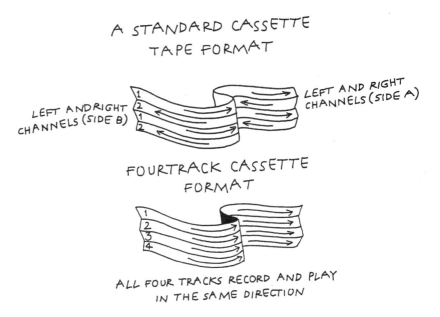

Fig 4.13

The *four-track* 'porta-studio' (e.g., by Tascam, Yamaha or Fostex), uses the full width of tape in *one* direction only.

Digital

Note: Betamax should not be confused with **Betacam**, which is a current industry standard video format.

Over recent years, a range of digital audio recording formats have been developed, with major commercial battles underway to capture the lucrative domestic market, in a struggle which echoes the VHS/**Betamax** 'wars' of the 1970s between JVC and Sony.

R-DAT (Rotary-head digital audio tape)

Professional digital recorders tend to use the R-DAT system where the inner workings in some ways resemble the VCR, with tape pulled out from the cassette and wrapped around a fast-rotating drum (2,000 rpm) that 'writes' at high speed.

S-DAT (Static-head)

DCC: Digital Compact Cassette

S-DAT has been developed for the domestic market, with Philips' **DCC** system proving the most marketable, because the same recorder will also play conventional analogue cassettes. Sony's market bid is a mini digital audio floppy disc. The smallest, most compact of formats to date, while affording over 70 minutes of digital recording per disc.

Advantages of the digital system

ISDN: Integrated Services Digital Network — a system of conveying high quality digital audio signals over the public telephone system.

Digital audio provides an 'incorruptible' format that does not degenerate through copying, editing or transmission, if a digital network is used (e.g., **ISDN**).

Professional DAT machines are also extremely quick in rewinding, cueing and accessing material. Combined with a suitable computer, the audio equivalent of non-linear video editing becomes possible, with all its advantages.

Industrial working practices

Basically, learning how to **operate equipment according to industrial working practices** will provide you with a valuable discipline, so that you are always sure that you have got the best from your equipment, the best from your crew, and that you approach the recording process in a systematic and organised way (which will also give the person you are recording confidence). You will also be able to *transfer you skills* to any situation, whatever the equipment.

Monitoring sound

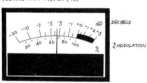

Fig 4.14 VU Meter

Modulation: Variations in recording or transmission/play-back levels.

Led: light emitting diode

To ensure that you have a high enough level to make a satisfactory recording, and to check that levels are appropriate to avoid distortion, you must monitor your sound recording. The most likely form of sound metering you will use is the VU (volume unit) meter. These meters, while useful for 'approximating' or averaging a sound level, are *very* slow in responding to surprise *peaks* in sound (the human voice is full of them!). Consequently it is best to *underestimate* to make allowances. If your levels are peaking into the red above 0 dB, the chances are they are higher still, and might well be

over-saturating your tape, causing distortion or 'break-up' (higher quality tape has more tolerance here). Aim to average your VU needle around −3 dB rather than 0 dB or 'supposed' full **modulation**.

Other cheaper versions of the 'needle' meter involve an **LED** column, with green turning to red in the 'peak zone'.

Peak programme meters (PPM)

PEAK PROGRAMME METER (PPM)

DARK BACKGROUND

EACH NUMBER
ON THE SCALE
REPRESENTS A RISE
OF @ 4dB

Fig 4.15

A more accurate (and expensive) meter, the PPM responds quickly to peaks, with each number on the scale representing a rise of 4 dB. (Levels for speech should be averaged at 4, peaking at 6). These meters, because of their accuracy, are used extensively in radio broadcasting, where the 'ride out' level from the sound desk must be consistent (unlike in the case of television advertisements, where levels are deliberately boosted above the surrounding programming, to the annoyance of many).

Using headphones

You should also double-check the sound quality using headphones, both at the recording and post-production stages. Sometimes, if you are using domestic equipment with no visual meter or display, you will have to rely solely on headphones to monitor your recording, which is not particularly satisfactory, but better than the naked ear!

Recording interviews

The production techniques for recording interviews require three levels of simultaneous activity:

- interviewing technique;
- microphone technique;
- recording technique.

Interviewing technique

See Unit 2, 'Conducting the interview'

Chat to the interviewee for a few minutes to put them at ease, then move to the interview with as little ceremony as possible, so that the relaxed relationship you have established is preserved. If the response to a question is somehow 'fluffed', or there is a noisy interruption, try to re-run the question, perhaps rephrasing slightly or explaining why you need a repeat.

Microphone technique

Having selected the right microphone for the context, the success of your recording is now down to its *handling*. Through familiarity with your microphone's characteristics, you should know the best distance at which to hold it from the mouth to maximize levels, but avoid 'popping', (the explosion of 'b', 'p' and 'd', known as 'plosives', causing break-up in the recording), and 'sibilance', (the excessive hiss of 's').

With each question and answer, the microphone should be moved from interviewer to interviewee. Remember, any hand movement on the microphone or cable is likely to be picked up as rumble, especially on cheaper models. Keep your hand and wrist locked, with movement only at the elbow. Also, when interviewing outdoors, be prepared for wind rumble, and take a foam windshield with you.

Fig 4.16

Recording technique

If you are using a portable cassette recorder (e.g., Marantz), your cassette should be wound on beyond the clear or coloured 'leader' tape which takes up the first few seconds of playtime. For total accuracy in cueing tape, (useful for playback purposes), you should wind this leader tape on manually with a finger or pen until the brown magnetic tape is just past the centre of the cassette. This checklist should now be run through *before* you leave the studio for your interview and is applicable to a Marantz recorder:

Checklist:

- Check tape type and length (e.g., ferric, chrome, etc.).

- Set the recorder's 'bias' switch to match the tape.

- With condenser microphones, check the battery.

- Check the recorder's battery level (VU meter on the Marantz doubles as a battery level meter).

- Check 'pitch' level is centred.

- Check Dolby Noise Reduction is off.

- As this is a mono recording, check your microphone jack is plugged into the left socket, but with stereo/mono switch in mono position. This ensures that you record mono across the full width of both channels (L and R), rather than on half the available tape.

If you are using a portable reel-to-reel (e.g., Uher), the procedures are broadly similar, with battery checks, cueing up and test recording. In addition, you should be aware of the running time of your spool and plan accordingly. You also have the choice over tape speed.

As with video, tape spools and cassette cases should be clearly *labelled* with production title, your name, date, etc., and stored after the recording in a safe place away from magnetic fields. In addition, the tabs can be removed from cassettes to **protect your recording**.

Recording actuality

For best results here, a number of factors come into play:

■ The nature of the sounds to be recorded.
■ The acoustic properties of the location.
■ The microphone type.
■ The effect you wish to achieve.

As with the recording of video wild-track, and 'synced' ambient audio, you should be aiming for as healthy a level as you can achieve without pushing up the recording gain to noisy levels.

Atmos: background sound at any location.

Choose microphone type according to whether you are recording a general '**atmos**' or trying to distinguish specific sounds — you need to determine where to get the right **ratio of background noise to your intended sound signal**. For the ambience, you might scout around, using you ears to determine the best spot to pick up the general reflected sounds, without the influence of other unwanted noise, (eg traffic, music). Having found the right spot, position your microphone, to take full advantage of its directional properties.

Remember: Recording background music (e.g., in pubs) still requires copyright clearance.

Recording drama

There are three main aspects to recording drama:

■ Performance — the effective delivery of dialogue.
■ Techniques within the studio.
■ Sound effects and reverberation.

Performance

Here, careful casting and dialogue rehearsal are vital. Although performers are able to read their lines during a take, they still need to become familiar with the phrasing and stresses to get the best out of their performance. Marker pens again can be useful to underline and accentuate on the script. As elsewhere in radio, silence can play a dramatic role itself, allowing the full message of a line to sink in. Also, pacing needs to change in keeping with the sense of the scenes.

Techniques

If you are working with performing arts students or actors with stage rather than radio experience, they will need an introduction to basic studio techniques. For instance, radio drama tends to be recorded in much longer takes than television, so performers must remain still and quiet when 'off mic', unless required by the producer to create 'noises off'.

Secondly, **microphone technique** must be learnt by the performers, keeping speech at a constant direction to and distance from the microphone, while avoiding 'popping'. This can be helped by the holding of scripts in front of the microphone stand, so that they are not looking down or to the side. Before a take, the corners of script pages should be creased over as 'dog ears' so that the pages can be turned with minimum effort and rustle. Using higher grade, thicker paper helps here too. A sense of movement and space can be created through lines being delivered at varying distances from the microphones.

Fig 4.17

Pan-pot: Panoramic potentiometer — a control on the studio mixing desk which places a source to the left or right when a stereo effect is required.

If a stereophonic effect is to be created then two or more microphones will be required, which may need to be recorded via a **mixing desk** on to tape. 'Pan pots' on the desk can also send the signal from left channel to right and vice versa, and this could be left as a post-production mixing effect rather than as a physical movement between microphones in the studio.

Sound effects and reverberation

Depending on the nature of your production and your equipment, you might choose to run the entire production more or less 'live'. In other words, all sound effects (SFX) would be created there and then in the studio, accompanying the performers' dialogue. If this is so, then a whole array of strange devices must be invented to create the required sounds, such as trays of gravel to walk in, coconut horseshoes, etc. Equally, if you intend to spend time mixing your recording down on to another tape, you can leave all these SFX until post-production, and then either use your own sourced recordings of 'the real thing', or SFX from a CD collection, mixing these in at appropriate levels with your dialogue on to your master.

Reverberation (reverb): The continuation of a sound after its source has stopped.

The same applies to the use of any artificial digital **'reverb'** that you might wish to add to enhance your studio's natural acoustic. This 'reverb', or other SFX like 'delay', 'chorus', 'gate', etc., can either be added 'live' or in a post-production remix.

Location recording

Alternatively you might decide to leave the studio out altogether, and record all your dialogue in the *actual* locations intended, ensuring the right ambience throughout. However, this presents a less controlled environment, harder to plan and schedule, and also subject to interruption and sound continuity problems between takes.

Sound mixing

This can either be a 'live' process during recording, or a re-mix when dubbing your initial recording on to another tape as a post-production process. Mixing is used in most genres of radio, but is at its most complex and sophisticated in the mixing of multi-track music recording.

Mixing desks

These can cover a vast range, from simple 'boxes' that mix two sources into one, varying the levels with faders, to 32 and 64 channel 'starship' consoles. In operational terms, however, the number of channels is irrelevant, as if you understand the basic controls of one channel, then all the others are mere duplications.

Controls

The illustration shows the typical channel controls on an 8 or 16 channel desk. The audio signal path flows from top to bottom, via the various knobs or 'pots', as follows:

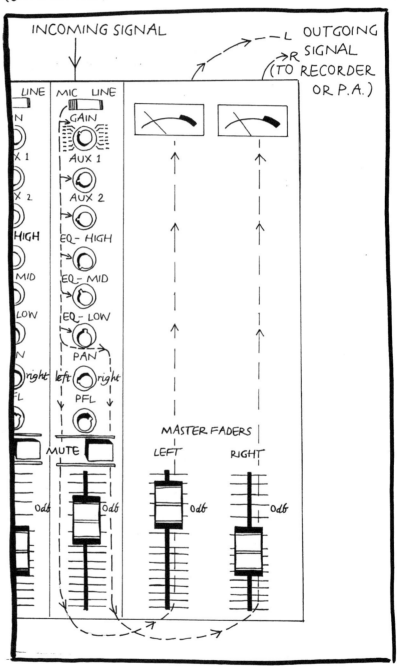

Fig 4.18 Mixing desk layout

- **Input select:** microphone signal or 'line' (e.g., from tape or CD).
- **Gain control:** to even out the variations in the level of signal strength from different sources. Also known as 'trim'.
- **Auxiliary level pot:** used where you have an effects unit 'looped' in with the desk. This pot can gradually mix a pre-selected effect (e.g., reverb) in or out. Often desks have two auxiliary pots, allowing for a choice of SFX.
- **Equalisation (EQ) pots:** these give you the option to boost or suppress certain frequency levels in your signal. If you intend to remix your recording on to another tape, always record a 'flat' signal, with all EQ pots centred, giving you as clean and unaffected a signal as possible. This then leaves you the full choice of the EQ range in the remix. Once you have removed a frequency range from your signal, you can't put it back again!
- **Pan pot:** this pot allows you to assign a signal anywhere across the left to right spectrum.
- **Pre-fade listen (PFL):** the main function of this is in radio desk work and allowing you to cue up a tape/disc/CD without the audio signal being transmitted through the desk as 'output'.
- **Mute:** this button cuts out the channel from the mix at a stroke.
- **Channel fader:** these are carefully engineered to fade levels up or down very smoothly, giving you a sensitive control over the variance of level for that channel.
- It is important to avoid getting dust into the faders by covering the desk in between use.

On more expensive professional desks, each channel is metered for its level, but the norm for smaller desks is to meter the 'ride out' level for left and right channels, controlled by the master faders to the right of the desk. If a desk is in a separate sound-proofed booth, recording can be monitored through amp and speakers, the desk having several line outputs for recording and monitoring. If not, headphones are used.

Setting a level through the desk

If you are using the desk for multi-track work (to be remixed later) each channel level should be working to full modulation (as near 0 dB as possible). However, if you are recording a 'live' mix, or a remix of pre-recorded material, then the different channel levels must be set in relation to each other according to *how it sounds to you*. Good quality monitor speakers need to be carefully positioned in relation to the room and your ears before you can begin to 'trust' the mix you are hearing.

Health and Safety

The health and safety of your crew, of your contributors and of the public are of paramount importance. You will have drawn up a risk assessment for your production, now you must implement the steps you have identified to minimise hazard in the recording situation. This is also important in terms of protecting your equipment. Likely steps you will have to take involve ensuring that microphones which are not to be handheld are rigged on a weighted stand; that cable is taped to the microphone stand and that cables do not obstruct doorways and are not loosely trailing on the floor.

Note: remember that behaviour can also become a safety issue as can not undertaking detailed checks on the circumstances in which you are going to record. For example, it is unwise for you to go alone to someone's house to interview them, unless they are known to you — always take at least one other crew member with you.

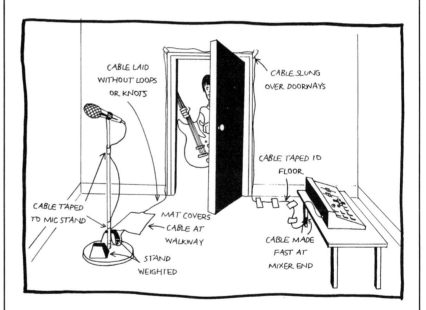

Fig 4.19

4.3 EDIT AUDIO PROGRAMMES

There are two ways of looking at editing: you can either see it as a way of removing mistakes, or you can see it as a creative process, in which you juxtapose speech, music, sounds and silence. In fact, the most likely approach to editing is somewhere between the two, where you can take out technically unacceptable, repetitive or uninteresting material, as well as rearranging your recording and enhancing it with a range of post-production techniques.

Before you can make any final editing decisions, it is first essential to play back through all of your recorded material and **log** it. The logging process should involve noting down the content of the tape and matching it to time or counter readings, with an extra column for notes on its technical **recording quality** as well as its relevance to your programme. You may also wish to note where you might use a particular sequence to the best dramatic effect, not forgetting that the **narrative context** refers both to fiction and non-fiction forms of storytelling.

In terms of checking the technical quality, you will need to check that the material you wish to use has been recorded at an acceptable level and note any problems that might have been caused by **handling noise** or **popping**.

In the case of actuality recordings or interviews, you may need to transcribe your material word for word so that you can structure your programme on paper precisely. Certainly, you will need to select your material carefully, having considered all of the above, and produce an edit script.

The edit script

Your edit script should be clearly laid out to include technical instructions, running order of items if appropriate, as well as durations. This provides you with a blueprint of your final programme before you begin the technical process of editing.

Editing processes

Dub: To copy material already recorded.

Editing audio recordings takes three main forms: **splice**, **dub** and **digital**.

Splice editing

This is still used as the main news editing process, especially in local radio. Splice editing involves actually cutting and sticking together selected lengths of audio tape using special adhesive tape, a sharp blade and a splicing block. While very fiddly at first, with practise and regular handling, this can become a quick process, especially with 'vari-speed' editing machines.

- ■ **Advantages:** it can be a very accurate form of editing; removing sniffs, grunts and coughs from speech. Also, your edited programme is still *first generation*. No copying has occurred yet, though in news desks, for ease of playback, the programme will have been copied down on to a '**cart**'. Splice editing can also be performed on very basic, old reel-to-reel recorders with little expense.

Cart: 1/4-inch tape cartridge.

- ■ **Disadvantages:** it can be a fiddly process. Also your original tape becomes hacked to pieces and cannot be retained for archive or for other edits, nor for recycling. If your field recording is on cassette, you have to dub footage down on to reel-to-reel before editing.

You must first release the tape spools from the motor drive. This enables you manually to 'rock and roll' the tape over the playback head by twisting the spools to and fro to fix exactly where words begin and end. You should use a 'chinagraph' pencil to mark the position over the playhead, indicating where to cut. You should use the diagonal groove on the splicing block to cut along, as this diagonal splice helps prevent a 'pop' on the edit by effectively creating a mini 'cross-fade' (lasting about $\frac{1}{60}$ of a second).

SPLICE EDITING

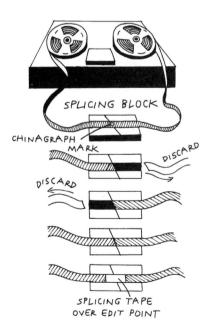

Fig 4.20 Splice Editing

Dub editing

This form of editing is more like video 'crash' editing, in that it involves copying or 'dubbing' selected extracts across from one tape to another, controlling the process by using the play, record and pause buttons. At its simplest level it can be achieved on any twin cassette deck although they tend to work on automatic gain control rather than record level control, so recording can be rather 'noisy'.

The compilation of a dance tape for a party is in effect a 'dub edit', involving the selection and ordering of songs from tape, disc or CD.

With a simple mixer, you can mix two sounds together and edit them on to another tape, something that would certainly enhance documentary and feature work, but which requires careful cueing of the tapes, and swift fingers on the pause/release buttons! It can save time if you 'zero' the tape counter each time you cue up cassettes or tape, avoiding fast-forwarding and rewinding to and fro to find the point again.

Dub editing also allows you to 'treat' your original audio recording with an effect such as *reverberation*, by simply passing the signal via a reverb unit, broadening the possibilities for enhancing your edit, while if your mixer has EQ pots, you can 'clean up' your original recording, e.g., by removing unwanted bass rumble, treble hiss or by boosting mid-range audibility.

In a radio station, if a producer is working with a sound engineer in mixing down a documentary or feature, dub editing is used, with a number of reel-to-reel players cued up with different source spools, which can automatically be set running by the faders on the mixing desk, allowing for cross fades, etc. With the journalist/narrator in an adjacent sound booth, commentary and links can be recorded 'live' as first generation on to the edit master, with actuality fading in and out, creating a more 'seamless' production.

- **Advantages:** it can be performed on very simple equipment, while dubbing via a mixer and/or reverb unit can give additional sound enhancement. It allows the direct copying from a variety of sources (CD, cassette, reel, disc.). Also your original recording is preserved intact.

- **Disadvantages:** with more basic equipment, accuracy is a problem. Cassettes are much harder to cue up exactly. You cannot 'rock and roll' them and players do not have a 'vari-speed' facility. Also, in copying, a generation is lost. If original levels, tape quality or equipment are not brilliant, this further reduction will be noticeable to the ear.

Digital editing

Digital editing systems have the immediate advantage of no generation loss, as the binary code is transferred intact in the process. The whole process is quick, flexible and accurate. There are two main forms of digital editing, DAT to DAT and computer-based digital editing.

DAT to DAT

Here the machines are synchronised and controlled in almost exactly the same way as a video editing suite, where 'in' and 'out' points on player and editor are assigned. As with a video suite, this can allow for highly accurate 'inserting' or 'punching in' of sound into sequences, and equally accurate erasure. Because of the recording's time coding, digital players can also be 'locked' to a video editing suite, and can be controlled by a three-machine edit controller, allowing originally 'synced' sound to be separately worked on and mixed with other material, (SFX, music), rejoining the video pictures in perfect sync.

Computer-based digital editing

'Sound cards' for PCs and Macs are becoming more available and, with sufficient memory, source recordings can be 'downloaded' on to the computer's hard disc, where, as with non-linear video editing, it can be accessed and manipulated almost instantaneously, and assembled or reassembled at will. A very high degree of edit accuracy can also be achieved through the soundwaves being graphically displayed on screen. Word shapes, intakes of breath and other sounds can be distinguished, and with a mouse control, in-points and out-points can be assigned, along with different fade and cross-fade times. A similar system, using a mouse and on-screen display can run as a multi-track digital recording studio too.

Multi-track recording and mixing

The main application of multi-tracking is in studio music recording, though it could also be used for creative fiction or feature work where a 'multi-layered' sound is required.

Recording

Multi-tracking allows you to record a sound on to tape, then rewind and record another sound on top of it *without erasing the original sound*, while also listening back to that original recording. Consequently, performance can be timed 'in sync' with the sound. This process can then be repeated for as many times as you have spare tracks on your recorder, (4, 8, 16, 32, etc.). For this process to be possible, very different erase, record and playback heads are required, with the facility for them to be *selectively* switched in or out on different tracks.

Mixing

Having separately recorded all the tracks you need, recording each at as near full modulation as you can, you now have the added freedom of *mixing down* these tracks on to another tape recorder as a form of dub edit. The 'freedom' results from the fact that your separately recorded tracks, when played back through the mixing desk, are all separately controllable in terms of:

For examples of the creative potential of this remix dubbing, listen to reggae 'dub' by groups like Dub Syndicate (On-U Sound label) or the remixes by Bristol group Massive Attack.

■ their relative level (through positioning the faders);
■ EQ (through the EQ pots);
■ 'position' in a stereophonic picture (through the pan pots);
■ additional digital FX (through the auxiliary pots).

Consequently, with the same multi-track source, you can rework 'versions', giving prominence to different instruments, adding reverb or delay to different sequences or voices, and even removing instruments altogether.

Mixing techniques — music recording

The basic techniques are the same, whether you are working with a 4-track 'porta-studio' or with 16-track gear. Indeed, much can be achieved with a 4-track machine recording with healthy levels and good quality tape. Recording a band, it is advisable to record drums and bass first, often playing together, as the bass provides the music's structure, while keeping them on separate tracks. This can be followed by a 'guide vocal' to help give an idea of verse, chorus and instrumental sections. (This guide can later be erased and taped over with the final lead vocal.)

If using a drum machine, then this should be laid down first. Equally, a 'click track' might be laid down first, purely as a rhythm guide, but later recorded over.

Direct input

Bass, lead and rhythm guitars, along with keyboards, need not be separately recorded. Their jack-to-jack leads can be plugged directly into the desk. (This applies equally to a porta-studio.) Sometimes, though, the amplified sound might be particularly wanted (e.g., from an old valve amp).

FX or no FX?

If you are working with a studio with numerous FX units, it is best to record the audio signals 'clean', leaving you the choice in the mixing stage of adding a variety of digital FX to several different channels simultaneously — e.g., 'small hall' reverb on vocal, 'multiple delay' on drums, 'stereo phasing' on lead guitar, etc.

However, if you have just the one unit, but wish to treat several different tracks, you need to pass the signal *via* the FX unit so that it is recorded *with* the selected effect.

Equalisation

You should record a 'flat' signal with EQ pots centred, as any EQ needed can be added in the remix.

Noise reduction

Recorders come with a variety of different noise reduction systems (e.g., Dolby B, Dolby C, Dolby X), designed to reduce tape hiss. However, you should only switch in the noise reduction if you know that your entire audio production suite includes the *same* Dolby system throughout and that it is switched in throughout, otherwise sound problems arise. This seems particularly marked with Dolby X.

Stereo

Stereo involves far more than simply assigning sounds to the left or the right (which is technically known as 'panned mono'), it is about building a sound 'picture' in space, working on the assumption that sound will be played back through two speakers set apart at a certain distance in a room of a certain size.

When mixing, the pan pots can assign sounds anywhere between left and right 'poles', making a complex picture that corresponds to our own stereophonic hearing perception, involving direction and distance in space. This stereophonic recording is at its most skilful with the recording of symphony orchestras where, at its best, and through a good hi-fi system, with closed eyes you should be able to 'sense' the relative positions of the instruments as they would actually be arranged in the live concert auditorium. With groups and dance mixes, your stereo mix can be open to experimentation. However, there are basic conventions that tend to be followed in the mix-down:

- **Drums:** often drumkits might be recorded with three or four directional microphones set close to particular sounds (e.g., high hat, snare, toms). If they are separately tracked on the recording, they can be mixed down with a 'spread', suggesting

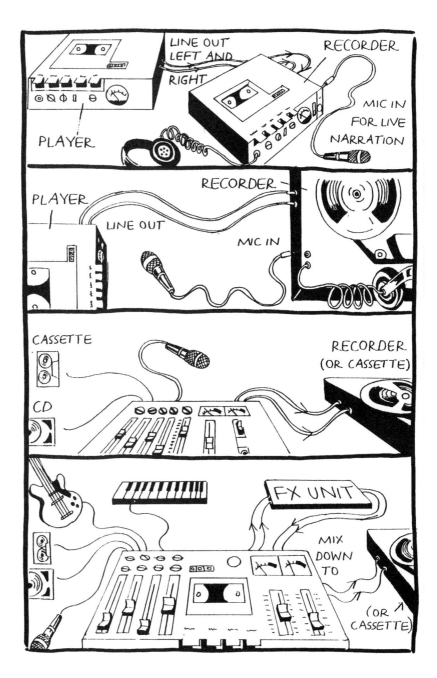

Fig 4.21 Mixing Techniques

the kit's spatial layout, but with the main bass beat centre-panned down the middle.

■ **Bass:** as part of the overall rhythm, this too tends to be centred in the mix. Also our ears are less sensitive to the directivity of the lower frequencies.

■ **Lead vocal:** this tends to be placed fairly centrally, though backing vocals might well be panned left or right.

■ **Guitars, keyboards, wind:** the important principle here is *separation*. When instruments (or voices) share a very similar frequency range, separating them left and right helps distinguish their identity in the mix. Hence lead guitar might go right while rhythm guitar goes left. Failure to separate these kinds of sounds can create an audio 'mush'.

Preparing tapes for playback

The colour of the leader is coded depending on the type of recorder — the BBC, for instance, uses yellow.

The edited tape should begin with several feet of *green* 'leader' tape, allowing length for spooling up, while also giving a clear visual cue for playback. The final edit should be with several feet of *red* leader. The green and red then clearly mark beginning and end and it is vital to follow this practice as, unlike a cassette, a spool of brown tape in itself gives no indication of whether it is wound back to the beginning or is 'end out'.

You must ensure that you label your tape, identifying the edit master and the dub as well as the name of the programme, duration, etc., so that you can easily store and retrieve your tape when required.

4.4 REVIEW AND EVALUATE YOUR AUDIO PRODUCTIONS

Process and Product

Evaluating the success of a production is not simply an educational activity — it is a vital part of the industrial process, and is particularly important as a market research process, especially for commercials. Reviewing and evaluating is also the main way we learn to overcome weaknesses and problems, and to progress.

In evaluating the process, you should be able to identify the successes and weaknesses of the way in which you and your team tackled the project objectively. In doing this, you should also be able to devise strategies to help you to overcome the problem next time. A technical problem might mean that you need to do some research, say, around the most appropriate equipment to use for a particular situation; or you may simply need to practise your microphone technique. Problems associated with programme structure could be a research issue — or could mean that you need to listen to much more of the particular form of radio so that you become familiar and comfortable enough with it to adopt (or challenge creatively) its conventions.

Ask yourself these questions:

Evaluating the process

■ Did the production meet the agreed deadline? If not, why not?

■ Did the ongoing production process run to your production schedule?

■ How was your own and your team's time management?

■ How effective were you as a group?

■ How effectively did you fulfil your own role and responsibilities? You will need feedback from the rest of your team and your lecturer.

■ What have you learnt from the mistakes made?

■ What would you improve on next time?

Your production log and minutes from production meetings should help you with evidence here.

The production log

Throughout the production process, from the beginnings of the idea of the presentation of the product to the audience or client, it is a good idea to keep a personal production log with a record of accurate dates and times. Although in some senses, the log could take the form of a sort of diary — like a ship's log — which will help you to pinpoint particular activities (or track down the sources of particular mistakes), you should be careful not to allow yourself to indulge simply in recording when other members of your team let you down.

Helping you to learn

The log should be an informative and helpful document, to assist *you* to understand what you have learnt through making an audio programme, and to help *you*, when you begin the next, to *action plan* to avoid the same mistakes, or to explore further a particular technique which you felt was interesting or successful.

Group accountability

Accountability of your group can be proven through the **minutes** of the production meetings, which will document who was present, who gave apologies (with good reason) and who was, simply, absent. They will document your decisions with reasons, and record who has agreed to do what. Minutes of previous meetings always form the first item of the agenda of the next, so you can easily see, as a group, whether you have met your identified targets and whether particular individuals are consistently letting you down.

Develop now ideas

Production logs can also be the place where you try out new ideas, or keep a note of things that interest you which you think might be good 'programme fodder'. These might happen anytime, anywhere, and be inspired by, for instance, a poster you see from a bus window, or a conversation you overhear on the way to school or college. In a way, the production log can become as much an '**ideas book**' as a means of recording how you went about tackling a project. The programme upon which you are currently working, for example, may also spark new ideas, both in terms of content and how, technically, you might go about achieving the effect you want.

Learn your equipment

When you are choosing or configuring a particular piece of equipment, it is a good idea to document why you chose it. This means jotting down, for instance, a microphone's technical qualities and why it is appropriate for your needs. This will also help you to learn your equipment well enough to be successful in the unit tests, as well as giving you your own reference which can help you next time. The first time you use a piece of equipment, you should document, with diagrams, how you put it together and the various steps you took.

Evaluation of the technical quality of the programme

From listening to your final programme, discussion with other members of the group and your tutor, and your production log, you should be able to draw up an accurate technical evaluation which identifies the strengths and weaknesses, and presents a solution for use in further projects where possible. You can either use a similar format to the log sheet where you go through the programme sequentially, or, perhaps more usefully, you could use the following headings to organise your evaluation, using your log or the script to identify where the problem occurred (or even, where the quality was particularly good):

Technical quality

■ Sound level (modulation) — high, low, patchy?

■ Mixes — smooth, accurate, appropriate?

■ Accuracy of editing — words cut off too soon, too late?

■ Microphone technique — popping, sibilance, rumble, moving from interviewee too soon?

Evaluating team and individual effort

This is probably where it is most important to take an objective view of your own as well as your team's performance. Criticism should be constructive, not adversorial. As well as your minutes, which should form a collectively agreed record of who did what and when, as well as an action plan of tasks to be undertaken prior to the next meeting, a frank discussion with your team at the end of the process will help you assess your strengths and weaknesses. In terms of assessing your role, it is necessary for you to be completely familiar with what is expected of that role.

Did you overspend?

Broadcasters would also evaluate programmes against cost and if you have worked to a budget you should compare your estimated costings (equipment, time, etc.) against what the production actually cost and work out whether you were on target or in deficit. Using a spreadsheet could help you here.

Evaluating the product

Measuring the relative success of your programme can be very vague and subjective. To avoid this, you need to combine three

The station completes 1 and 2 before distribution.

LFVDA Radio

1. Programme title . . . .
2. Date/time of broadcast . . . .
3. Do you listen to this station? (circle) every day/most days/once a week/once a month/never
4. Did you hear this particular programme? (circle) yes/no
5. If no, go to Question 11. If yes, did you listen to (circle) all of it/most of it/parts of it/a little of it?
6. What did you think of the programme? (circle) excellent/good/fair/poor.
7. What did you like most about it?
8. What did you dislike about it?
9. Is the programme broadcast at a suitable time for you (circle) yes/no
10. If no, what would be a better time for you? (circle) on the same day/on a different day
11. If you did not hear the programme, why was this?
12. If you did hear the programme did you do anything as a direct result?

Some information about yourself is very useful since it enables us to contact you for follow-up if necessary, and it helps us to know more about our audience. However, this section is optional and you may leave if you prefer. Any information you give is for the purpose of programme evaluation only and is regarded as strictly confidential.

Name . . . . Sex M/F
Address . . . . Married/Single
. . . .
Age (circle) under 15/16-24/25-39/40-59/60+
Occupation . . . .
Hobbies and interests . . . .
. . . .
Other Radio Stations listened to . . . .
Newspapers/magazines read: . . . .

Fig 4.22   Audience Research Questionnaire adopted from McLeish (1994) *Radio Production*, Focal Press

different responses to your work from:

- your client/commissioner/lecturer;
- a sample of your intended audience;
- your own critical analysis of the programme's technical quality and relevance of content.

Client/audience feedback can be gathered through discussion, questionnaire or written review, but think carefully about the questions you ask. The vaguer the question, the vaguer the answer. Fig. 4.22 is an example of an audience research questionnaire of the kind frequently given to listening panels by broadcasters.

Finally, the clearest measurement you can use is asking: 'Did it meet the agreed brief? Did it achieve what you set out to achieve?'

A quality programme?

In your evaluation, you should also ask yourself about the success of the programme in terms of its aesthetic qualities. It is perfectly possible to produce a technically competent, well researched programme in which everyone has carried out their roles perfectly but which is completely unimaginative and boring! Do not forget to assess the quality of performances, whether they are actors or interviewees or musicians; did you use techniques which did not just 'do the job', but enhanced the production and delighted the audience?

How does your programme stand up?

Comparing your productions with existing broadcast or recorded material will help you analyse the way in which you have understood the conventions of the genres or formats you have employed. This does not mean that, if you have departed from the 'rules' governing programme construction, you are wrong-if you have fully understood the conventions and worked against them in an innovative and exciting way, which further enhances your production, all the better. Writing a detailed analysis of 'professionally produced' audio material, in which you not only compare your work in terms of style, technical quality and so on, but also in terms of, say, issues of representation, narrative style and structure will also help you in gathering evidence for your portfolio for Unit 1.

EVIDENCE COLLECTION POINT

Each of the following assignments provides a way of collecting complete evidence for the assessment of Elements 2.3 and all of Unit 4. They can either be individually produced or as part of a small group production. The assignments also provide plenty of scope for gathering assessment evidence for the core units.

You should check carefully the **evidence indicators** in each element and ensure that you carry out the necessary tasks described in the performance criteria to produce the requirements.

REMEMBER:

To achieve a distinction grade, you need to have carried out a range of **complex tasks**, which means that you must be familiar with all of the activities associated with planning and production and **apply** them to your project, without expecting your teacher to break the assignment down for you.

The activities here range from assignments which give you a reasonable task guide through them to, simply, scenarios which depend on **you** to draw up the necessary tasks.

ASSIGNMENT 1

Planning and producing a radio commercial

You are required to produce a 30-second commercial for a specific product or service to meet an agreed deadline. Carry out the following tasks:

- Research into the nature of the product and who the main market is for the product to construct an audience profile.

- Decide on the best way to appeal to that audience, in terms of style and imagery. This may involve analysing other commercials aimed at a similar audience.

- Script a radio commercial, giving an exact breakdown of fictional dialogue, SFX and music. Check your script for copyright implications and for negative stereotyping. Does it make false claims about the product?

- Plan for production by booking, scheduling and casting.

- Record material for editing. Also secure any additional pre-recorded music or SFX.

- Log your footage and edit.

- Prepare a questionnaire for a sample of your target audience.

- Evaluate the effectiveness of your commercial by playing it to a sample of your target audience and gathering their feedback through questionnaire and interview.

- Produce your own evaluation of the production process and product, taking into account the feedback from the audience questionnaire.

- Present for assessment an entire production file, including research notes, production meeting minutes, scripts, logs, audience feedback and evaluation, together with your clearly labelled master tape.

ASSIGNMENT 2

Planning and producing a local news programme

You are a journalist working for a local independent radio station whose main output is dance music, and the majority of the audience is aged 14–21. The station has hourly news headline updates, with more in-depth coverage at 1pm and 6pm, with news bulletins lasting 10 minutes. Working as part of a small team you will:

■ Identify current local topical issues and list them.

■ Carry out research and assess the information in terms of relevance to the issues, topicality and human interest.

■ Plan the 10-minute programme, breaking it down into items and links, using the appropriate planning format, and taking account of your audience in terms of selection, order and presentation of items. You must be clear as to the duration of each item, as well as the likely length of each link. This forms the **programme brief** from which you are to work.

■ Decide who in the team will cover what and, individually, carry out any further research required prior to recording material for your item, including compiling contacts lists covering a range of opinion to identify potential interviewees, arranging your interviews, and so on; compiling questions prior to interviews or vox pops, etc.

■ Plan for your production by scheduling interviews, booking equipment and arranging transport. Where appropriate, schedule a time and location for vox pops.

■ Record material including, as appropriate, interviews, vox pops, actuality.

■ Log your taped material, writing transcripts of interviews and highlighting likely excerpts.

■ Script and record intro, outro and linking narration to tie your programme together.

■ Edit your material to the agreed brief, following the conventions of local radio news.

■ Prepare a questionnaire for a sample of your target audience.

■ Evaluate the effectiveness of your programme by playing it to a sample of your target audience and gathering their feedback through questionnaire and interview, and comparing it with broadcast radio news.

■ Produce your own evaluation of the production process and product, taking into account the feedback from the audience.

■ Present for assessment an entire production file, including research notes, production meeting minutes, scripts, logs, audience feedback and evaluation, together with your clearly labelled master.

ASSIGNMENT 3

Radio drama production

Taking either your own original script, developed through Unit 2.3, or your adaptation (from a play or short story), produce the script into a fully edited recording, following these tasks:

■ Agree the programme brief in terms of duration, format, deadline and resources.

■ Mark up the script for production, following industry conventions.

■ Schedule the production to meet the deadline.

■ Minute your production meeting throughout the process.

■ Decide upon your cast, and agree recording times with them.

■ Book appropriate equipment and studio time.

■ Allocate production roles: producer, sound recordist/engineer, editor. (You might be doing all three!)

■ Rehearse and record the drama, following safe working practices for cast, crew and equipment.

■ Log and edit your recording to meet the brief.

■ Play back your drama to an appropriate audience and monitor their response (by interview or questionnaire).

■ Produce an evaluative report on process and product, measuring the product against existing broadcast programmes of a similar genre.

■ Present your production file, complete with script, schedule, research notes, minutes, log, audience feedback and evaluation, together with your edited master programme, for assessment.

ASSIGNMENT 4

Extended radio documentary/feature

Advertisement — local evening paper:

Radio Switch FM
Turning on more listeners

Burning to broadcast? Got a great idea? Sick of programmes not talking to *you*?

SWITCH FM is under new management and seeking fresh, original material. Our output is largely speech-based, and we are keen to attract a wider, younger audience. We are looking for bright new talent, with relevant skills and oodles of ideas.

SWITCH FM invites *you* to submit a sample of your radio work. We require a 7-minute package which will be judged by our documentary/feature management team. Please submit all of your planning and research documentation with a copy of the finished tape, which must be fully labelled.

See also Element 2.3.

Developing ideas and research from earlier in the chapter, answer the above advertisement, using the process of appropriate tasks as outlined in the above assignments, producing production documentation, audience feedback and evaluative report, together with the final edited master tape to an agreed deadline. You will then be called to interview to discuss your submitted work.

5 PRODUCING MOVING IMAGE PRODUCTS

As with all of the production chapters (3, 4 and 5), you may already have begun the process of thinking about producing moving image products. If you are following the GNVQ on a unit-by-unit basis, you will almost certainly have produced treatments and scripts for **moving image items**, which might form part of a larger production you can develop as evidence for this unit.

The range of moving image media includes film, video, television, computer graphics and interactive multimedia. Animation can be generated on any of these forms and all would be acceptable media on which to produce products for the GNVQ, although the unit itself is focused primarily on video production, this being the most likely format to be found in schools and colleges.

This unit concentrates on the three stages of production — pre-production, production and post-production — as well as introducing some of the technical principles of video. This should help you to understand better the various processes that go to make for successful recording. However, you should remember that the creative, imaginative work does not simply come from cameras, microphones and editing suites, but is dependent on strong scripting, a strong message to our audience and in making sure that we get the best out of limited resources.

Moving image production is very much a collaborative activity, depending on a *team approach*. You will need to experience all of the roles in production, and may find that you are particularly strong in, say, camera or directing. Crewing on fellow students' productions will help you develop your skills and, possibly, specialise in your strongest area.

5.1 PRE-PRODUCTION — PLANNING THE PRODUCTION PROCESS

Choosing the right medium

- Television?
- Video?
- Film?
- Tape-slide?
- Multimedia?

Moving image (audio-visual) productions can take a number of different forms, each with its own qualities. You are most likely to be using video, within which there is also room to include computer-generated captions and animated sequences, which you could originate on film or by computer. Less familiar forms, such as tape-slide production (involving 35 mm slides, carefully sequenced and projected in synchronisation with an accompanying audio tape) have been used frequently for corporate presentations, or you may have seen them in museums. Multimedia production is an exciting interactive form which incorporates video, audio, graphics and text, edited together on a desk-top computer, using many of the editing codes of television.

Television, video and film language

It is a useful first step to make clear the differences between television, video and film as media forms. They all share many of the same conventions, but have differences in audience and in conditions of reception. Try asking the questions: *who*? *how*? *where*?

- *Who* is intended to watch and listen? (Audience.)
- *How* is the programme to be shown? (Broadcast, video playback or screen projection.)
- *Where* is the programme to be shown? (Context: homes, conferences, cinemas, schools, post offices, etc.)

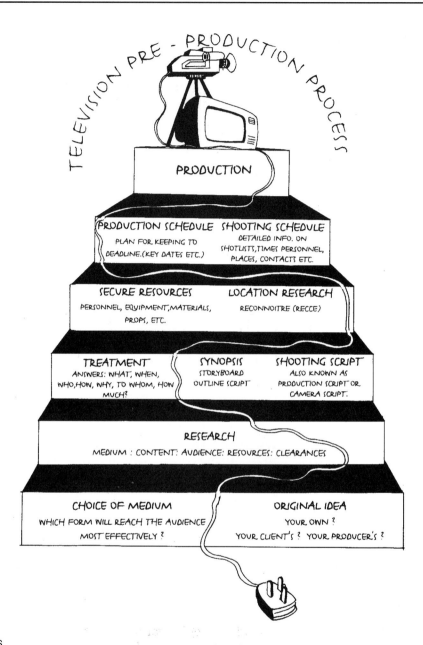

TELEVISION PRE - PRODUCTION PROCESS

PRODUCTION

PRODUCTION SCHEDULE
PLAN FOR KEEPING TO
DEADLINE.(KEY DATES ETC.)

SHOOTING SCHEDULE
DETAILED INFO. ON
SHOTLISTS,TIMES PERSONNEL,
PLACES, CONTACTS ETC.

SECURE RESOURCES
PERSONNEL, EQUIPMENT,MATERIALS,
PROPS, ETC.

LOCATION RESEARCH
RECONNOITRE (RECCE)

TREATMENT
ANSWERS: WHAT, WHEN,
WHO,HOW, WHY, TO WHOM, HOW
MUCH?

SYNOPSIS
STORYBOARD
OUTLINE SCRIPT

SHOOTING SCRIPT
ALSO KNOWN AS
PRODUCTION SCRIPT OR
CAMERA SCRIPT.

RESEARCH
MEDIUM : CONTENT: AUDIENCE: RESOURCES: CLEARANCES

CHOICE OF MEDIUM
WHICH FORM WILL REACH THE AUDIENCE
MOST EFFECTIVELY ?

ORIGINAL IDEA
YOUR OWN ?
YOUR CLIENT'S ? YOUR PRODUCER'S ?

Fig 5.1

Codes: Signs (words, gestures, sounds, pictures, etc.) that are understood and agreed between senders and receivers of messages.

Conventions: Ways of doing and saying things that have become established through repetition and habit, and which, like codes, depend on a shared understanding.

Revising your knowledge of the different kinds (**genres**) of programme will help you to develop ideas which utilise or experiment with film and televisual **codes and conventions**. While it would be true to say that we live in a society which is highly visually literate, able to pick up complex storylines and hidden messages from, say, the quickfire images of a 30-second advertisement, it is another thing altogether to express ourselves in that language. Becoming familiar with the *codes* and *conventions* of film television and video is, consequently, as vital as learning how to use the equipment.

Basic visual codes

Planning a production involves detailed visualisation. The following questions should help you to envisage how your final production should look and plan to achieve such results.

- Framing
- Camera angle
- Camera movement
- Colour and resolution
- Lighting
- Frame content
- Graphics
- Editing

Framing

How much of the scene do I include within the rectangular frame? What do I choose to exclude?

The human eye sees almost 180 degrees, compared to a typical wide-angle lens of 60 degrees. This angle decreases dramatically when zooming in to select something within the screen. Another feature of framing concerns *aspect ratio*, in other words how high the frame is compared to its width. Cinema films are at 16:9 ratio (the same as 35 mm negatives and slides), while television and video are at a ratio of 4:3. This explains why some films are 'letterboxed' with black strips top and bottom when shown in full on television (Fig. 5.2)

New high-definition television is now recorded on a 16:9 ratio, like film.

Camera angle

Where is the camera set up in relation to the main subject of the scene? Is it above, below, level with, near to or distant from the subject?

This is not simply a theoretical question, but can have a major influence on the effect upon the viewer, whether applied to fiction or non-fiction. For instance, a person shot from a **low angle** will appear to dominate (adding potential fear and menace, if this is the desired effect), while someone shot from a **high angle** might appear smaller, weaker and more vulnerable.

low angle: camera is placed low and placed up at subject
high angle: camera is placed high and is placed down at subject.

ASPECT RATIO

A) 16:9 RATIO OF FILM COMPARED WITH 4:3
RATIO OF TELEVISION

B) 4:3 TELEVISION SCREEN WITH
16:9 "LETTERBOXED"

Fig 5.2 Aspect Ratios

Camera movement

*Is the **camera** or **lens** moving?*

Movement from a wide shot into a close-up *directs* the viewers'
attention, taking them from establishing a scene into a detail the
director wants to select. Often the slower and more subtle the movement, the greater the effect.

Basic movements

- Tilt up/down.
- Pan left/right.
- Zoom in/out.
- Track/dolly in/out.
- Elevate/depress.
- Handheld (with/without Steadicam).

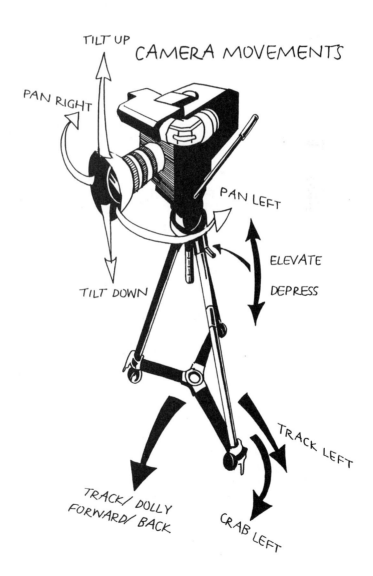

Fig 5.3 Basic camera movements

It is rare for the zoom to be used in fiction productions (though it enjoyed a brief season in made-for-television films in the 1960s, perhaps because it is regarded by directors as an unnatural device, as the human eye cannot zoom in and out. (Neither can it fade to black, dissolve, edit or run in slow motion, yet these 'unnatural' devices appear to be acceptable!)

Colour and resolution

Are the images in black and white or colour? If in colour, what hues and shades? If in black and white, are they sharply defined or grainy?

Choices here might be as a result of technical constraints (e.g., only black and white film available at the time) or production conditions (low light levels tend to produce grainy images for both film and video). Equally, choices might have been deliberate to create effect, (e.g., grainy black and white images suggest authentic, 'raw' documentary realism). Also the frequent presence of certain colours can create effects relating to certain moods (e.g., reddish hues: hot, bluish: cold). Coloured lens filters can enhance this.

Lighting

Where is the light coming from? Where are the shadows cast? Is the light coloured in any way? Is it from a natural/artificial source?

Designing the lighting for film, television and video is a highly skilled craft, and can add greatly to the meaning of what is being shown on the screen, while also serving to direct the audience gaze to significant detail.

Frame content

What is positioned in the frame in the foreground? In the background?

Although the human face is often the most dominant element within the frame, clothes, furnishings, decor, cars, streets and landscapes all can signify relevance to the central message or story. Cars in particular take on obvious symbolic meaning in films (as in life). Compare Columbo's beaten-up old convertible with the Ferrari in *Miami Vice*. What does it say about the owners? Because of the vital importance of set, props, costume and make-up to an image's potential meanings, the people responsible for these roles are well respected as part of the production personnel. Above all, though, it is the careful way that people and objects are positioned, lit and framed by the lens that gives impact, while directing the viewer's gaze towards specific details.

Graphics

How does graphic style anchor or enhance meaning?

Horror films, where the title letters tend to use a gothic font and drip ghoulish red drops, or detective thrillers where the font is a rough-edged type like a police statement are well-worn examples.

Of all the codes, graphics tend to be the most specific in meaning, usually providing answers to the basic questions: *who? where? what? when?* At best, the introductory graphics sequences to a programme are an art form worthy of study in themselves. (Look at Saul Bass's graphics for *Psycho* (Hitchcock, USA, 1960) for instance.) Often there is a perceptible link between the choice of letter font and colour with the nature of the programme. These title graphics play an important role for the audience through inviting them to anticipate a certain kind of story.

Editing

See Unit 5.3 for full description of transitions

Cuts Fades? Dissolves/mixes Wipes are the most used *transitions*, and over the last century these devices have established their own agreed connotations. One thing is common to all editing though; it involves playing with *time*.

Camera-effect edits

These are effectively 'cuts' from an editor's point of view, but their effect is achieved through actually shooting footage in a way specially intended for an edit effect, and though not often used, are well worth experimenting with. An example of this is the *whip pan* where, at the end of a scene, the camera is 'panned' right or left

(Examples: *Man from U.N.C.L.E.;* and *Bad Timing*, Nicholas Roeg, UK, 1980).

at great speed, creating a rushing blur on screen. When it comes to the editing, this blur then cuts to the next scene, suggesting we have been 'beamed' across to it at supernatural speed.

The *focus merge* is another example, where the end shot of one scene is pulled fully out of focus. This is edited to the next shot which begins fully out of focus and is pulled sharply back in. The effect here on the viewer is more psychological, suggesting a loss of consciousness, perhaps, which is then pulled back sharply into a new reality.

The tasks which follow in this section can reinforce media analysis work connected with Unit 1 (especially Element 1.3), as well as providing a critical foundation for Unit 2 (especially Element 2.4) and for Unit 5.1 (pre-production).

Test your understanding of visual codes

TASK

- Record five brief extracts from a range of TV programmes, or cue up extracts from pre-recorded video tapes that illustrate these visual codes.

- With each extract, prepare a brief presentation which explains why that series of codes has been used and the meanings created.

- Present the extract and your findings to your group.

TASK

■ Choosing two very different television genres, e.g., documentary, soaps, record the opening sequences (no more than two minutes).

■ Play through the extracts, hitting the pause button each time the shot changes, making rough sketches of each frame on to black storyboard sheets.

■ Note which of the above codes you can identify, and account for why the programme makers have used them, entering your answers next to your sketches.

Basic audio codes

■ Dialogue

■ Music

■ Sound effects (SFX)

Turn the sound down on any programme and its power is instantly reduced. Visual images that previously seemed to flow together now appear interrupted and 'bitty', while fiction scenes lose drama and emotional impact.

Dialogue

Who is speaking? To whom? How is it said? What is being said?

Who is speaking?

This could be a person within the frame, where the speech may be in synchronisation or 'sync' with the lip movements (lip sync). Equally it could be a speaker whose voice is separately recorded from the accompanying visuals. Here, speech is used as narration (voice-over), and is a convention used in every genre, whether fictional or non-fictional.

To whom?

The speech might be addressed directly to someone within the scene, directly to the audience or to someone within the narrative indirectly, for instance, through spoken diary or letter intended for the future.

How is it said?

The tone of voice can carry considerable meaning, as can the choice of words. In the case of audience address, the 'how' is very important in terms of establishing the audience's position. Is it, for instance, as caring, responsible citizens, future voters, fun-loving tearaways, as fellow conspirators sharing a secret, as rich achievers, as poor consumers out for a bargain? On a more basic level, is the audience addressed as adults or children, male or female, heterosexual or gay, informed or ignorant?

What is said?

The meaning behind the actual words used is the most direct and powerful code. However, there are important variations. If irony or sarcasm is being used, then the implied meaning might be the opposite of the literal one.

Music

(Silent films were never really silent, but were accompanied by live music and even commentary from the film's distributor.)

From the very beginnings of cinema, music has been a key element accompanying the visual projection. Music can bind together separate visual cuts, reinforce the mood, tension and action. It can either be established in and grow out of the scene itself as *diegetic* sound (e.g., a car radio, a transistor, jukebox or danceband), or be purely an accompanying soundtrack that comes as a source from outside of the 'story space' of the programme (*non-diegetic*).

It is also now the main driving force behind a whole genre of music videos, where some of the most innovative experimentation can be found. Many Hollywood films feature a popular song as a key part of their narrative, effectively promoting the song, while each airing of the song on radio or television promotes the film.

Soundtrack music is likely to be at its most effective, though, where it has been specially composed for the pace, mood and action of the film or programme itself, and may often take a very simple form such as single resonant notes or treated sound effects.

TASK

Discovering sound

- Choose an extract from three programmes or films you have on video which you feel use music effectively to convey different moods or atmospheres. Note why you think the music works, describing it as exactly as you can (e.g., the dominance of certain kinds of instrument, etc.).

- Cue up your video cassettes and play back music to your group with the screen hidden.

- Ask them to write down what impressions and images are formed, then show them the extracts again, this time with picture. Do their impressions change, having seen the picture? Does the music anchor the picture's meaning or vice versa?

Sound effects (SFX)

This is a general term, covering a wide range of sounds other than the synchronised sounds in the original production recording; in other words those sounds that have been 'mixed' in during editing to create an impression or illusion. These may be natural sounds that you record yourself as follows:

■ **Wild-track:** Sounds relating to a certain location or action but which are not recorded in 'sync' with the pictures. (e.g., waves, traffic, pubs).

■ **Ambient track:** (also known as 'buzz track'): Every location, interior or exterior, has its own ambient sounds. Recording a few minutes of this sound can help provide a 'seamless' background soundtrack or ambience behind edited shots, smoothing out the sound edits.

TASK

The 'sounds of silence'

a) Close your eyes for a minute or two and listen purely to the sounds of 'silence' in the room around you.

b) List the sounds you hear.

A vast range of sound effects are now available on CDs, but record your own where you can.

■ **Synthesized sounds:** These have been electronically produced, and can be highly effective in creating moods or 'sound pictures'.

■ **Treated sounds:** Natural sounds can be treated by passing them through a digital effects processor to add echo, reverberation, delay and a whole host of other effects.

Note: Conventions also vary according to different cultures

Note: In the television industry, independent producers approach *commissioning editors* with their original ideas, or proposals, which are then commissioned by the channel.

There is one last thing that is important to bear in mind: conventions are not *rules*. However, they have gradually evolved over the last century and because they are so generally understood, they can provide quick 'shorthand' ways of communicating. But what causes them continually to change, acquiring increasing sophistication, is programme-makers' willingness to *experiment, challenge* and *take risks*.

This section recaps on the two main processes in generating ideas and helps you undertake the planning process necessary to realise them.

Proposals: fiction

For simplicity, think of your own, original ideas as proposals and ideas that are given to you to develop as commissions.

You may have already developed your fiction proposals separately, as evidence for Unit 2.4, you may be developing these ideas further or simply starting afresh. Whatever the case, here are some reminders to give you inspiration — you should go back to Unit 2 for a thorough approach to researching and scripting.

- **Themes And 'triggers':** Individual or group 'brainstorming', perhaps around key words or phrases that have particular meaning for you.
- **Spider diagram:** Use the trigger themes to make associations; link related ideas; try sequencing, remembering the classic narrative ingredients of cause, effect and time.
- **Towards a story:** From the spider diagram, is it possible to construct a classic story using the *conflict — development — resolution* formula? (Do not forget, sometimes *conflict* is instead expressed as *enigma* — suggesting a mystery posed that is gradually solved through the film or programme.)
- **Breaking the rules:** A 'linear story' may not be the inspired result of your creative labours, but instead, a more challenging, perhaps thematically linked fiction piece. There is no reason to be constrained by established genre or narrative forms, although it is important to maintain a sense of audience if you decide to experiment.

Adaptations

Do not forget that many successful films or television dramas began their lives in another form, for instance, a short story, play or poem. Translating ideas from one media to another is a creative process which would doubtless provide real challenges, especially when working with limited resources, perhaps with actors who are all of a similar age, if they are fellow students.

Proposals: non-fiction

The first stages in putting together an idea for a non-fiction production such as a short documentary might seem 'safer' or less taxing on creativity than 'coming up with a story'. However, the challenge to imagination and storytelling are just as strong in shaping 'reality' into a form that will interest a wider audience.

You may have already developed non-fiction proposals separately, as evidence for Element 2.4, or you may be developing these ideas further, or simply starting afresh. Whatever the case, here are some reminders to help you formulate your ideas.

- ***Observation:*** The situation for documentary-making does not necessarily need to be a 'big issue' — the raw material for programme ideas can come from detailed observation of everyday life and the presentation of this afresh.

■ **Process:** Situations likely to prove fruitful for documentary recording are where people or places are going through some kind of changing *process*, as this is likely to provide a deeper story structure embracing the *conflict — development — resolution* narrative formula.

The programme brief

For fiction, the programme brief is, basically, the proposal and treatment you devise, summarising the aim of the programme, audience, content and style of the programme. Fiction treatments can be written in a variety of ways, and it is important to capture the essence of the story in a way in which will catch the eye of a commissioning editor.

Commissions

The needs of the *client* have to be taken account of in preparing and agreeing the **programme brief** for commissions, whether they are advertisements, campaigning videos, promotions or informational programmes. It is not unlikely that you may be asked to undertake a 'live brief' for a real local client. This is excellent experience, although projects of this nature are probably best tackled, when you have established your skills.

Drawing up programme proposals, briefs, treatments, etc., is covered in detail in Unit 2

Agreeing the brief

Whether you are working with a commissioning client, setting up a project with a teacher or lecturer, or working with fellow students in your production team, the first ideas can be extremely vague.

Checklist: The brief

■ Target audience (could influence style).

■ Viewing context (where and how it will be seen).

■ Deadline (can you do it in time?).

■ Budget (planning, research, recce, shooting days, edit, etc.).

■ Overall Length.

■ Content/Information.

■ Purpose.

■ Duplication, packaging design, distribution.

The budget

BECTU: Broadcast Engineers and Cinematographer Technicians' Union.
Equity: Actors' union.
NUJ: National Union of Journalists.
MU: Musicians' Union.

Essential to providing you with 'real world' production experience is budgeting your own productions. Even though you might not see how much, in actual terms, it costs your school or college in equipment maintenance, stock, etc., for you to produce a video, as a producer you would not be able to access the resources to make your programme without a realistic budget. You need to account for time and equipment hire, not forgetting copies for distribution, if required. The following rate card gives you some idea of current rates for commercial and non-commercial equipment hire. Rates of pay for personnel can be obtained from the appropriate unions.

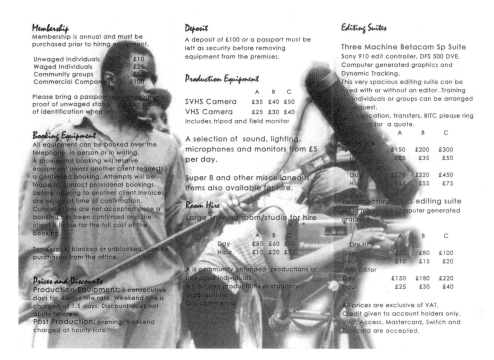

Membership
Membership is annual and must be purchased prior to hiring equipment.

Unwaged Individuals	£10
Waged Individuals	£25
Community groups	£50
Commercial Companies	£100

Please bring a passport size photograph, proof of unwaged status and two proof of identification when joining.

Booking Equipment
All equipment can be booked over the telephone, in person or in writing. A provisional booking will reserve equipment unless another client requests a confirmed booking. Attempts will be made to contact provisional bookings before offering to another client. Invoices are issued at time of confirmation. Cancellations are not accepted once a booking has been confirmed and the client is liable for the full cost of the booking.

Tape stock, blacked or unblacked, can be purchased from the office.

Prices and Discounts
Production Equipment: 5 consecutive days for 4 days hire rate. Weekend hire is charged at 1.5 days. Discount does not apply to crew.
Post Production: Evening/Weekend charged at hourly rate.

Deposit
A deposit of £100 or a passport must be left as security before removing equipment from the premises.

Production Equipment

	A	B	C
SVHS Camera	£35	£40	£50
VHS Camera	£25	£30	£40

Includes tripod and field monitor

A selection of sound, lighting, microphones and monitors from £5 per day.

Super 8 and other miscellaneous items also available for hire.

Room Hire
Large Training room/studio for hire

	A	B	C
Day	£50	£60	£70
Hour	£15	£20	£25

A is community unfunded productions or unwaged individuals
B is funded productions or statutory organisations
C is commercial

Editing Suites

Three Machine Betacam Sp Suite
Sony 910 edit controller, DFS 500 DVE, Computer generated graphics and Dynamic Tracking.
This very spacious editing suite can be hired with or without an editor. Training for individuals or groups can be arranged on request.
Duplication, transfers, BITC please ring the office for a quote.

	A	B	C
Day	£150	£200	£300
Hour	£25	£35	£50
Day	£270	£320	£450
Hour	£45	£55	£75

Two machine SVHS editing suite
A 30 mixer and computer generated graphics.

	A	B	C
Dry Hire			
Day	£50	£80	£100
Hour	£10	£15	£20
With Editor			
Day	£150	£180	£220
Hour	£25	£30	£40

All prices are exclusive of VAT.
Credit given to account holders only.
Visa, Access, Mastercard, Switch and Eurocard are accepted.

Fig 5.4 Rate card courtesy of Connections (Communications Centre Ltd)

Whatever rates you decide to use, the following points need to be established and agreed:

■ **Pre-production:** How much *time* in hours (at £xx per hour) will be taken up in researching, scripting, planning and scheduling? How much on telephone, post and transport (e.g., recces)?

■ **Production:** What recording format? What equipment (hired or in-house)? How many crew? Transport costs, crew expenses, materials (e.g., cassettes), insurance, performers' fees and expenses. How many days of location shooting, how many in the studio?

Note: These calculations are best done as a separate paper exercise, without the client being present.

Research

Note: You may need to research additional material to complement items you have already developed in Unit 2.

- ■ **Post-production:** Amount of time to produce 'off-line' edit (plus edit suite hire), time to produce 'on-line' fine cut (plus edit suite hire), cost of music clearance, if required, additional graphics and digital video effects (DVE).
- ■ **Packaging and duplication (if required):** Design and graphics for cassette sleeve and labels, number of cassette copies ('dupes') to be run off.

The kind of research likely to be undertaken in the pre-production stage involves finding the appropriate locations, gaining permissions, organising caterers, scheduling actors or presenters, etc.

A reminder about clearances

Do not forget, where it is intended to use *other people's work* as part of your programme's material (recordings, etc.), then various **clearances** might be needed. For purely educational productions, fees are sometimes waived; however, if the programme is commercially commissioned, or might enjoy a wider audience, it is well worth remembering that this clearance is a *legal* requirement. It is possible, though, to gain access to music and other material that is 'public domain'.

Permissions

Never assume that it is fine to film anywhere with a crew. If you have a full crew, complete with sound boom, cables and tripod, this can be seen as causing an obstruction in a street or shopping centre. To avoid arguments, it is good practice to contact the police beforehand to let them know your plans. Certain locations tend to be highly sensitive to cameras. Ministry of Defence sites and prisons are particularly fruitless areas for documentary projects unless you are prepared to undergo months of letter-writing with the relevant government ministries. For very different reasons, gambling amusement arcades are exceptionally resentful and paranoid of video recordings, while, more surprisingly, shopping centres can be highly suspicious of crews at work. Again, a prior request for permission can avoid tangled cables and frayed nerves!

Release forms

When recording people, especially in interviews, permission should be gained in writing on a *release form* allowing use of their 'performance' on the agreed terms. A token payment of, say, £1 can be made to make the clearance 'binding'. This is particularly pertinent in the rare event where you have a budget to hire 'talent', (professional performers), and here, Equity or Musicians' Union agreements may be relevant. The most practical and cheap way round this 'maze' is to create an informal co-operative with fellow students on music and performing arts courses, who will often appreciate the opportunity to extend the range of their own work and experience for the price of a VHS copy of the finished programme!

The recce

How to find appropriate locations is covered on p. 95.

The recce of a location, whether for drama or documentary, has two main purposes. Firstly it should establish whether the location is the most appropriate one for the programme's context. This could be for aesthetic impact or purely informational reasons. Secondly, the location should be 'reconnoitred' from a technical recording point of view, when a checklist of problem areas should be run through, answering the following:

- **Light:** Will it be day/night; interior/exterior; daylight or tungsten? If daytime, is the sun's angle important (am/pm)? Will portable lights be needed? Battery or mains?

- **Weather:** Is one kind of weather critical? If exterior, is there a bad weather contingency plan? What time of year is it? Hot or cold?

- **Sound:** What interference is likely (e.g., roadworks, traffic, exposure to high winds)? What microphone(s) will be most suited?

- **Health and Safety:** Are there potential hazards for crew, performers or public? If so, can the risk factor be removed by careful planning and forethought?

■ **Logistics:** Are transport, parking and access straightforward? For extended shoots, is there refreshment/toilet provision nearby?

Production/shooting scripts

See 'Rockall' script, Unit 2

You may have already produced your draft scripts — if not, you should follow the guidelines in Unit 2.

The **shooting script**, also known as the **production script** or **camera script**, is a further stage on from the original drafts, with the *director* having worked into it the appropriate 'technical' visualisation through the addition of camera, lighting and sound instructions. In effect, it is a storyboard in words. The format is usually off-set to the right, allowing for additional camera instructions, sketches and notes.

SHOOTING SCRIPT - giving directions for single camera set-ups

(Lines indicate suggested cutting points for editing)

12. INT. NIGHT CLIFFTOP COTTAGE FRONT ROOM

SHOT 1)

BCU George's face — pull back slowly to 3 SHOT, silhouetting Gabriel and Angel against the window

GABRIEL AND ANGELA SIT IN THE WINDOWSEAT, KEEPING VIGIL OVER GEORGE WHO LIES UNCONSCIOUS ON THE MADE-UP COUCH. THEIR CLOTHES AND THE BLANKET ARE GREEN. OUTSIDE, THE WAVES CAN BE HEARD BEATING ON THE CLIFFS BELOW.

GEORGE

I'm going now.....if I don't go now.......

2)
Cut to CU. George's hands on the radio

3) *Cut to 3S (as shot 1)*

HE TRIES TO RISE, GRASPING THE TRANSISTOR RADIO. THEY RESTRAIN HIM AND FORCE HIM BACK INTO BED.

GABRIEL

You're going nowhere until you get your strength back. Here....(GIVES HIM A FLASK) Drink

4) *Cut to MCU Gabriel from George's p.o.v.*

this...it will calm you down.

5) *Cut to C.U. on George.*

GEORGE

But I've had no news for so long....just weather....no news.......

Fig 5.5 Shooting script extract — (extract from 'Rockall' P.A. Kaspar 1996)

FADE OUT

Non-fiction Scripts

The degree to which non-fiction programmes are pre-scripted can vary greatly according to style, content and purpose. A carefully researched historical documentary series such as *The World at War* will certainly have been tightly scripted for two reasons. Firstly its style is heavily dependent on a scripted voice-over narrating events, and secondly, much of the visual material is pre-recorded archive footage, interspersed with key interviews with survivors. More observational documentary, however, will rely less on scripted narration.

Sequencing images: storyboards

The main reasons for preparing storyboards are as follows:

■ To give yourself and others an idea of the visual sequence and how shots will edit together.
■ To give framing and movement indications to the camera operator.
■ To give an indication of *mise-en-scène*.

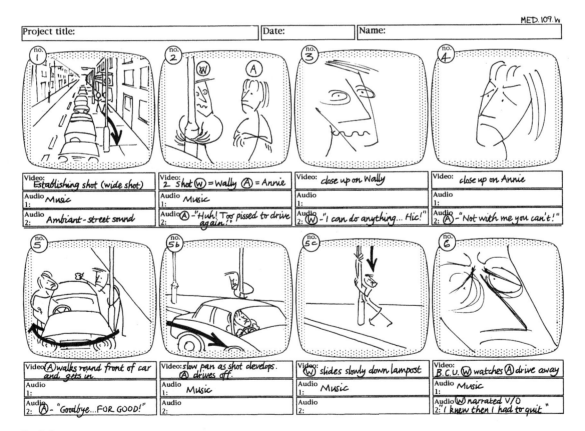

Fig 5.6

■ To allow for the testing of sequences (e.g., in advertising) on a client or sample target audience prior to committing cash for full production.

The exception is with advertising storyboards, where the look and the design need to be close to the intended end product. Here a graphic artist and/or photographer would be commissioned to produce the storyboard.

Detail in storyboards

People, can be easily represented by stick-drawings, and you do not need to be an artist! However rough they may be, a certain degree of accuracy must be there to reflect the following points:

■ **Framing:** Characters and objects must appear in the same relative scale in the sketch as they are intended to in the final recording.

■ **Identity:** A 'shorthand' way of identifying people can be simply achieved by writing in a name or initial.

■ **Movement and direction:** Any movement within the frame of a person or object needs to be indicated clearly. This can be shown either by an arrow within the frame, or by using two or more frames to show how action develops within the shot. To avoid confusion, the same frame (shot) number should be kept, with the development indicated by using letters (e.g., frame 3a, 3b, 3d). These details can also be spelled out in words alongside the frame for added clarity. This also applies to the storyboarding of a camera movement (pan, track, zoom, etc.) where what we see at the beginning of the shot develops into a very different framing (and content). The direction in which people are looking is also an important detail, and you should try to indicate whether people are in profile, three-quarter profile, facing left, facing right, etc.

■ **Shot sizes:** Because the majority of film and television is about people, the various framings are based on the proportions of a person included in a shot. If inanimate objects are being recorded, we simply translate accordingly. It is worth remembering that if these shot size instructions accompany a sketched storyboard, they are largely superfluous in terms of helping us to visualise a sequence as the pictures do that. Their main function is in a *written* script to give indication of likely framings. Consequently, they are not an 'exact science'. One person's BCU is another's ECU.

■ **Dialogue, music and sound effects (SFX):** This information needs to accompany the relevant frames, written either below or alongside the frame. Dialogue need not be in full, but beginning and end 'cues' can be used to save space.

SHOT TYPES

VISTA SHOT OR
VERY LONG SHOT V.L.S.

LONG SHOT L.S.

2 SHOT

MEDIUM SHOT M.S.

MEDIUM CLOSE UP M.C.U.

CLOSE UP C.U.

BIG CLOSE UP B.C.U.

EXTREME CLOSE UP E.C.U.

Fig 5.**7** Shot Types

Planning a visual sequence:

This section is best approached in conjunction with an early production exercise as a practical camcorder task.

For this to be achieved in a documentary shoot, fast camera work is needed. See documentary techniques.

Fig. 5.8 is an example of a sequence from a gangster spoof:

- **Establish the scene. (frame 1):** In fiction and in documentary, it can be useful first to establish the *context* with a wide shot.
- **Cut in. (frame 2):** Attention is now drawn into an area within frame 1. This then might be followed by a further cut in **(frame 3)**, directing attention to specific detail within frame 2. This storyboard suggests that these cuts follow the rules of *continuity*.
- **Cut away. (frame 4):** from the established scene to another shot (this could be to a different location), but still the suggestion is that time is continuous — there have been movements forward or back in time. The cut away (or 'cutaway' as one word) is a standard news and documentary device, often used to 'illustrate' an on-screen interview; in so doing, adding extra visual information and also avoiding an excess of 'Talking Heads'.
- **Point of view. (P.O.V.) (Frame 5):** Literally, the camera lens becomes the exact P.O.V. of the audience, who are invisible

Fig 5.8   'Gangster' spoof storyboard

spectators. However, where the camera is placed and angled in relation to people and action can be very significant.

- **Associated P.O.V. (Frame 6):** In fiction, when the central character(s) are not on screen, action is often shot broadly from their P.O.V., as though from over their shoulder. The effect of this is gradually to increase our identification with their role. A classic convention often used is the Look/P.O.V. sequence, where we see the actors turn to look, and then cut to what they are seeing.

Other shot types include:

As background research, watch Hitchcock's *Psycho*, which experiments with montage (c.f., shower scene), and, more subtly, with literal P.O.V. (c.f., traffic cop sequence and final scene with Norman Bates and the fly).

- **Literal P.O.V.:** Here, the camera lens is viewing exactly what a character is seeing. The impact of this in fiction can be highly dramatic as, in effect, the audience share the eyes of the character. Because of the strong emotional impact of literal P.O.V., it is most often used in horror movies, psychodramas (often using hand-held camera) or for dream sequences and generally 'altered states'.

- **Reverse shots and matched framing.** It is a standard convention to try, when shooting a conversation or confrontation between two people, to shoot 'reverse shots' that are similarly proportioned within the frame, so that when 'intercut' during editing, dialogues between *giants and munchkins* are avoided! This applies equally to news-style interviews.

REVERSE SHOTS

Fig 5.9 Reverse Shots

"GIANTS" AND "MUNCHKINS"

Fig 5.10 Talk Space

- **Matched eyeline:** Similarly, when intercutting between closer shots of two people facing each other, it is important to retain on screen the illusion of direction, by matching their regard in relation to each other.

- **Talk space:** Your storyboard should suggest this kind of framing that allows performers or interviewees to talk into frame space, adding to a sense of direction and a wider space outside the frame.

For research, watch Jean-Luc Goddard's *A Bout de Souffle* (France, 1960) the original working of the more recent *Breathless*. Goddard deliberately uses jump cuts, drawing attention to the fact that continuity is a Hollywood convention.

■ **Jump cuts:** This is the jargon for cuts that somehow break the illusion of continuity for the audience, drawing attention to the technical production rather than the content. This visual disruption can be produced in two ways: (a) continuity lapse, (b) a cut (e.g., from one angle to another) that only slightly changes a person's size and position within the frame, creating the impression of a slight 'jump' on screen. This does not necessarily break continuity, but still jolts us. A significant change in frame size, (e.g., M S to C U will usually avoid this effect.

Developing your skills

These four tasks will provide you with valuable exercises in planning and shooting simple sequences. You should use these as opportunities to gather evidence for Unit 5, and as a chance to practise using video equipment in different production roles.

TASK 1

Developing 'reading' skills

■ Choose a short sequence from either a fiction or a non-fiction programme that involves 'continuity' conventions.

■ Using blank storyboard sheets and a finger on the VCR pause, storyboard this sequence using sketches, with appropriate terminology. This must also describe what is happening on the soundtrack.

TASK 2

Storyboard and shoot practise sequence 1

■ Select an action or activity from your immediate surroundings and break it down into approximately ten-shot sketches on a storyboard in a way that covers the 'action' and which should edit together as a continuity sequence. (Suggestions: Making a cup of coffee; entering a room; answering the telephone; getting into a car and driving off.)

■ Try to work some kind of 'twist in the tale' in your final shot.

■ Now, with tripod and camcorder (plus built-in microphone), working as a group of two or three, shoot the sequence, following your storyboard. You can either record shots in strict chronological order as an 'in-camera' edit, or with a view to editing on a suite, in which case, remember 'pre-roll' time on your takes. If you are to use a suite, this frees you to shoot your story out of sequence, which may save time in your camera 'set-ups'.

See shot list, p. 290.

TASK 3

Storyboard and shoot practise sequence 2

■ Devise a storyboard and accompanying narration that demonstrates a simple process as a short training video. (Suggestions: Setting up a camcorder; loading a 35 mm film.)

■ Shoot and edit your sequence, then dub on your narrated voice-over.

TASK 4

Script, storyboard and shoot practise sequence

Devise a script involving dialogue, based on a short dramatic situation (e.g., domestic argument). Storyboard your script and together with crew and cast, shoot and edit the sequence. (An appropriate microphone will be needed to cover the dialogue, e.g., boom microphone or pressure zone microphone (PZM).

In Tasks 2,3,4 above, carefully evaluate how well your sequences cut together, and, where appropriate, make amendments to your original storyboard or draw up a new one to show how continuity might be improved.

Scheduling

Effective scheduling can save time, energy, money and sanity. it generally divides into three levels:

■ scheduling the overall production, from script to screen.

■ scheduling the script into the logical order for scenes and shots to be tackled;

■ scheduling specific shoots.

Getting this planning right is a key to good production management, and is one of the main roles of the **production assistant or PA.**

Scheduling the overall production?

This involves analysing how long the production process might take, then working backwards from the ultimate deadline.

Scheduling production components

■ Research.

■ Script development.

■ Recces.

■ Rehearsals (if appropriate).

■ Production shoots.

■ Off-line edit (fine cut).

■ Sound dub, additional graphics.

■ Packaging, duplication, marketing (as appropriate).

Scheduling the script?

It is not necessary to shoot a story in chronological order, so scenes can be broken down and re-ordered according to other factors that make production quicker and easier, such as **location, time of day, weather, availability of performers, availability of resources, (equipment, crew, props)**.

Scheduling specific shoots?

An obvious illustration would be the shooting of a telephone conversation, where the finished edit will inter-cut between the two characters' dialogue. To shoot this in chronological order would take all week! However, the point is just as relevant for inter-cutting between two people in the same room.

This takes the above schedule one stage further. Careful planning of a day's shoot *before* setting off with the full crew and cast saves time and avoids embarrassment. The storyboard or shooting script of the scenes to be recorded can be further broken down and tackled in an order that requires the minimum of camera set-ups. For fiction, each set-up is a time-consuming process involving director and crew in constructing a new *mise-en-scène*, involving cast, props and lighting, with sound levels rechecked each time.

Shot list

When the best order has been worked out, this is written up as a **shot list** and is circulated to camera operator, crew and cast.
    You are now finally ready to roll some tape!

SHOOTING SCHEDULE (CALL SHEET)

PRODUCTION:

DATE/TIME:

RENDEZVOUS LOCATION:

TRANSPORT ARRANGEMENTS:

CAST:

CREW ROLES:

SPECIAL REQUIREMENTS (EQUIPMENT/PROPS):

CONTACT TELEPHONE NUMBERS:

WRAP TIME:

Fig 5.11 Shooting schedule (call sheet)

SHOT LIST (RUNNING ORDER)

PAGE	SCENE	SHOTS	D/N	CAST
16	3	3,5,7	NIGHT	Terry, Julie
16	3	1,2,4	NIGHT	Terry, Julie
16	3	6,8	NIGHT	Terry, Julie
19	5	1,5,6,8	NIGHT	Terry

ETC......

Fig 5.12 Shot list (running order)

5.2 PRODUCTION – RECORD MOVING IMAGES

The eye and the camera

About seeing

Light is reflected from objects and particles into the eye in varying degrees of colour and shade. The eye's **lens**, through the muscular control of the **iris**, focuses vision on chosen subjects, while opening and closing the pupil's **aperture** to let in more or less light. The lens projects an **image** of the external world on to the retina, where microscopic **light-sensitive cells** called rods and cones align in different ways according to the shapes and colours that fall on them. This visual information is **encoded** into minute **electrical pulses** that travel along the optical nerve to an area of the brain where they are **read** by our conscious mind, which then gives feedback to the eyes to tell them what to do next. It is no coincidence that a number of the highlighted words in this description are common to the principal functions of the camera.

Persistence of vision

Though the eye appears to transmit an uninterrupted stream of visual information, in reality it is more like a series of 'snapshots', merged together. The retina actually reads pictures at about 11 frames per second (fps). However, if the brain received them 'unmixed', our perception of sight would be like a flashing strobe or slowed down film projector. Instead, the individual snapshots are joined seamlessly together by a phenomenon known as *persistence of vision*. If you have ever written your name in the dark with a

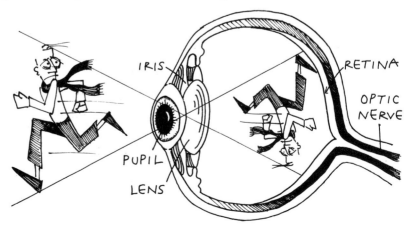

Fig 5.13 The eye

burning sparkler on Bonfire Night, you will have experienced a more exaggerated form of this, which is a kind of 'afterburn' effect on the retina.

In fact, the very *illusion* of moving image media depends entirely on persistence of vision merging together the frames.

Frames per second (fps)

For film to give the illusion of movement on screen, early inventors had to meet the challenge of both photographing and projecting images at a much faster rate than the eye can handle. The higher the fps, the smoother the illusion of movement and the less flicker. With the further mechanisation of cameras, 24 fps became established as the industrial norm.

How the video camera works (Fig. 5.14)

It is useful background knowledge for video production to understand the basics about how the system works, without going into the higher realms of electronic engineering. At the very least this can sometimes help with simple problem-solving when you fail to get a picture on screen.

The camera's equivalent of the retina where this encoding happens, is the **CCD** silicon chip (Charge Coupled Device). More domestic level camcorders are likely to have one CCD chip to encode RGB, while higher resolution industrial cameras are more likely to have three (one for each of the primaries). Like the retina, these CCDs are made up of photoelectric 'picture cells' or 'pixels'. As the light falls on a pixel, a minute electrical charge is created, varying according to the intensity of the light. The higher the camera's **resolution**, the more cells needed on the CCD plate, with broadcast cameras relying on several hundred thousand cells on plates little bigger than thumbnails.

Resolution: Ability to record fine detail.

Primary colours (additive and subtractive)

You might well have experimented with colour combinations in art classes, where the basic primaries with paints are not red, green and blue but red, blue and *yellow*. This is true for mixing dyes, where you are using 'subtractive' colours which *reflect* light. With television, the primaries we are dealing with do not reflect light, they *are* the light source. These primaries are known as 'additive' colours, where red, blue and green combine to make white light. They also combine to form other colours in the way shown.

If your studio or edit suite has a vision mixer with back colour or matte facility, you will be able to click through and choose from: red, green, blue, yellow, cyan, magenta, black and these also make up the colour bar test signal that industrial cameras emit.

From the lens to the screen

Just as happens with the eye, the light, having passed through the lens, must be **encoded**. For this to happen, the light must be split up into its separate **components**, which are then encoded either into fluctuating electrical signals known as **analogue,** representing the varying amounts of the three primary colours, red, green and blue or **RGB**, or now with most recent technology, directly into **digital** code, which, if then edited and transmitted on a digital system, loses *no* resolution in the entire process from lens to screen.

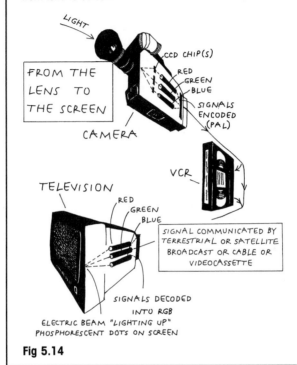

Fig 5.14

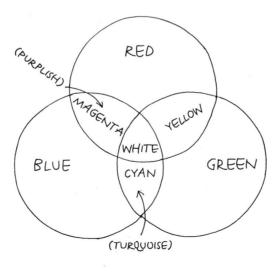

Fig 5.15 'Additive' colours, where red, blue and green combine to make white light

Colour temperature, filters and white balance

A mixture of 30% red, 59% green and 11% blue is necessary to produce a white light on screen. The camera is not as sensitive to colour as the human eye, so filters and circuitry must be adjusted to retain the right **balance** of RGB to recreate white light on screen.

The colours of objects change dramatically according to the kind of light that reflects from them. At extreme levels, logfires and candlelight impart a soft, warm, orange glow, while bright snowy mountain sunshine gives an almost bluish clarity. If you have ever taken photographs indoors, using normal 'daylight' colour film, with only electric household bulbs for illumination, you will have noticed that the prints show people with orangey faces. A bluey-white flashbulb, however, will give you similar colours to natural daylight. This is due to **colour temperatures**, which are measured in degrees kelvin (K), a scale similar to centigrade, but beginning at absolute zero rather than at water's freezing point. In simple terms, the higher the temperature, the wider the spectrum of colour produced, with the 'blues' at the upper end of the scale:

Light source	Degrees kelvin (K) @	Colour
Midday sunshine	5,500	Bluish
Fluorescent tubing	4,000	Greenish
Tungsten studio (e.g., 800 W)	3,200	Yellowish
Household	2,600	Orangey
Sunset	2,500	Orangey
Candlelight/firelight	1,900 or less	Reddish

Filters

If you are working with industrial rather than domestic cameras, you can immediately help to **balance** your camera to the lighting conditions by choosing the appropriate **filter** from a selection of two or three on a filter wheel, The choice is a simple one usually, between daylight or tungsten (5,500 K or 3,200 K), but can have disastrous results if neglected. Shooting by daylight with a tungsten setting will result in pictures awash with blue, while making the reverse error can result in a sunburnt, jaundiced look to the fleshtones.

White balance

In addition to choosing the appropriate filter, industrial cameras will require you to perform a **white balance (WB)**. (The selection of filter/WB on domestic camcorders is combined into a single, less accurate choice of daylight/artificial through clicking the appropriate icon in the viewfinder. Alternatively auto WB, like autofocus, can be selected as an 'idiot-proof' approach, though this can present problems. A full WB, proportioning red, green and blue, is a simple process, but vital if you are to record accurate colours.

This is done by holding up a white card or sheet in the same lighting conditions as you intend to shoot, and by pressing the WB button until icons in the viewfinder tell you 'OK.' This process must be repeated each time you set up in a new, differently lit situation.

Black balance

With industrial cameras it is also required to 'tell' the camera what it should read as black. This is simply done by pressing a black balance switch which closes up the aperture totally, registering black as what it is — an absence of light.

Focus

The earliest optical lenses for astronomy were being developed by Islamic scientists eight centuries ago around Baghdad and Basra, at a time when the English were just emerging from the Dark Ages.

As with 35 mm stills cameras, the video lens has several mechanisms that influence the focusing of a chosen image. The focus ring itself, when turned, will bring the subject into or out of focus. Industrial cameras also have a control for the aperture (iris), whereas domestic cameras will often only have auto-aperture. The more open the aperture (i.e., in darker conditions), the shorter the **depth of field** within which objects remain in focus, while the tighter the aperture (lighter conditions), the greater the depth of field.

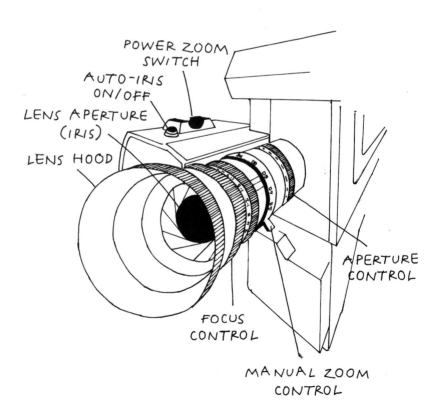

POWER ZOOM SWITCH

AUTO-IRIS ON/OFF

LENS APERTURE (IRIS)

LENS HOOD

APERTURE CONTROL

FOCUS CONTROL

MANUAL ZOOM CONTROL

Fig 5.16 Video Camera controls

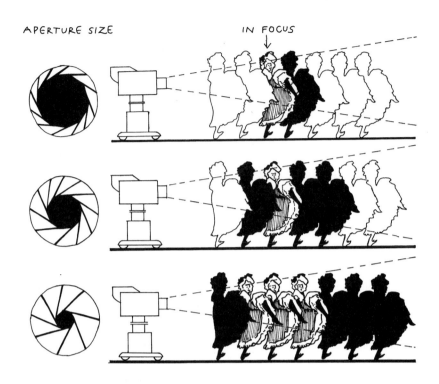

Fig 5.17 Depth of Field

Before the zoom lens became a standard in the 1960s, lenses had to be unscrewed and exchanged for others of different focal lengths according to the shot required. A later innovation involved several different lenses on a revolving 'turret'.

Finally, the **zoom** lens has a profound effect on depth of focus. When zoomed fully in on a subject, depth of field is at its minimum, while when zoomed out, depth of field is at its greatest. A shallow depth of field need not be a problem, particularly if the subject is two dimensional or not moving, and can be turned to creative advantage in two ways:

- **Creating depth:** A sharply focused object against a blurred background can give that object presence making it seem more three-dimensional.
- **Focus pull:** A shallow focal depth allows us to 'pull focus' from foreground object to background (or vice versa). This is best achieved when the lens is fully zoomed in and focus is at its shallowest.

Camera operation — industrial working practices

The job

Note: although the basic principles of camera operation are common to almost all video cameras, be sure to read the manual for your particular equipment

Camera operators must be increasingly multiskilled people to earn a living. They must be technically adept, understand light, have a photojournalist's eye, a weight-lifter's shoulders and a head for business as freelancers. Sound-recordist's ears are also often required, as the shrinking of crew sizes, added to the 'dockable' combination of camera and VCR, has resulted in two jobs becoming one when budgeting and profit margins are very tight.

> **Checklist: Setting up**
> - Power.
> - Position.
> - Light.
> - Focus.
> - Frame.
> - Practice.
> - Record.

■ Power

Your recce or schedule notes should have told you whether you are powering from mains or battery. If you are on camera for the shoot, it should be your responsibility to check this *the day before* to ensure batteries are to be fully charged or that all leads and power-adopters are available and *working* (never assume anything!). If powering from mains, 'gaffer' tape should be brought too, for **health and safety** reasons, as trailing leads can be dangerous, and should be taped to the ground where they might present a trip hazard.

■ Position

See camera tripod movement, p. 302.
See handheld techniques, p. 305.

Wherever possible *use a tripod*, as good hand-held camera work takes years of practice to develop. According to the shot required, set up the tripod first in the most likely stable position. Then mount the camera and attach power, video and audio leads as required. For handheld shots, refer to the section below.

■ Light

See Lighting for video, p. 306.

Select the correct filter setting for the lighting conditions, then white/black=balance the camera. According to the size of your crew, you might also have a major say in arranging appropriate lighting and applying 'gels'.

■ Focus?

For health and safety reasons, you should only do this for more static set-ups, as if you are moving around with handheld work, you will need your full stereoscopic vision, and cannot rely purely on the viewfinder for orientation.

As a standard procedure to ensure sharp images, follow these steps. Firstly, **zoom in** fully (as far as it will go), on your chosen subject. **Adjust focus** so that it is as sharp as you can make it. Then **zoom out** to the framing you require. Your subject will remain in focus throughout the range of the zoom, from telephoto to wide angle ('T' to 'W' on the zoom control). If when you do this operation, the subject, when fully zoomed in, will not focus sharply, the likelihood is that your lens is too close, i.e., shorter than its minimum focal distance. You should either move back the camera (or the subject, whichever is easier), or, if this is not possible, try adjusting the **macro** ring on the lens.

If you wear glasses, you might find them a hindrance when peering into a small viewfinder. If so, then having taken them off, you can adjust the viewfinder to your own vision by moving a viewing lens or 'diopter' accordingly (standard on most cameras.)

Remember, *at wide angle, the lens only covers a third of your own vision!*

■ Frame

Unless you are shooting instant-response documentary footage, you should carefully frame up the shots *before* rolling tape. This avoids wading through hours of wobbly, out-of-focus rubbish when you come to edit your work. It also saves tape. The framing of the shot is not always down to you, but might be according to a director's wishes, and must also take into account lighting and sound, with the positioning of the microphone boom.

See framing techniques, p. 303.

■ Practice

If your shot involves a camera movement of some kind, (e.g., zoom, pan, tilt, etc.), again, to avoid wasting tape and edit time, practise your shot until it works smoothly and you are ready to roll.

■ Record

This is either down to the camera operator (if operating a camcorder), or a separate VCR operator. Either way, it is usually a good idea for all concerned to be aware that tape is rolling. Here an agreed procedure for the shoot is necessary, with clear instructions like: 'Roll VCR,' followed by the response: 'Rolling!' This should then be followed by a count-down of ten seconds to allow for pre-roll.

See editing video, p. 329.
See documentary approaches, p. 322.
This procedure is not appropriate for more 'fly on the wall' documentary work where it can be counter-productive to draw too much attention to the camera and crew.

While you are in the ten-second count-down period, it is useful — and usual — to ensure that there is also a visual reference to the shot. You should use either a clapperboard, or a white board, or even a piece of paper with the shot number and take marked clearly to identify visually the shot you are currently filming. You can also add an audio reference by calling 'shot three, take two,' for instance, while the clapperboard is on-screen. This helps enormously during editing, as it can be very difficult otherwise to work out which take is which, if there are only subtle differences between them.

Again, to assist in editing and to avoid 'clipping' action or words, do not be too hasty to 'cut' or pause VCR at the end of your shot. Let four or five seconds pass by, then cut. This is particularly important with camcorders which 'backspace' to varying amounts of time, when paused, cutting back into the end of the previous shot. A way you can calculate this 'backspace' is to record a clockface's second hand, pausing at key times. Playback should show you how many seconds are being cut.

Note: to count seconds without a second counter on a watch, count 'five hundred, four hundred, three hundred, etc.'

Fig 5.18

The clapperboard is used in film production to identify the beginning of each shot visually and to enable sound and vision to be synchronised. In film, sound is recorded separately from vision. As the clapperboard is closed, the point at which the 'clap' can be heard on tape is clearly identifiable with the visual 'clap' on screen as the board is snapped closed.

How to be an effective camera operator

Tripod techniques

The tripod 'head' has various levers that will either 'lock off', or 'release' movement in both vertical (tilt) and horizontal (pan) plains. You must be able to adjust these to the right degree at speed if you are to avoid missing shots, and this requires regular practice.

More expensive professional tripods (e.g., Vinten or Sachtler) have 'fluid heads' (hydraulics) that dampen down the movement, allowing for smooth pans and tilts; but again, practice is needed to get the best from them. These tripods also have a built-in spirit level to ensure a horizontal 'platform' for your camera.

Setting up procedure

■ Set up the tripod at the required height

The standard convention for people shots is to have the lens at your subject's eye-level. Alternatively, if a very low ground-level shot is required, forget the tripod altogether and rest the camera directly on the ground, propping up the front end with a book or cassette box to gain the required angle. This can be very effective for exaggerating perspective with roads, pavements, railway tracks, etc.

Two situations where an exact bubble-up is vital are when the sea's horizon is framed or when straight vertical buildings are in shot. A downward sloping sea might look good for water skiing, but will cause either laughter or tears in the edit suite.

■ 'Bubble-up'

This involves raising or lowering tripod legs to ensure that the spirit-level bubble is centred so that the camera will be exactly horizontal.

RESTING CAMERA ON THE GROUND

BRICK

Fig 5.19

■ Mounting the camera

The camera should be securely screwed to a base plate and mounted on the tripod after bubble-up, as it is much harder and potentially more hazardous for the camera if tripod legs are being adjusted with the camera in place. The only exception to this is where the tripod is on soft ground, where the additional weight of the camera might influence the horizontal levelling.

When mounting the camera, *always* keep a firm grip on the camera's handle throughout the process and check that it is firmly attached before letting go, as this is the stage when most camera 'casualties' happen.

■ Still shots from a tripod

For really steady camera work, where there is likely to be little or no movement (e.g., static interviews, landscape cutaways), it is a good idea for you to remove your hands altogether from the camera, once the shot is recording. This avoids the transmission of shake or breathing movement to the camera, as this can be a real problem, especially if you are tense or nervous about 'getting it right'. However, try to keep the tripod head released, so that should you need to make a slight adjustment to the framing, you do not jog the tripod in trying to move the levers.

■ Camera/tripod movement

Camera movements and zooms can easily become distracting and gratuitous, and are the bane of video editors for one reason in particular: they cannot be cut short without the viewer sensing a 'jerk' or lack of continuity. Consequently, pans and zooms, if they really must be included, need to be carefully timed so that they do not last more than five or six seconds.

It is a *very* good idea to practise the movement first. This avoids bumping into fellow crew members as you pan round, and also allows you to choose the beginning and end frames of shots, avoiding the unpleasantness of pulling out from a well-composed landscape to reveal the rear bumper of a Morris Ital, glinting in the sunset.

SHOT 1A   SHOT 1B

THIS SHOT INVOLVES A ZOOM OUT WHILST

Fig 5.20   SIMULTANEOUSLY TILTING DOWN AND PANNING LEFT.

Framing techniques and movement

The suggestions here mainly relate to framing people. Refer back for guidelines on shot composition. The framing of a subject according to a storyboard becomes complex when we introduce movement into the picture, either through the subject moving or the camera. A typical pull-out (zoom-out) will often involve more than a simple pressure to the zoom control. The picture within the frame often must be recomposed for it to end with a suitable image. This can be a real test of skill and tripod control, in that, while zooming out, the camera might need to be tilted and panned slightly in a continual recorrecting of the frame. Effectively you are doing three things here: zooming out, panning and tilting, all at same time.

Following a moving subject can be equally demanding, e.g., a running person or a dancer. Here, as with 'talk space', we should allow space in the frame for people to move into, so they are not pushing up against the frame's edge. You will find there comes a point where you are likely to lose your subject. Try to predict this point, and stop the camera movement, allowing the subject to move out of frame, as this provides a good editing point.

Test your camera skills

TASK 1

Having set up a camcorder on a tripod ready to record, choose five objects in the room or studio. (e.g. clock, doorhandle) focus and frame on the object in CU. When framed steadily, then pull out until you have framed a wider shot of your choice in the room. Practise this on all five objects until the movements and tripod adjustments come naturally. Now record them and watch them back on screen, identifying and correcting any faults in your camera work.

> **TASK 2**
>
> In pairs, practise camera movements following each other, with one of you on camera, the other walking or running. Try to maintain a constant framing throughout. Record, review and evaluate.

Tracking/dolly shots

To see this fluid camera at its best, look closely at the opening few minutes of *A Touch of Evil*, (Orson Welles, USA, 1958). Hitchcock's *Rope* (USA, 1948) is also well worth close study, being shot entirely in eight-minute takes (this being the running time of a 400-foot reel of film), where all the changes in framing are by camera rather than by edit.

Higher budget fiction and corporate productions often involve '**tracks**' and '**cranes**' or '**cherrypickers**' to ensure fluid camera work. Here, the camera and operator are mounted on the mechanism, then raised or lowered, pushed or pulled (by 'grips') according to the desired effect. (Remember, zooms are almost never used in fiction.)

It is worth looking at low-budget versions of the tracking shot, all of which, however, are dependent on a reasonably flat, smooth floor surface over which to travel:

- **The studio dolly**. This involves mounting the camera on a wheel base, the sophistication of which can vary greatly from hydraulically elevating smooth gliding machines to simple sets of casters attached to the tripod legs. These will track successfully over 'lino' surfaces and short pile carpet, but remember to align the wheels *before* moving to avoid the 'supermarket trolley effect'.

- **The wheelchair**. Old wheelchairs with pneumatic tyres can be very successful for moving shots, and will tolerate slightly rougher surfaces. The camera operator sits in the chair and is pushed.

- **Handheld movement**. Unless you have a Steadicam harness, the last resort for moving camera is the walking handheld (shoulder-mounted) shot, which, with some practice, can come

Fig 5.21 Hand-held movements. An assistant holding a belt round the camera operator's waist can prevent nasty accidents

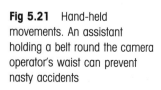

out quite smoothly. This is most likely to work with the zoom lens on wide angle, as the telephoto position magnifies any jerks or unwanted motion. Again, there are very real health and safety considerations here, due to the restricted view of the camera operator.

Further handheld techniques

For steadier, more effective (i.e., less distracting) work, there are some straightforward techniques that can be developed with practice:

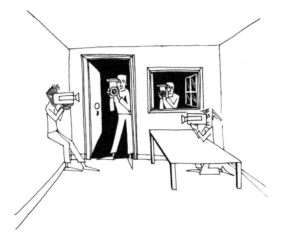

Fig 5.22

■ To steady the shot, always look for some support against which to prop yourself, creating a form of tripod. Walls, tables, doorframes, trees or windowsills are ideal for 'jamming' yourself against to create that extra stability.

■ Wherever possible, shoot using wide angle (zoomed-out) as the zoomed-in lens exaggerates the slightest movement. If you need a closer shot, it is better that *you* move in, (circumstances allowing).

■ Make sure you are fully at ease with your camera, and have sorted out a comfortable way of holding and operating, adjusting straps, viewfinder position, etc.

■ Try to control your breathing to avoid the movement affecting your footage.

Rostrum camera

Whether recording for two-dimensional animation, captions, graphics or still photographs, a simple rostrum set up can be very useful. An old darkroom enlarger rostrum can be ideal, providing easy adjustability. Because of the closeness of the subject to the lens, a *macro* setting is required on your video camera, which will often allow you to within an inch of your subject. As a result, you

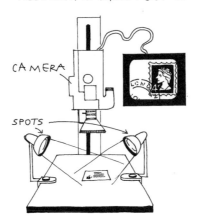

Fig 5.23   Rostrum camera
set-up

can fill the screen with an object little bigger than a postage stamp. The depth of focus is very shallow though, and requires a flat object.

Lighting for video

Unlike lighting for film (not dealt with here), where film speed and type, lens speed and filters are major factors, with video, what you see on screen is what you get.

Lighting problems

Unlike theatrical lighting, where your eyes tell you of the overall effect, with video you need to use a video monitor or television screen to gauge the lighting. Understanding this first principle is vital to successful lighting.

Added to this is the problem that the television screen is a two-dimensional, flat image. The challenge is to give the illusion of *depth* and a *third dimension*. Essentially then, you need to try and 'sculpt' with light and shade — not an easy task.

Basic studio three-point lighting

Although broadcast studios might have banks and banks of suspended lights, they are all working towards achieving a common end: to produce the illusion of depth and solidity. This depends on a principle shared with stills photography: *three-point lighting*, and can be successfully achieved using portable lighting kits.

Key, fill, back.

Artificial lighting is often an attempt to imitate natural (daylight) conditions, where there tends to be one particularly strong source of light (the sun), which is then either filtered through cloud or directed through a window, but is still the dominant, **key** source.

BASIC STUDIO THREE POINT LIGHTING

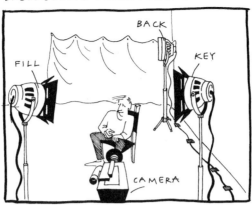

Fig 5.24 Basic studio three-point lighting

This light bounces or reflects from a variety of surfaces (especially white walls and ceilings), **filling** in much softer lighting from a number of directions, front, side and **back**, this backlight outlining the subject, adding to the 'depth' of the image. The illustration shows how you can recreate this by positioning lights on their stands. You need to experiment with different positions and directions until you are happy with what you see *on the screen.*

Portable lighting techniques

The most usual general purpose lights to be found in education and industry are the 800 W portable lamps known as **'redheads'**. Bulkier 2,000 W lamps, known as **'blondes'**, similarly hark back to the sexist roots of the industry! With modern CCD 'low lux' cameras, 800 W lamps are usually ample to give adequate light levels, unless a very large area is being lit from a distance. These redhead lamps can be highly flexible and adaptable. Here are some techniques and features:

- **Spot/flood**: The back of the lamp has a variable knob that adjusts the bulb position either to focus or disperse the lighting according to needs.
- **Barn doors**: The beam can be directed or blocked out by adjusting the metal flaps or 'barn doors'.
- **Gels**: There are a variety of gels that can be attached to the barn doors to change the coloration or intensity of the light.
- **Diffusion**: If a less intense light is required with softer shadowing, then an opaque diffusion gel can be attached, or 'scrim', which is like a wire gauze, breaking up the beam.

Reflected or 'bounced' light

To create the light and shadow that three-point lighting achieves, you do not have to have three lamps. Often, bouncing a light off a white wall or ceiling can give a very effective fill, softening the shadows created by your key. In fact, with suitable reflective surfaces, you can produce well-lit shots with a single light source. An old white cotton sheet has often proved a vital part of a 'minimal' lighting kit, as this can be quickly draped or taped in an ideal position to bounce light back on to the subject.

Mixed lighting

Often it is necessary to mix daylight with artificial light, especially when shooting indoors. If you refer back to the section on white balance, you will realise that this is going to create problems with the way the camera encodes the colours. (In short, you are mixing 'blues and oranges', and your camera will be confused.)

There are several solutions. The most common is to place pale blue gel over your lamp, changing its colour temperature to that of the daylight coming through the window. However, you need to make a decision as to whether you use the window light as the key, with your tungsten as a softer fill or vice versa. Having 'equalised' your light, you should now white-balance your camera, using the 'natural daylight' filter setting.

A more 'fiddly' alternative can be to use pale orange gel stuck over the window, changing daylight colour temperature to tungsten. (The orange filters out the blue.)

BLUE GEL

Fig 5.25

Shadows

Too strong an overhead light can give deep black shadows beneath eyebrows, nose and chin. Worse still, twin overhead lamps can give a double nose shadow, combined with a luminous halo of hair. Also, if your interviewee is too close to a back curtain or a set 'flat', the more frontal lights can cast distracting shadows on the backdrop. Two techniques can be used here to avoid this:

- Simply move your subject away from the backdrop until the shadow falls too low to be in shot.
- If you do not have the room for this, try to direct a light on to the shadow itself to soften or neutralise it. If positioned with care, this rear light can also spill on to the rear of your subject producing an effective backlight, adding to the impression of depth in your image.

Hot spots

Using high-wattage lamps can create particularly bright areas in your shot, especially where two beams are overlapping or falling on to a more reflective surface. This should be avoided, as the effect on your recording will be of over-exposed or 'bleached out' areas. This is at its worst where you have a darkish scene or studio set, and it is your subject's face that is bleaching out. While you have some control over this through closing your aperture, this might also result in darkening the rest of your scene to unacceptable levels. Instead, try to reposition your lights, and set them on 'flood' rather than 'spot'. Also you might try to *diffuse* the light through a scrim or gel, or by bouncing it indirectly.

A more literal 'hot spot' is often created for the poor interviewee, as several thousand watts of light create a considerable heat. Bear this in mind and stop whenever possible for a cooling-off break, switching off lamps when you can. Paper tissues and some talcum powder are also useful for removing highly reflective glistening sweat. (A glass of water is appreciated too.)

Anti-reflective spray can be sprayed on other glinting objects, such as chrome microphone stands.

Outdoor

Wherever possible, location interviews are recorded outside, in daylight. This provides strong light levels and usually sufficient reflected light to fill in the shadows. Points to remember:

- Make sure you set up positions so that sunlight is coming from *behind* the camera, on to the subject's face, avoiding silhouetting.
- Avoid very strong direct overhead sunshine, as this can create too contrasting a picture, with dark black nose and jaw shadows.
- Avoid shooting your subject against the sky, as again, this likely to cause silhouetting.
- Watch out for patchy cloud, as this can cause sudden bursts of strong sunshine, which will bleach out your image unless you adjust the aperture in time.

Fig 5.26

- On dull, wintery days, a battery-powered 100 W portable light (e.g. Pag or Sachtler), can give a little 'lift' to the subject's face, and is very effective in giving reflective 'points' in the eyes, making the face come alive. This technique is also ideal for lighting the journalist's *piece to camera* (PTC).
- When framing your shot, try to give a background context that is somehow relevant to the interview.

Indoor

Wherever possible, available light sources should be used, not only because it cuts down on cumbersome lighting set-ups, but also it is likely to be more 'naturalistic'. Points to remember:

- Try to use the light from a window as a *side* key, as this is likely to be your strongest available source, but avoid at all costs having the window *behind* your subject, unless you want to create the silhouetted freedom fighter effect!
- If the room is not very reflective and you need a fill light, remember to use blue gel to balance the colour temperature.
- Draping a sheet on the interior side of your interviewee can create an effective fill by bouncing the window light back on

Fig 5.27

KEY   REFLECTIVE SHEET

Fig 5.28

to your subject's face, filling the darker shadows. This uses *no* artificial lights, but creates a very successful result.

■ Try to avoid direct sunlight falling on to your subject, as the contrasts are likely to be too strong.

■ If levels of light are sufficient, switch off any ceiling lighting strips, as these add another colour to the mix, and will be picked up as a distinct 'hum' by a sensitive microphone.

■ Try to choose a 'backdrop' context that provides some visual information about the interviewee.

Lighting effects

For fictional drama work and experimentation, creative lighting can be a very suggestive part of your visual storytelling. Here are some techniques you can experiment with to create impressions and illusions.

■ **Watching television in a darkened room**: To recreate the flickering blue light of the television set, blue-gel a low positioned light source, and wave a sheet of card in and out of the beam. In a darkened room or studio, this will give the required effect. (Using a real television set just does not cast enough light for the camera.)

■ **The open fire**: Use a similar technique to above, this time with orange gel. You can add to this by deliberately choosing the wrong camera filter!

■ **Candle light**: Often candles are simply not bright enough to give the required effect on screen. You can 'cheat' by boosting the orangey light with a household table lamp. (40 W), positioned on the floor. This will give a warm, low light which, with a candle or two in shot, gives the required atmospheric lighting.

■ **Fractured shadows (blinds and bars)**: To recreate the film noir *mise-en-scene* on the cheap, strips can be cut out from stiff card like a stencil. Taped to the barn doors of a redhead, this will cast clearly striped shadows like those authentic venetian blinds or prison cell bars (Fig. 5.29).

CUT OUT CARD

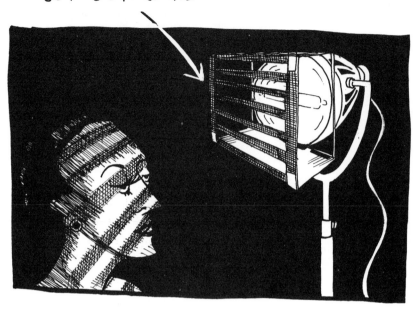

Fig 5.29

Rostrum lighting

When lighting two-dimensional graphics for rostrum work, it is important to position two lights in a way that will avoid reflections up into the lens, and will spread light as evenly as possible. At close range, two 'feature' spotlights can be adequate. A similar set up could be used for stop-frame animation work.

Health and safety with lighting

Portable redheads are potentially the most dangerous video equipment you are likely to work with. However, if you have carefully assessed the hazards and followed good working practices, you can reduce the risk to zero. The hazards are as follows:

■ **Problem 1**: The bulbs and surrounding lamp casing become *very hot* after a relatively short time, and will burn if touched.

  Solution: Before handling or packing away the lamps, allow to cool for five minutes or more.

■ **Problem 2**: Bulbs have been known to 'pop', showering redhot splinters of glass.

  Solution: A heat-resistant safety glass plate should be fitted as standard practice across the front of the lamp.

■ **Problem 3**: The 'telescopic' light stands are unstable, particularly when the lamp is extended at six feet or more. This is made even more dangerous by

Note: Health and safety issues cannot be emphasised too strongly, particularly if you are shooting in a public place, or where people are likely to be ‚ passing. Remember, in addition to the guilt you might feel at having maimed someone, it is **YOU** they will sue!

the relatively short power leads, which tend to trail to the nearest mains plug at ideal trip height, giving the potential for a red-hot lamp with metal barn doors to come crashing down.

Solution: Avoid over-extending the stands if possible. Also, position one leg of the stand so it is directly beneath the lamphead's weight. This adds to stability. Make sure you bring an extension power lead to the foot of the light stand, and **tape** this lead and any others down with 'gaffer' electricians' tape, avoiding any trailing leads and trip hazards.

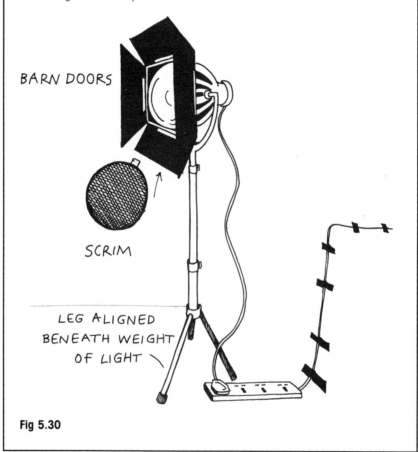

BARN DOORS

SCRIM

LEG ALIGNED
BENEATH WEIGHT
OF LIGHT

Fig 5.30

Test your lighting skills

TASK 1

Using material you have prepared in Unit 2, set up an interview situation in a studio, if you have one, or in an interior location if you have not. The interview should be between two people. Position your subjects and position your lights appropriately for three-point lighting. Make a note of where exactly they are (either on the lighting grid or on a floor plan of the area). Using a video monitor linked to the camera(s), switch the lights on, and record any adjustments you make until you have the lighting conditions you require.

TASK 2

Using some dialogue you have created in Unit 2, use one of the 'illusion' techniques above, or one of your own invention, and shoot the scene. Repeat, using a different 'illusion' and compare and evaluate the results in terms of the lighting's mood and impression.

Separate VCRs

If your role is to operate a separate VCR, whether portable or studio/mains, you are very much at the heart of the crew, with all the 'lifelines' coming to and from your machine. The first thing you should learn, then, is how all the cabling connects. This falls into three areas: **power, video** (in/out) and **audio** (in/out).

■ **Power**: If working on location, you should be ready to run from battery as well as being familiar with the mains adaptor connections. It is *your* job to check that batteries are charged beforehand, and are in sufficient quantity for the shoot.

■ **Video in**: This will either be through a thick multi-pin cable connected to the camera (known as the 'umbilical'), or through a BNC cable connected to 'video in' on your VCR.

■ **Video out**: To monitor the camera's image, as well as to cue up the tape or replay shots, you will need to take a BNC cable from 'video out' to a monitor. If you are using a portable monitor, *remember batteries.*

■ **Audio in**: The standard input for microphone cables is the XLR three-pin connector. If you are using a single microphone, you have the choice of two channel sockets to plug into. Always use *channel 2* for the following reasons:

(a) when editing, you will know where the sound is recorded;
(b) channel 2 is slightly protected through not being on the edge of the tape. This does not apply if your VCR is recording in hi-fi mode, as here the audio is encoded with the video signal across the width of the tape.
(c) Many VCRs have the option switch on *channel 1* to monitor the camera's video signal and/or the battery charge level. Hence it is useful to leave this channel free.
(d) With appropriate equipment, channel 1 can be used for recording a *time-code* signal.

In certain circumstances, you might be recording sound through a mixing desk, especially where live performance using several microphones is involved (e.g., live bands or studio discussions). While on some models, the same audio input might be used, it is vital to switch the *impedance* setting from microphone to *line* setting, as this will match the signal output from the mixing desk.

■ **Audio out**: This tends to be simply a headphone ('cans' in the jargon) socket for you to monitor sound. However, if you are recording from a separate, sound-proofed recording gallery or studio, you may also take audio lines (XLR or phono) out to an amplifier and speakers if a number of you wish to listen in. Alternatively you might use a headphone junction box (common in language departments) from the headphone socket, allowing up to six sets of cans to listen in.

Camcorders and 'dockable' VCRs

Many of the same connections apply here, though, depending on your crew and equipment, you may well involve a separate portable audio mixer, as the audio metering levels on the back end of a camera are difficult to adjust while a shot is in progress, especially with handheld work.

Tape handling

You are in the line of fire for any mistakes or misrecordings made on shoots, so you need to be very organised in tape management.

■ It is down to you to see you have sufficient tape for the shoot. Check with the director.

■ If you are recording on to tape that already has footage on that you wish to keep, you must carefully **cue** the tape to the last piece of recorded footage. For safety, run on in 'search' mode to check in case there is any extra footage. Having found the last frames recorded, run the tape on in 'play' mode for several seconds before putting into 'record/pause' mode ready for rolling. Remember, normally peace-loving people become psychopathic when you record over their footage.

■ As the shoot progresses, you should give an indication to the director as to how much tape is left on cassette, to avoid having to break in mid-take. if you have a production assistant taking a footage log on a time-sheet, check the totals. This is particularly relevant when using short tape formats (e.g., U-matic 20s, Betacam SP 20s or SVHS 'C' format).

■ When cassettes are finished, or at the end of a shoot, it is down to you to **protect** the cassettes by removing the recording 'tab', ensuring the tape cannot be recorded over by accident. Also both the cassette and its box should be clearly marked with relevant information, e.g., project title, tape number, date,

Note: *Never* put tapes on top of loudspeakers or television sets as the speakers incorporate powerful magnets that can damage your footage.

location, and possibly a reference to content (such as scene numbers or interviewee names). This latter task could equally be a PA's role (If you have one).

■ Completed tapes should now be re-wound and stored in a safe place known to the director, away from magnetic fields and extremes of temperature.

Sound recording and monitoring

Setting a level

Note: On a film shoot, the sound recordist would be responsible for recording the sound-track on a separate tape recorder.

Too often on a shoot, directors are so preoccupied with getting the visuals sorted that they neglect sound until the last minute. So you need to make your presence felt early on in the process of setting up. This is particularly so when a boom microphone is used (i.e., for most fiction/drama work), as the boom must not appear in shot, and *neither should its shadow*. This means that the boom should be held in position *before* any lighting design is finalised.

Positioning the boom

Positioning the boom is a complex process involving four people's agreement: VCR operator, boom operator, camera operator and director. As a sound recordist, you need to argue for the microphone being as *close* as possible to provide you with strong sound levels and optimum signal-to-noise ratio. However, this tends to be compromised by the visual demands, as if a wider shot is required, this inevitably means the microphone is further away from the subject. Usually a compromise is struck between ideal frame and ideal sound. The positioning of the boom, known as *fixing edge of frame* is a vital discipline which, in fiction work, must be followed all the time, while in documentary shoots, this must become an almost telepathic understanding between camera operator and boom operator.

■ Once the camera has framed up the scene and subjects to be recorded, the boom microphone should be slowly lowered until it just appears in shot in the monitor/viewfinder. The boom operator should be clearly told that this is 'edge of frame'. The boom should now be raised slowly until it disappears from screen, then raised a few more inches for safety. (Some monitors 'scan' more widely than others, while the boom operator might 'droop' slightly on a take.) Exactly the same procedure should be followed with a boom in low position coming up from the bottom edge of frame.

■ A sound level should be taken now, with boom in position, with the person who is to talk either running through lines or responding to an interview 'warm-up' question. If you find that you are having to boost the recording level dial to 8 or 9 to gain a healthy level (with the VU meter averaging at around –3 dB),

EDGE OF FRAME

Fig 5.31

then you must let the director know that the microphone should be closer (or the talk should be louder). Failing to do this could result in 'hissy' or 'noisy' sound through trying to boost a weak signal. The point at which recording levels become noisy will vary according to the quality of the equipment, and you need to get to know the tolerance of the gear you are using.

Using VU meters (see Unit 4)

These meters are broadly standard, whether built into video or audio equipment, and are there to help you avoid over- or under-recording. Where possible, then, try to take a 'sound check', and adjust your meter level so that the needle is averaging around -3 or -4 dB (roughly the vertical position) with only occasional peaks that might stray just into the red area of the meter (above 0 dB or 'full modulation').

The tape recording will tolerate occasional peaks into the red, but if your levels are consistently working into the red, and even peaking off the scale, your recording will have distortion and sound 'break-up' and will be unusable. Again, *you* will be held responsible when this is discovered in the edit suite. Equally, too low levels (e.g., around–10 dB) will give poor results, especially for speech, as when it comes to the editing sound dub, these levels will have to be boosted to the–3 dB average, which will also boost tape hiss and noise.

'Riding' the levels

Once you have set your levels, the job does not end there. Sound levels fluctuate with speech and music, and you need to make ongoing corrective adjustments to the metering level. This is particularly so when using tie-clip microphones, as the sound level can dramatically change if the subject suddenly talks with head lowered or tilted to the side on which the microphone is attached, sending levels through the roof.

Audio limiters

Some VCRs have audio limiters which, when switched in, will prevent peaking and break up. However, these should only be switched in *after* a sound level has first been taken with them off, as otherwise the limiter could 'camouflage' a horribly over-modulated signal, resulting in a strangely clipped, 'compressed' sound. This technique applies equally to their use in post-production when editing sound.

Portable sound mixers

These are particularly useful if your sound metering is on the back end of your camcorder. The mixer allows you to adjust the levels separately, feeding in a carefully adjusted level to the VCR. Before recording, you can set the VCR meters to a constant tone from the mixer (usually at 1 KHz), and from then on, all adjustment is done on the separate mixer, where there is another VU meter, rather than on the VCR itself. The same procedure should be followed when editing sound if you are editing through a mixing desk with a 'tone generator'.

In documentary and news gathering interview work, often the person adjusting sound levels is also holding the microphone, either on a pistol grip or short boom. This has the added benefit of being in the best position to re-direction the microphone for maximum pick-up.

Monitoring techniques

Good use of headphones is a key part in sound recording. Firstly, it is essential that the cans block out as much *external* sound as

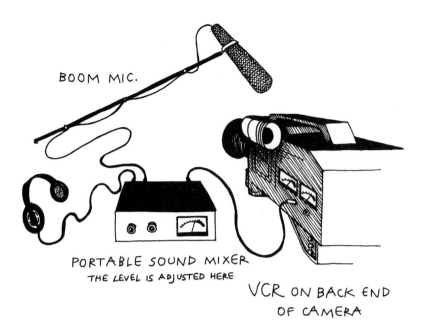

Fig 5.32 Portable sound
mixer

possible, so that you are only listening to what the microphone picks up. For this reason, small personal stereo' phones are virtually useless. At critical moments the sound exclusion can be helped by cupping your hands over the 'muffs', for example, to see whether a passing aeroplane noise has been lost by the microphone. A psychological aid to this can be to close your eyes, as this helps focus purely on your hearing. Another technique when recording speech is to try to avoid looking at the speaker's mouth, as your subconscious lip-reading abilities can compensate for a lack of audio clarity, filling in the 'grey areas'.

Headphone sockets often have a volume control. Remember this has *no* control over the recording level, but is purely for listening. Consequently, the only way to *ensure* adequate recording levels is to go by what the VU meter reads. Finally, to underline the importance of audio recording, sound recordist/VCR operators are the *only* people in a crew apart from a director who can interrupt a take by shouting 'cut' if they hear a major sound problem. They are effectively the director's ears and are relied on to make critical decisions.

Microphone techniques

See Unit 4.

The properties of different microphones are covered in the audio section. However, there are a range of microphones specifically designed for video use:

■ **The rifle (gun) Microphone**: This is a very *directional* condenser microphone, usually battery powered, and is probably the most multipurpose microphone for general production work. For best effect, it should be mounted in a shock-proof cradle that comes attached to a pistol grip. This in turn can be handheld for close-up vox-pops and piece-to-camera (PTC) work, or screwed on to the end of a telescopic boom. For outdoor work, a windshield is recommended, and further insulation from wind rumble can be achieved by enclosing this in a special artificial furry fabric, affectionately known as the 'dead sheep'.

■ **Tie-clip microphone**: These are ideal for more 'static' interview and discussion work, and can provide excellent sound levels through being placed close to the speaker's mouth, without obstructing the camera's view, due to its tiny size.

■ **Radio microphones**: When concealed in clothing, tie-clips are sometimes used with a small radio transmitter in fiction shoots, especially where dialogue occurs in a wide, panoramic shot that rules out any boom use. Equally, in news and documentary PTCs, their use can be effective in placing the presenter in the midst of a crowded scene, beginning the PTC on close-up, then slowly zooming out to reveal the full scene, with the camera at up to 50 yards from the journalist.

In addition, any of the full range of microphones outlined in the audio section can be used as required. The general point to remember with them all is that wind noise and any 'handling' of microphone or cable will be picked up as a distracting rumble.

Fictional approaches

Because drama production, especially on 'minimalist' budgets, is likely to be largely location work, many of the techniques outlined below under documentary approaches will apply. Above all, the question: *'Will it cut together?'* should be continually applied to each take.

Continuity

As well as closely observing action and detail, there are some techniques to help the flow of continuity. Firstly, it is agreed that cuts from wide shot to close-up draw attention to themselves far less if the cut is on the action (e.g., opening a door, drinking from a glass, taking out a wallet). To record the two shots in a way that ensures a smooth cut 'on the action', the action needs to be repeated *in its entirety* in the WS as well as the CU. This allows you, when editing, to choose the best possible moment, where hand positions and directions are near identical.

The imaginary line

If you are to maintain continuity and avoid audience disorientation, it is important not to 'cross the 180° line'. For example, if you are shooting a conversation between two people, the camera should remain on the same side of the imaginary line, otherwise the eyelines will not match and the participants will appear not to be talking to each other.

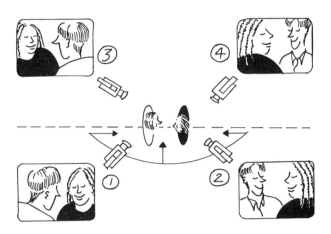

Fig 5.33 Crossing the line

The 'safe' approach

This tends to be used for dialogue scenes, with two or more characters, and involves shooting the whole scene three or four times through, using different angles and framings for your set-up each time. Imagine now that you have to shoot a tempestuous 'love triangle' scene between **Jim**, **Eric** and **Dorothea**.

See pp. 286–287 for explanations of P.O.V, Associated P.O.V, etc.

- Shoot the 'master scene' on a WS.
- Shoot MS or CU from associated P.O.V. of **Jim**.
- Shoot MS or CU from associated P.O.V. of **Eric**.
- Shoot MS or CU from associated P.O.V. of **Dorothea**.
- Shoot any BCUs or cut-ins as required.

This leaves *all* decision making about the 'look' and pace of the sequence to the editor, (or director/editor team) who effectively has to 'rescript' the visual sequence.

It is far better to have made decisions about P.O.Vs and camera angles *before* shooting the scene, so that you shoot the images you want to end up with, allowing for continuity 'overlaps'. Not only is this cheaper on time and patience, but also it is more likely to create a more purposeful, stylish working of the scene, with more sustained performances from the cast.

Performers

The general 'rule' for screen performance seems to be that *less is more*. The more that is done by *suggestion* (aided by the *mise-en-scène* and sound-track), the greater the realism and impact.

Working on dialogue and rehearsing with the cast the most 'natural' way for them to say things is time well spent. If the words sound false or 'bookish', change them.

It is very easy to become preoccupied with getting sound and vision technicalities sorted, meanwhile ignoring the performers. It is a good idea, once crew and set are sorted, to have a scene run-through, allowing for final touches to performance. Also, keep actors informed about progress, delays, etc., as it is very dispiriting to be kept hanging around, not knowing when you are on call and when you can relax.

Lighting

If you are trying to achieve 'realism' and 'authenticity', poor lighting is one of the first things to give the game away. Remember, you are lighting purely for what is on screen. Study carefully the monitor, checking for unnatural gleams and shadows, especially the boom microphone! Does the light look as if it is coming from natural sources? If not, change it until it is believable. As a research task, compare the lighting for *Coronation Street* (Granada TV) (studio-based overhead glare) with *Brookside* (Mersey TV) (shot with 'available light').

Documentary approaches

Documentary is 'the creative treatment of actuality'. John Grierson, (1932), 'First Principles of Documentary', *Cinema Quarterly*, Winter.

Moving away from purely technical operations, there are certain ways of going about productions that can help or hinder the programme's impact. Documentary directors' styles can be just as marked and distinctive as those of fiction directors. However, at the risk of over-simplification, they can generally be divided into two main approaches, which could be called 'interventionist' and 'non-interventionist'.

Interventionist approaches

The moment you begin to interview someone, your production is intervening in the world you are documenting and creating a new reality that relies on a kind of 'performance' from the interviewee who, faced with camera, microphone, crew and possibly lights, inevitably acts out a 'role', however genuine this role may be. This 'intervening' in reality also can apply to the recording of actions or activities as well as speech, particularly, as is often the case, if there is some kind of agreement between crew and subject as to how, when and where an activity can be filmed. (In other words a 'set-up'.)

A further level of intervention in portraying actuality occurs in the very obvious way the programme is *constructed* through a series of highly selective choices on a number of levels, arguing against any notion that documentaries are a 'window on the world' or a 'slice of life'.

Selection and construction

- The first level of selection happens with the choice of a situation for documentary production. This tends to be combined with an 'angle' the producer/director might have (For example, the feeling of an untold story that needs telling.)

- Individuals and locations are selected or discarded either for purely logistical reasons or according to whether they fit in with the 'angle' or story. This is no less true even if the programme is aiming for editorial 'balance' of views.

- Once recording is underway, the camera itself is selecting within a narrow frame, to the exclusion of the majority of the 360 degrees of vision around you, and the microphone is doing the same from an audio perspective. In both counts, *positioning* of the crew can place a vital slant on the recorded 'truth'.

- Time itself becomes another selection process: when to roll tape, when to pause. Similarly, the final edited programme is likely to have to meet a set running time.

- The final, perhaps most visible construction through selectivity occurs in the editing suite, where footage is chosen or discarded, combined in sequences to create new meanings, and ultimately an ordered *story* with conflict, development and resolution imposed on the random chaos of everyday life. Scripted voice-overs might be added, interpreting events on the audience's behalf. This is an example of 'mediation' where the programme makers are explaining or re-presenting the documented evidence to us, rather than presenting an 'open' text for our own personal interpretation. Add to this the varying levels of censorship and constraint under which programme makers work combined with the increased demand by broadcasters to entertain more than inform, and you end up with a highly refined, constructed version of the original actuality.

'Non-interventionist' approaches

No film-maker believes it is possible to avoid in some way influencing the actuality you wish to document, other than by purely concealed camera techniques, (which raise a host of ethical questions). However, certain film-makers have tried to keep their intervention to an absolute minimum.

The documentarists who set out to minimise the intervention, mediation and construction of their genre all had certain techniques in common:

- Never interviewing people (this being classed as 'performance'), but finding other ways to portray this personal information.
- Avoiding any 'set-ups' or reconstructions purely done for the camera's benefit.

■ Only using available light sources, and keeping the film crew presence to an absolute minimum to limit its influence.

■ Avoiding using any scripted voice-over in the editing of the final programme, leaving the footage to tell its own message and the audience to draw its own conclusions.

One of the best examples of this tradition of film-making is director Roger Graef, who has talked about other techniques he has used to limit 'intervention'. One such trick is to avoid all eye contact with people during a filming session, as this helps towards people gradually coming to regard the crew as simply 'part of the furniture', resulting in the likelihood of a more 'authentic' recording.

Note: Another common factor in this style of film-making is two-person crewing.

The following points will, be relevant whichever approach you adopt:

See Units 2 and 4 for interview techniques.

■ **Trust:** People you are filming need to trust you and your motives. Time must be spent on establishing this as a priority.

■ **Knowledge of subject:** Only careful, thorough research and familiarisation with the situation will reveal the hidden 'story' or the possible relevance of details to the overall structure.

■ **Interviewing technique:** Unless attempting a deliberately 'adversarial' interview, you should try to put interviewees at their ease, as the whole process is extremely nerve-racking. It is a good idea to have been interviewed yourself, with camera, microphone and lights to understand fully the tension involved.

Shooting for the edit

For documentary and drama, whatever approach you adopt, your footage will need editing into a sequence and structure that make sense to an audience. While 'shooting for the edit' cannot be taught as a straight 'lesson', it must be continually highlighted as a reminder to you to find the shots that will help weave a visual story in post-production. Your edited storyboard tasks should have shown you what 'cuts together', and similar guidelines apply, whether you are shooting fiction or non-fiction. Here are some practical points:

■ **Cutaways and cut-ins:** These are essential not only to illustrate points raised in interviews or narration, but also to provide edit 'links' or to mask 'jump cuts' created by editing out footage. If you are shooting a sequence of someone working, cut-ins (e.g., close-ups on hands or face concentrating on the task) also provide valuable edit links.

■ **'Three-in-one' shot:** If you intend to use a camera movement, (e.g., zoom, pan), there is a simple technique you can apply to provide *three* possible shots for the editing stage. Firstly, having framed up on your starting shot, roll VCR for ten seconds pre-roll, then keep it rolling for another five seconds before beginning your movement (which should itself take no more than five seconds), keep the VCR rolling on your end shot for a further five or six seconds. This gives you three possible shots to choose from in the editing stage.

■ **Interview shot sizes:** When shooting interviews that follow a fairly clear question/answer format, agree an approach with your camera operator whereby with each new question, the camera reframes to a significantly different shot size. This should be done for two reasons:

(a) When editing, all the unwanted camera reframing movement can be edited out, along with your questions.

(b) It allows you to cut into the answers, making possible visual edits (say from MS to CU), that actually work on the eye as a 'continuity' cut, while allowing you to condense your interview considerably. (This is a standard news interview technique.)

Interview as narration

If you are using interview speech as part of your narration, it is advisable to interview your subject *first*, then arrange a shoot that will 'illustrate' the issues raised in the interview, providing you with a match between 'commentary' and relevant cutaway footage.

Buzz track

See Unit 1, p. 22 interview with Mandy Rose.

When shooting on location, background or 'ambient' sounds are continually changing. In cutting together a sequence (i.e., making jumps in 'real time'), we might achieve continuity in the visuals, but the audio track is likely to crash all over the place in both levels and content. As a technique to give the illusion of audio continuity, it is standard practice to record a minute or so of purely continuous 'atmos' sound-track at a constant level on to your videotape. (Use the opportunity to pick up some extra cutaways at the same time.) When you come to edit your sequence, having cut the visuals together, you can now lay down a continuous sound-track which will create an even stronger illusion of continuity on your audience, enhancing your programme's impact.

Background music

As well as this technical consideration, there is also a legal one: recording the music, even from a jukebox in the background, constitutes a potential copyright infringement. Does your budget cover this?

If you are shooting in a location with music on in the background (e.g., a pub), you should try to have the music turned off while you record. Failure to do this means that when you come to edit, the song in the background jumps from mid-verse to mid-chorus and back again in a highly distracting, comical way. In the edit, if you wish to recreate the pub 'ambience', lay down a continuous piece of music.

5.3 POST-PRODUCTION — EDIT MOVING IMAGE PRODUCTS

The post-production process

Before you begin the final edit on the 'fine cut', there are a number of stages to go through to order your material and save time and money:

- Reviewing and logging footage.
- Doing a 'paper edit'.
- Arranging additional material (voice-over, music, SFX, captions, graphics, etc.).
- Producing a 'rough cut' (off-line edit).
- Editing the 'fine cut' (on-line).
- Screening (to colleagues, client, audience sample).

Reviewing and logging footage

This process should be ongoing throughout the production stage, so that any necessary re-shoots do not disrupt the process too dramatically. **Logging** involves playing back footage, pausing with each new shot to make a note on your logsheet of the shot length, a brief 'shorthand' description and some comment as to its value and

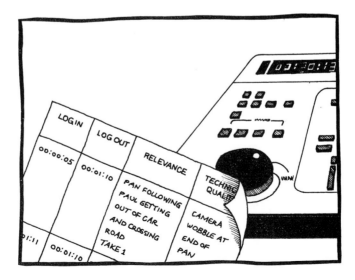

Fig 5.34 Logging footage

suitability in terms of vision and sound. If your recording has on-screen time-code, this helps greatly; otherwise you can use the 'real time' counter from the edit controller, having 'zeroed' it at the tape's beginning. If neither of these are available, use a standard VCR counter (although you should be aware that unless they are referenced to actual time, it is rare to find two VCR counters that match).

The paper edit

Going through your logsheets with a highlighter pen, you should now be ready to make choices, selecting and discarding shots according to relevance, content and technical quality. If you are working to a tight script or storyboard (e.g., for fiction or commercials), then the next stage, actually putting the shots into a running order, becomes relatively straightforward. If, however, you are working on a documentary or more experimental form, then this stage is possibly the most difficult, as you are trying to create order and narrative 'sense' out of your gathered material. A tried and tested technique to help this process is to use small adhesive 'Post-it' cards, writing different shots or 'items' on to them, with their time code, until you have covered all the shots you intend to use. From your pre-production research and treatment, you should have some notion of the main blocks or elements of your programme. Divide up a large sheet of card into these sections, and begin to stick the 'Post-its' on to the sections to which they seem most relevant. With a little more sifting and ordering within each section on the card, you now have the makings of an **edit decision list (EDL)**, and can write them up as a straight list of shots to assemble. This list is also known as an 'edit script' or 'shot assembly list'.

Arranging additional material

You need to have all the basic constituents of your programme ready before the fine cut. This might involve:

- Deciding on music/SFX (including clearances).
- Arranging for captions/graphics/rostrum work that cannot be produced in the edit suite.
- Scripting and recording any additional voice-over narration (e.g., on to reel to reel tape).

Producing a rough cut

This stage is optional in the process, but is a normal next step in professional production, and is strongly recommended if time and resources allow. Firstly the source footage is copied on to other cassettes, usually of a cheaper, lower format like VHS or Lo-Band Umatic. Where possible, these copies will have the time code 'burnt in' on screen. You can now go away and do the most time-consuming part on a cheaper edit suite that costs the same to hire for a week as a full broadcast on-line suite costs for a morning. Also, continually searching through, forwarding and reversing tape can cause wear and tear and 'drop-out'. Consequently it is better for this to happen on rough copies rather than the precious master footage itself. The master tapes remain safely boxed until the fine cut.

The rough cut need not involve all the mixes and SFX of the finished product. Indeed it might be purely an 'assembly' of the material into a working 'draft'. What this rough cut provides though, if you are working for a client, is a vital document for feedback. The client can watch the cut and make any suggestions as to suitability of content, reinforcement of messages, etc. Consequently, any problem can be ironed out *before* the fine cut, the client is content at having been consulted and involved, and you should now be free to get on with it without interference or comeback!

Fine cut (on-line edit)

Post-production technologies are continually up-dating with 'non-linear' digital equipment becoming the norm as a professional facility. However, the craft of telling stories or communicating effectively with sound and vision is still down to your imagination and creativity, and this will not change. The fine cut pulls together all the elements you have been working on: sound, vision, SFX, graphics, voice-over, etc.

Screening

As soon as your fine cut is complete, it is useful to show your programme to others immediately for feedback. This screening could be to colleagues, a client or a targeted audience, and it is important to listen to and evaluate any constructive criticism. Remember that you have been working so closely to your material that you can become blind or deaf to some mistakes which you might still *just* have time to remedy or improve.

Video editing techniques

There are two basic modes: **insert** and **assemble**. To understand them requires an introduction to videotape and how it records video and audio signals.

Videotape format

Like audio tape, videotape is made up from a fine coating of tiny magnetic particles upon a plastic backing strip. The recording process involves minute electrical signals from the record heads (video and audio) aligning these microscopic particles according to the signal's 'message'. This process is known as 'writing'. The aligned particles can then be 'read' by playback heads, converting back into an electrical current that can be amplified and reproduced through screen and speaker.

Video signal

Although invisible to the eye, the tape surface divides into different areas, where separate signals are recorded. By far the largest area of the tape is taken up by the video signal, written on to the tape by a record head on a fast rotating drum, spinning at high speed against the tape in a 'helical scan', writing diagonal lines on the tape, each line representing one line of television picture.

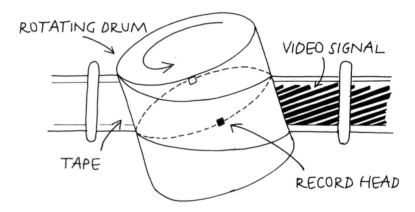

HELICAL SCANNING

ROTATING DRUM

VIDEO SIGNAL

TAPE

RECORD HEAD

Fig 5.35

Audio signal

The two separate audio tracks can be recorded as linear tracks on to the tape in exactly the same way as a conventional cassette recorder.

Hi-fi audio

Increasingly, professional and 'semi-professional' machines can also record audio in hi-fi mode, where an FM audio signal is encoded beneath the video signal, the wider bandwidth and faster writing speed resulting in 'near CD' quality sound recording. (You still need healthy sound levels though.)

Control track

Along the edge of the tape, regular synchronising (sync) pulses are recorded which allow for accurate scanning and playback of the video track, in the same way that sprocket holes on film keep the frames steady on screen. Should damage occur to these pulses, such as by copying down 'generations', through magnetic exposure or tape 'drop out', (magnetic particles becoming detached from the tape), then the television picture will shake and roll at these points.

A basic edit suite

Although it might seem daunting, it is a very useful exercise to strip down the external cables from an edit suite and reconnect according to a diagram and to your logic. This can prove invaluable in practical problem solving such as tracing faulty cables/connectors that might otherwise delay progress.

The edit controller

This is the heart of the suite, and simply duplicates many of the familiar control buttons on the front of the VCR for ease of use. In addition there are other key controls specifically to do with the editing process: for example **assemble/insert**. You can choose the mode in which you wish to edit. Unless you are in a hurry and cutting together a very basic sequence, choose insert mode, as this provides you with far more flexibility.

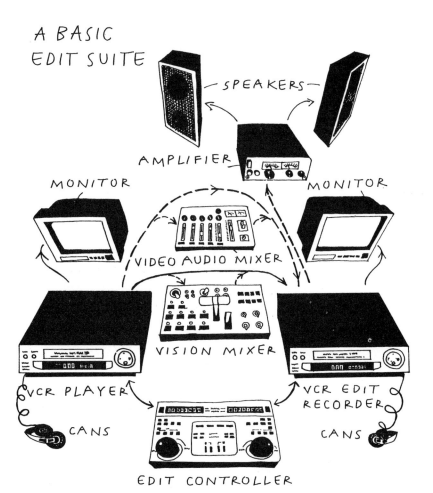

Fig 5.36 A basic edit suite

Insert editing

This presents you with options regarding exactly what you wish to record on your edit master tape. You might wish to lay down sound and vision together, but leave one audio channel free for later insertion of music, voice-over or buzz track. Equally you might want to lay down a soundtrack first and then edit visual images that cut in time with the beats. (Many music videos are produced this way.) Or you may simply wish to lay down a video image on its own.

However, in order to do this form of editing, it is first necessary to 'sync' up the tape on which you wish to edit. This can be done by recording a constant camera signal through the length of the tape, either with the camera set to 'colour bars' or 'blacked' with closed aperture or lens cap on. Equally, if you have a vision mixer that can supply a 'black burst' signal, you can take a video cable from this, plugging into 'video in' on your VCR.

Once recording is underway, it must not be interrupted or paused, as this will break the continuous sync pulse, resulting in picture roll or break up when you come to edit over this part of the tape. Having 'synced' or 'blacked' your tape, when you now 'insert' edit, you are leaving the control track pulses intact, and merely inserting video or audio signals on to the tape.

Assemble editing

This works in the same way that standard recording operates. An erase head wipes all before it, then video, audio and control track are recorded together, the control track losing a generation as it is copied across. Each new edit simply picks up the pulse from the end of the previous one.

The art of editing

A book cannot teach the mechanics of editing. This requires personal demonstration by a skilled trainer, practice and play to reinforce techniques on the equipment itself. However, there are certain techniques that can usefully be learnt:

- Selection and cutting points.
- Timing and pace.
- Transitions (audio and video).
- Digital video effects (DVE).

Selection and cutting points

The critical choices should have happened at the 'paper edit' stage, but there is more precise fine-tuning in selecting within a particular shot. Here, cutting points are critical, and learning where best to begin and end a shot becomes an art in itself. The main guideline should be according to the interest of the *content*. In documentary work, choose the part of the shot where there is most relevant movement or activity. Avoid cutting during camera movements, (pans, zooms, tilts, etc.), and allow them to run in their entirety. If they are too long, scrap them! Be prepared to abandon some beautiful shots of which you are justifiably proud, because they simply might not be relevant or usable, or might duplicate what you have already.

Timing and pace

By speeding up the number of your edits, using shorter cuts or by slowing them down, you can dramatically alter the pace and impact of your programme. Pace need not be constant, and it is good to vary it. But this 'gear change' should complement the content and message of the shots, rather than being a random decision.

Transitions

How you get from one shot to the next is a major part of the editor's craft, and might involve four main devices: **cuts, mixes, fades** and **wipes**.

- **Cuts:** These are the most frequent device used, and entire programmes can be made without resort to any other device. They are at their most effective when creating the illusion of continuity, but equally can create an interesting 'counterpoint' when cutting between different locations (or times).
- **Mixes:** This device is beyond basic two machine editing, as it requires two separate source images (from separate VCRs) to be 'mixed' or 'dissolved' together as a transition from one to the next. This requires a three-machine edit suite and a vision mixer to achieve, though with trial and error, much is possible through manually cueing up and operating a third VCR (allowing for pre-roll time), as long as the edit does not have to be too accurate. (A vision mixer is still unavoidable though.)
  A mix provides a smoother, more 'hypnotic' transition, particularly suited to a slower pace of editing, but also suggestive of a shift in continuity of time and place. The slower the mix transition time, the 'dreamier' the impression. Leaving the mixer level in mid-position will create a super-imposed image.
- **Fades:** Most programmes begin and end with a fade to and from black. As a transition, it is a simple way of moving on in time and place.
- **Wipes:** These come in a variety of styles, some of which are frankly grotesque! In some ways, they represent 'turning a page', and consequently tend to be more suited to a more regimented presentation of information, such as news or informational training programming. As pure 'techno-flash',

however, they are much used (and abused) in corporate 'promos'.

■ **Digital video effects:** Many vision mixers, as well as having the potential to mix and fade, also have a sometimes bewildering array of special effects, typically including assorted **wipes, strobe, 'mosaic pixellation', chromakey, etc**. It is probably a good idea to have a really self-indulgent 'binge' on them, and then after that to use them *sparingly* and with good reason.

See also multi-camera techniques, p. 336.

Editing sound on video

This is the area where most care needs to be taken if you are to produce professional quality video work, as it is a bad sound track that can reduce an otherwise good-looking programme to a poor, 'amateur' level. Areas to concentrate on are **sound levels** and **transitions**.

Sound levels

The first principle is that you should take just as much care over sound editing as over visual images. When recording sounds from source footage (or elsewhere) to the edit master tape, check the sound level on the VU meter through a **preview** edit first, making necessary adjustments. Speech that is intended to be 'up front' (e.g., narration, interview, foreground dialogue), should be set to the usual level, averaging at approximately–4 to–3 dB.

If your suite has a sound mixer with a tone generator, then, for most consistent results, you should set your edit VCR's VU meter to 0 dB as the setting for the constant 1 KHz tone. Thereafter, all sound level adjustments should be done by using the mixer's faders, not the VCR's level pot. It is also good practice to record several seconds of this tone at the beginning of your edit master tape, as this helps with setting levels for duplication or transmission.

However, because you have *two* audio channels to play with, remember that if you want speech on one channel, you will *not* want fully modulated sound on the other channel (e.g., music, SFX, actuality), as this will 'do battle' with the speech channel on playback, and you will struggle to distinguish what is said. Consequently, when laying down non-speech audio, it is best to do this *after* having recorded the speech channel, so that it can be 'mixed under' the speech, (say at–10 dB), then 'mixed up' again when speech ceases. For this reason, it is a good idea to try to keep all speech to the same channel throughout the edit.

Transitions

These are audio equivalents to the visual fades and mixes that are just as effective and necessary to the programme's impact.

■ **Fades:** Where possible, fade sound in and out to accompany scene transitions. It can also be a good idea with individual edits to 'snap in' the sound (fade up quickly), if there are differing levels of ambient noise, as this prevents the impression of sharp audio cuts, as one 'wall' of sound meets another. A separate sound mixer is useful for this, as it gives more control over the fade than the VCR's recording level pot.

■ **Cross-fades:** An even more 'seamless' way of drawing your audience from one scene into the next is by making full use of both sound channels, by slowly bringing up the sound of the next scene subtly before the previous scene is over, while allowing the sound of that scene to fade under the next. This takes practice, but is very rewarding in its psychological effect.

Non-linear editing

Conventional editing of videotape from one VCR to another, involving spooling through footage to find each shot, is a 'linear' process, as the edit itself is dependent on one shot after another being locked into a particular time and place on the tape. These shots cannot be removed without leaving a gap to fill, while any reordering of shots requires an entirely new edit. Non-linear editing (sometimes known as **random access editing**), has similarities with new multi-media technology, using a computer and vast digitised memory storage. In simple terms, it works in the following way: selected source footage is digitised into binary code, by playing the footage in through video and audio input connectors in the computer, (just like copying on to a VCR), and is stored there on hard disk.

(Each frame of video image is 'memory hungry', requiring considerable storage.) The higher the resolution of the image, the more memory is required.

There are several major advantages to this system:

■ Through calling up any shot's time-code, it can be instantly accessed (as opposed to spooling through yards of videotape).
■ Edit decision lists (EDLs) can be 'typed' in, and left to the computer to assemble and play back to you, complete with fades, mixes, DVE and digital sound mix. (Typically, 16 channels of digital sound recording and mixing are available.) Any shots that you want to lose or reorder simply requires a quick alteration to the EDL.
■ With the arrival of digital sourcing through digital cameras, the entire process need never leave the digital medium, resulting in *no generation loss whatsoever*, given that digital broadcasting down Telecom lines completes the picture.

Non-linear editing is now becoming the norm in post-production facilities companies and broadcasting.

Health and safety with editing

The main issues with editing are similar to general VDU operator guidelines. Eyestrain, fatigue, headaches and disorientation can and do result from extended editing stints. To reduce this, regular breaks, at least every two hours, need to be taken, preferably going outside where you can focus eyes on horizons and freshen ideas. Chairs should give adequate back support and be at an appropriate height for arms to rest on the desk-top to use the edit controller without strain or discomfort. Monitors should ideally be at head level, and about three feet away from eyes.

Multi-camera studio techniques

Relatively low budget vision mixers can now 'lock' two camera inputs together to allow you to mix 'live' between two cameras, creating the basics for a multi-camera studio. Add to this a simple talk-back system, extra monitors to view the separate camera frames, appropriate microphones, and you have something approximating a multi-camera studio set-up.

This equipment rig need not be tied to any one building, but can be set up as an 'outside broadcast' exercise to cover events such as theatrical productions, live bands, dance, sports, etc., giving a whole new dimension to production work, while placing a strong emphasis on effective crewing in large teams.

Fig 5.37   Multi-camera set up

Basic studio procedures

An agreed 'language' (instructions) must be understood by all. Having overseen crew, lighting, camera positions and sound requirements, the director's role is to give a continual stream of instructions to camera operators and vision and sound mixers. (In fact, in a small crew, if the director can vision mix too, that cuts out one level of communication.) Through quick thinking and careful 'juggling', it is possible to achieve the impression of a complex four-camera shoot with just two. Instructions must be quick and accurate, though.

Instructions

The first two camera shots can be set up in advance, sound levels checked and the VCR set to roll. Immediately the intercom instructions begin and will sound something like this:

'On camera one.' (Camera one's shot is being recorded.)

'Camera two, find a close-up on guitarist's left hand.' (Waits for shot to steady itself in the preview monitor.)

'Cutting to camera two.' (Warning vision mixer and alerts camera two to hold shot steady.)

'On camera two.' (This frees up camera one to find next shot.)

'Camera one, find a two-shot of bass and drummer.' (Waits for shot to steady.)

'Mixing to camera one.' (Warns camera one and vision mixer.)

'On camera one.' (This frees up camera two.)

Another production that allows more planning of shots can be a short scripted studio drama, where camera shots, angles and moves are planned in advance so that the operators and vision mixer are working to shot lists and dialogue cues. With careful rehearsal, this kind of live studio drama could be produced even if you lacked a studio talk-back system.

The 'safety' shot

Inevitably, mistakes are made, such as cutting to a camera while it is still wildly searching for the next shot. Given that you can edit your footage, it can be a good idea to have a third camera/camcorder set up for the performance that is recording a separate take. You can now drop in or 'insert' (video only) the relevant footage to 'mask over' your errors, creating a more polished production, and adding yet another camera angle.

5.4 REVIEW AND EVALUATE MOVING IMAGE PRODUCTS

Process and product

See pp. 255 to 260

Exactly the same procedures and concerns described in Unit 4.4 should be applied here. The production log, again, is an invaluable record of the process as well as being an excellent way of constructing your own personalised production manual. When evaluating the technical quality of your video you need to consider:

- framing;
- focus;
- camera movements;
- transitions (sound and vision);
- accuracy of editing (continuity, too soon, too late);
- microphone technique ('popping', 'sibilance', 'rumble', moving from interviewee too soon, etc.).

How does your programme stand up?

Comparing your productions with existing broadcast or recorded material will help you analyse the way in which you have tackled your project. As suggested in Unit 4, it is a good idea to use one of the concepts introduced in Unit 1, for example, narrative, representation or genre, and write a detailed critical analysis of films or television programmes into which you incorporate your own production, thereby gathering further portfolio evidence for Unit 1.

EVIDENCE COLLECTION POINT

A number of fictional and non-fictional themes have been suggested throughout this unit. In addition, you will have developed a number of ideas as evidence for Element 2.4. By following the production process from conception of the idea through the three stages of production, and review and evaluation, you will have ample evidence for all of Unit 5, as well as Element 2.4. You should check carefully the evidence indicators in each element and ensure that you carry out the necessary tasks described in the performance criteria to produce the requirements.

ASSIGNMENT 1

Planning and producing a magazine programme

You are a production company, producing items for a magazine programme aimed at a 'youth' audience (14 −21). The programme is transmitted on Channel 4 twice a week, between 11pm and midnight. The programme consists of several features on topics that would be of interest to a 'youth' audience. Bearing in mind Channel 4 remit to be innovative in its presentation and style, and to address issues that would interest minorities, you are required to research, plan and produce a two-minute feature for the programme. Timing must be exact — there is no room for error.

■ Carry out research to establish the style and content appropriate for this programme slot (audience questionnaire, studying existing 'youth' programming, magazines, etc.)

■ Prepare treatment, for approval.

■ Prepare necessary pre-production documentation, as appropriate for item (script for fiction/shot list for non-fiction, budget, etc.).

■ Carry out production research and plan the shoot (recce, permissions, risk assessment for health and safety, schedule, call sheets, obtaining appropriate equipment and resources, etc.).

■ Shoot and edit the piece, following industrial working practices.

■ Screen and present items to your class.

Optional:

■ Discuss ways in which items could be linked to form a complete show.

■ Design graphics, title sequence, presenter links if appropriate.

■ Shoot additional material and produce a complete programme, incorporating all of the links.

■ Screen to a 'youth' audience, and obtain feedback to be incorporated into your evaluation.

This assignment could be done as individual pieces (obviously, you will need a crew for the shoot, but the items could be devised, planned and edited individually), or as group assignments. You may wish to keep each 'item' as a separate piece of evidence, or you may wish to take the optional steps to make a complete show.

You could choose to produce pieces relevant to other parts of the GNVQ course. Items on jobs in the media, or issues of censorship, for instance, could help you produce evidence towards Unit 8 requirements.

ASSIGNMENT 2

Planning and producing a training video 'in the style of.'

You have been commissioned by the local Post Office Cadets Training programme to produce a health and safety training video. The video should communicate the various hazards that might face a post office worker on his or her rounds (this could be anything from lifting heavy weights correctly to dealing with over-zealous guard dogs). The audience is aged primarily between 16 and 20 and you have been asked to inject a note of humour into what can, otherwise, be a dull, if essential, aspect of the training programme.

You have decided that one way to do this is to use a recognisable genre, such as thriller, romance, horror or silent movie, as a device in which you can both get the message across, and entertain your audience.

- Carry out research to establish the issues that need to be covered.

- Carry out research to confirm your understanding of the codes and conventions of your chosen genre.

- Plan, produce, edit and present your video to an audience. (It would be excellent if you could encourage your local post-office trainers, or employees to come and view your efforts, providing you with real client feedback to incorporate into your evaluation and review).

- Compare your video with other training videos and evaluate the effectiveness of both.

You may be able to make use of this project as evidence for Element 1.3.

ASSIGNMENT 3

Planning and producing a promotional video

Recent research undertaken by Skillset, the Industry Lead Body for Film, Television and Video has demonstrated that women continue to be underrepresented in the industry, particularly in the technical grades.

Your media department at college has noticed that it has recruited very few young women to the GNVQ Media: Communication Production course. The college has an equal opportunities policy and actively tries to encourage girls and women into traditionally male domains.

You have been commissioned to produce a three-minute promotional video for the college open days, and subsequent visits to local secondary schools, which encourages young women to apply for the course. Your audience is 15–16 years of age.

Using the evidence checklist to guide you through the process, plan and produce this promotional video. If it is possible for your school or college to make use of it in a real marketing situation, you will have excellent feedback to incorporate into your review and evaluation of the product.

Information gathered in the making of this project will be useful to underpin some of the requirements of Element 8.4.

You may wish to adapt this brief to look at other areas of underrepresentation, for instance, to encourage boys to do secretarial courses, or nursery nursing; girls into engineering., etc.

ASSIGNMENT 4

Planning and producing a regional news programme

You are a journalist working with the regional news team for the commercial station in your region. After the 6pm networked news, there is a ten-minute regional news slot. Working as part of a small team, you will:

■ Identify current local, topical issues and list them.

■ Carry out research and assess the information in terms of relevance to the issues, topicality and human interest.

■ Plan the ten-minute programme, breaking it down into items and links, using the appropriate planning format. This forms the programme brief from which you are to work.

■ Decide who in the team will cover what and individually carry out any further research required prior to recording the material for your item.

■ Plan for your production by scheduling interviews, vox-pops, booking equipment and arranging transport.

■ Record material, including, as appropriate, interviews, vox-pops, actuality.

■ Edit each item into a 'package', order them, construct the links and produce the entire programme.

If you have the facilities, you should endeavour to 'play in' each package to live links from the studio. If not, you should edit the packages and links together to produce a pre-recorded programme.

To get a real sense of the immediacy and pressure of news programming, you should try to undertake this exercise as a one-day project, transmitting at 6.15pm on the dot!

ASSIGNMENT 5

Different ways to tell a story

Choose a story from the daily newspaper and summarise it. Take the summary and use it to plan and produce:

■ A news report.

■ A piece of scripted drama (no more than two minutes).

■ A 30-second advertisement (you may wish to take the scenario and adapt it to sell a product; or you may wish to use the essence of the story as a campaigning advertisement, for instance, if it is about pollution, or cuts to the health service).

ASSIGNMENT 6

Brief Endeavours

Brief Endeavours is a regional production scheme aimed at new talent. It is operated by your local Regional Arts Board or Media Development Agency and has additional funding from the regional commercial television station. Brief Endeavours commissions new work which demonstrates an innovative — possibly experimental — approach to a regional theme. Six five-minute shorts are commissioned each year and they are transmitted during the spring schedule, after the regional news headlines at 10.45pm. The budget is up to £10,000.

Some regions fund cultural or arts-based film and video projects through a Regional Arts Board (e.g., North West Arts, Eastern Arts). Other regions have Media Development Agencies to deal with cultural film and video production e.g., London has the London Film and Video Development Agency; the South West has the South West Media Development Agency, based in Bristol). Detail of this arts funding structure can be found in Unit 8.

■ Prepare an outline and treatment and submit it to Brief Endeavours for consideration (your tutor could role-play this function, or you could set up a panel of representatives from your school or college's art department, media department and literature department to make the selections). With your outline and treatment, you should include your curriculum vitae and, if available, a showreel of your best work to date. You should also prepare a budget, costing your production as though you were able to shoot it on broadcast-standard equipment. *This part of the assignment should be carried out individually.*

■ If your treatment is selected by the panel, you will act as director for the production. If your treatment is not selected, you will act as a crew member for another member of your group.

■ Plan and produce your commissioned 'Brief Endeavour', and present it to the selection panel for feedback and evaluation.

Note: You are required to keep full production stills as a condition of the grant from the Arts Board or Media Development Agency, and equal opportunities is an absolute requirement in terms of your working practice (how you recruit and deal with your crew, for instance).

6 INVESTIGATING AND CARRYING OUT AUDIENCE RESEARCH AND ANALYSIS

Anyone who lives in a technologically-based society has a massive experience of being part of innumerable media audiences.

It is not surprising then that this aspect of our lives is discussed not just in Media Studies but in many other academic disciplines as well, such as sociology, anthropology, law, government and politics and in the better English courses. More than any other area of Media Studies, ideas about audiences have a wide circulation particularly when it comes to the fraught question of the influence or 'effects' certain kinds of media texts have on society. You are as likely to hear views on this issue from politicians, the church, feminists, from media workers, from parents, teachers, community leaders and social workers.

Another enormously important player in this arena is the advertising industry. Advertising is a multi-billion pound industry and clearly the people involved in the process of making, placing and (especially!) paying for adverts have a keen interest in knowing the size of the audience reached and the effects of their efforts on the buying public. For this reason, finding out about media audiences has become a commercial enterprise with huge amounts of money spent on research daily.

The different concerns of commercial audience research and sociological/psychological research on media audience behavior are explored in this unit.

By the time you begin your own audience research project you will have realised that the area is a very complicated one. It can be easy to get lost in the welter of research methods and academic theories, hypotheses, results, research organisations, etc. To make matters simpler it is worth keeping the following questions in your mind whenever you encounter a piece of audience research:

- Who is researching?
- What topic?
- Why are they doing it?
- Who is paying the bill?
- What are the methods being used?
- What are the conclusions drawn?
- Do their methods and conclusions seem justified?

6.1 INVESTIGATE THE USE OF AUDIENCE RESEARCH IN THE MEDIA

The main areas of concern for this element can be summarised by this set of questions:

- To what uses is media research put?
- How is it carried out? What methods are used?
- How is the audience subdivided (into 'children', 'target markets', into different kinds of categories)?
- Who carries out this research? What groups, what agencies?

The uses of audience research

Commercial users of research are motivated by the need to sell a product or service. They need audience information to know where best to locate their advertisements and how to design their message. Audience figures help them to make these decisions and help the media to prove that a particular purchase of advertising time or space will be effective. Advertisements that go out at times of peak viewing/listening or are placed in the most advantageous position in a magazine will cost more, so research into audience size helps to establish a kind of currency for buying and selling advertising space. In broadcasting, for example, there is the concept 'cost per thousand' (CPT): audience members likely to be reached by a particular advertising slot.

Media organisations themselves (or at least the majority which carry advertising) are also therefore 'commercial users' of research, since they need the results to price and sell one of their products — advertising space. Organisations like the BBC may also need research for commercial reasons, like convincing the government of the value of the licence fee.

Academic or social users of research are more interested in the relationship between media and society. Their questions will be motivated by social and intellectual concerns. A typical question might be: how well are particular communities served by the media? Do media broadcasts affect behaviour like voting patterns or attitudes to women at work? There is no direct commercial benefit to asking these questions. They are motivated by a concern for people or just a simple desire to know, so these questions tend to have a more philosophical tone. As a general rule, commercial users of research will be very interested in audience figures (quantities) while academic and social users will be equally or more interested in the less countable aspects like the effect of a TV report.

However, these distinctions between the two kinds of users are rather crude generalisations. A university, for example, might be sponsored by government to do a piece of research about comics and children — social research — but its motive for taking it on may be largely commercial — to bring in funds. Also we should not think of all commercial research as just head counting. Sometimes commercial researchers seek to uncover very subtle and deeply

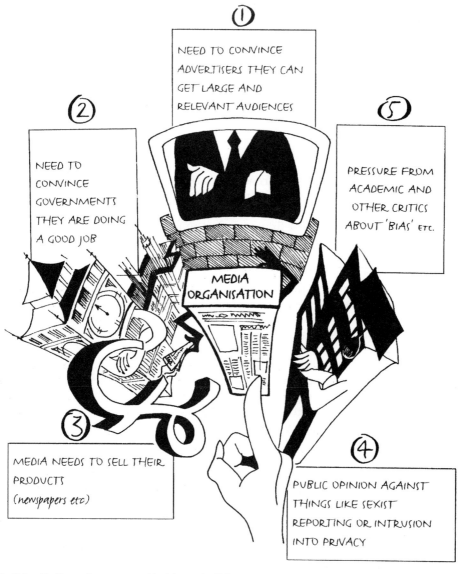

Fig 6.1 Media audiences are subject to contradictory pressures

held attitudes like the kind of values and associations that spring to mind in relation to a particular brand name (fresh? cheap? sexy? reliable? fun?). As well as this, commercially produced work like the audience figures for the numbers of people watching top TV programmes per week produced by the Broadcasting Audience Research Bureau (BARB) are widely used in academic research projects. So there is a movement between the worlds of commercial and academic research. The main difference between the two lies not so much in the kind of material uncovered as in the reason for asking the particular questions.

The place of the media itself

These two agendas, the commercial and the academic/social can sometimes leave the media itself in a difficult position. For example, on the one hand, there may be a need to convince advertisers that audiences are deeply affected by advertising at the same time as denying responsibility for other kinds of undesirable effects that might be produced by other media content. Media owners have sometimes to tread a careful line between the influences represented in the figure below.

Commercial audience research

See p. 371 for more detailed impormation on BARB.

In general commercially based research is carried out by specialist agencies which then sell on the information to regular buyers.

Media owners and media corporations

Organisations like cinema chains, magazines, radio stations, commercial TV channels need audience facts and figures for two reasons. The first is to check how they and their competitors are doing in the market and to look out for any trends up or down in audience size. The second is so that they can price and sell their advertising space. For both purposes they need, ideally, information that extends beyond audience size (though this is crucial) and says something about the types of people regularly listening, watching or reading. The importance of advertising revenue is enormous. As consumers we tend to think of advertising as taking up a small part of the media, so many minutes per hour or so much space per page. However, in economic terms it is much more important. The national paper you buy probably gets up to 70% of its revenue from advertising, obviously a much higher percentage than it receives from selling newspapers. Your local free-sheet is 100% dependent on advertising. If that stops coming in, the business folds. This means that newspapers and other media organisations need to operate in two markets: the market for advertisers and the market for buyers. (This does not mean that the market for buyers is less important, however. Rather the opposite, because it is the size of this market that 'delivers' the advertisers to their door.)

Advertisers

For the same reason, advertisers have very similar needs for audience information. They need to be convinced both about the potential size of their audience but also its relevance to their product in terms of age, gender, geographical area and, importantly, class and income.

> **TASK**
>
> Take two daily newspapers that are obviously aimed at different social groups (e.g., the *Sun* and the *Guardian*, the *Daily Mail* and the *Financial Times* and write a page and a half on each analysing the advertising content alone. Can you deduce the kind of person the newspaper and its advertisers see as their 'typical reader(s)' from the advertisements alone? You could test your own analysis against the assumptions made by the newspapers themselves by obtaining their rate cards and descriptions of target audience.

Demography: information about the characteristics of groups of people.

On the basis of this kind of **demographic** information, the advertiser needs to make some risky judgements. Increasing the spread of advertising on any one day may increase the number of people exposed to the advert ('coverage'). On the other hand, the message might be more effectively reinforced by targeting a smaller group initially but then increasing the number of times the ad might be seen by repeating it over a number of days or weeks ('frequency').

Advertising agencies

Usually a company will have a good idea of the kinds of people it is hoping to talk to through advertising — its target market — although it is not unusual for a larger concern to commission a research project from a market research company to find out, for example, if there are other markets it has not thought about or if its advertising campaign is reaching the right people. When it comes to designing and placing advertisements, however, most large companies seek professional help from advertising agencies. These agencies base their advice on a knowledge of the psychology of advertising and, importantly, a knowledge of media consumption patterns. This knowledge will come form three sources:

- Previous experience in working for other clients;
- The agency's own market research;
- Market information bought regularly from research agencies like BARB, RAJAR, CAA. These commercially run research

See p. 371.

agencies specialise in producing information on audiences for a particular medium (eg. radio or posters) and selling it on to people who need it. Sometimes information collected overnight — like how many people were likely to have seen a particular advert on television on any particular evening — can be dumped 'raw' (i.e., as unanalysed statistics) on the agency's computers ready for it to analyse and present to its clients the next morning.

Users of audience data — media professionals.

The launch of *The Sunday Planet* was imminent at the time of writing.

Many of the people who work in the media need to use audience information to carry out their day-to-day jobs. Newspaper editors need to know how their paper is selling against the opposition. For example, the tabloids recently went through a fairly vicious price-cutting war to try to encroach upon each other's markets — a fact that is commented on the article below. Knowledge about potential media audiences is also clearly crucial to the development of new media products and this is one reason for the TV mini-series: it allows a chance to gauge audience response to the new product before launching into long-term production. In the article below, the journalist Roy Greenslade questions whether the people at the new Sunday publication, the *Planet on Sunday*, have made correct calculations about the existence of an audience in an already crowded market-place.

Latest figures show that the Sunday newspaper market is declining by 10 per cent a year. So what possible chance has next month's launch of Planet on Sunday, a new middle market tabloid with an environmental agenda? Even if it has bought the rights to the Dan Dare comic strip.
Roy Greenslade reports

Saving the Planet... can the Eagle's famous comic strip character, Dan Dare, ensure a safe take off for next month's launch of the new tabloid title, Planet on Sunday?

Why on earth?

JOURNALISM breeds optimists. No matter that total Sunday newspaper sales are declining at the rate of 10 per cent a year. No matter that the Mail on Sunday is on the crest of a wave. No matter that the only national paper ever to adopt a Green perspective, Today, quickly dropped it. For next month sees the launch of the Planet on Sunday, aimed at the middle market with an environmental agenda.

Editor Austin Mitchelson, whose previous claim to fame was launching Sunday Sport, is seeking 250,000 buyers for his 48-page tabloid at a cover price of "65p or thereabouts". He says: "We're going to compete directly with the Mail on Sunday and Sunday Express. We'll have strong conservation and wildlife content, taking up issues that people are really interested in and which affect them, like BSE."

It is a self-consciously shoestring operation with a launch budget of just £500,000, funded by its owner, Clifford Hards, a holiday and travel business entrepreneur. Apart from Mitchelson's deputy, another ex-Sunday Sport editor, Drew Robertson, the staff of just 12 are all relative novices. The sport content will be provided by the Press Association as eight camera-ready pages.

There will be columns by Guardian environment correspondent John Vidal, former Daily Star executive Sue Blackhall and Fleet Street veteran John Austin — astrology will be provided by Nicholas Campion. One ace Mitchelson is counting on is the return of the comic strip hero, Dan Dare. He has bought the rights to the character who helped sell the Eagle to a million youngsters in the 1950s. Sidney Jordan, the artist behind the Daily Express's Jeff Hawke strip, will draw new Dan Dare adventures.

There will be no paid-for TV advertising to announce the launch, nor a poster campaign. Mitchelson is relying instead on his public relations advisers to win him interview time on every TV and radio outlet across the country.

Nobody likes to quell this kind of boyish enthusiasm, and there is certainly a lot more sense in this small-scale venture than the spendthrift multi-section Sunday Business, but it is going to be a tough fight to win readers.

The latest official circulation figures reveal just how difficult it is to sell papers, even with expensive TV promotion and the add-on cost of giving away thousands of copies free to hotels and fast-food chains.

Throughout this year the beneficial (sic) effects of the price war have begun to unravel and the daily papers together sold fewer than 14 million a day last month, a further step back towards the pre-price war circulation total. The situation is worse for Sunday titles where gentle but inexorable decline is now the norm for all but the Mail on Sunday and the Sunday Times.

Some owners have a great deal to worry about. Conrad Black, for instance, must be alarmed that the Daily Telegraph is once more selling fewer than a million copies a week. The headline figure shown in the chart below includes 35,107 bulk sales. The Sunday Telegraph is also slipping, again bolstered by bulk giveaways, though its revamp may help to stem the tide.

Lord Hollick also has a headache. The two Express titles have changed dramatically but the sales declines continue as before. If the strategy of appealing to a younger, more intelligent audience is to work then the flight by the old readers has, at some stage soon, to be matched by signs of new ones coming aboard. The Daily Star, by contrast, is holding its own: my forecast at the end of last year that it would close within six months has proved hopelessly wide of the mark. Sincere apologies to its editor, Phil Walker, who has done well to maintain its 750,000 average.

The Star's sales consistency has been achieved without TV advertising and few resources. That cannot be said about the Daily Mirror, which has spent lavishly but without reward. Its inability to keep its head above 2.5 million while the Sun regularly sells more than 4 million shows just how far it has slipped these past couple of years. Editor Piers Morgan has improved staff morale, impressing with his energy and commitment. But the content is too predictable, a relentless round of royal scoops that hardly deserve the exclusive tag and interminable celebrity trivia. He has adopted the Sun's agenda, with the only difference being knee-jerk support for Labour at a time when the Sun is also anti-government.

Mirror Group's chief executive, David Montgomery, cannot expect much else. He has wowed the City, and other newspaper owners, with his ability to cut costs and improve margins. But he doesn't appear to have the touch necessary to forge a great newspaper. Sales on the two main Mirror titles have declined ever since he took over.

Lord Rothermere, by contrast, has presided over an era of enormous success at the Mail group. In April, when circulations usually fall because of the Easter holiday, the Daily Mail was the only daily to add copies. The Mail on Sunday did well. Rothermere's long-term strategy, based on investment in journalism and a steady nerve, has paid off.

Rupert Murdoch's Wapping titles are undoubtedly doing well. But there must be some concern at the Times, which is suffering from post-price cut blues. Indeed, the story of the price war is fascinating: in June 1993, the month before the first cut — at the Sun — Britain had 11 national daily papers which between them sold an average of 13,060,151 copies every day. In April 1996, the most up-to-date audited figures available, Britain had 10 national daily papers which between them sold 13,181,062. In other words, there has been an increase of 120,911 copies over that period, a rise of just 0.95 per cent. Thanks, Rupert.

National newspaper circulation

	April 1996	March 1996	% change	Nov 1995-Apr 1996	Nov 1994-Apr 1995	% change
Dailies						
Sun	4,023,127	4,101,117	-1.90	4,068,091	4,069,459	-0.03
Daily Mirror	2,461,065	2,480,231	-0.77	2,490,618	2,460,826	1.21
Daily Record	725,709	738,432	-1.72	738,544	749,835	-1.51
Daily Star	741,946	748,773	-0.91	753,766	740,383	1.81
Daily Mail	2,061,803	2,055,775	0.29	2,016,072	1,772,733	13.73
Daily Express	1,243,017	1,255,293	-0.98	1,261,671	1,286,152	-1.90
Daily Telegraph	1,033,566	1,042,647	-0.87	1,041,172	1,062,345	-1.99
Guardian	394,000	400,245	-1.56	400,107	401,854	-0.43
Times	654,213	669,366	-2.26	669,028	621,539	7.64
Independent	276,029	280,396	-1.56	284,948	287,794	-0.99
Financial Times	292,296	308,914	-5.38	304,176	293,635	3.59
Sundays						
News of the World	4,546,298	4,561,607	-0.34	4,614,032	4,614,032	-3.35
Sunday Mirror	2,402,663	2,401,109	0.06	2,438,172	2,511,441	-2.92
People	2,066,809	2,031,339	1.75	2,059,844	2,077,301	-0.84
Mail on Sunday	2,118,799	2,112,016	0.32	2,096,621	1,950,623	7.48
Sunday Express	1,253,933	1,280,567	-2.08	1,295,504	1,423,090	-8.97
Sunday Times	1,291,386	1,306,518	-1.16	1,289,655	1,256,643	2.63
Sunday Telegraph	651,462	658,892	-1.13	659,867	676,927	-2.52
Observer	457,775	458,815	-0.23	461,080	474,413	-2.81
Independent on Sunday	301,564	305,764	-1.37	311,914	317,627	-1.80

Source: ABC

Fig 6.2   Courtesy *The Guardian* May, 13, 1994

TASK

Read the article, 'Why on Earth', and then answer the questions which follow.

■ In a few words, describe the proposed publication: the *Planet*.

■ Using as much information as you can find in the article, sum up what you learn about the target market/envisaged audience for the new paper.

■ What strategies is the editor Austin **M**itchelson using to promote the paper?

■ In about a page, summarise the reasons why the journalist Roy **G**reenslade believes 'it is going to be a tough fight' for the paper to win readers.

■ Lord Hollick is described as trying to reposition his paper in the market. In what way?

■ Compare the recent fortunes of the *Daily Star*, the *Mirror* and the *Sun*.

■ What reasons are given for the *Sun's* comparative success?

■ What is the point of the journalist's final remark: 'Thanks, Rupert'?

Scheduling: In relation to magazines and newspapers, it is not quite the same as applied to television. Schedulers decide which magazines/newspapers advertisements would be placed in, and when, and then organises this to happen.

The people who **schedule** time-slots on TV and radio (a much more skilled job than it might at first appear) also need to keep a watchful eye on audience data. If, for example, a particular slot attracts a large youth audience, then there may be a way of encouraging that audience to stay on into the next programme if it is something appropriate. This applies equally to the BBC as to the commercial channels. Clearly, to make these kinds of decisions about scheduling, planners need audience information that is more sophisticated than just gross numbers.

Deregulation and the need for audience research.

Deregulation: Taking a service out of state control or opening it up to private companies to run commercial channels in competition.

Across Europe over the last 20 years, there has been a pattern of '**deregulating**' parts of the media, notably in broadcasting. For example, in 1955, BBC television, which was the only service and was run by the government, was opened up to competition from ITV which was paid for by advertising. Since then other European countries have followed the same path. One result of this has been a huge increase in the number of channels that viewers and listeners can tune into. The UK now is about to have its fifth major terrestrial TV channel, Ireland has three, Portugal has three, Belgium has 22, Italy has 25.

Now we have not only new channels but also new means of communicating with audiences — Internet, cable, satellite, etc. At the same time, there has been a fragmentation of audiences. There is more choice in which media to consume and audiences have become more selective about finding things that they want. An example might be the enormous numbers of specialist magazines you can now find in most newsagents. The more complicated the media market becomes, the greater the need for audience research.

Academic and Social Research

'My favourite programme is *Minder*. The programme is packed with fighting, swearing and women.' Fourteen year-old boy quoted in government report, 1983.

The main difference between academic/social and commercial research lies in the kinds of questions being asked. Academic and social research is less linked to business and profits, and its results are usually available free, or at least for the cost of an academic book or a government report. A typical piece of social research might be the 1983 report written for the Department of Education and Science, called *Popular TV and Schoolchildren* which covered what young people said they had watched on TV over a particular period of time. It was written by a group of schoolteachers and dealt largely with the experiences of their pupils. It is introduced in the following terms:

> *The concern of teachers and others involved in educational provision about mass media and television in particular is of long standing. It is based on both awareness of their potential as educational tools and anxiety lest they be negative influences on the attitudes and behaviour of young people.*

While the report is careful not to jump to conclusions about the effects of the media, none the less, the research project is clearly framed in terms of a social concern: the proposed use of the research is for the benefit of society, it has a social agenda. It aims to produce knowledge or to stimulate discussion among teachers, parents, politicians and the wider society with a general aim of contributing a positive influence on what might be a social problem. So although on a small scale the methods it uses — interviews, quotes, measuring patterns of audience viewing, etc. — are not dissimilar from those used in commercial research, it is clearly different because of the purpose and language of the report. It goes on to express concern about the amount of TV children watch and in particular that percentage which depicts violence, particularly violence that goes unpunished or is even rewarded: 'We are very concerned about the cumulative effect on young people over a period of time.'

The report also noted the 'emotional violence' and 'triviality' displayed in soap operas, the constant use of sexual innuendo employed by game-show hosts, the portrayal of homosexual men as effeminate and the romantic aura that was seen to surround some petty villains, sparse representation of ethnic minorities, and missing or negative representations of old people.

Problems with this assumption are discussed in the next element although you can probably begin to see what they might be.

In these concerns the report is fairly typical of work with a 'social agenda'. Like a lot of such work it is anxious about the effects of the media, particularly on the young. It is also typical in that much of its analysis is of media content (eg. what is on TV), from which it envisages particular effects may arise.

Academic research may also take a wider, less applied line. One common question researched and debated nowadays is: what is the best way to understand and describe the relationship between the media and a member of the audience? Another way of putting this question is to ask: who is boss when it comes to deciding what a media text means: the media text itself or the viewer/consumer/reader? This may seem at first to be a rather obscure question, but, if you think about it, it is the question we need to answer before we can evaluate statements like those from the teachers above.

See Unit 1.

> **TASK**
>
> The account above has made a distinction between three different kinds of use of media research: commercial, social and academic. In about two pages, summarise the difference between the three types considering:
>
> ■ the typical kinds of questions asked;
>
> ■ the typical reasons for asking these sorts of questions;
>
> ■ who the researchers are likely to be;
>
> ■ the motives of the researchers;
>
> ■ the use of the results.

Methods of research

Problems of method for audience researchers

Media consumption is on the whole an individual choice and can be carried out in private locations like the home, the car or even between you and the earphones on your Walkman. How is the researcher to gain access to information about what goes on in these private domains?:

What is media consumption?

Sarah is in the bath glancing at one of the teenage magazines her younger sister always leaves on the floor. Downstairs somebody is listening to the news on the radio and she can catch the occasional headline. However, because of what happened at work today, Sarah is not really concentrating on anything except the thoughts in her own head.

See 'Open The Box' (Jane Root, Comedia/C4 1986)

This imaginary scenario typifies one of the main problems in media research: what constitutes consuming the media? Films taken discretely in people's homes show that all sorts of activities go on while people are 'watching' the TV including:

■ doing the ironing;
■ reading the paper;
■ having family rows;
■ headstands and bouncing on the sofa;
■ playing the flute with back turned to the set;
■ snogging, etc.

In the example of Sarah, she did not buy the magazine she was reading so her use of it will not show up in sales figures. However, an advertiser using that magazine is interested in the total audience, buyers or no. This is a major issue for research about reading habits. Studies from the 1960s onwards show that newspapers, books and magazines are likely to change hands, often more than once. It is well known now, for example, that many men are avid consumers of their partners' magazines although they probably would not walk around with *Cosmo*. However, their consumption is often marked enough to interest advertisers of mens' products and to encourage brief experiments like *Cosmo for men*.

(See Unit 2.)

TASK
Describe the progress of a well-used piece of media entering your home, e.g., a videotape, a magazine, a music tape. In a few sentences describe what happened to it. Who used it?

Problems of recall

Sarah could hear some of the news broadcast, but if asked in a recall survey the next day if she had listened to the radio news, she would probably reply 'No.' If she did remember what she heard, she might well have no idea what channel she was listening to.

A study in Canada discovered, by stopping drivers in their cars, that 60% of those with the radio on could not name the channel they were tuned to. However, this is exactly the information the channel owners will want to learn — one reason for all those repetitive station jingles.

The media form such a taken-for-granted aspect of our lives and are encountered in so many ordinary places that we are often not conscious of our own consumption. Problems of recall are more pronounced for those media we consume as we are also doing something else. We remember going to the cinema but how many of us could name the products advertised in the posters we passed yesterday? Yet advertisers know that poster advertising is a very effective way of communicating to certain social groups. Some researchers try to get round the problem of memory by using prompts. People involved in readership surveys, for example, often carry the logos and mastheads of the publications they are researching to encourage people to remember if they have seen them. However, even this attention to detail is not guaranteed to produce foolproof results. One survey found that when shown the logos for non-existent magazines, a percentage or respondents remembered reading and enjoying them!.

One proposal for newspaper research was that a thin microchip be inserted inside the pages of target publications which would be activated by the act of flexing the page as happens naturally in the act of reading. The activity would be logged on a specially adapted wristwatch worn by a representative panel of readers. The patents exist for this piece of research but perhaps not surprisingly it is too expensive to fund

Problems of selection

Despite, or because of, the wide range of media products available to us, people are quite selective about what they give their attention to. They may listen to the news, but only the headlines. They may buy a daily paper but read only the features and horoscope: fine, except for the advertiser who has just spent thousands on space next to the sports report. How much people select from what they are offered is a question that is of interest to both academic and commercial researchers but is very difficult to answer.

TASK

Watch people on the bus, train, etc. Is there any pattern to the way they approach printed material, like skipping pages in a novel, starting at the back of a newspaper, reading a page and then staring into space with a magazine? Report your observations back to your media group.

TASK

You have been employed to find out how much of their newspapers daily buyers actually read. Write a one-page research proposal (i.e., a description of the research you intend to do) specifying your methods.

Problems of scale

The media-using audience is vast and the resources available for any research is always a finite sum. It is rarely possible to research the whole of a relevant population so the answer in almost all research is to ask questions of a relevant sample.

Sampling

Sampling in research (as in music) means taking out a small section of the whole to use for your purpose. BARB, for example, reports on the TV-viewing habits of the nation. Since 97% of the population own at least one TV and people watch TV on average for over three hours per day, that implies an enormous amount of research. BARB surveys, not the whole population of the UK but a sample which consists of 4,700 households. (This is a considerably larger panel that the ones used in other European countries, partly because of the need to report accurately on viewing in each of a number of Britain's television regions.) The households on the panel are chosen because their members appear to represent major features of sections of the British population. A certain percentage will be young, a certain percentage will be working class, a certain percentage will have a particular number of children and so on. This kind of matching up goes on in all 'representative' samples and is carried out for most major pieces of commercial research and also for a percentage of academic research. The theory behind representative sampling is that the behaviour that is observed in the sample can indicate likely patterns in the wider population. When we hear, for example, that 16 million people watch *Coronation Street*, this figure has been estimated on the basis of the much smaller number in the BARB panel because their behaviour in this respect is believed to mirror the likely behaviour of others like them.

Not all sampling is done on this 'mirror' principle. It is most often a feature of 'quantitative' research where the researchers want to count the likely numbers of people who think or behave in a certain way. Some samples are drawn by advertising for people to respond which clearly attracts certain types of (unrepresentative) people. Others are defined by time like: the first 150 people to enter a new supermarket. There are clearly problems with non-representative sampling. Is the behaviour of these 150 keen shoppers likely to say anything about the way the rest may behave? There are also, however, problems with representative samples: for one thing, it is actually quite hard to make them really representative. Two people may be the same sex, age and social class, but does that mean they are going to watch the same things on TV?

A lot of student research is spoiled by the temptation to go for easy samples, like 'my friends' or the 'people in my class'. This is fine if this is indeed the relevant audience but you cannot then conclude (as is often seen done) that, for example: 'the TV programme/my project was very effective because 100% of my sample said so'!

Element 6.4 gives some advice about how to avoid these problems.

Qualitative and quantitative methods

Ien Ang (1986), *Watching Dallas: Soap Opera and the Melodramatic Imagination*, Methuen.

Having said that, there are media research projects which make no attempt to be representative and yet which contribute significantly to our understanding of the media. An example might be Ien Ang's work. on the very popular 1980s TV soap opera about very rich people: *Dallas*. Ang drew her sample of *Dallas* watchers by placing an advertisement in a women's magazine in her home country, Holland.

Forty-two people replied and her book *Watching Dallas* consists of a very detailed analysis of the motives they gave for loving or hating *Dallas*. Clearly the responding group is not a representative sample. However, because of her innovative and imaginative analysis of the letters, Ang's work helps us understand the pleasure people get from seemingly 'unrealistic' programmes.

David Morley (1986), *(Family Television: Cultural Power and Domestic Leisure,* Comedia.

David Morley makes an attempt to draw on a wider sample, though numerically smaller than Ang's, in his work on the effects of the home and family relations on the way people relate to TV. With the couples he selected, he carried out informal in-depth interviews with many open-ended questions. This produced a lot of quotable, but not much countable, material. He is very clear in the introduction to his book that the sample of couples he interviewed in south London, all of whom were white and living in nuclear households with partners and children, is far from representative of the UK population as a whole. None the less, his methods drew praise from the well-known cultural theorist, Stuart Hall who calls the book a 'seminal piece of research'.

Stuart Hall, Introduction to Morley (1989), *Family Television.*

TASK

The individuals in David Morley's sample are described in the chart below. Write a two-page commentary on this sample explaining its main features. In what ways would this group (i.e., the 'heads of households' referred to and their families) make and/or not make a good base for doing research on TV and the family in your view?

Quantitative methods are based on counting things. This could be audience size or, for example, the number of people who prefer

Family		Family Income	Job (Head of Household)	Age left Education (HoH)	Home Status	Years in Residence	Hoildays in Last year	Political Preference	Approximate Age of youngest child
	F16	£11k	Builders (S-E)	19yrs	Owner	$8\frac{1}{2}$	1	Con	6
	F11	£12k	Manager	18yrs	Owner	10	1	Lab	6
B	F8	£15.5k	Carpenter/Builder (S-E)	15yrs	Owner	18	1	Con	12
	F4	(?)	Furniture Dealer	19yrs	Owner	10	1	?	18
	F9	£16.5k	Salesman (S-E)	15yrs	Owner	11	1	Lab	12
C_1	F14	£11.5+	Caretaker	16yrs	Owner	$1\frac{1}{4}$	1	Con	6
	F15	£17k	Decorator (S-E)	16yrs	Tenant	$1\frac{1}{2}$	2	Lab	6
	F17	£12k	Fitter	17yrs	Tenant	10	1	Lab	12
	F13	£12k+	Caretaker	15yrs	Tenant	10	3	Lab	12
C_2	F18	£7.5k+	Builder (S-E)	15yrs	Tenant	3	2	Con	18
	F12	£13k	B Telecom Technician	15yrs	Owner	20	2	?	18
	F10	£10k	Postman	17yrs	Tenant	2	3	Lab	6
	F7	£8k	Service Engineer	14yrs	Owner	28	6	Lab	12
	F6	u	Ex-builder	16yrs	Tenant	13	0	Lab	18
	F5	u	Ex-ambulance worker	14yrs	Tenant	17	1	Con	18
U	F3	u	Ex-landscape gardener	15yrs	Tenant	7	0	Lab	6
	F2	u	Ex-decorator	15yrs	Tenant	5	1	Ecol	18
	F1	u	Ex-caretaker	16yrs	Tenant	$\frac{3}{4}$	0	Lab	6

Notes:

1. The class categorisations have been made by means of what is, in the end, an intuitive judgement, whereby class is assessed as a factor of income × educational background × cultural capital × home status. A simple income calculation would produce a different categorisation. I am using the standard ABC, etc., classifications merely as a descriptive short-hand to give a rough indication of class position.

2. The sample is, unfortunately, rather restricted at the top end of the scale. It lacks any substantial representation of the higher educated, professional classes.

Source: NORLEY, Family Television, Comedia 1986

Fig 6.3

Who's Who in

CORONATION ST

4,400 visitors in June

Welcome to Who's Who in Coronation Street - webpages all about everyone and everything in Coronation Street - the world's most successful drama serial.
You can currently look up indexes of:

Actors Characters
Places

Actors Characters Places

and pages for **Scriptwriters and Producers** will be added at a later stage.

Updates

Episode synopses by Glenda Young and Paul Baker. Contains reviews of the last episode, reviews for the current month, and an archive of back issues. **WARNING !!** As both of these are written in the UK, non-UK readers may see these as spoilers

NEW !! The Street - the whole story. A complete set of storylines since December 1960, appearing here over the next few months

The Kabin

Unlike Rita and Mave's Kabin, you can read all day long here without buying a thing
· · · ·

Fig 6.4   The *Coronation Street* newsgroup webpages. Not only do over 16 million people watch *Coronation Street*, but 19,225 visited this website to interact with other *Coronation Street* junkies. A newsgroup (sometimes called a usenet) is a discussion group on a subject on which you can participate via the Internet. It consists of a number of different 'threads' — a series of messages on the same topic

E.R. to *Casualty* or it could be the percentage of those asked who dislike hospital dramas, etc. The advantage of quantitative methods is that they can give you answers in a form that can be compared to other answers. Perhaps you want to find out the percentage of women enjoying hospital dramas compared to men? With numbers you have a basis for doing this. Or you might compare your research results with those in a previous study. Again numbers make this possible. The disadvantage of these methods, however, is that people can put too much faith in the results. Because they take the form of numbers ('57% said . . .') they feel very solid, scientific and true whereas in fact they are no more true than any other way of representing a picture of people's opinions. Number-based answers are only as useful as the questions producing them were subtle and intelligent. Unless you are careful however, this can lead the research off in a rather simple-minded direction. For example, while the BARB total audience figures can tell you with some likelihood of accuracy that 16 million people watch *Coronation Street*, they cannot begin to deal with the much more interesting question of 'why?'

TASK

How could audience researchers make use of newsgroups?

How would you analyse the audience's desire to discuss the series, Are they 'using' — forming 'virtual relationships with others, etc., via sharing views on — or are they victims of the 'hypodermic effect' — indulging in the escapism provided by a fictional world?

Qualitative methods, like Morley's in-depth interviews, produce uncountable material. For example, asking an open-ended question like: 'what do you like about your daily newspaper?' will get a range of answers from which it will be hard to produce statements like '57% said . . .'. On the other hand, this method may reveal something unexpected and might uncover some of the more subtle motivations for buying a paper. The disadvantage of qualitative methods is that they produce material that requires a lot of interpretation and this can open up a space for the subjective views of the analyser to take over.

On the whole, the large commercial agencies, whose work is described at the end of this chapter, seek to produce statistics about audience size. This is because many advertisers favour this kind of 'hard' information. But while the fact that millions of people saw a particular advertisment seems to indicate an impressive level of publicity, it cannot tell you what those readers made of the ad and how effective it was in making the product attractive. For that kind of information, qualitative methods are more useful.

Types of research method

Good research projects will often mix up methods using one set of answers to check on the reliability of another.

Interviews

These can be carried out face to face or by phone. Phone calls are often used where the need for information is immediate ('would you mind telling me how many radios are switched on in your house at the moment?') or where the questions do not require a lot of difficult answers. Usually readership surveys, where the respondent's memory may need to be jogged with images and which often take a long time ('tell me everything you read yesterday') are carried out face to face. The presence of the interviewer encourages the respondent to stick with it.

Questionnaires

Questionnaire design in Media Studies is rarely as simple as just asking what you want to know directly ('are you easily influenced by what you see on TV?' for example!). Often a more subtle pattern of questioning is called for.

The question is based on the premise put forward by some sociologists that crime, because of its sensational appeal, is over-reported in the media with the result that some old people become trapped in their homes. In fact statistics show that the majority of street violence is directed at young men — but this may be because they tend to be more present on the streets than other groups.

TASK

You want to find out if programmes like 'Crimewatch UK', where real crimes are discussed in the hope that the public will help find the suspects, make some groups in society feel anxious about going out after dark. To carry out this task, you have decided to use the same questionnaire with a group of old people, a group of young men and a group of middle-aged women.

- Write a page outlining any difficulties you perceive in finding out the answer to the question with these groups.

- Draft a questionnaire (also known as an 'interview schedule' when used alongside an interview) of between 10 and 20 questions including both closed and open-ended questions. Next to each question add a note explaining (to your GNVQ assessor, not the respondent) why you have chosen that question. What information exactly do you hope it will give you?

Focus discussion groups

These are often used by advertising agencies and others to get a general feel for a topic or a set of attitudes. For example, a supermarket chain might sponsor a series of discussion groups with (what they still call) 'housewives' to find out what is most important to them when they shop. Is it fresh produce? Friendly service? Good price? Easy parking? The chosen feature could then be played up in advertising. Once again the approach needs to be subtle and the chairing of the group carefully handled. A good chair will be able to move from the general ('What supermarket do you use?' 'Why that one?') to the more specific ('What is more important? Fresh food? Friendly service?'). The earlier parts of the discussion may well elicit underlying attitudes. As with most qualitative methods, it is a technique that requires sensitive, intelligent analysis and a good 'ear' for what people are really saying. Sometimes such sessions would be tape-recorded to allow later in-depth analysis.

Focus discussion groups were used during the design of the (then) new magazine *'Marie Claire'*. It was discovered that women in the groups did not like the proposed spine slogan which indicated the product was for 'thinking women' (because it implied that there were other women who did not think!).

Panels

Panels are pre-selected groups of people whose views are regularly sought or whose behaviour (e.g., watching TV) is regularly monitored. They are usually chosen to be representative of a larger group. People agree to participate out of interest, or sometimes there are small rewards, like being entered for a prize draw each week. One problem with panels is that they need to cover a whole range of behaviour, for example, from obsessive newspaper reading to none at all, but there is very little motivation for the people in the latter category to answer regular questions about something they rarely do. Another problem is that being on the panel can actually change people's natural behaviour. ('I never realised I watched so much TV. I'm going to cut down on it in future!') Panels are the main focus of much quantitative media research and they are also good at uncovering trends since the same people's behaviour is repeatedly monitored.

Electronic devices

These can be used to measure what equipment is switched on in the home and who is in the room if they declare themselves present, e.g., by pushing a button. Some devices can sense how many people are in the room and even make assumptions about who they are, since people tend to sit in the same seats. Some ideas for measuring equipment for the future are positively futuristic: e.g., a watch worn by a volunteer which picks up and registers each radio station they hear or the aforementioned microchip newspaper.

Diaries

Survey participants can be asked to keep up regular diaries about their media habits. This is a practice that is widely used in research and, before the electronic 'peoplemeter' now used, was the standard way of 'capturing data' about TV viewing. Diaries are useful in that they can report on both quantitative data ('how often . . .') and qualitative ('I thought it was rubbish!') but the difficulties are obvious. People forget what they have listened to or watched or read, they can get bored filling in the diary or even lie about their habits.

Someone who said a particular programme was rubbish may not feel comfortable owning up to the fact that they then watched it again the next week. To make matters simple for the respondent, most researchers give a pre-printed diary format to be filled in.

TASK

Persuade five people to be part of a diary-based survey about one particular form of media for a week (this could be part of a larger research topic if you want). Design a pre-set diary sheet for them to use. At the end of the week:

■ write up any problems you and they encountered with the diary form of research;

■ what did the diaries tell you about patterns of consumption in your group?

Hint: this exercise works best if you start with a hypothesis or idea you are testing out like: 'people watch more hours of T V than they think they do,' or 'a lot of people buy newspapers they don't read.'

See Unit 6.2.

The halo effect

All researchers, whatever their methods, need to be aware of the dangers of the 'halo effect'. People responding to requests for information may 'dress up' their normal behaviour to try to impress the researcher — as if they really wore an angelic halo. Personal taste in media is still a very class-based issue in our society and quite possibly also gender related. David Morley found that a number of the women in his survey group felt they should apologise for watching the soaps and that their husbands and partners often put them down for doing so. If someone in your research tells you that they 'only watch documentaries and nature programmes', this may indeed be true or it may be a secret quiz-show addict putting on a 'halo'.

Observation/participant observation

Observation studies can be set up to monitor people's behaviour in relation to their media consumption. For instance, it is not surprising to learn that many people use the advertisement break to go to the lavatory or to make a cup of tea. Even the water companies are known to count on extra water use at the end of particular popular TV events. Another example might be to observe the behaviour of a class of schoolchildren after they have seen a particular programme or read a particular kind of story.

Simulations

A simulation is an artificial situation created by the researcher. When David Morley and his research partner Charlotte Brunsdon wanted to test the hypothesis that different social groups would 'read' a particular news documentary programme differently, they set up a number of sessions during which different groups, for example, trade unionists and students, were shown the same videotape of the pre-recorded programme. Their subsequent discussion was analysed for its main concerns and opinions. Other researchers have deliberately exposed an audience to a particular kind of media information and then observed later whether their views on a number of topics vary from those who have not seen the stimulus piece. Simulations are artificial situations deliberately set up by the researchers in the same way as students of the physical sciences set up experiments in the laboratory. However, because they involve real people, they need careful handling so as not to abuse the trust of their participants. The researcher also needs to remember that often the experimental situation creates types of unnatural behaviour, such as people feeling they should have views on topics that in reality mean little to them.

Using resources

The resources needed for a piece of audience research can be as minimal as a pencil and paper or as large as a huge team of qualified interviewers and suites of computers. One constant resource in all research is time: the researchers and other people's. Things to think about during resource planning include:

- your time;
- other people's time;
- physical resources like pen, paper, tape recorder, question-naires;
- photocopying;
- computers and computer-access time;
- transport (timing and costs);

TASK

You want to find out if a recent government poster campaign, aimed at letting unemployed people know they are entitled to dental treatment at reduced costs, has been successful in increasing awareness. You have designed a short questionnaire to use with 60 local people in three different benefit offices. List all the resources you would need — down to the last pencil.

All research projects, however funded, are shaped and limited by the availability of resources. Here David Morley describes how this issue shaped his choice of sample for the work on families and television:

David Morley is a well-known authority on audience research. He is currently Professor of Communications at Goldsmiths College, University of London. David Morley (1986), *Family Television: Cultural Power and Domestic leisure*, Comedia.

CASE STUDY
Extract: Interview with David Morley

J.P.: Research is always limited by resources ...
D.M.: Very true!
J.P.: What resources did you have to research for *Family Television*?
D.M.: As I remember it, I finally got about six-and-a-half thousand pounds out of the research arm of the Independent Broadcasting Authority who usually did mainly statistical number-crunching research on numbers of viewers. But at that time, the IBA had a head who was slightly more sympathetic to 'weird' research like mine. He was more of an academic and more sympathetic than most, but it still took two-and-a-half years badgering away at them.
The money mainly went on the cost of recruiting the sample and the cost of transcribing the tapes because I paid a local market research company to go round knocking on doors until they had recruited enough appropriate people for me to interview. I didn't have the time or the skills to do this myself. I

don't think I'd be very convincing standing on the doorstep! Similarly with the transcription. They reckon it takes eight hours to transcribe a one-hour tape so you have to pay quite a lot for 30 tapes at two hours each. So there wasn't much left to me to do the interviews, and all the analysis was something I did unpaid in the evenings after work. It was almost like a hobby.

J.P.: What other resources did you need?

D.M.: I needed a good tape recorder and I needed to remember to put batteries in it. Also, I needed to remember to switch the tape on and to turn it over during the interview which sounds really stupid, but I have ruined so many interviews in my life by forgetting to do those very simple things. So my advice to your students would be things like make sure you figure out the journey beforehand; make sure you arrive on time and that you've practised with your tape recorder at home before-hand so you can work out its radius and how far you'll need to put it away from the person you are interviewing. You want it near enough to pick up their voice but not so you have to hold it under the person's nose, otherwise they will always be conscious that they are being recorded and you'll get less articulate answers.

Segmentation of the audience

We tend, in media theory, to talk about *the* audience, but it would actually be more accurate to keep using the plural word: **audiences.** As we have seen in this and other chapters, owners, advertisers, programme-makers and schedulers are acutely aware that their work is 'targeted', aimed at particular segments of the potential audience. The article on p. 352 raised doubts, for example, about whether the new paper, the *Planet*, could find room in the already crowded 'middle market'. If you think about your own media consumption you will be aware that there are all sorts of media products that you never consume or purchase (the *Financial Times*? Body-building magazines? Quiz shows? Plays on the radio? Health and fitness videos? Romantic novels? Cartoon films?)

Our society is divided into taste groups in a very complex; way. This is partly because we are all individuals with our own person-alities however, there are also very perceptible 'patterns' in taste and choice, and researchers have different methods of describing these divisions.

Gender

The *Daily Mail*, is a paper that has a wide female circulation, a fact that was played on in the recent advertising slogan: 'every woman needs her *Daily Mail*.'

Female and male engagement with the media appears to be different in a range of ways. We know that men and women show different patterns in buying and consuming products — not always but often. It has also been argued that even within the same product, the sexes may often respond differently. A simple example may be which character one chooses to identify with in a particular fiction.

Social class

There are clear class patterns in media consumption, however class is defined in a variety of ways — for example, by income, education level, occupation group.

Age

Obviously people interact with media differently at different stages in their lives. This is not just a question of biological age. Advertisers in particular are interested in the stage people are at in a 'typical' life cycle. For example, whether people have children is a crucial piece of information for particular types of selling. Also people are richer or poorer at different stages of their lives, hence marketing concepts like Yuppie ('young, upwardly mobile professional' — used to describe careerists in the 1980s) or Dinky ('dual income, no kids yet' to describe couples with a high level of disposable income) or 'Empty nest' (people whose children have grown up and left home thus liberating more money for the parents).

Personality/psychology

Advertisers may target their appeals to particular types of personality or **aspiration**. Adverts showing products in the context of a sophisticated dinner party may be targeting people who live a life that involves posh dinners or, and more likely, people who would like to lead this kind of life or at least enjoy imagining themselves doing so.

Different companies will use different ways of categorising the psychological needs and profiles they are appealing to but the following are not uncommon: self-improvers, worriers, status conscious people, conspicuous consumers, sociables, social resistors (rebels or people who would like to be rebels), explorers (people looking for excitement), experimenters, people wanting to belong. Sometimes this kind of socio-psychology will be used deliberately, and at other times unconsciously as advertisers imagine what would appeal to 'such and such a kind of person'.

Lifestyle

This is obviously related to aspirations but may well include practical descriptions like how a person travels to work. People in cars are more accessible by radio than those on public transport, for example.

Social grading scales

A widely used concept in describing a target group or market is that of social class. Many students shy away from this concept in their own theoretical and practical work for the very understandable reason that they feel uncomfortable about putting people into categories where one group may appear to be 'better' than another. However, while we may not like the fact, it is true that the UK, like most other industrial countries, has a stratified social system and factors that are traditionally associated with class descriptions, such as levels of wealth, ownership of property, levels of education, income, type of job, are very different for different individuals. To say that someone is 'middle class' or 'working class' does not imply that they have more or less value as human beings, but it does imply a lot of other things about them which media owners, advertisers, etc., want to know.

The most commonly used system to describe these differences within media and sales is the **JICNARS** social grading scale. This scale, which is largely self-explanatory, is reproduced below. It was originally devised as a way of measuring newspaper audiences.

JICNARS: Joint Industry Committee for National Readership Survey.

The six categories of the JICNARS social grading system are as follows:

Social grade	Social status	Occupation	% OF ADULTS OVER 15, 1986
A	Upper middle class	High managerial, administrative or professional	2.7
B	Middle class	Intermediate managerial, administrative or professional	14.5
C1	Lower middle class	Supervisory or clerical, managerial administrative or professional	22.7
C2	Skilled working class	Skilled manual workers	27.6
D	Working class	Semi-and unskilled manual workers	7.6
E	Those at lowest	State pensioners or widows (no other earner), casual or lowest-grade workers	14.8

Despite its wide use in the media, there are a number of difficulties with this scale, not least its use of the concept of 'head of the household' which is assumed to be male . The scale was devised at a time when it was more accepted that a man was automatically the head of a household, when fewer women worked and when there were fewer single-parent households. Feminists would object to a woman's status being pegged to a man's in this way especially when it is not unusual for women in some households to earn more than their partners. In JICNARS the Head of the Household is usually the person who owns or rents the home. If there is not a male person to whom this obviously applies or if that person has not been in work for the last two months, then the title passes to the senior working person in the household. Retired people are classified according to their previous occupations. However, despite difficulties with the scale, a number of researchers who are not completely happy with it still use it so they can compare their results with those of others.

Another commonly used scale for social class is the Registrar General's Classification of Social Class and Socio-economic Groups which was developed in 1911 by the Government Office of Population Census and Surveys. This scale is used more by some sociologists and in government surveys, but less in media-related research. The scale identifies six groupings but puts more emphasis on skill and education levels and less on assumed levels of income related to jobs. Both systems can potentially be applied to individuals rather than households, although JICNARS is rarely applied in this way. This is perhaps understandable from the point of view of advertisers and the media organisations that depend on them for income. Advertisers are interested in potential customers in terms of, among other things, their disposable income and this is often organised around the household. For example, the family or household buys dog food — not each individual within it.

Registrar General's Classifications of Social Class and Socio-economic Groups — (developed by the office of population, census and surveys)

Social class	Example of occupations
I Professional	Doctors, lawyers, chemists, clergy
II Intermediate occupations	Most managerial and senior administrative posts (including teachers, nurses and MPs)

III Skilled occupations:	
(N) Non-manual	Typists, clerical workers, sales representatives
(M) Manual	Cooks, railway guards, bricklayers, foremen/forewomen in engineering
IV Partly skilled occupations	Bar staff, bus conductors, canteen assistants, telephone operators
V Unskilled occupations	Office cleaners, labourers

Sociologists argue that society has become more structured in a more complex way since the days when it was possible to draw a clear line between management classes and the workers. At the same time, there has been a huge increase in the amount and type of media available. The impact of these trends acting together has been to make the structure of audiences more and more complicated and hence to increase the need for good quality research.

Research bodies

Many different kinds of organisations do media research. These include:

- UK government departments;
- European Community researchers;
- charities and campaigners;
- educational and social agencies;
- university departments especially those of sociology, anthropology and, of course, film and media studies;
- students at all levels of the education system from primary to postgraduate
- the media;
- advertising agencies
- specific commercial research agencies like, JICNAR, BARB, etc.

The list above includes a wide variety of types of people and it is worth making three points about these differences:

- These organisations have different agendas and different motives for doing research.
- They all have different levels of resources for research, ranging from an individual student grant or loan through to huge budgets for the larger commercial organisations.
- They have different levels of independence. While a university student, following advice from his or her tutor, can develop virtually any line of enquiry, someone working for a commercial organisation, despite a larger budget, will need to confine the

research to the kind of data that companies are likely to buy. For many reasons, this still tends to be quantitative data, although there is a slight shift now towards an interest in more qualitative factors. Government research is often directed through either research agencies or through universities but in both cases, the sponsor obviously retains a guiding hand in shaping the project.

Commercial research agencies

BARB

The TV ratings are the best known results of audience research. They are often referred to by TV commentators and reproduced weekly in the trade press. Producing figures which refer to the behaviour of millions of viewers is far from simple and is the work of BARB: the Broadcasters' Audience Research Board. The scale of the research task it faces can be gleaned from a few basic facts and a bit of history.

The UK has had television since 1936 when the BBC came into being but broadcasting has become a more complex industry since its original days. Commercial TV — television that is dependent not on the licence fee but on advertising — began with the ITV in 1955. Further channels have been added during the period between the 1960s and the 1980s including BBC2, Channel 4, regional TV, breakfast TV, etc. The audience picture is further complicated by the growth in video use and the arrival of satellite and cable TV. Now:

In 1936, users had to pay a licence fee of £2 a year!

- 96% of the population of the UK have a colour TV set in their home;

- 74% have remote control;

- 53% have two or more sets;

- 65% of families with children have two or more sets;

- 61% of households own a video.

BARB, the organisation that researches this complex situation, is a private limited company owned half by the BBC and half by ITV. BARB commissions the research it wants from private research companies who compete for the contract, but BARB itself lays down very precise guidelines for the things it wants to know. BARB then pays the researchers for their work from the income it makes from people who buy the resulting data. This model of subcontracting the research to expert companies is a common one in commercial media research.

BARB's methods

BARB has the same methodological problem as haunts much media research: what constitutes 'watching'? Does just being in the room when the TV is on count, or if you press a button to say you are there, watching a whole programme or watching a small fragment as you hop channels? The method chosen since 1991 is called a 'peoplemeter', an electrical device which is installed in each TV set in every one of the 4,700 homes selected to make up a panel representative of the population of Britain. All panel members are asked to push a personal button each time they start to watch and each time they stop. From there on, the peoplemeter logs what is being watched in the room, which channel, whether the channel was changed, the exact time of day, if the video was switched to record or play, whether it was playing material previously recorded from TV, what it was, and so on. This information is collected for each of the TV sets in the home and passed from the various units on to a central storage system that is stored discretely in the house, usually in a cupboard or behind furniture. This storage unit is attached by modem to the household's telephone from where information is retrieved by a silent phone call from a central computer in London between 1 and 5 o'clock in the morning.

The BARB panel

The panel consists of all the household members of the selected who are over four years old. The panel is spread across Britain but not equally. It is adjusted to represent the possible viewers in any particular TV region. Also, interestingly, the sample is slightly weighed to give larger numbers (i.e., a wider base of data) in those categories of people that buyers of information most often ask about: younger people, 'housewives' and 'housewives' with children'. One group, known in the trade as 'C2DE early inactives' (i.e., unemployed school leavers in households where there are no other wage earners) are deliberately under-represented by two-thirds. Here we have an interesting example of an agenda at work. BARB may find this kind of data hard to sell (for the obvious reason that these people have low purchasing power), however, a sociologist or a media academic might be very interested in the uses of the media by the young unemployed, particularly given the theories which exist (and are disputed) about the extent of media influence on those who lack other 'message' sources like those which come from work or family.

About 25% of the BARB panel change each year either because their circumstances change or they move home or they prove to be bad at remembering to log on!

Analysing the data

The data that the peoplemeters generate can indicate which channel was playing and to whom for any 15 second slot of a day's broadcasting. In reality BARB can only report on the behaviour of its panel, but since its panel is 'representative' it is taken to indicate the habits of the nation and figures are rounded up to represent 'national viewing'. Since BARB has also collected information about the panel's age, sex, class, etc., it is possible to relate these sets of data together with viewing patterns for the

MILLIONS VIEWING, WEEK ENDING APRIL 21

BBC1			ITV		
1	EastEnders (Thu)	15.26	1	Coronation Street (Mon)	16.13
2	EastEnders (Tue)	14.31	2	Coronation Street (Fri)	15.75
2=	EastEnders (Mon)	14.31	3	Coronation Street (Wed)	13.37
4	National Lottery Live	13.03	4	Police, Camera, Action	12.71
5	Antiques Roadshow	10.42	5	The Bill (Fri)	12.59
6	Hamish Macbeth	9.80	6	Peak Practice	12.58
7	Birds of a Feather	9.42	7	Emmerdale (Thu)	12.39
8	News and Weather (Sun 20.52)	9.22	8	Emmerdale (Tue)	12.23
9	Naked Gun 2½	9.19	9	The Bill (Thu)	10.85
10	Madson	9.12	10	The Bill (Tue)	10.42
BBC2			**C4**		
1	The X Files	6.69	1	Brookside (Tue)	4.36
2	Have I Got News For You (Fri)	5.46	2	Brookside (Fri)	4.19
3	Top Gear	5.13	3	Brookside (Wed)	3.77
4	Food and Drink	4.80	4	E R	3.59
5	Gardeners' World	4.58	5	Father Ted	3.22
6	Home Front	4.03	6	NYPD Blue	2.94
7	Ready, Steady, Cook (Fri)	3.89	7	Red Rock West	2.82
8	Ready, Steady, Cook (Thu)	3.85	8	The Real Holiday Show	2.80
9	Ready, Steady, Cook (Tue)	3.75	9	An Inspector Calls	2.74
10	Star Trek: The Next Generation	3.69	10	Cybill	2.55

Where programmes appear in omnibus or repeat editions, ratings for the highest single showing only have been included. Source: BARB

Fig 6.5 BARB ratings. BARB publishes this data on a weekly basis in the press. (Source: the *Sunday Times*, 5 May 1996)

possible 16,000 programmes and 60,000 adverts shown in an average week. The data can be presented to buyers of information in a number of ways: by region, age group, how often a particular group of people saw a particular ad, and so on. While some of these correlations may seem obscure, it is not hard to imagine how desirable information could be about, for example, what particular kinds of credit-card holders watch what, or how many ads are seen by dog-owning families and at what time of day. In fact BARB subcontracts many of its analysing functions to other companies, notably to AEB and Donovan Data Systems, which use it to advise their clients on, for example, the best commercial break slots to buy on TV.

This account of BARB is very much a summary of its main work. The organisation carries out a number of other tasks including a surveys of 'audience appreciation' particular programmes.

For a fuller account, read Raymond Kent (ed.) (1994), *Measuring Media Audiences*, Routledge, to which this whole chapter is much indebted.

The National Readership Survey

Measuring what people read in the UK has been going on for 60 years. During the Second World War, for example, the government, with its eye on public opinion, sponsored a number of surveys to find out where people were getting information about daily events. Now the interest in these questions is more likely to come from commercial sources. However, readership of magazines and news-papers is very hard to research for reasons that have already been discussed. While people may remember a TV programme because it stands out in their minds as a particular event, they are less likely to recall an article they saw in a magazine at the hairdresser's or read over someone's shoulder on the bus. The NRS, however, sets itself the difficult task of finding out what people in the UK have been reading by using regular in-depth interviews with a sample of adults (over 15 years old) taken from across Britain. The research is mainly **quantitative** in character asking less about the actual activity of reading and understanding and more about the number of opportunities people may have had to see particular adverts. The sample size is approximately 37,000 individuals.

To jog the respondents' memory, interviewers use a series of prompt cards showing the logos and mastheads of various publications. The respondents sort these cards into piles of those they have looked at 'for a couple of minutes or more' over the last year and those they have not. The researcher then takes the pile referring to magazines, etc., that have been seen and asks questions to establish what the respondent has seen over the last week and 'yesterday'. Questions are also asked about the person's lifestyle like who does the shopping in his or her household and how much is spent. Other questions establish 'demographic details' like age, sex, class etc.

During these interviews, the interviewer enters the replies directly on to a keyboard, ready to be analysed by a computer.

Fig 6.6　NRS survey regions

ABC: Audit Bureau of Circulation

You will notice that the article about the *Planet* on p. 352, which is about the commercial survival of papers and therefore concerned with sales figures, takes its data from ABC (see the table).

This organisation counts not readers but sales of particular newspapers and magazines. As a general rule, advertisers are more interested in readers because they want to know how many people saw their advertisement. Newspaper and magazine proprietors are often as interested in circulation numbers (i.e., sales) for obvious reasons. One of the ABC's main roles is to stop newspaper proprietors from bumping up their circulation figures by, for example, including those papers given away free to hotels, etc. It is therefore regarded as giving more reliable information on circulation than the media organisations themselves who, for reasons of pride and to attract advertisers, will be tempted to inflate sales figures.

JICPAR

JICPAR: the **J**oint **I**ndustry **C**ommittee for **P**oster **A**udience **R**esearch.

As you read on about media research organisations, you will notice a lot of them begin with the initials JIC. What these initials tell you is that, in this particular medium, relevant organisations have got together to create one overriding research body from which they can all then buy information. Obviously the creation of one research organisation will cut costs for everybody and allows the research to be carried out according to one set of procedures rather than everybody doing it their own way. **JICPAR** includes representatives from all those interested in outdoor advertising including the media owners, the advertisers, the advertising agencies, the people who select poster sites.

A separate organisation known as the Outdoor Advertisers Association represents the people who own the advertising sites or who are responsible for renting them out, but this organisation does not now carry out any research. Instead it gets its information, like all other interested parties, through JICPAR.

OSCAR: **O**utdoor **S**ite **C**lassification **a**nd Audience **R**esearch.

Together these two organisations have agreed a model known as **OSCAR** through which they do their research. OSCAR's title just about sums up what the research tries to achieve. It evaluates the effectiveness of particular poster sites in terms of visibility, amount of traffic passing and so on. It also counts the kind of vehicles which pass and the number of pedestrians. All this information is integrated to produce a score for a particular poster site and this helps determine the price that is set to companies who want to rent it. It also indicates to advertisers which sites it would be wise to try to rent. For example, advertising a new series on TV — something that poster campaigns do well — will work best on the known routes to work of people living in a particular TV region.

Cinema Research: CAA, Gallup and CAVIAR

Research about the numbers of people who attend cinemas is easier to carry out than for other media because it is not difficult to count admissions. The work on this topic is commissioned by the

CAA: Cinema Advertising Association. You will probably have heard of Gallup because they carry out a lot of political opinion polls as well.

CAVIAR: Cinema and Video Industry Audience Research.

Cinema Advertising Association and carried out by a research agency called Gallup. The research is carried out by telephone. Cinemas representing about 70% of the nation's total number of screens are phoned each week for information about their box-office figures. One interesting feature of cinema attendance is how far factors other than the film being shown impact on numbers attending. These can range from the weather, what is on television and the timing of the school holidays. However, a particularly popular film can also have a massive impact on attendance. The release of *Ghost*, for example, in October 1990, nearly doubled the numbers of people going to the cinema compared with the previous weeks. Another research project is also commissioned by the CAA, called **CAVIAR**. This research is less concerned with total audience figures and more interested in who is going to see what or watching what on video. CAVIAR is an annual survey covering 3,100 respondents over five years old. As well as 'films seen', the survey discovers the usual demographic details of age, sex and socio-economic class.

Radio research: RAJAR

Radio audience research suffers from the same problems of recall as readership research. In some ways the problems are worse for radio researchers because radio listening is an activity which often accompanies other acts like driving or doing the ironing so people are, by definition, half distracted. The result is that people tend to underestimate significantly the amount of radio they have heard.

RAJAR: Radio Joint Audience Research.

RAJAR is a joint industry committee for the whole of radio. Its research is carried out through using a pre-printed diary sheet which respondents fill in indicating all their radio listening. One problem with this is that radio is often regionally based so respondents in different areas need a different pre-printed checklist. Every week different households fill in the diary and four times a year, when the total number of respondents has reached about 14,000 adults and 2,400 children over the quarter, the results are totalled and analysed.

Ways forward in commercial research

As can be seen from the account so far, the emphasis in most commercial research is the production of numbers which indicate consumption figures, or at least numbers indicating people who have the opportunity to consume because they make contact with the medium in question. However increasingly, agencies with a commercial agenda are seeing the relevance of qualitative questions. They want to know not just if people viewed, heard or read, but what this experience did to them. Did it increase brand loyalty? Did it make them want to change their spending habits? One growing concern at the moment is to establish whether context (i.e., what an advert appears next to) has been underestimated as an influence. Does a programme or feature that produces positive feelings in the consumer create a context in which these feelings can be transferred to advertised products? If so which contexts are most productive? These kinds of questions will lead commercially based research to extend down some of the same avenues as academic and social research because in both cases the question being raised is a psychological one.

6.2 EXPLORE THE RELATIONSHIP BETWEEN MEDIA AND AUDIENCES

Introduction

- What *is* the relationship between the mass media and its audiences?
- Do the media have effects on society?
- If so, how does this work?
- Are their effects good or bad?
- How much choice do we have in interpreting what we see, hear and read?

Another way of putting these questions is to ask: 'what is the best **model** to describe the relationship between people and the media?'

A model is an abstract construct that is used to describe and explain how something works. For example, a model of an aeroplane or of a water dam will show in miniature how those machines function. In the same way, a sociological or Media Studies model can show in a simple way how something happens in society. In these subjects, the models are made in words or sometimes in diagrams. They represent a theory in simplified form.

The media is pre-constructed for audiences

A radio producer quoted in Helen Baehr and Michelle Ryan. (1984), *Shut up and Listen*! Comedia/Campaign for Press and Broadcasting Freedom.

'We call our average listener Doreen. Doreen isn't stupid but she is only listening with half an ear and she doesn't necessarily understand long words.'

Before we start talking about what happens when a 'reader/consumer' comes into contact with a piece of media it is important to remind ourselves that all forms of media are already constructed with a specific audience in mind. Media producers would no doubt vary widely in their opinion about the potential effect of their work on society, as widely as those academics whose views on this subject are discussed below. None the less, one thing is sure, they will do their best to appeal to the audience and to engage their interest in the text that they are making. This is true of journalists, advertisers, designers, photographers and all those who make their living from media production. Consider, for example, the following extract from *Creative Newspaper Design*. The writers, one an ex-Fleet Street designer, the other a current Fleet Street journalist, are

Creative Newspaper Design Vic Giles and F.W. Hodgson (1990), Butterworth-Heinemann.

discussing the layout on a front page of the *Birmingham Post* which shows a picture of a train being winched from a crash site. Below, among the written text, are two small images of people involved in the story.

The news page from the tabloid Birmingham Post shows how to get the best out of a handful of pictures supporting a dramatic

One of the carriages derailed in Saturday's crash at Purley, Surrey, is hoisted above the houses before being taken away for examination. Five people were killed in the accident.

Warning to egg producers

By NIGEL HASTILOW

The Government last night promised tough legal action against food producers who continue to sell infected eggs.

After months of criticism of the Ministry of Agriculture's delays in responding to growing public concern over salmonella in eggs, a clear warning was issued to producers last night.

Mr Richard Ryder, the Junior Agriculture Minister, told producers: "Clean up your act or face the full brunt of the law."

He was speaking during a Commons debate on the Government's £19 million package of assistance to the industry which came after the slump in sales caused by a remark by the former Junior Health Minister, Mrs Edwina Currie, that most egg production was infected with salmonella.

Mr Ryder rejected the claim by the all-party Commons agriculture select committee that his department had been negligent.

He said the Ministry had put forward 17 new measures to control salmonella in eggs, the most comprehensive package in the world.

Though egg sales were still down by 30 to 35 per cent, the Government's rescue package had restored stability.

He said: "Consumer sovereignty is the key to the market place."

"It can be threatened by monopoly and cartels, trade protectionism masquerading as protection, or neglect of public health standards."

Earlier, Mr John Biffen (Con Shropshire North), the former Cabinet Minister, condemned Mrs Currie (Con Derbyshire South), for her reluctance to give evidence to the select committee and described her as "a political health hazard."

Sir Hal Miller (Con Bromsgrove) said some caterers had still not reacted positively to the Government's measures to improve egg quality. Some small farmers were still finding their supplies to caterers were down by 60 per cent.

Dr David Clark, the Labour agriculture spokesman, accused the Government of mishandling the whole affair by "incompetence, excessive secrecy and delaying tactics."

"By their failure to act speedily, they have allowed the problem to become exacerbated."

Driver 'failed to report Clapham signal change'

A British Rail driver could have prevented the Clapham disaster in which 35 people died by reporting signal irregularities he noticed only minutes before the crash, the inquiry was told yesterday.

But Mr George Christy did nothing, it was claimed.

The reason was that he should not have been driving the train, but had agreed to an "illegal" swap with another driver, said Mr Benjamin Browne, a lawyer.

Mr Christy rejected the allegations from Mr Browne, who was representing Mrs Sue Rolls, widow of the driver killed in the crash, Mr John Rolls.

In an emotional gesture yesterday, she handed back the union badge her husband was wearing when he died.

Mr Tony Staton, district secretary of the Associated Society of Locomotive Engineers and Firemen, told her to keep it, but she said between sobs: "I am sorry, you don't understand. They have let everyone down."

It is understood she was upset at the union decision not to cross-examine Mr Rolls's fel-

Mr George Christy: denied 'illegal' swap as driver.

Mrs Sue Rolls: handed back husband's union badge.

low drivers about the failure to report the signal irregularities.

The inquiry has heard that a wiring fault during signal modernisation caused the fault, which the driver of a Basingstoke train stopped to report. The signals then allowed a Bournemouth train — driven by Mr Rolls — to run into the back of it.

Mr Christy, aged 60, said he had driven a Bournemouth-Waterloo train past the spot just 10½ minutes before the crash in December.

But he dismissed Mr Browne's claim that the swap he had agreed to — by taking over the train from another driver — was "illegal."

However, he admitted it was unauthorised and a disciplinary offence had the management found out.

He did not report sudden changes in the lights shown by the signals because he thought they were no more than unusual. He thought the reason was that a Clapham signalman had rerouted a train in front.

Mr Browne said: "If you had realised the importance of what you had seen and reported it this tragedy would never have occurred, would it?"

Mr Christy said he did not know how to answer — there was a signal irregularity, but he was not aware of it at the time.

Mr Browne said: "May I

suggest that you are so anxious now to say that this wasn't an irregularity and didn't report it at the time because you were well aware that you should not have been driving that train and, had you reported it, you would have got yourself into trouble?"

Mr Christy: "That isn't the case. If there had been an irregularity I would have reported it."

Mr Christy, of Hammond Close, Basingstoke, Hampshire, said he had seen three signals approaching the one at the centre of the crash, number 136, change to green as he approached the first of them.

Then signal 142, the one before 136, suddenly "flicked" from green to yellow, he said.

A BR official responsible for supervising signals modernisation said he had feared there could be more loose wires like the one that caused the crash.

Mr Alfred Court was being questioned by Mr Michael Spencer, counsel for the bereaved and injured, about why he had agreed to cut off part of the old loose wiring responsible for the disaster after signal engineers found it within hours of the crash.

Mr Court, aged 46, signals supervisor for new works, based at Wimbledon, said he had carried orders from senior engineers to make the wire safe by cutting it and had left it in their hands.

Mr Spencer, asking why Mr Court had not left it in place to be photographed and examined later, said: "You appreciated the importance of this evidence, did you not?"

Mr Court said: "Yes, but I had just finished 16 commissions similar to this one and I was a bit worried about wires on my job hanging loose."

Mr Spencer said: "You were worried that some of the wires that you have been involved in could be in the same state?"

Mr Court said: "I was worried. But when we checked there were none."

He said the remaining wire, still connected at the other end to a fuse, was taped up with black tape with a marker to distinguish it.

The next day two senior engineers asked him to remove the wire completely, but he refused. He cut off a short length and gave it to one of the engineers.

The inquiry continues today.

Fig 6.7   Courtesy The *Birmingham Post*

page lead. The decision to top the page with the most vivid one of a crashed train coach being hoisted past a house establishes an instant eye-catcher, and takes the reader straight down through the headline to the intro. [The page] benefits, with its left to right movement, by being placed on the left-hand side of the page. At the same time the two single column pictures of people involved give a human dimension to the text of the story and provide a middle of the page breaker. The cropping in all cases is impeccable, accentuating in particular the composition of the main one [i.e., main photo].

TASK

Summarise in your own words why the two authors approve of the design of this newspaper page.

Here, in this professional talk between two newspaper men is a clear assumption that the designer's job is to draw in the reader through any means possible. In fictional media, the attempt to engage the audience is even more marked. Think, for example, of scary music in films, or the point-of-view shot, whereby we the viewers are shown scenes and people as if we were actually standing in the characters' own shoes. These techniques encourage our empathy, our feeling of being involved. Even a factual text like the TV news has stories which are scripted in a way that heightens their impact and a structure that presents them in bite-size manageable chunks to keep us alert and stimulated.

Addresser and addressee

The pursuit of audience engagement by the mass media has led some critics to abandon terms like (media) producer and (media) consumer in favour of terms like 'addresser' and 'addressee' (i.e. the person being addressed or talked to by the text.) The link between the two words, like the link between employer/employee or trainer/trainee, suggests a particular kind of relationship between text and audience, one in which the addressee, like the employee or the trainee is less powerful than the other half of the pairing. Although employees and trainees are not always obedient, their freedom to do what they want is limited by their position. By calling the media consumers addressees, the same restrictions are implied — the term suggests they are restricted in the interpretations they can make of texts. The issue is: how restricted?

TASK

Discuss the following pairs of words. They are often used in Media Studies. Each pair has a subtle difference of emphasis in what it implies about media and audiences. Working in threes, see if you can pin down the differences and when you have made some progress, share it with the rest of the group.

Producer	Consumer
Maker	User
Text	Reader
Addresser	Addressee
Sender	Receiver

Models of audience

The 'hypodermic' model

The model is sometimes also called the stimulus/response model because it implies that, just as when you tap someone's knee-cap, his or her leg will automatically jerk (stimulus and response), so when an audience receives a certain piece of media, they will automatically respond in a predictable way (hence the phrase 'knee-jerk reaction').

Sometimes described as the 'simple effects model'. In its most basic form, the 'hypodermic' model would see the audience member as entirely passive — the classic couch potato. Messages from the media would enter the person's mind where they would have a straightforward influence on what the person thought, believed and subsequently did. If, for example, that person was shown racist reporting or exposed to violence that was shown as exciting in the media, they would become (more) racist as a result or go out looking for violent fun. The simple effects model is also called the 'hypodermic' model because it is comparing the media effects process to a hypodermic syringe. With the hypodermic model of media effects, media content is 'injected' straight into the person's mind like a kind of uncontrollable indoctrination.

You have probably thought already of many objections to this model. For one thing, it does not seem to take into account the fact that audiences are offered a myriad of contradictory impressions from the media. Some representations may be racist, many are not and some are determinedly anti-racist, so which of these effects will be hypodermically syringed into us? It also seems to underestimate the power of other factors in our lives. If we have been brought up to believe that racism is a negative force and/or we are black and/or we have good friends from many different racial groups, we are unlikely to be turned around by opposing influences in the media. We are much more likely to use our previous experience to produce an oppositional reading of any racially biased material.

The above summary of the hypodermic model is quite a crude one. It would be hard to find anyone who really believed absolutely that the media worked in this way to create simple effects directly on society. But although the model in its simplest form is unconvincing, none the less, many people seem to imply that it is what they believe when they talk about 'copycat' behaviour or

See 'Fabulous Powers:
Blaming the Media', in *Television
Mythologies: Stars, Shows and Signs*,
Comedia/MK Media Press, Ian
Connel, 1984

relate extreme acts of violence — like the James Bulger Case — to violence depicted in the media, as if one directly caused the other.

However, theorist Ian Connel argues that, automatically blaming the media for social problems can have a negative effect because it can make people feel helpless. How, they might feel, can they act to change society against such a powerful force as the media if it has such 'fabulous power'? It is also a way of getting off the hook, because you can avoid looking for other reasons for society's ills.

See fig. 6.8

David Morley (1986), *Family
Television*, Comedia.

TASK

Below are three separate excerpts: one from The Guardian and two from interviews. Each refers in passing to media effects. Read each one carefully and answer the following question, writing about half a page for each extract.

How far do you think either the people involved/speaking or the journalists are drawing on the hypodermic model? Justify your views in each case.

Excerpt 1

Patrick Wintour and Madeleine Bunting, 'Natural Born Killers Video Held Back', the *Guardian* 14 March 1996.

Excerpt 2

Interview recorded for *Family Television*. A mother is talking about what she allows her children to watch on TV — some of the references to TV programmes are a little outdated but it is still easy to see what the speaker is getting at.

> *Mother: I put my foot down on very violent films – like The Long Good Friday – but things like The A-Team or Nightrider – no one dies in it and I don't think the children take it more seriously than they do with Tom and Jerry cartoons. [About Grange Hill – a serial set in a secondary school]. It's good – because they always get their come-uppance, the bad children. They always come to sticky end. The wrong is always righted and there is a lot of anti-racism in there. It's very good, I think. It can be quite frightening to fear going to secondary school, but if you see what it could be like and the sort of things you're going to meet, it could take some of the sting out of it.*

Excerpt 3

Interview recorded for Family Television.

> *Father: We could sell these [UK series] abroad, rather than import the American rubbish we do . . . with the violence – the silly violence. I don't like children to see some of the violence. Being an ambulance man, I've seen violence. TV has a lot to answer for with children. I have to take them to hospital, I've got to pick them up from police stations and they have been imitating the characters on television. You see an old lady get cracked over the head on television and you don't see what happens afterwards.*

DUNBLANE MASSACRE | 5

Deaths halt film centred on couple's murder spree

Natural Born Killers video held back

The screen

New questions over impact of cinema violence

**Patrick Wintour
and Madeleine Bunting**

WARNER Brothers yesterday deferred the video release of Oliver Stone's controversial film Natural Born Killers, in which a couple go on a two-week random killing spree.

The killings yesterday at Dunblane have rekindled the debate about the impact of violence seen on television and at the cinema and are certain to unleash a torrent of self-searching about moral and social breakdown.

The decision to hold back the film by Warner Brothers Videos, conveyed yesterday to David Alton, the Liberal Democrat MP who has led the campaign to prevent its release, will strengthen the hand of campaigners who urge control over violent videos.

Michael Heap, managing director of Warner Brothers, told Mr Alton by phone from California that it would not be appropriate to release the film at this stage in the light of the Dunblane massacre.

More than 80 MPs, including former ministers, had planned to table an Early Day Motion condemning the video release — due on March 22 — after it was given a certificate by the British Board of Film Classification.

A furious Mr Alton said: "If this film is not appropriate to be released as a video because of this horrific incident, it is not appropriate to be shown at any time. All the evidence shows that these videos lead to a culture of violence and we need to stop it."

Mary Whitehouse, former chairwoman of the National Viewers and Listener's Association, said yesterday that the use of violence as entertainment desensitised people. "There have always been lonely, bitter individuals. The difference now is that they are particularly vulnerable to the images of violence as entertainment which is an approved and accepted part of our society.

"The chasm we have crossed in our day is using as entertainment violent images which used to shock us."

But David Selbourne, a writer on civil ethics, argued that the killings were a ghastly illustration of social breakdown in which individuals could become totally estranged from their fellow human beings. Only in such isolation are individuals vulnerable to the television diet of violence.

"Out of estrangement comes a sense of individual entitlement without moral restraint to impose your own ego on others," he said. "We have become habituated to . . . a gush of blood from an innocent body on the screen. If you gaze on these things in isolation . . . with no bonds of family or friends, you come to think this is a human norm."

Fig 6.8   Courtesy *The Guardian*
14 March 1996

Conspiracy theories

Conspiracy theorists believe there is a well organised attempt among a powerful élite to affect what the media says and hence to control the way that we think and stop us seeing the truth. Again this can be a view that comes from a left-wing or a right-wing source (depending on what is seen as the media's main political message). Belief in the existence of big conspiratorial secret groups has little credibility with most Media Studies theorists, because it is hard to believe that such well organised plotting among so many people could be kept a secret. However, this is not to say that there is not considerable manipulation and attempted manipulation of what the media says by public relations experts, government and by people with something to sell.

Hegemonic model

A more sophisticated version of the conspiracy model is the Marxist model of **hegemony**. This would argue that, while there may not be conscious, devious conspiracies, it is true that the more powerful people in society, including those who direct and own the mass media, tend to come from a similar upper or upper middle class background and for that reason they may have similar attitudes views which then find their way into our media. Here the conspiracy is not seen as conscious but rather the unconscious act of a particular class working in its own self-interest. Antonio Gramsci argued, for example, that in democratic societies the dominant classes hold their power not through force (as would be the case under a military regime like Burma) but by persuading the rest of the population that what was good for themselves — i.e., good for the dominant classes or groups — was the best for everyone. In other words they established a kind of agreed **ideology** or set of values which are then adhered to by most social groups. He called this process **hegemony** — establishing the hegemonic values of society. The mass media, Gramsci argued, have a powerful role to play in maintaining this hegemony. To take an example: from a Marxist point of view, the role of Queen is over privileged and unnecessary, and her position as our sovereign reinforces the second-class status of ordinary people. However, the media on the whole report the news about the Queen with respect and affection (although this is increasingly less true of other royals). A Marxist might argue that this pattern of reporting creates a hegemonic belief among most members of society that the Queen is a good thing and therefore by implication it is quite normal that some people have great wealth while others are poor. Some Marxists use the term 'false consciousness' to describe beliefs that are widely held but which do not seem to be in the self-interest of the people who hold them. An often quoted example of this is the belief that trade unions have too much power and cause trouble which can be found among those who might well benefit materially if there were more powerful trade unions.

The problem with the idea of false consciousness is the implication that one group of people (in this case Marxists) can see the truth while others (notably the working classes) are taken in by ideology put out by the media.

Agenda setting

Stuart Hall took Gramsci's ideas and developed them in a slightly different way. It is not so much, he argued, that the media tell us directly what to *think* as what to *think about*. They define the shape of public debate by putting certain things on the agenda and downplaying others. So, for example, unemployment is often featured as a sad social problem in the popular media but its causes are less frequently discussed. An 'agenda', in a meeting, also organises the discussion by putting things in groups. However, the media categories produced in this way can be questionable. See, for example, a previously discussed tendency to bracket news involving young black Britons as automatically related to the 'law and order' category.

Finally while both the hegemonic model and the agenda-setting models may seem quite persuasive when we look at media **content**, but the same problem remains for audience theory. These models still cannot reveal what sense a media audience makes of that content in their minds. Is it the case that the mass media has the power to make us believe things and act in ways which we would not were it not for their influence?

Trivialisation

'Today's Television and Tomorrow's World' essay in Len Masterman, (ed.) (1984), *Television Mythologies. Stars, Shows and Signs*, Comedia/MK Media Press

For a number of media critics and people in the public, a major concern is the belief that the media tend to trivialise things that deserve to be taken more seriously, that they place too much emphasis on **entertainment** at the expense of information and debate. Kevin Robins and Frank Webster, for example, are very critical of the television science programme *Tomorrow's World*. They believe the upbeat, jaunty tone of the programme does more to overstimulate viewers than to increase their understanding of science.

> *There is a distinct trivialisation of many of the topics covered, as entertainment comes to prevail over information. The viewer, it is assumed, is not too bright.*

Another argument around trivialisation concerns the saturation of the schedules with trivial programming, designed to appeal to a mass audience. This is often referred to as the 'lowest common denominator', implying that in order to find a common ground of appeal to a mass market, the programming of Saturday nights is going low down the scale of good taste and deliberately excluding programmes that are more intelligent or challenging. 'Lowest common denominator' is a phrase that often appears in discussion about popular media forms, but it is a potentially dangerous one because while it appears to be talking about 'taste' it is often really talking about social class. It suggests that minority programmes and high culture is good while popular entertainment is low and bad.

TASK

Tape-record a conversation/in-depth interview with a chosen person (not a Media Studies specialist) about their views on the relationship between the media and society. You will need to think up some well phrased, open-ended questions to encourage them to talk at length and express their opinions. After the interview, listen to the tape carefully and write a summary of the person's opinions on this topic using plenty of quotes. Are there points at which they seem to be adopting (either consciously or unconsciously) any of the models so far discussed?

Audience (or 'subject') positioning

The audience-positioning model, which grows from the same academic roots as the language of addresser and addressee, comes from psychology and the study of psychoanalysis. It stresses the way that a text can 'fix' us into a position and so seriously reduce the choice we have in interpreting its message. Perhaps we have all experienced an example of this when we find ourselves moved nearly to tears by something we know in our hearts to be tacky and sentimental.

The theory of audience positioning is most advanced in film studies. Some feminist film theorists have been interested to find out how female spectators respond to the classic Hollywood film which is often quite masculine in its content. For example, a voice-over narrative in a film, which is most commonly the voice of a man, dictates how the text should be read by telling you what you are seeing and often what it means. At a deeper and less resistible level much camera work offers a male point of view. This can be because the hero is the one carrying the story forward (we go where they go) or more literally that we are offered point of view shots through which we see the action and characters as if we are looking through the man's eyes. If, for example, the hero meets a new woman and the camera runs suggestively up her body indicating her sexiness (and his interest), we in the audience have little choice about how to read that shot whether we are male or female, feminist or not. In this passing moment of the story we will have taken on the message of 'she's sexy' or 'cor!' even if in our everyday lives this is not how we automatically evaluate the women we meet. At the same time, the camera has told us that the purpose of this woman is to be looked at: It has positioned us as voyeuristic spectators.

A brief summary of the models discussed so far

The models discussed so far are different in their emphases but they also share a number of features.

■ They all seek to define the nature of the relationship between the media and its audiences.

■ Some, like the hypodermic model, are specific about how they see this relationship, while others — like trivialis-ation — assume how the audience will respond from what is *in* the media, its content. For example, the critics of *Tomorrow's World* seem to assume, without really proving, that if the programme is trivialising or patronising, then this will make the audience think trivially and feel intimidated.

■ They all, to different degrees, assume the audience is passive. The simple effects model assumes that we are utterly passive. We do nothing in our minds with media messages except to absorb them. The messages are boss and we are their victims. Other models, like the agenda setting model, credit the audience with a little more power to negotiate their interpretations. But none the less, the emphasis is still on what the media *does* to people.

Texts and readers

See Unit 1 on semiotics.

Using the term 'reader' already creates a picture of a more active audience member than does the language of 'effects' and 'receivers', etc. However, most semiotic approaches stress the codes and conventions at work in the text which are likely to encourage particular kinds of reading because the reader has 'learnt' what those codes mean.

Dominant, negotiated and oppositional readings

S. Hall *et al.* (eds) (1980), *Culture, Media, Language,* Hutchinson

Stuart Hall's influential article 'Encoding/decoding' developed his work on agenda setting by introducing a number of new terms to help us think through what may be happening when media consumers read texts. Certainly he argued texts are coded and constructed in particular ways and in his view these were usually ways which supported a right-wing cultural hegemony. However, he also argued that readers are not naive or stupid. They come to a text with their own opinions and their readings are influenced by previous experiences. To take an obvious example, a feminist is unlikely to be very impressed with 'page 3'. Although the text has been constructed (encoded) both visually and verbally to emphasise a particular view (desirability, availability, 'good clean fun for the lads', etc.) the feminist reader is likely to decode this text in a very different way. She might feel angry that this was a 'typical' example of sexism in the media. Her reading would be **oppositional** to the intentions or unconscious assumptions of the text.

Hall's way of looking at things here opens up a useful new space in audience theory because it encourages a two-stage approach to texts and readers. The text may say one thing, he argues, but the reader may respond differently. This simple proposition, called the encoding/decoding thesis, is useful because it allows us to consider what the text is doing ideologically, including its possible effects, without at the same time assuming that the audience are a uniform bunch of idiots.

Meaning, in Hall's model, arises from the encounter of the codes in the text with the life experiences of the reader. Hall hypothesised that this encounter might produce one of three types of reading:

Note: David Morley and Charlotte Brunsdon's work tests out these ideas and further develops them. "Family Television: Cultural Power and Domestic Leisure" (1986) is a very interesting and accessible read — highly recommended!

- **An oppositional reading:** As discussed in the page 3 example. Here the reader not only reacts against the text but does so from an oppositional system of views. For example a number of people reacted very negatively in June 1996 to the *Daily Mirror*'s reporting of a forthcoming football match between England and Germany. 'Achtung!' said the first page and from then on continued over three pages in this pseudo war-time style demanding that Germany 'remove its [football] troops from these shores' and so on. Complaint from readers was so strong that the *Mirror* was obliged to climb down and send a hamper of goodies to the German team to show it was all just in fun. The people making these oppositional readings were doing so from a particular worked out standpoint. They were pacifists, they felt the war should be forgotten or they were concerned about the effects of xenophobic reporting on volatile football supporters. They read the article through a system of (already) oppositional views.
- **A negotiated reading:** Here the reader may buy into part of a text's message but not the whole implication. For example, a trade unionist may be persuaded by the negative coverage of a particular strike yet not relinquish their adherence to the trade union movement in general.
- **A dominant reading:** Here the reader agrees with the line taken in the text because both the text and the reader are influenced by the same dominant ideology.

Hall's model of encoding and decoding was useful because it helped pull audience theory out of the hypodermic rut. However, there are problems with it, and he has altered his own views to some degree since he wrote the original article. First it is a theory that grows out of a (left-wing) concern with political reporting about strikes, race and social protest where, Hall believed, the dominant ideology in the reporting supported the dominant ideology of the (then) Conservative government. You can see how his three kinds of reading line up with the three main political responses or

Fig 6.9 Oppositional, negotiated and dominant readings

See Introduction, in David Morley (1986), *Family Television, Cultural Power and Domestic Leisure*, Comedia on the ever changing audience member.

parties — the left: oppositional and rebellious; the middle ground: less revolutionary but still asking questions; and the right (then): politically dominant and working hard to hegemonise the interest of a particular class. However, the model is harder to apply to non-news-based media. What would a 'negotiated reading' of *The Clive James Show* look like? It also leads to a tendency, although this was not its intention, to divide the audience into two camps, those who 'see through' the media and those who do not. But this is a rather static view of the individual media reader. As Hall himself later put it: 'We are all in our heads, several audiences at once.'.

The uses and gratifications model

The uses and gratifications model is one that we often use casually without being aware that we are doing so. We might say: 'I always flop down with that programme when I come home from work — it's a great way to unwind,' or 'I want to catch the last part of the news tonight to see who won in the football.' Here we are defining in everyday language how we are seeking to *use* that piece of media and what gratification or enjoyment we expect from it.

These may be just some of the gratifications that we look for. Reading the news in a newspaper may allow us to escape from the day's pressures and it may also make us feel good that we are 'on top of' the world's events, that we are keeping up. McQuail and his research colleagues wanted to put this model to the test by seeing if they could discover what uses people were making of television quiz shows. They used a questionnaire with a large number of different statements on it which people could tick if they felt they applied to themselves like 'I like the excitement of a close finish,' or 'I like to learn something new.' They concluded from their research that there was a pattern in individuals' responses and that most of the audience's replies were clustered into one of four categories. These are summarised below:

■ **Self-rating appeal:** People whose answers fell in this group tended to enjoy quiz programmes because it made them feel

D. **M**cQuail, **J**. Blumler and R. Brown (1972), *The Television Audience: A Revised perspective.*

good about themselves. They ticked replies like 'I like to imagine that I am on the programme and winning,' or they were pleased that they had been backing the top team or, more callously, they liked to laugh at the contestants when they made a mistake. The central feature of their response was that they were using the quiz programme to help define themselves to themselves.

- **A basis for social interaction:** In this category, people tended to use the quiz shows to talk about with family and friends. Some liked the way the programme brought the family together and provided a common topic of conversation with their children. This is an interesting result because it implies that, far from destroying communities — something that the media are often accused of — the quiz shows were providing a focus for communal interaction.
- **The excitement of quiz shows:** People in this category are the adrenaline freaks. They reported enjoying close finishes and getting emotionally involved in the competition.
- **Educational appeal:** These people stressed how much they learned from quiz shows. They also said they respected people who got the answers right and said that it was pleasant when the shows made you see that you knew more than you realised.

(One of the appealing features of the uses and gratifications model is that it does at least allow for the idea that the media might be pleasurable. Effects models on the other hand sometimes sound as if they consider media usage as some kind of social problem!)

These categories have been added to by other uses and gratifications theorists who have also discerned particular tendencies for users to seek functions from the media such as:

- diversion: escape from everyday pressures;
- developing personal relationships: either imaginary ones between consumer and media characters, like newsreaders and soap stars, or real ones as the media is used as a topic of conversation with friends;
- personal identity: for example, comparing the user's life to those of people depicted in the media.

TASK

Choose a type of media product (newspaper sports pages, horoscopes, phone-in radio, etc.) Using the same method as **M**cQuail, write a number of statements for your respondents to agree or disagree with about why they use this type of product and what they get out of it. Try out your questionnaire on two different groups of people like men and women, or young and older people, or people from two different ethnic backgrounds, teachers and students, etc. Can you, like **M**cQuail, find a pattern which puts their answers into different clusters? What explanation can you give for any patterns which you perceive? Write up your experiment under the headings:

- methods used;
- questionnaire results;
- commentary and interpretation of results.

If we now look back and compare the uses and gratifications model with the models of simple media effects, you can see that it is almost as if we have come full circle. Now it seems the viewer/reader/consumer is the boss. Just as you might go into a supermarket and pick out what you want so, the uses and gratifications people seem to suggest, you can 'go into' a media text and take what you want or need. The emphasis here has switched to active choice on the part of the reader rather than passive response. There are, however, questions to ask about this model. One book suggests this sounds too much like *laissez-faire* economics, overemphasising our freedom of choice.

*'Watching Dallas': [Ien Aug (1985),Watching Dallas: Soap Opera and the Melodramatic Imagination, **M**ethuen].*

It is the TV networks which decide which programmes are to be broadcast and which not. The audience can only wait and see what menu it will be served. In this sense the TV audience is passive.

*(**J**ohn Fiske: (1982), Introduction To Communication Studies, **M**ethuen*

A second reservation about the uses and gratifications model, at least in its most basic form, is that it may be too individualistic. It seems to imply that we are all free to pick and choose meanings according to our individual personalities. This contradicts what we know about the patterns that exist in media consumption along the lines of sex, age and class. Fiske, for example. points out that McQuail's respondents were all working class and lived in council housing estates. Perhaps, he suggests, there is a pattern running across their responses because all their 'uses' could be seen as a form of compensation, compensating for low social status or for the fact that many of them were early school leavers. Later researchers in the uses and gratifications school have put more emphasis on the way particular **groups** might use the media.

There is some statistical evidence, however, to support the perspective that individuals quite consciously use the media to fit around other aspects of their lives. For example, we know that patterns of media consumption (amount, timing, type of, etc.) depend on the seasons, the weather, school holidays, etc. It is also worth noting that, while the amount of media available has escalated enormously — television now broadcasts for many extra hours of the day — people are still watching the same number of hours per person as they did before this happened. Again this suggests that people use the media to fit in with their other patterns of life.

EVIDENCE COLLECTION POINT

While reading this element you will have found some of the models of media and audience more convincing than others. Choose an area of this theory you find interesting and design an experiment which will put a model or an aspect of it to the test in a practical piece of research. This task is left deliberately open-ended to encourage you to think imaginatively about how you might design such an experiment and which aspect of the theory to choose. Write up your experiment under the following headings.

- Hypothesis (the idea you are testing out, your angle in the experiment).

- Experiment design.

- Comments on experiment design — e.g., does it now need rethinking?

- Experiment results and implications for audience theory.

EVIDENCE COLLECTION POINT

A large part of this element has been concerned to investigate the possible influences the media may have on society. In an extended essay, in your own words (approximately 1,500 words) evaluate the main models available to describe this relationship and explain, with good reasons, which you find the most convincing approach.

TASK

Write a letter, as requested in the article below, in reply to the editor of the *Independent* giving him your views on his dilemma on how to deal with reporting disturbing facts. Use ideas on audience research you have gained from this element to help you construct your argument.

LETTER *from* THE EDITOR

The reassuring thing about editing is that the difficult decisions turn out to be ethical ones, or at least about values in a general way. This is how it should be. The biggest problem coming up for us here may be the Sophie Hook murder case – the sex-murder of the seven-year-old girl who was snatched from a garden tent.

It seems clear that the evidence will be lengthy and horrible. My preference is to avoid most of the evidence, covering the main developments in the case in an episodic rather than daily way, and steering clear of the nasty bits. This time, that's what we will do.

But plenty of my colleagues think this is plain wrong: we are a newspaper and should report all the facts, no matter how unpleasant.

They have a point: many readers, however much they shudder, want to know everything there is to know about such crimes. And sometimes, the telling detail matters or resolves some important unknown. The Fred and Rosemary West trial, Dunblane, the Bulger case – these could not have been properly reported without some terrible stuff.

So there is no point in telling you that we have an answer for, or a formula to, what has become almost a weekly dilemma, if not yet a daily one. If anyone has suggestions or strong views about it, I'd be glad to hear them.

Fig 6.10   *Independent* 29 June 1996, Letter From the Editor

TASK

Comprehension

Read the following interview with David **M**orley and answer the questions that follow.

Interview with David Morley.

J.P.: Why did you want to do this research for *Family Television*?

D.M.: It was supposed to be part of our original project on *Nationwide* [see above for description of this research]. We said then we wanted to interview people not just in an artificial setting, like where they went to college — artificial in the sense that that is not where they normally watch television. We said then we wanted to interview people at home. But we just didn't have the money to do it. Also I had got more and more interested in a kind of anthropological approach which involves observing people do things in the places they normally do them.

With the *Nationwide* research the context was quite artificial, for example, in some instances I was getting people to give interpretations of programmes that they wouldn't normally have considered watching! So what was the validity of the data? With *Family Television* I was after *a more contextualised understanding of the activity of watching television*. I began to understand that the actual watching of television is in itself quite a complicated activity. In most families it is governed by all kinds of complicated rules to do with who sits where, who gets to choose the programmes, who watches which programmes with which other members of the household, what kinds of conversation are or are not permitted or encouraged as an accompaniment when who is in the room and all that stuff about who gets to have the remote control. It's just like anthropologists who study the rules of society by, for example, watching the family meal to understand who cooks it, who serves it, who eats at what time and so on. Television watching is just as complicated as an activity. It is at the centre of household life in so many cases that it needs to be taken seriously. So rather than just looking at the interpretations of programmes I begun to think I needed to look at the nature of the activity. It's not a random activity. It's a thoroughly rule-bound activity and you need to understand what the rules are which is what the study was designed to bring out.

J.P.: Were you surprised by your findings about the gender differences in watching TV?

D.M.: What can I say that isn't in the last chapter of the book on gender?! ... The whole thing surprised me. I had not imagined when I designed the research that its principal focus would be on gender differences. I thought that the principal differences would be class differences. I hadn't anticipated for a moment the extent of the gender differences. It literally, in that old-fashioned way, emerged from the data. Again and again. Almost everything about men and women's relationship to television was different. There were exceptional cases that are written up in the book like the household where the woman worked and the man was unemployed, but the main patterns were very marked.

J.P.:   Why do you think these differences exist?

D.**M**.:   It's not to do with biological differences, we're not talking about 'maleness' and 'femaleness' here, we're talking about cultural categories, masculine and feminine subjectivities and ways of inhibiting those subjectivities. I think it's about differences in the relationship with the home in that, in our culture, the home is women's work, the sphere of feminine expertise and competence and also the sphere of labour for these women. Their husbands regard the home as a place they come back to when they've been to work. For the women 'coming home' did not mean resting. It meant a different kind of work. Even though many of them worked outside the home as well, they saw themselves as primarily responsible for the domestic work. Obviously this might be different in different families and in different classes. But among the white working class families I interviewed, there was a very traditional gendered division of labour and this determined the different relationship to television as far as I could see.

J.P.:   If I said your book fell within the uses and gratifications school of thought, what would you say?

D.**M**.:   I would say: 'rubbish!' What I am trying to do is *not* uses and gratifications. That model is a very individualistic one about the way different individuals use the media as a consequence of their different psychological make-up. It's completely non-sociological and non-cultural. Johnny does this and Jimmy does that — well what can you do with that?! My work was about categories of people. These were women who inhabit a particular cultural mode of femininity which means that they understand their obligations in the home in a particular kind of way. It was systematically the same for all the women in the sample. It's nothing to do with individuality. What you *do* want to extract [i.e., positively] from the uses and gratifications approach is that people do make choices and they're not passive, but you can't leave it at that individualistic level.

J.P.:   When you're teaching about media and its possible 'effects', how do you go about it?

D.**M**.:   I look with my students at a number of different models and evaluate them. So we look at the hypodermic model and talk about what's wrong with that, and then we go to the other extreme and look at the uses and gratifications model and talk about what's wrong with that and — lo and behold! — I take the line that the truth is somewhere in between, that the media are very powerful, that they do set agendas, they do provide the conceptual categories with which we will tend to think in the absence of anything else. They do have very profound effects. It's pointless to imagine that they don't have effects, but at the same time we're not just a load of zombies soaking up whatever the media point at us. We're making choices within what's available to us and we make interpretations of what's available based on the cultural resources that we have available. So we are active, but within the limits of our circumstances. Marx said people make history but not in the circumstances of their own choosing. So people make interpretations of the media, but only with the resources at their disposal.

Questions:

- What does Morley mean when he says he wanted a more *contextualised* understanding of the *activity* of watching television? Why did he want this?

- Why, in his opinion are there differences in the relationship of men and women to television? Looking back over the summary of his findings in *Family Television* (above), do you agree with his interpretations of the reason for these differences or are there other factors you feel should be considered?

- What is Morley's view on the issue of media effects? Explain this in your own words.

- Reread the interview above. What do you think of the questions asked? Are there other questions that you would have asked or other lines of enquiry that you would have pursed and if so what are they?

6.3 ANALYSE AND INTERPRET PUBLISHED DATA

'Information' on its own is relatively useless. What is important is how pieces of information are put together, how they are **analysed** and **interpreted** and what action follows on from the analysis. From the analysis of data on media consumption, some far-reaching decisions can be made. A television company might redirect its programming, a newspaper might change its staff, an advertiser might spend millions of pounds on a campaign or an academic might produce a radically new theory.

The analysis of audience data needs to be able to uncover the appropriate **sources** of information, sift through the data, rejecting what's irrelevant and put what's left into a meaningful order. They also need to keep an open mind, following new lines of enquiry when inspiration strikes!

In commercial research, there is usually a marked division between the people who collect audience data and the people who make sense of it in order to advise on subsequent action. Perhaps not surprisingly this second category of workers tend to be much better paid. People who can extrapolate significant trends from bland-looking information are very useful not just in the media industries but in the many business ventures which can benefit from predicting changes in the market. With academic research, the researcher and the analyst may or may not be the same person but it is still true that their work is judged on the strength of its conclusions, and drawing conclusions is an interpretative act.

Elements 6.1 and 6.2 outline a number of sources of data and approaches to research. The following tasks should enable you to begin to apply them.

NB Don't forget to refer to the GNVQ performance criteria for 6.3 when carrying out these tasks.

Feasibility report on new cinema development

The sports and leisure department of your local council has commissioned you to produce a detailed report on the feasibility of building a new cinema in your area. The cinema would form part of the council's overall economic regeneration programme and aims to create new jobs and add to the social and cultural life of the area. As an independent researcher, you will be required to present the information back to the council, who will use it both to underpin the economic strategy, and to present the area favourably to prospective cinema owners. You have been supplied below with a limited amount of published data on national trends in cinema-going, which

You may decide to ensure that your information is right up-to-date by sifting though the trade press or BFI's Film and Television Handbook to add to that provided.

Note: Make sure that you take account of the number of *screens* rather than simply the number of cinemas.

You may also wish to prepare a presentation to the council, as evidence for Unit 7.4.

should enable you to forecast growth or decline of future audiences. You will also need to carry out your own local research, to establish:

- the number of screens in your area (in a rural area or small town, you would research the number of screens within a 30-mile radius);

- the kinds of screens available (multiplex? arthouse?);

- the number of cinema seats available;

- whether the growth of one kind of cinema development has led to a decline in another (e.g., has an out-of-town multiplex opened and a local cinema closed?);

- the demographics and cinema-going habits of local people compared to national trends.

The council has asked you to pay special attention to the following questions:

- Is a new cinema likely to attract good size audiences?

- What kind of audiences might they be?

- What sorts of films would help make the cinema commercially successful?

- What sort of cinema might work well for the area/projected audiences?

- Where might it be located?

Present your findings as an illustrated report of not less than 1,500 words.

A&R = Artiste and Repertoire

Some advice on conducting audience research

Use: Use the sources available. Using a source is very different from reproducing it. With audience data, you need to use only those parts which are really appropriate. A fact or a quote is only as useful as the argument it is supporting so anything you use must be there for a reason.

Focus: The detective approaches the scene of a crime with a few central questions in their mind (like 'who did it?!'). Because they are focused on the key issues they are able to organise their material as it arises. The first thing you need to do when you approach a complicated research and analysis task is to ask yourself: what am I being asked to do exactly? Boil the problem down to a few basic questions. Try explaining to a friend what you are doing. If they cannot understand, it probably means you are not clear enough in your own mind and a foggy approach to a complicated problem leads to foggy and unfocused results.

Trends: As you work through it, bear in mind that spotting trends, be it in music, fashion or media consumption can be a very well-paid job. **A&R** people in the music industry will spend quite a bit of their time lurking around in clubs. Here they can watch out for the new and talented bands but they are also on the lookout for something more subtle — a feel of where things are going next. In the assignment you, or your employers in the council, are going to ask a cinema chain to invest up to six figures in a new venture based on future media consumption so you need to make a convincing argument about trends.

Synthesise: This means 'bring together and mix' but it is the key to a good research-based report. When you have selected the pieces of information you want to use, try arranging and rearranging them on the table. What bits go together to produce a creative and convincing argument? Can a well-chosen quote punch home a largely statistical argument? Or can you construct a diagram or chart which just sums up the arguments you are making so the reader gets a very clear picture?

Tone: This assignment gives you a few problems about tone, the feel of your writing. On the one hand, it has to be a report which is usually a rather formal, closely argued document. On the other hand your council wants to use this document to persuade the cinema chains, and persuasion is usually more emotive and sensational. This is a dilemma for you to solve, but feel free to be creative!

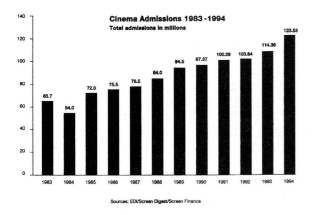

Fig 6.11

UK Sites and Screens 1984–1994		
Year	Total sites	Total screens
1984	660	1 271
1985	663	1 251
1986	660	1 249
1987	648	1 215
1988	699	1 416
1989	719	1 559
1990	737	1 685
1981	724	1 789
1992	735	1 845
1993	723	1 890
1994	734	1 869

Source: Screen Digest

Fig 6.12

Annual Trends		1985	1987	1989	1991	1993	1995
All ever go to cinema (7 + popn.)	%	49	54	60	61	69	75
Ever go 7–14	%	86	88	85	80	93	96
Ever go 25–34	%	62	65	72	70	82	87
Go once a month or more 15–24	%	23	26	30	33	35	37
Go once a month or more 25–34	%	7	7	11	15	18	19

Source: CAVIAR 13 1995.

Fig 6.13

Cult hits lure public back to the big screen

LOUISE JURY

A sharp 35 per cent rise in attendances at the start of this year confirms that the British public is returning to the cinema.

The spectacular success of the home-grown hits *Trainspotting*, based on the cult Irvine Welsh novel, and Emma Thompson's *Sense and Sensibility* was highlighted by the film industry as a key factor in this revival.

The figures provided yesterday by the Office for National Statistics showed 32.2 million

Top 10 UK films

1 (1) Up Close and Personal (£350,710) US
2 (2) Now and Then (£228,591) US
3 (3) From Dusk Till Dawn (£22,391) US
4 (4) The Juror (£22,342) US
5 (9) Fargo (£130,965) US
6 (6) Vampire in Brooklyn (£21,814) US
7 (-) How to Make an American Quilt (£89,990) US
8 (5) Spy Hard (£83,078) US
9 (7) Secrets and Lies (£71,530) UK
10 (8) Muppet Treasure Island (£63,440) US/UK

Chart, supplied by Screen International. Figures show individual grosses for last week.

cinema tickets were sold in the first three months of the year, an increase of more than one-third on the 22.5 million admissions during the same period last year.

The period does not include National Cinema Day, on 2

June, when cut-price tickets marking the 100th anniversary of the cinema attracted 1 million people.

Tony Slaughter, of the British Film Institute, said they were delighted at the figures and looked forward to 150 million admissions in the near future as the film industry adapted to please the market. "There are now better films, they are better marketed and we are delighted that there is a higher UK presence among them," he said.

The re-emergence of the family film had helped, with movies like *Jumanji*, *Toy Story* and *Babe* being specially targeted at younger viewers.

Mr Slaughter said: "In the Eighties, family films were not where the market was, but now the film-makers have realised it is very important to get a younger audience."

There had also been more investment in cinemas, as companies like Virgin opened modern multiplexes with top facilities. David Cole, of Rank Organisation, which owns 75 Odeon cinemas nationwide, said: "The films have been strong this quarter and there has been a noticeable upsurge."

Sense and Sensibility, Thompson's production of the Jane Austen novel, starring a big-name British cast that included Hugh Grant, seems to have encouraged people back to the cinema. "It brought a lot of people out of hiding and hopefully they will re-establish a cinema-going habit," Mr Cole said.

Cinema attendance reached its lowest point in 1984, but has since gone up by more than 300 per cent, pushing the turnover in Britain's 470 cinemas to more than £100m in the last year.

Mr Cole said a summer of blockbusters, including Walt Disney's version of the *Hunchback of Notre Dame* and *Independence Day*, a special-effects spectacular, starring Bill Pullman and Jeff Goldblum, should enable the trend to continue.

Fig 6.14

6.4 CARRY OUT AUDIENCE RESEARCH FOR MEDIA PRODUCTS

Introduction

It is unlikely that you have got this far in your Media Studies career without having done some audience research. The purpose of this element is to make sure that, during your advanced GNVQ, you do a sustained and focused piece of audience research work: a major project. Much of this unit has been spent criticising the approaches and conclusions of other writers and researchers in the media — now it's your turn! *You* decide the questions, *you* find the respondents, *you* decide the methods and *you* derive the conclusions.

You may react to this sudden freedom in a number of different ways. Here are some typical kinds of reactions made by people at the beginning of their personal research projects:

- 'Great! I know what I want to do so now leave me alone to get on with it.' Admirably confident, this person clearly has ideas. But a word of warning — inspiration on its own will not see you through. You need to plan carefully or your project can change rapidly from inspired innovation to disorganised disaster!

- 'I can't think of anything interesting to research about audiences.' Don't worry. Very few of us have ideas that spring out of thin air. Hypotheses are created through the connections between ideas, and later parts of this chapter will help you to get the connections working.

- 'It sounds boring.' The word 'research' can summon up the image of a dry old academic rustling through bits of paper. But your research project here is about the **media** — one of the greatest sources of pleasure in modern life — and about **audiences**, in other words people. The only thing that will make your research boring is if you ask questions that you do not really want to know the answers to.

Research rewards people who are methodical, for example, in the way they construct their sample, and patient because in any project, there are always unexpected frustrations that arise and which need working through. When it comes to analysing the data, you need a mind that is clear enough to keep focused on the original research objectives, logical enough to perceive whether these have been proved or disproved, but open enough to see any new or unanticipated patterns emerging.

Research Stages:

■ identify the objectives of your research;

■ develop methods and instruments (tools) to carry it out;

■ carry it out with an appropriate sample;

■ log any relevant information you get;

■ analyse your findings and draw valid conclusions.

Not surprisingly in those agencies that specialise in research, much in the design and carrying out of projects depends on teamwork and members of the team are often selected for the specific qualities they can add into the group mix. Good managers deliberately create teams which include an 'ideas' person (to start the ball rolling), an 'evaluative' person (to make sure it rolls in the right direction), and a 'finisher' (to make sure it does not roll to a halt).

Consumption and attitudes

The element asks you to produce two pieces of audience research, one about media **consumption** and one about **attitudes**. These are fairly loose terms but the purpose is to allow you to reproduce the range of approaches we have come across so far in this unit, especially in Elements 6.1 and 6.2.

The idea of **consumption** encourages you to look at how a piece of media is taken up by the public. Who uses it? How often? What kind of people are they? These might be typical questions here, as they are for the commercial agencies like BARB. These questions seem to encourage a **quantitative** approach, although possibly not on its own. Here are some imaginary projects that deal with patterns of consumption.

"Research project ideas — consumption".

You want to find out:

1. if the total volume of media consumed goes down for students when they begin to prepare for exams.
2. the real age groups of consumers for 'age range' magazines like *19*.
3. if it is true that women consume more fictional media than men.
4. if people's reading habits change significantly according to the seasons.
5. if parents know about and implement the 9 o'clock watershed for material considered suitable for children.
6. the sex, class and age of the groups most likely to use the Internet.
7. how many people have been made aware of your local supermarket's special offer campaign by its poster and advertising campaign.
8. if David Morley's observations about men being in charge of the remote-control device is true for more middle class families.
9. how many people watch party political broadcasts and what kinds of people they are.

All these projects have two things in common. First they are all looking for information about the consumption of media (its take-up, its use) and they are all looking for patterns within a group or groups of people. In this way they are asking quite *sociological* questions.

When it comes to looking at **attitudes** we are likely to be asking more **qualitative** questions. Getting at people's attitudes implies research with a more psychological frame of reference. This does not mean that you will not use quantitative methods as well. For example, a research project that wanted to find out if a video that you made yourself had been successful in changing viewers' attitudes to a particular topic might well ask a lot of detailed questions to elicit subtle changes in people's opinions, but you might then also want to count up these answers to see if there was a pattern you could perceive across the group. On the other hand, you might take the view that, given the resources you have or the types of questions you want to ask, an in-depth unstructured focus group would be more informative. This latter method would give you a lot of qualitative information but no 'countables'. Typical projects looking at **attitudes** might be:

Research Project ideas:

You want to find out:

10. if regular TV viewers have found a new pilot series engaging enough to justify the production of a full series.

11. whether one of your local cinemas is more successful in attracting customers because of the films it screens or because of its facilities.

12. if different kinds of student groups (e.g. art students and English students) respond differently to the visual and verbal content of a newspaper.

13. if men or women get more enjoyment out of comparing notes about favourite TV programmes and if the two sexes converse on the same TV topics.

14. if children brought up in households which have a regular daily newspaper are more interested in and knowledgeable about current affairs than those who do not.

15. what kind of publicity campaign will encourage people in the UK to feel positive about a new unified European currency.

17. whether older people feel embarrassed/threatened/ indifferent/interested about new media like the Internet.

Testing out media models

Both research projects about media **consumption** and **attitudes** are capable of being used to test out the audience models which have been presented in other parts of this unit. Project 13, for example, will take you into the territory of the **uses and gratifications** model as does Project 3. With Project 15, you will have to think about media **effects** and so on. Research that is grounded in some aspect of theory will have more bite, so do not forget what you have learned from the views of others about audiences. If you have found yourself passionately agreeing or disagreeing with any of the theorists encountered in this book or elsewhere, this might give you a very good starting point for designing your own project to prove them right or wrong.

Finding ideas and setting objectives

For many people, getting started can be the most difficult part of the research process. Any number of projects come unstuck because people have grabbed at an idea because it would 'do' and then spend weeks being bored to death. You must be excited about the ideas you are researching or your project will feel tired both to you and its readers. Some ways of starting to get interesting ideas together are suggested below:

- ■ Think back to moments in your Media Studies class where you have felt involved and either did, or wanted to, participate in debate. What was the idea that grasped your imagination? Could this be worked into a project?

- ■ Is there a particular form of media/media product you enjoy or particularly hate? Are there questions to be asked about how other people consume it or their attitudes to it?

- ■ Are there any audiences to whom you have a natural access? For example, you might live near a video club, do a paper round, work at a cinema or a pub with a TV, know someone with a newspaper stand or do a lot of babysitting. Can you profit by your connections with these audiences?

- ■ Are there groups in the audience you are particularly interested in, for example children, teenagers, etc.? If so can you build these interests into your research?

- ■ Are there any topics, for example, in the news or in current debate, that particularly interest you? You might be able to find out how media reporting is affecting the views of the wider population on this or related matters.

- ■ Is there an aspect of the media you find particularly interesting like image, sound, writing, new media? Is there scope around this for an interesting project?

- ■ Is there anything happening with your local media that suggests a project idea?

- ■ Have you produced a piece of media on your course either alone or with others, or are you planning to do so? If so, bite the bullet and consider making your research on audiences about your own audience for this piece.

- ■ Can you get a real client for your research? Colleges nowadays, for example, are very interested in finding out how their marketing is going down with potential students, the local supermarket probably really would like to know who is reading about its special offers in the papers. These people may not pay you for your work, but they might talk through your objectives with you and will certainly listen to your findings. All this will provide you with useful experience and help to focus the research process.

When you have run through this list of 'idea provokers' you may find that a few ideas are forming. Jot them down in the order they come to you and do not worry at this stage if they are very vague. It can often take days to 'see' a shape in your own thoughts (it is said that 'sleeping on an idea' can help rearrange it in your mind) so do not leave the ideas part of the process until the last minute or you will not have time to let these ideas settle into something more concrete. When you think you have a rough idea of an interesting area to research, find someone to talk to about it. The ideal person might be a friend who is a good listener or your teacher/lecturer. Talk through your idea without worrying if at this stage it is full of "ums" and "ers" and does not really sound like a project. Hearing yourself explain your general area of concern will start to clarify things. The next step is to take a pen and start thinking in terms of **objectives**.

Objectives

Objectives are the point at which **hypotheses (ideas which are to be tested out in your research)** become specific. One way of organising your objectives is to have two or three main statements about what you are aiming to do like: 'find out if older people are intimidated by new media,' followed by a number of sub-aims, like 'find out if they all tend to say the same thing about it,' 'find out if they feel negative or positive about computers,' etc. Do not be afraid to make your objectives sound simple. It is hard enough to test even straightforward theories and the bravest research is often very direct. You do not need to be over-ambitious but a question like: 'does violence on television make children act violently?' is not beyond your means to research. You are unlikely to come up with the definitive answer but, if you plan your research well, you may contribute to the debate. On the other hand you might want to take a much more finely tuned objective like discovering what kind of people had been appealed to by a media campaign to sell a particular product and why. Whatever questions you start off with, make them very specific.

Resources

When you have settled on a topic, ask yourself a very simple question: do I have the resources to find the answer? A question about the behaviour of the nation's audiences is rarely with in the scope of a student to answer. You just do not have the time or the person power. However, there is nothing wrong with boiling down a question like: 'are children affected by violent television programmes?' to a question like: 'is there any evidence that the children in my two sample groups were affected by the violent television they saw on the dates I was observing them?' A lot of research works like this, taking a general question and then applying it within the frame that is available to you locally. Perhaps you can only observe working class children? Or children between the ages of 8–10? You only need to be honest about this and draw conclusions about this group specifically. You may hypothetically extrapolate from this group in your conclusions (like wondering out loud if other children might be the same) but your final comments need to be clear about what you can genuinely say that you established in your particular project.

TASK

Take the Projects 1 to 17 above and put them into three categories according to how far you feel they are achievable by a GNVQ student researcher. The three categories would be 'yes, possibly achievable', 'touch and go' and 'no, not possible to achieve'. Share your judgements with the rest of the group along with your reasons for reaching these conclusions. Then look carefully at the last two categories. Would a slight change of emphasis or phraseology make these projects possible for a student without having to abandon their original interest? If so rephrase their project for them so it could be achievable.

Choosing a method and a sample

This unit requires you to carry out real research with real people about their patterns of media consumption. You could not do the project based on secondary sources alone (see next section). So first you need to decide what kind of people will make it possible to find out what you need to know. There are a number of possible pitfalls here:

■ Thinking too narrowly. If you want to know about the effects of TV on children, you might want to set up a session where you observe them at play, another session where you watch them watching TV, another session where you talk to teachers and another where you talk to parents. Some of these might be loose unstructured chats or observations and the others might have a tight questionnaire format. This way of approaching a problem, whereby you get a lot of information from different sources and then compare it, is called **'Triangulation' — checking one kind of information against another**. So both in your method and in your choice of sample just ask yourself one key question: what (groups of) people can tell me what I need to know? Often you may find it is not just the target group for your project (e.g. in this example 'children') who can help give you the answer.

TASK

Take four of the imaginary projects in the list 1–17 and describe the sample(s) that you could construct to get information relevant to the project's goals. Be very specific: how many people would you need to talk to/observe/invite? How would you get in touch with them? What controls would you need in terms of age, class, etc.?

See 6.1 p. 357 on sampling.

■ Thinking too narrowly: To get started on the issue of methods, reread the section about the methods used in commercial and academic research. In student research, there is often a rather limp over-reliance on the 'yes/no' written questionnaire. Think about other methods like the qualitative ones and observations or simulations. Better still, think about how you can approach the problem with a range of 'triangulated' methods.

> **TASK**
> Take the list of projects that you categorised in the 'touch and go' category in the previous task. What methods could you suggest to the researcher that would allow them to carry out their project?

See D. Morley's comments on his sample in 'Family Television'.

- Being too ambitious. You are unlikely to be able to construct a sample that adequately represents the whole of UK society. Even if you try hard to reach a range of classes, ages and both sexes you will still find it difficult to cover more than a few geographical areas. You have to choose an accessible sample and make it clear that this may lead to limited wider application of your results. That does not mean, however, that your results have to be small scale or unimaginative.

- Being too lazy: If you want to know about the uses and gratifications offered by the news or by *E.R.* you will not find the whole picture by just interviewing your friends or the people in your class. Make an effort to go out and find others who are relevant to the question but not in your natural social circle. Think where you might find a group of *E.R.* watchers who are not very much like you and find out what *they* get out of the programme.

Primary and secondary sources

In this research you will be going out, with very few exceptions, to primary sources for information. In other words you will be going 'straight to the horse's mouth' and asking real people about their own media consumption and attitudes to it. This does not mean that you need to ignore secondary sources, the other people or organisations who also have views or information on your topic. There may already be useful research in your area of concern to which you can relate your findings. If you are testing out an aspect of one of the models offered earlier then you will certainly be using that research as a source of ideas.

Logging information

During the course of this research work you need to keep track of a number of different types of information. Some of these are the kinds of information you would need if you had been employed to do this for real, for example, you would need to record what the respondents said and your final analysis of it; others are the kinds of information that your GNVQ assessors need to see so they can understand your thought processes as you went through the project. Your teacher/lecturer will guide you about this according to your own project topic but the following are pieces of information you certainly need to keep and probably to write up in some form:

- Your objectives and why you think they are worthwhile.

- Your influences in choosing these objectives.
- Your thinking about how to go about the research including all the stages in developing your choice of sample and your methods of research.
- Your raw data, e.g., filled in questionnaires, the tapes of interviews or other types of recording made with respondents.
- Your processed data, for example, graphs, charts, sample quotes.
- Your analysis and conclusions.

As a basic piece of advice — keep everything! Even a few notes taken while you were on the phone may help shape your thoughts later.

Analysing and drawing valid conclusions

This part of the process can seem intimidating — the work is all done, but what does it *mean*? Well this is the bit where science meets art — in fact one of the most interesting bits. All your snippets of information may be true and factual but until the human mind gets to work, there is no pattern. Here you have considerable leeway. Someone once said that you could describe a glass which contained half liquid and half air as either 'half full' or 'half empty', and that what you choose to see said a lot about your personality. Well it is the same with survey results, there is a lot of space for interpretation. However, there are also some rules:

- Do not fly in the face of the data. If your data is saying one thing, even if it is not what you want to hear, do not turn it around and make it say something else. Be honest, but register your doubts elsewhere if they remain.
- Do not be afraid to admit if the data is contradictory. Some of the best ideas grow out of people trying to resolve contradictions. Just ask yourself what these contradictions might mean and if you are not sure, say so.
- Do not become obsessed with your original objectives. Research projects have a life of their own and can grow like plants into unexpected shapes. You must report back on what you found out about your original hypotheses, but do not get over-tied to these if something else interesting crops up. A number of scientists have stumbled across their most important discoveries when they were actually on a completely different track.
- Be imaginative — if there is a hint of something there, draw it out and have a look at it. Not everything has to be proved 100% before it appears for consideration.
- Finally, reflect on the process you went through. The world at large may benefit from your findings, but the first purpose of this research project is that you should benefit from having done it. That is the best argument for keeping going when things get difficult. Afterwards think both about what you learned

about your topic and what you learned about doing research. And measure yourself by what you achieved, not by what went wrong!

EVIDENCE COLLECTION POINT
Use some of the ideas in this element to apply the methods discussed in this unit on a research project of your own making.

7 INVESTIGATING AND CARRYING OUT MEDIA MARKETING

Films, television programmes, magazines — all media products, like any other product — need to reach their markets or audiences. It can be quite daunting to consider what needs to be done to create these markets for new products. For instance, if you want to launch a women's magazine aimed at the 'independent 1990s woman who knows where she's going', how do you try and ensure that she will buy *your* product rather than one of the competing ones?

Quite obviously, it is important to research the needs, desires and aspirations of the target audience well before a new media product is developed. It may look as though the selling of a new publication, new film or new TV series comes after the product has been developed and produced. However, in order to convince investors to spend the time and money required for new product development, the marketing process must start before the product has even reached a prototype stage. This unit will help you to understand the importance of the role of marketing. You will see many connections with other units, particularly Unit 6 which focuses on audience research. You will also begin to understand that marketing is in itself an important media industry. There is a range of opportunities to use your practical skills to present 'marketing products', for example, media packs and advertisements.

7.1 ANALYSE THE ROLE OF MARKETING IN THE MEDIA

Advertising, Marketing, Publicity — What is the Difference?

The concept of marketing:
'Marketing is the management process responsible for identifying, anticipating and satisfying customer requirements, profitably.'
The Chartered Institute of Marketing

Advertising, marketing, publicity — they are all part of the same general principle: to make your product visible in the public eye. Marketing involves the promotion of products or services through a range of activities, which could include promotional materials, staged events and advertising. Advertising is paid-for persuasive communication through posters, television, magazines, radio, while publicity is free, taking the form, perhaps, of film stars talking about their latest movie on chat shows, or stories in the tabloids about soap-opera actors.

What is marketing for?

Everybody has heard the old adage "the customer is always right." When a new film, TV programme or publication is being developed, however brilliant the idea might seem to the person who wants to make it, if it is not what the audience wants, it will never be made. Marketing is all about putting the customer's (or audience's) needs first, thinking about *who* they are and *what* they want. Only then is it possible to know who to target and what kind of product to produce.

The **aims** of marketing are concerned with serving the customer by providing the right kind of product at the right price in the right places, combined with ensuring that the organisation producing the product is able to meet its needs. These needs are not necessarily profit, but could be, for example, the raising of public awareness around the dangers of drug abuse, or political campaigns to win votes rather than to sell goods.

When developing a new product, how is it possible to forecast how many customers are likely to buy the product and how often? All of the factors which could influence the audience have to be identified and monitored regularly to see if, for example, some old habits are dying and new ones being taken up. **Anticipating audience needs** is vital in terms of making decisions about how much to produce. For instance, *Hello!* magazine could have been published monthly, but audience research suggested that there were enough women interested in reading about personalities' homes and interests to sustain a weekly publication.

Audience research is also used to forecast what people are likely to do and want in the *future*, anticipating their needs so that existing products can be adapted to suit them, or new products developed.

Another satisfied customer

Finding out if customers were satisfied and why is vital to ensure that they will buy the product again. Everyone has different reasons for liking a particular magazine, newspaper or television programme. Maybe it is a magazine's special interest content, or the price and design of a packaged music video. Successful marketing will **satisfy audience expectations**, building up loyalty to the product, rather than raising false expectations and generating disappointment.

TASK

Preview time

Trailers are one of the main ways in which audiences have enough of a 'taste' of a film to want to go and see it. Carry out the following tasks next time you go to the cinema, or rent a videotape:

1. Carefully watch the trailer of a film that you intend to see. Make detailed notes on:

    ■ the length of the trailer;

    ■ which key scenes/shots were used;

    ■ which part of the storyline was emphasised;

    ■ the use of trailer or voice-over to tell the audience about the film;

    ■ the use of sound (very loud/recognisable theme music/sound effects, etc.).

2. Compare the trailer with the poster displayed in the cinema. What are your expectations of the movie? Write down:

    ■ the genre of the film;

    ■ a summary of what you expect the story to be;

    ■ what roles you expect the main characters (stars) to play;

    ■ the pace of the film.

    For each, describe what in the trailer or poster leads you to draw these conclusions.

3. Watch the complete film. Compare your expectations with the finished film. Were they accurate? Did the film live up to what you had been lead to expect? Did the trailer/poster make more of certain aspects of the film to attract the audience? Were you disappointed in any aspect of the film, because your expectations were not met?

Who are you up against?

If a product is attractive to a large audience, it is unlikely that there will be only one of its kind in the market-place. Think about how many women's magazines there are on the shelves. Consider the growth of home-produced and imported soap operas jockeying for position on prime time television. One of the aims of marketing is to **manage the effects of change and competition**, adapting the product or at least its image to make sure that people continue to buy it when faced with a choice of many similar products. Monitoring the competition is vital, looking at what products are being introduced and how they position themselves in terms of content, image, price and availability. Only by knowing who your main competitors are and how well they are doing can you make a judgement about the success or otherwise of your own product. This is known as marketing intelligence and research, involving tracking and monitoring your competitors' progress, their marketing strategies and sales. If a major source of income for your newspaper, for example, is advertising, then you would monitor the advertisements your competitors are running, check the rates at which advertisers are buying space and, as a result, work out their 'market share' — i.e., the amount of advertising revenue that each competitor paper is attracting.

New technology — keeping up to date

Technological developments are hugely important not only to the production of media products, but also in terms of distribution. At the simplest level, new technology may enable a product to be produced more quickly, to a greater quality or more cheaply. A good marketing strategy will take account of the potential of **technological developments**. For example, the onset of electronic publishing is providing new opportunities for developing new kinds of products, or "re-purposing" existing products: what might have started out as a printed reference book can now be published on CD-ROM, containing not only text, but also quick-time video sequences, audio, animated graphics, etc.

How do people see you?

Companies also spend money on **enhancing audience perception** of the organisation and/or its products, raising awareness about the merits of the products so that consumers will be tempted to buy or use them. Money spent on this comes out of a budget allocated to **marketing activities**. A good example of this can be seen in the BB1 and BBC2 Identity Case Study. The current television campaign to convince the viewing public of the value of paying the licence fee is another example.

CASE STUDY
New channel identities for BBC

In 1990 (the same year as the Broadcasting Act) the design consultancy Lambie-Nairn was commissioned to develop new on-screen identities for BBC1 and BBC2. The brief was:

to make the BBC's two television channels appear fresher and less institutional following changes among commercial stations; to safeguard the perception of the BBC as the provider of quality television in Britain.

Extensive market research revealed the following general perceptions about the BBC:

■   The British pet-name for the BBC — 'Auntie' — revealed both an affection from the UK public, but also had overtones of the corporation 'knowing what's best for you'.

■   People in the UK are proud of the BBC, with the phrase 'British television is the best in the world' being frequently voiced more as an assertion of faith than a statement of fact.

■   The BBC has immense strengths, but they are also its weaknesses — it is seen as overstaffed and overconfident by some.

In terms of public perceptions of the channels themselves, BBC2 emerged as 'weak' and 'negative', while BBC1 looked better but was 'old-fashioned'. Until 1990, the BBC's presentation of itself was make-shift and suggested 'an avuncular air of authority'. Change was forced upon it by the late 1980s tide of slick retail design and corporate identity. The impact of the Broadcasting Act, increased competition from satellite television, and the ever-present threat of non-guarantee of public funding underlined the need for the BBC's on-air appearance to smarten itself up.

Lambie-Nairn's proposal

The original proposal centred on the representation of the channel numbers in letters: O, N, E and T, W, O, creating a sense of 'brother and sister' between the two channels, while leaving ample opportunity for variations.

The core of the thinking was based on the perceived need to create brand identities for the two BBC channels within the overall corporate identity. This, however, proved problematic for a variety of reasons, not least of all the confusion as to what the product actually was — the channels or the programmes? The brand identity had to be broader than a corporate mark, expressing personality more than corporate identity. It was also decided that the channel identities should be in keeping with what is broadcast on those channels. Lambie-Nairn worked closely with the head of presentation at the BBC and the controllers of the two channels as the designs progressed. The final designs were far simpler, based on the numerals 1 and 2, rather than the letters, as originally proposed.

Martin Lambie-Nairn said:

Complicated designs tend to look dated very quickly. Many years' experience in branding has taught us that starting from a strong and simple mark provides the greatest opportunity

Fig 7.1   Recent BBC ident sequences. Source: BBC TV Graphics Design Dept.

for creating lively and exciting on-screen imagery while maintaining the power and integrity of the brand identity.

The channel identies

The notion of the two channels as 'brother and sister' is maintained. Both channels have a common clock, programme schedule, and special announcement formats. Both use Futura typeface (easily read and neither traditional nor modish).

The Lambie-Nairn research had shown that BBC2's reputation for experimentation, high quality and informative programming was recognised, but that it was also seen as dull, boring and old-fashioned. The final BBC2 identity was designed to accentuate the positive and eliminate the negative. The BBC2 sequence exists in several forms which are in use at the same time. Their names are based on 'raw materials' which could be associated with arts and artistry — "blade", 'paint', "silk", "water", "copper", etc. The sequences are used randomly, but some thought has gone into selection, for instance, the 'water' sequence is playful; the 'silk' more serious.

More sequences have gradually been added designed by BBC in-house designers, but based on Lambie-Nairn's concept.

source: BBC TV Graphics Design Dept.

It is not unusual to get coverage in the trade press when a company changes its image or embarks on a major marketing campaign. With an organisation of the scale of the BBC, particularly one that is publicly funded, the marketing strategy and the amount spent on the marketing activity becomes newsworthy, attracting a significant amount of coverage in the national press. Press coverage and PR are also ingredients in a good marketing strategy.

Research

Of course, no decisions about any the four Ps can be made without **research**. We live in a climate which is continuously changing, affected by the ebb and flow of the business world and political, social and economic shifts. Short of employing the services of a crystal ball, it may seem hard to predict such events which may affect the consumer's demand for products. Planning ahead to try and anticipate them, however, is vital: decisions taken *now* will inevitably impact on future profits. It is important to maintain an eagle eye through constant and consistent market research.

See unit 6 for approaches to market research

The marketing environment

If nothing ever changed, making marketing plans would be easy. The factors which affect this changing environment can be easily remembered using the initials **PEST**:

Political/legal	Political influences can led to legislation that will restrict or open up opportunities for marketing
Economic	Economic factors, not only nationwide, but globally can affect the market-place, including changes to interest rates, taxes, etc.
Social	Social trends include, for example, the increase in population of the elderly, representing a potential new market, or the growth of the "pink pound" (i.e., the gay market)
Technological	Technological changes can have drastic effects and are difficult to forecast, for example, the marketing of a product based on a new technological development could be either a market leader, or become obsolete very quickly by a new development

The marketing mix

The marketing mix: The marketing mix is a planned mixture of the elements of marketing. It includes the product, its price, the place where it is available (or how it can be obtained), promotion or advertising and (where relevant) after-sales service. The 'mix' combines these ingredients in such a way as to achieve the greatest effect at minimum cost.

Marketing activities used by media and other industries are known as the "marketing mix".

The marketing mix can be remembered, quite simply by the four Ps — Product, Price, Place and Promotion, not forgetting after-sales service. The balance in marketing mix activities

Product	The range of media products designed to reach its designated target audiences through effective product design and sales packaging
Price	Price is linked to product value. The audience must equate the price with the benefits it provides. It can position a product in the market-place, e.g., a low price can suggest that the product is 'downmarket', while a high price will suggest exclusivity
Place	Whereas you would expect to find popular daily newspapers in most of the usual outlets, specialist publications may only appear in certain areas where there is likely to be a demand (e.g., foreign newspapers at airports or major railway stations; special interest television programmes in off-peak times)
Promotion	Includes the whole area of communication (advertising, PR, sales promotion and direct selling)

Fig 7.2   The four Ps

should never be set in stone. Marketing is dynamic, changing to suit the requirements of the customers, and mindful of the competition as well as the external environment.

P for product

A vast selection of media artefacts is available and **product design** is based on the requirements of the target audience, with **sales packaging** fashioned to capture the attention of that audience. It also helps build a product's identity and to advertise it, differentiating it from other similar products around.

Take magazines: although the picture on the front cover may change, it is still recognisable on the bookstalls because its packaging looks much the same. The name is the same, the typeface and the overall style and design are consistent for every issue.

Some companies use symbols or 'logos' which identify the name of the company and provides some information about what it does. It can also be a 'signature', a shorthand way of communicating to an audience who actually made or commissioned something. For example, BBC2 and C4 use different logos, or 'channel idents' to promote each channel's identity. Sometimes the graphics will change with the seasons, for example, Christmas. The closing of a programme may include a credit to the production company (the people who made the programme) and the channel which commissioned it and transmitted it (Fig. 7.3).

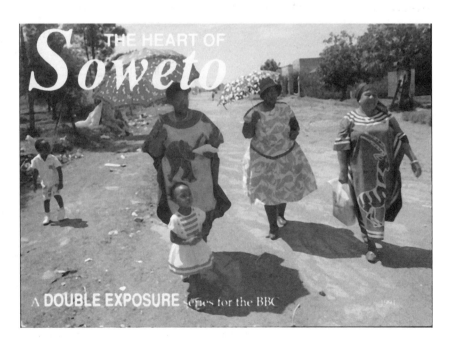

Fig 7.3 Production identification: A Double Exposure film for the BBC

The mastheads and overall layout of newspapers are enough to identify the style of journalism and the type of story likely to appear in the paper. The font or typeface used can suggest that a paper has 'serious' content, or more popular stories, gossip and photographs.

P for price

This may refer, for example, to the price of a newspaper. In terms of *customer satisfaction*, price is one of a set of reasons for our choice of product. It is linked to product *value*, which will mean different things to different people. For instance, you may decide that a particular magazine is too expensive: 'it isn't worth it,' i.e., its value does not equal the price.

Price on its own is rarely the sole issue when it comes to selecting a publication. It can be linked to a particular style of editorial with which the reader feels comfortable, or specialist content, for example, football fanzines, film magazines or the music press.

Upmarket vs downmarket

Price can actually position a magazine in the minds of people. Low price is associated with more mass-market titles and high price with the more upmarket publications. A low price means that it will be more accessible to many more people, while a high price suggests exclusivity. Not least of all, the price of the competition will be a major determining factor in pricing a product (particularly in print media). The price wars between newspapers over the last few years are a classic example of this.

Fig 7.4 Newspapers Price Wars

Source: *Financial Times*, 6 January 1995

CASE STUDY
Newspaper

The newspaper price cutting war first started in July 1993 when the *Sun,* the largest selling tabloid paper, reduced its price from 25p to 20p which increased copy sales to over 4 million — a figure last seen in 1989. That same year News International (owner of the *Sun*) reduced the price of another of its papers, *The Times,* from 45p to 30p which has had the effect of pushing circulation up to over 600,000 for the first time ever (although circulation is now down to over 500,000). Each of these price cuts were announced to consumers largely through television advertising.

As a result of the cut in price of *The Times,* a number of other national newspapers have seen a fall in circulation particularly the *Daily Telegraph.*

At the beginning of the 1980s, the *Daily Telegraph* was selling, on average, 1.4m. copies a day. This fell to below 1 million in Spring 1994 and lead to a reduction in cover price from 48p to 30p, in the June, with TV advertising. Results from this price cut pushed circulation over the 1m. mark. *The Times* retaliated by cutting the price further, to 20p and sales continued to climb. Meanwhile, the *Independent* was forced to match the *Telegraph* at 30p.

The **Guardian** held its price at 45p and suffered little. It has built up a loyalty amongst its target audience. [This is referred to as "brand loyalty".] Buyers of the *Financial Times* are also brand loyal which means that existing consumers are quite satisfied with the products produced. The *Daily Mail* kept its price the same. In an article in the *Financial Times* in January 1995, Lord Rothermere, publisher of the *Daily Mail* was quoted as saying "If you produce good newspapers you don't need to cut the price."

The increase in the cost of newsprint prices is likely to mean an easing of the price war as some of the extra money needed for newsprint is recovered by increasing the cover price of the paper.

But there are other alternative ways to recover the extra costs. Some papers have reduced the number of their pages. *The Times,* now offering advertisers larger audiences, has increased its advertising rates to advertisers while News International is looking for cost savings in the distribution of all of its papers.

P for place

The *place* refers to how the product is distributed and where the consumer buys it. In general terms — not just in media industries — distribution is the process of transferring goods from the producer to the consumer or end user.

Some producers distribute their goods by two different methods. For example, magazines are distributed to the wholesale trade, which will then sell on to the retailer or supermarket. They can also be sold directly to the consumer via subscriptions that are delivered directly through the post.

The local newsagent will be influenced by a number of factors in determining which publications they stock. For instance, a newsagent situated near to a major advertising agency in London will stock the major advertising trade journals such as *Campaign, Marketing, Marketing Week.* One situated near a college would

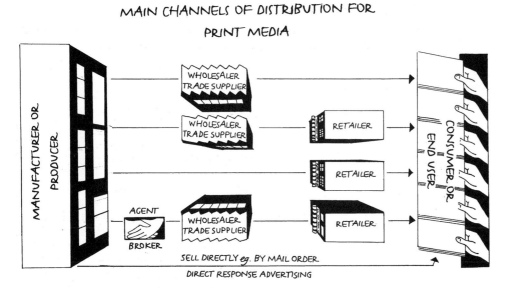

Fig 7.5 Main channels of distribution for Print Media

display a selection of publications which appeal to the 16–18 year old reader as they will be more likely to be in demand. In an area where there is a high ethnic population, specialist language papers will be available. For those who are aspiring to become involved in feature films, the famous *Soho Runner* is only available in the Soho streets of London.

TASK

Class activity

Visit the newsagent nearest to your home and conduct a survey to establish the range of publications on sale. The easiest way to do this would be to make a checklist of all of the national dailies, weeklies, Sundays, plus local publications and photocopy for the whole class. Leave a space for 'other', where you can add specialist titles. Depending on where you live, it may be that your local newsagent stocks particular publications of interest to certain occupation groups (for instance, if you live in a rural area, you may find agricultural publications on the shelves; if you live in a large city, you may find ethnic publications; if you live in certain parts of Wales or Ireland, you may find Welsh language or Gaelic publications.

Collate all of this information and present your findings. You could do this diagramatically, by identifying on a map of your locality the outlets visited and the publications stocked.

You could compare this with another part of the country by linking up with another college doing the GNVQ course and asking students there to carry out the same experiment. If you are 'on line', you could perhaps make contact and exchange data using the Internet.

P for promotion

Promotion is about **communication**, which includes **advertising, public relations, sales promotions** and **direct selling**.

DEFINITIONS:

Advertising	The use of paid-for space (in the press, on posters) or time (on TV, radio, cinema) usually as a means of persuading people to take a particular course of action, buy a particular product, or reach a point of view.
Public relations (PR)	Publicising different aspects of the company to different audiences (or sections of the public). A company may employ a PR agency to do this, or may use a well-known spokesperson to talk with the media, e.g., Richard Branson, who is synonymous with Virgin.
Sales promotions	Concerned with the promotion of sales of the product. Sales promotions are usually available for a short time with the objective of enhancing sales demand (i.e. encouraging people to buy the product by offering something extra). This could be as straightforward as a price reduction or a free gift.
Direct selling	Selling directly to the target audience. With publications, this could be special price reductions for people who take out a 12-month subscription, rather than buy 12 issues at the newsagent — this ensures that 12 issues will be purchased. Some media products are not available in the high street, but may be ordered directly from the company by mail order (e.g., specialist videotaped programmes or audio cassettes).

The sales and promotion department of newspapers are responsible not only for improving and maintaining sales of the publication, but also for generating revenue. Promotional activities may take various forms, for instance, offering a cut-out coupon in a daily newspaper to present for cut-price purchase of a Sunday paper owned by the same group. Competitions and prize draws which depend on at least one week's purchase of the title to enter are another way to try and bring new readers. Reader offers give 'added value' to a newspaper, but can also be income generators in their own right. For instance, reader travel schemes provide the newspaper with a commission for sales; offers on particular products usually provide percentage on sales back to the newspaper.

TASK

Study a range of publications to find the promotional activities. Cut them out and analyse them in terms of:

- how they fit the target market;

- whether they are an incentive for readers to continue to buy the publication;

- whether they are an incentive for new readers;

- whether they are income generators in their own right (through, for example, special offers on other products; information services with 0891 telephone numbers, which generate profit on phone calls).

Frequency of marketing activities

Obviously, to sustain an audience's attention it must be advertised more than once. **Frequency of activities** for terrestrial television stations (BBC1, BBC2, ITV, Channel 4) is on-going to let consumers know of the forthcoming programmes. This is achieved by advertising on the same or sister channels, for example, BBC1 will promote forthcoming programmes throughout the day and will refer at intervals to what is being shown on BBC2. BBC2 does much the same, as does ITV and Channel 4. This is known as a "cross-promotion".

Another example of cross-promotion can be seen in the products relating to specific television programmes which are publicised at the end of the programme, for example, sell-through videotapes of characters from soap operas (e.g., *Brookside*).

TV and satellite programmes are listed each day or week in all newspapers and some magazines, promoting what is available on each channel. Specialist listings publications provide the most detail, e.g., *TV Times*, *Radio Times*, or *Time Out*.

With print media, the retail outlet represents a powerful vehicle for them for communication and advertising. This is particularly the case when the outlet, for instance, W. H. Smith, is in the high street where large numbers of people are passing by their windows. Of course, the packaging of the titles displayed on the shelves speak for themselves.

Although there is no direct link between press media owners and news-trade outlets, they enjoy a "dotted line" relationship. The media owners' circulation sales force will visit retailers to try and increase copy sales by way of various in-store activities such as sales promotions. They will also check to see that their publications are displayed in the right place and that there are sufficient numbers of copies available.

Dissemination

One of the most important **marketing activities** is to determine how well the marketing mix has worked by looking at the **dissemination** of the product. If a magazine has recently introduced a new subscription offer, what motivated its take-up by readers: price reduction? The product itself? The convenience of home-delivery? The persuasiveness of the advertising of the magazine? All media products are constantly monitoring and measuring the effects of the **marketing mix** elements to see which combinations increase audience demand more than the others.

In relation to the development of new media products, there is no past dissemination information to go from. However, information can be gained, for instance, from similar products available.

The cost of marketing

The marketing 'spend' for new product launches is extremely high, especially if there are many competitors. The high expenditure is invested largely in the product and in the advertising to ensure that the target audience hears the message communicated, buys or uses the product and is satisfied enough to use it again. Price may be used to tempt over consumers from competing products.

When the woman's weekly magazine *Bella* was launched in this country, it was introduced at a price far below the other available women's weeklies so that women would be tempted to try it. The price was promoted through an extensive advertising campaign. The high spend in these two areas ensured that the product was stocked by newsagents and much money was spent on distributing it to these outlets.

Once *Bella* became established among consumers, less money was spent on advertising as word of mouth spread and loyalty built up. Later, its price was raised to a realistic level to coincide with similar products on the market. **M**oney continued to be spent on distributing the title and improving the publication.

How do media products attract advertisers?

All media have an advertisement sales force who call on both advertisers (clients) and advertising agencies on a regular basis to sell their products.

The sales force is armed with the product or outline of their service, a *media pack*, which includes the **ratecard** which shows space costs, as well as all relevant media research data which can help them to argue their case. They will also give presentations to the prospective buyer about their medium.

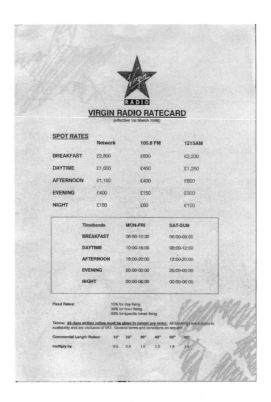

Fig 7.6 Virgin radio ratecard

When new (and favourable) media research data becomes available, advertisements appear in the advertising trade press to announce the results, so getting the message across quickly to the right target market.

Comparing marketing approaches

The prime concern of most media products is to maintain their audience levels so that advertisers continue to buy space or time in the products, providing them with income and profit. Sometimes, as with commercial broadcasting, this income is the only revenue coming in while in the case of print media it comes from two sources — cover price sales and advertising sales. There may be many factors which can affect the advertiser's decision to buy space in one medium rather than another. The major target groups of each medium are an obvious starting point.

Main Target groups

Television, radio, cinema

- Different sectors of the population, according to type of programme or film shown.
- Advertisers and advertising agencies who buy space or time.

Newspapers, magazines

- Different sectors of the population according to the editorial emphasis.
- Advertisers and advertising agencies who buy space.
- News trade (wholesalers, newsagents, supermarkets) which stock the goods

Posters

- Advertisers and advertising agencies who buy space.

Fig 7.7   Main target groups

Off The Record can only marvel at the might of Channel 4's publicity machine and the campaign for its latest Friday night shocker, Rapido TV's The Girlie Show. Not only has C4 enjoyed a mass of pre-show publicity from outraged Tory tabloids but its posters have managed to pique arch rivals like ITV's top girlie, Katie Puckrik. We hear that those wits at C4's ad agency BMP4 booked a site smack outside Puckrik's office, leaving her able to see little but les girls from her lair at Granada, where she is plotting her next Pyjama Party. Katie's ex-colleagues on The Word have also been got at by the snarling girlies – a poster having popped-up outside the bedroom window of Duncan Gray, producer of the dearly-departed Friday slot from Rapido's rival, Planet 24. Cynics might suggest there is no love lost between the two indies.

Fig 7.8   Source: Broadcast 2 February 1996

For instance, although terrestrial TV and radio programmes are not *bought* by the target audience, they have to be on at a time when the target audience is more likely to have the opportunity of seeing and hearing them. Scheduling, therefore, is of major importance.

When the creative treatment is right, the poster medium can deliver memorable campaigns. For example, *The Girlie Show* (Channel 4, 1996) combined frequent television trailing with a bold poster campaign in the weeks leading up to its launch.

7.2 PREPARE MARKETING PLANS FOR MEDIA PRODUCTS

If you have already made a video, or produced a magazine, you will know that the production process itself requires careful planning, but before a new product is even developed, media owners must plan ahead.

This element will lead you through the various stages required to produce a **marketing plan**. You should be familiar with some of the approaches to research from Unit 6. You will need to make sure that you are familiar with the key marketing issues covered in Element 7.1.

Why plan ahead?

Planning ahead reduces the risk of failures while ensuring that tomorrow's profits are secured. In a nutshell, planning involves making decisions about the future in terms of:

- what to do;
- how to do it;
- when to do it;
- who is to do it.

Research

See unit 6 for approaches to market research.

When developing a new product, deciding **what** to do, the first thing you need to establish is what is going on in the market place by undertaking a 'marketing audit' — i.e., you collect and analyse **research data** for the kinds of media products relevant to your proposed new magazine, or radio station, or newspaper.

Sales trends

To form a complete picture of where your new product (or, if it is a relaunch, of an existing product) is likely to be positioned in the market-place, you first need to look at **sales trends**, which will provide you with historic data and will give you an idea about the state of the market overall (e.g., whether it is increasing or declining). It will also give you information about the different products (e.g., LWT, Capital Radio, the *Daily Mirror*, etc.) within the market to see how they are performing.

Source: BVA *BFI Film and Television Handbook*, 1996

CASE STUDY
The UK video market, 1994

In 1994, the video market increased its sales by an overall 3%, to £1.14 billion. This kept the industry ahead of inflation, but behind the real rate of growth in the economy as a whole. This figure reflects both rental and retail (or sell-through sales), however, the rental business has been in decline since 1989, largely due to satellite and cable. The advent of digital television, Channel 5 and near-video-on-demand will further marginalise video rental.

However, while UK homes continue to acquire video cassette recorders, there will, obviously, be a place for rented cassettes.

The rental business is dominated by feature films, with the top-grossing releases (i.e. the films which have been major box-office successes in the cinema) leading the rental charts.

Top ten video rental titles in the UK (1994)

Title	Company
1. *The Fugitive*	Warner Home Video
2. *Jurassic Park*	CIC
3. *Demolition Man*	Warner Home Video
4. *Four Weddings and a Funeral*	Columbia TriStar
5. *Mrs Doubtfire*	Fox Video
6. *In the Line of Fire*	Columbia TriStar
7. *Sleepless in Seattle*	Columbia TriStar
8. *Cliffhanger*	Guild
9. *The Firm*	CIC
10. *Passenger 57*	Warner Home Video

Source: BVA

It is not surprising that US majors dominate the market, with Warner Home Video capturing a 24% share (19.5% the previous year), followed by Columbia TriStar (18.4%) and CIC (16%).

Distributors' share of UK rental transactions

Company	Percentage
Warner	24.0
Columbia TriStar	18.4
CIC	16.0
Buena Vista	10.2
Guild	8.3
EV	7.0
FoxVideo	6.9
Polygram	2.5
Others	6.7

Source: BVA/BFI Film and Television Handbook, 1996.

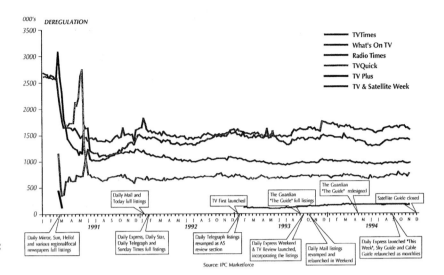

Fig 7.9 TV weeklies copy sales 1991–1994 source IPC market force

Customer Behaviour

You also need to know about **customer behaviour, customer buying patterns** and **customer preferences** so that you can design your product to meet their requirements.

CHECKLIST: CUSTOMERS BEHAVIOUR:

Questions to ask about prospective customers or audience:

■ **Who** is your audience?

■ **How big** is your audience?

■ Are there **more** or **less** of them than there were a year ago?

■ What are their **attitudes** to your products and to competitors' products?

■ Do they **respond** to advertising and promotion?

■ What **affects** (or could affect) demand?

Keeping an Eye on the Competition

You will need to use published data (eg., on sales trends) to help you identify what the competition is doing.

CHECKLIST:

What you need to find out about the competition

- What are the products?

- Do they make money?

- What do their sales trends look like? Up or down?

- Are their products better than yours?

- What are the target audiences?

- Are there more or fewer customers than a year ago?

- What affects or could affect customer demand?

- How often do they use the products?

- When do they use the products?

- How are they distributed?

- What price (if any) is paid for them?

- Do they advertise and promote? If so, what do they do and where do they do it?

The marketing audit

Before you can begin to put together a marketing plan, you will need to carry out and structure a marketing audit based on the factors listed above. You will need to carry out market research using the approaches described in Unit 6 which includes gathering published data on sales, circulation, ratings, etc. (according to product).

By analysing research data, you can learn from the past and make predictions about the next 12 months. This will help you to make your marketing plan as accurate as possible.

CHECKLIST:

Analysing research data

Sales trends	■ Historic data
	■ The market overall (TV, radio, press, etc.) — is it increasing or declining?
	■ Information about the different products within the market (e.g., LWT, Capital Radio, Virgin Radio, the *Daily Mirror*) to see how they are performing
Market information	■ It is possible from sales trends data to plot **changes in the product's market share** compared to that of the competition, revealing how successful (or not) the product is
Customer buying behaviour	■ Information about **customer buying behaviour, customer buying patterns**, together with **customer preferences** is vital so that the product meets their requirements
Competitor activities	■ What are the products, what are their sales trends, who is the audience?
Information about the marketing mix — the four P's	■ If the product is produced by a large company or media 'group', examine the marketing mix adopted for other (similar) products
	■ Compare with the marketing mix for competitor products

Check that your data is up to date

Developing a marketing plan

Marketing plans are concerned with making judgements about, firstly, the products on offer and then about the best possible way of combining place, price and promotion, with the aim of retaining existing audiences and persuading new customers to use an existing medium. In the case of new products, the goal is to

position the product in the market and then to persuade sufficient numbers of customers to use the product and pay for it so that it makes a profit.

Forecast: a prediction or projection of sales, audience figures and budgets to enable media organisations to predict what might happen, thereby enabling them to respond to future demands or changing circumstances.

What is the demand for your product?

The first stage in the planning process is to **forecast** the demand for it by its prospective audience. There is no sure method, mainly because of the uncertainty of how customers are going to react in real life. Once you have carried out a market audit, you will need to undertake some additional research.

TASK

Forecasting

■ Prepare the product design, both content and sales packaging, for a media product. (this could be based on work you are doing in the practical units)

■ Prepare a brief presentation, describing the product in terms of its content, style and packaging. This can be simply a list of points to help you describe the product verbally, or could be enhanced by using overhead transparencies or other visual aids.

■ Identify the target group and bring together 12 people who are a representative sample of that group. Divide the group into two focus groups and, with each:

a)   present your product description;

b)   through questioning and facilitating discussion, find out their reactions to the product and whether they would be likely to use it in its current form;

c)   through discussion, find out what product revisions are necessary to make it better;

d)   keep detailed notes throughout the focus group discussions (you could tape-record the discussions, transcribe them and select the most useful quotations from the focus group participants);

e)   write a report on the findings, including a proposal which develops the product further.

How reliable are forecasts?

It is worthwhile mentioning that most forecasts are estimates and will change with time. They can also change once you begin marketing mix activities. The pricing has to be right; the product has to be distributed widely; the audience needs to know it is available through promotion and advertising — all of these factors will affect the demand for the product.

What are your marketing goals?

Whether you are repackaging an existing product, or launching a new one, once you have forecast the demand, you need to set yourself realisable goals so that you can easily test whether you have your marketing mix right. In the trade, these are sometimes referred to as 'SMART' goals:

S Simple and clear
M Measurable, with figures attached
A Achievable
R Realistic and relevant
T Time (when objectives should be met)

Testing the Marketing Mix

Once the product is in circulation, the marketing mix balance is tested to see whether it was the favourable price at which it was on offer that increased demand. Or it may have been the powerful advertising campaign, or the superior quality of the product which was unique. It is important to measure each marketing activity that we select so as to see which ones work the best. This is how to maximise budgets efficiently.

Developing the marketing plan

The **marketing plan** is a formal report which gathers and arranges, in a systematic and methodical way, everything that can affect a company's future business. It includes all activities to do with communicating to the different customer groups (i.e., not only those who will buy the product, but those who will advertise through it).

Fig 7.10 The marketing plan gathers and arranges everything that can affect a company's future business. Not all activities are relevant to all products

Sales packaging	Advertising	Publicity
Sales promotion	Personal selling	Direct mail
Sponsorship	Exhibitions	Point of sale
Public relations	Merchandising	Word of mouth

Advertising objectives

Advertising objectives are about what the advertising has to do, or achieve. Advertising **strategies** are about the selection of media for the advertising campaign and the message to be put across.

Content of the marketing plan

As well as reviewing the situation to date and setting targets to be achieved by marketing the product, the marketing plan should answer the following questions:

- Why advertise? (objectives of the communications/advertising tasks)
- At whom is the advertising aimed? (target audience)
- What is being advertised? (product/service)
- How will the product be advertised? (the creative message)
- Where will the product be advertised? (which media)
- When will the product be advertised? (timing)
- How much will the advertising cost? (costs)

How will you monitor your plan?

Any advertising campaign or, indeed, any item of communication, should be evaluated after the campaign has taken place in terms of:

- Who saw it?
- How many times did they see it?
- How did they react to the message?
- Did it meet objectives?
- Did sales (and/or usage) increase?

The answers to these questions will provide you with the data required to assess the success of the advertising.

Justifying product development

When launching anything new, there is a high risk that the product will fail. All companies will therefore use their marketing management team to justify everything to do with the new product launch — the product, the forecast and the marketing mix of activities — in a formal report to justify the profitability of the product. This helps to minimise the risk of failure. It ensures research data that has been analysed and interpreted correctly and that, based on that data, the right decisions have been taken. The report should include all the existing research data — both secondary and primary — that supports the product launch by:

- pinpointing the target audience and their buying behaviour patterns;
- justifying product design and content, and sales packaging;
- providing evidence for its positioning in the market sector;
- comparing it with the competition;
- providing a well researched estimate of forecasted demand;
- giving reasons for the timing of the launch;

■ detailing the proposed financial investment in marketing activities
■ justifying this with the proposed financial return.

A word on costings

Do not forget to include *all* of the production costs in your financial estimates (equipment, materials, staff, reproduction). In the industry, you would also include the cost of sales staff who would be selling the product to advertisers.

Advertising budgets are split between those for advertising space costs and those for the production of the advertisement. The size and cost of advertising space for each medium, together with a dateplan is known as the media plan or advertising campaign plan. The total cost is worked out by multiplying the single insertion rate (i.e., how much it costs to place an advertisement once) by the total number of insertions, in each medium.

Medium	Size of insertion	Cost per insertion	No. of insertions	Total cost	Date plan
					Jan Feb Mar
Magazine	Colour page	£7,000	3	£21,000	X X X

You will also need to estimate the income. Some sample calculations of revenue are given below.

Circulation revenue from print media products

A new monthly magazine, priced at £1.50, is aimed at 15–24 year olds, both men and women. It is estimated that 50,000 copies will be sold each month. This will provide an estimated circulation sales income of £75,000 per month (£1.50 × 50,000). Over a 12-month period, this will add up to £900,000 (£75,000 × 12).

Advertising revenue from print media products

In order to forecast the revenue for print products from advertisement sales, you need to consider how many advertisements the title should carry, how many and how much should be charged for them — bearing in mind how many people are likely to buy and read it.

Advertising revenue from audio-visual products

For audio-visual products, a price must be set for the advertisement space to be sold within the programme's commercial break. If it looks as though the programme is going to be extremely popular with large numbers of listeners or viewers, it will be transmitted during peak viewing periods. At these times, advertising space is charged at the highest rate.

If the programme is going out nationally, then the cost to advertisers of commercials must be worked out for each of the ITV stations.

For example, a new half-hour programme is being produced to include clips from 1970s and 1980s UK and US pop concerts is scheduled to go out nationally, on Channel 4 at 9.00pm on Thursday evenings. There will be five, 30-second spots within the commercial break, each one will cost £150,000 with total revenue received from advertising of £750,000 (£150,000 × 5).

TASK

Select a print media product of your choice and obtain a media pack for that product:

■ count the advertisements contained within it (their size or length, colour or mono:

■ from the ratecard, calculate the costs for the advertisement space and time to arrive at the advertisement sales revenue;

■ forecast advertisement space and time revenue for the future.

Write a brief report to justify your forecasts. Show each of the steps you took to arrive at it, under headings.

Media packs can be obtained by contacting the publisher or broadcaster.

7.3 PRODUCE DRAFTS AND TREATMENTS FOR ADVERTISEMENTS

Advertising is the best way to get a product noticed. Advertising messages are clear and targeted. The marketing plan will have enabled you to identify an appropriate advertising approach. While inspiration for creative ideas might come in a variety of ways, they will always be rooted in the objectives identified in the marketing plan.

You may come up with several advertising approaches. When advertising agencies compete for a new account, they may well come up with entirely different creative ideas. However, each will have considered their approach in terms of:

- Relevance to product;
- Relevance to target audience;
- Content;
- Treatment;
- Resource requirements needed to produce the drafts.

In judging whether a creative idea is suitable for the product, you need to ask such questions as:

- Will the product be seen in a positive light?
- Does it put across the unique selling points of the product?
- Does it get across the brand name?
- Is it memorable?
- Is it available nationally or just regionally?
- Does it help to sell competitors' brands?
- Most importantly, does it fulfil the aims of the advertising?

TASK

Select a TV commercial for a national newspaper. Write down who you think it is aimed at. Describe the advertising approach in terms of its suitability and relevance to the target market. Suggest ways in which it could be *more* relevant.

When thinking about the content of advertisements, obviously the idea is to increase the target audience's awareness of the product. If it is a new product, then introducing the product is the key objective, with the advertising aims:

- to encourage product trial;
- to persuade the retail news trade to stock the product (in the case of a print product);
- to persuade consumers to write in for more information;
- to counter competitive activity;
- to advise and inform of the product's advantages;
- to create a strong brand image.

The **treatment** is about *how* the advertising objective is put across — for instance, by using humour, using a popular personality to endorse the product or by using memorable jingles or catchphrases. Selecting the one most suitable for the product depends on the following questions:

- What is in fashion, generally?
- What is fashionable for the product (new or old images)?
- Are words more powerful? Or pictures? or both?
- Is sound important? Combined with movement?
- Is the use of colour important?
- Do we need a long or short advertisement?
- What is the competition doing?

CASE STUDY

To focus your thinking on the idea of magazines, radio stations, films, etc., as 'products', look at the way in which a creative advertising idea is developed for a completely different kind of product.

Developing the creative idea for the Anchor brand

The Anchor Butter TV, campaign using Jersey Cows started eight years ago with 'Rapping Bull'. The creative team was inspired with the thought that Anchor cows had a very happy life, living in green pastures all the year round, which meant they supplied great milk!

Rosemary Poole, the TV producer working on the account since Saatchi & Saatchi first gained it, relates the story.

At the time 'dancing cows' in a commercial were unique and computer techniques were not as sophisticated as they are now.

The campaign proved highly successful and, as new products such as cheese and cream, became available in the UK the animal route was the obvious one to follow.

About three years ago, a commercial was shot for cheese using mice, but research showed that mice and food are considered rather an off-putting combination. In the latest commercial [1995] the central animal is a giant tortoise. The connection may seem obscure, but there is one! Anchor have a range of cheddars which have to mature sometimes for a long time — and giant tortoises live to a ripe old age!

Later on this year, we'll see a cat advertising Anchor Cream — an obvious choice, and the same cat, getting up to tricks, will be featured in the Anchor Custard commercial.

The essence of all of the commercials is fun — that's why they're so popular.

TASK

Tabloid newspapers have shorter articles and many more pictures than the quality press which is aimed at a more upmarket audience who prefer a more in-depth read. Select a newspaper of your choice and look at the content and treatment of the advertisements. Are they in keeping with the target audience and the editorial style?

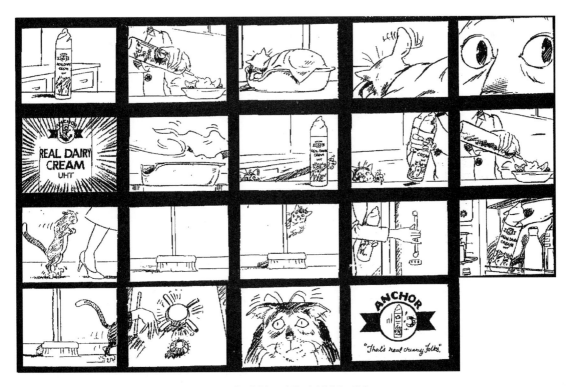

Fig 7.11   Anchor Cream storyboard courtesy: Saatchi and Saatchi Advertising

Fig 7.12   Anchor cheddar commercial courtesy Saatchi and Saatchi Advertising

Where to place your advertisement

The **choice of medium** (The 'where' in the communications mix plan). will depend on budget, target audience and whether the product needs particular features of the medium, like sound, colour, tone of voice, printed word, etc. The choice of medium can also dictate the kind of treatment.

TV	Radio
Immediate impact	Impact with repetition
'Real' time	'Real' time
Sound	Sound
Moving visual images	Stimulates imagination
Magazines	**Newspapers**
Permanent	Permanent
Static visual images	Static visual images
Excellent colour reproduction	In-depth approach
Time to read at leisure	Time to read at leisure
Specialist content	Topicality

Fig 7.13 Summary characteristics of main media

The many music stations on air in the London area — Capital FM, Melody, Classic FM, JFM and Kiss FM — cater for the people's different interests and tastes. The advertising, too, is on the 'same wavelength' as their listeners.

Many advertising campaigns will use a mix of media or media groups to provide different messages and levels of impact, over time.

Grabbing audience attention

The research you have conducted on your target audience will tell you enough about its characeristics and interests to enable you to **select the messages to be conveyed** about the product which will appeal most. As well as attracting attention, the advertisement has to hold the attention so that the target market is more likely to recall the product and be motivated to buy it, or watch or listen to it. As well as deciding on an appropriate and effective treatment, it is important to consider the use of language — it is crucial that the target audience interprets an advertisement in the way in which you intend. For example, the word 'wicked' can mean something quite different to a 16 year old and 60 year old.

Are you legal?

When selecting an advertising approach, you will need to be aware of legal issues, as well as bearing in mind ethical issues, which are largely articulated in the industry's own self-regulatory codes of practice.

The British Code of Advertising Practice lays down rules for press advertisements. The Advertising Standards Authority (ASA) is the body which monitors the code's practice to ensure that all press advertisements:

See unit 8, p. 507.

- ■ 'should be legal, decent, honest and truthful';
- ■ 'should be prepared with a sense of responsibility to the consumer and to society';
- ■ 'should conform to the principles of fair competition generally accepted in business'.

You can obtain copies of the various codes of advertising practice from the ASA, the Independent Television Commission and the Independent Radio Authority.

There is also a section which gives stringent guidelines for particular areas of advertising where special care is called for in the interests of the consumers, for instance, on direct mail advertising. Although these are not law, in the official sense of the word, if the rules are not adhered to, the advertiser will be asked to withdraw or to amend the advertising.

The Code of Advertising Practice does not apply to television and radio commercials. These are governed by the Independent Television Commission (ITC) and Independent Radio Authority, both of which are regulatory bodies.

See unit 8, p. 473.

TASK

Very often advertisements which put forward strong benefits of the product do so in such a way as to show up the competition in poor light. Also, they may infer that the competition is inferior. Can you think of any advertisements that have done this?

Many of the legislated Acts protect consumers' rights, such as the Trade Descriptions Act, Sale of Goods Act, Data Protection Act. Others, like the Race Relations Act and Sex Discrimination Act, provide legislation for equality and fair employment. There are many acts which have to be consulted to find out if they are relevant to the product being advertised.

There are also Acts which offer protection for Trade Marks (Trade Marks Act, 1994). The main focus of the Act is on names, logos and their design, but advertisers are now also able to protect music, sounds, colours and slogans by registering them as long as they can prove an association with the product. For instance, the Andrex puppy is now protected as a trade mark. This means that other products cannot use it. If they do, they are breaking the law. As with all media products, the copyright laws apply to advertising, should it make use of film, photographic, musical, artistic or literary works.

Product placement

The ITC Code of Programme Sponsorship guidelines forbids the inclusion of a product within a programme in return for payment. This is different to the paid-for TV sponsorship of programmes. Where the programme sponsor's brand is advertised before the programme starts and at the start and end of commercial breaks within the programme, for instance, Pepsi Cola sponsoring major movies on ITV, or Beamish Stout sponsoring the *Inspector Morse* series. Companies like Pepsi and Coca-Cola have dedicated inhouse divisions, actively seeking product placement opportunities in Hollywood.

"Advertising isn't just about selling products; it's also about showing us a world in which those products are needed, wanted, and used." *Advertising Pack – English and Media Centre*

Representation in advertising

This unit concentrates on describing marketing and advertising methods. However, as students of media you will also be aware of the way in which advertisements represent people, places, lifestyles and ideas. Stereotyping is the accusation most often levelled at advertisements. In a way, it is not surprising that stereotypical representations are attractive to advertisers, in that they very effectively and speedily convey a whole range of shared understandings, providing 'instant messages' to the reader or audience. Repetition of such messages serves to reinforce these dominant beliefs, particularly in the areas of gender, ethnicity, class, age and so on. However, it is also true that audiences are not passive sponges, and may read advertising images in a variety of ways. You might also want to make use of advertising methods to challenge stereotypes, or offer a different range of representations.

The study of representation and audience 'effects research' are covered in Units 1 and 6 and you should bear in mind the issues raised when developing advertising ideas.

Advertising agencies have also achieved some of their most notable successes precisely through taking risks, tapping into the cultural 'edge'.

One recent Levi ad featured a transvestite wearing the jeans. Though it was quickly taken off British TV, it was seen as a Bennetton-style attempt to maintain the reputation of Levi for striking ads at a time when the 'pink pound' or gay community's spending power is being sought by advertisers.

Such ads are neither simply irresponsible, as the NVLS [National Viewers and Listeners Association] has claimed, nor an abstract stand for a liberalisation of sexual attitudes. The processes of advertising's necessary attempt to keep up to the minute means that it will be driven to take such risks, which many would applaud as giving visibility to groups whose very existence has previously been censored.

Gill Branston and Roy Stafford. (1996), *The Media Student's Book,* Routledge.

The case study on *Marie Claire* on p. 451 provides an example of marketing practice, as well as material from which you could also begin to develop a project on representation of women as evidence for Unit 1.

Of course, having a conscience about issues of representation is not usually a top priority for the producers of advertisements — their role is to sell products, and in convincing a client that a particular advertising approach is appropriate for a particular target audience will inevitably mean that a limited range of key characteristics will be used to describe that group to prove that the image of the product, the image of the brand and the image created by the advertising all 'fit'.

Developing advertising ideas

See p. 358.

Animatics. *a fairly detailed storyboard is recorded on videotape, with rough voice-over and sound-track added, to give a sense of how the finished advertisement will look and sound on-screen.*

Most advertising creative concepts, particularly those for television, are researched by qualitative methods. Storyboards can be presented, or **animatics**; voice-overs and music can be played and the group's response to the creative approach can provide valuable insights. It is also a good idea to gauge the target audience's response to the type of person who is to appear in the advertisement.

Advertising agencies

An advertising agency offers the complete service, from analysing the advertising problem, through to devising a campaign, producing the advertisements and placing them in the appropriate media.

Usually, a major client will present the advertising problem to a range of agencies, who will then pitch to win the account. The pitching presentations are extremely important, as they can win agencies high-earning, high profile accounts. Once a new client is won, the Account Director will work with them to form some initial

HOW AN AD IS MADE

THE AGENCY WINS A NEW CLIENT
THE CLIENT (IE THE COMPANY WHO NEEDS TO ADVERTISE) MEETS THE ACCOUNT DIRECTOR OF THE AGENCY. TOGETHER THEY MAKE INITIAL SUGGESTIONS FOR AN ADVERTISING STRATEGY.

THE DIRECTOR HANDS OVER THE ACCOUNT TO THE ACCOUNT MANAGER
WHO NOW DEALS DIRECTLY WITH THE CLIENT. CLIENT AND MANAGER KEEP IN CLOSE CONTACT ABOUT THE WAY THINGS ARE GOING.

RESEARCHING THE MARKET
THEY USE MARKET RESEARCH INFORMATION ABOUT BOTH THE PRODUCT AND THE MARKET FOR IT TO HELP THEM TARGET THE CAMPAIGN AT THE RIGHT MARKET, AND TO SUGGEST THE RIGHT IMAGE AND APPEAL FOR THE PRODUCT

PLANNING THE STRATEGY
THE ACCOUNT PLANNERS DECIDE ON AN ADVERTISING STRATEGY AND A GENERAL CREATIVE APPROACH.

GETTING CREATIVE
USING THE BRIEF PREPARED BY THE ACCOUNT PLANNERS, THE CREATIVE TEAM NOW WRITE AND DESIGN IDEAS FOR THE ADS. THEY HAVE TO ENSURE CLIENT APPROVAL.

Fig 7.14 Making an Advertisement

suggestions towards an advertising strategy. The Account Director will then hand over the account to an Account Manager, who deals directly with the client and is the link between the client and all of the other agency functions. The Account Planners decide on an advertising strategy and creative approach, producing a brief for the creative team. This brief will draw on extensive market research about the product and the market, so that the product can be targeted with the right kind of image and appeal. The creative team, which usually comprises a copywriter and a graphic artist, design the advertisements and pass them on to the graphic and

TV production departments, which commission the appropriate suppliers to produce the advertisements (this could be for high quality artwork or photography, film production companies, etc.). The media department will include planners, researchers and buyers who will work with the planning and creative departments on a media strategy (i.e., deciding what media to use and how often) and will ultimately buy the advertising time or space.

Branding

Much advertising relies on branding or the brand image of the product. A brand is an established product name or company name. Over time, the brand name builds up features or characteristics that, collectively, provide it with a unique character or personality. This all helps to position it in the minds of the consumer.

When deciding on a new name, consider the following:

- Is it distinctive?

- Is it easy to pronounce?

- Is it memorable?

- Does it lend itself to advertising?

DID YOU KNOW

The earliest brand names are named after the founders of the company, e.g., **M**arks & Spencer, Sainsbury, Woolworth, Whitbread, while some family names have been reduced to initials — RH**M** (Rank, Hovis, **M**cDougall) — as mergers took place. **M**any products also took their product brand names from the company name: Coca-Cola, Ford, Cadbury's, **G**uinness. Some are first names: *Bella, Marie Claire.* Some are descriptions of the product content (*Homes & Gardens, Mother & Baby, Woman's Own, What's On*). Some have just been made up — Durex comes from the words DUrability, Reliability and EXcellence.

The brand personality can be built up by the physical aspects of the product (colour, shape, taste, name, packaging, etc.) and by any emotional aspects which come via the advertising (the treatment selected). Everything to do with the brand should enhance the product's required image to give it an identity. This is known as "brand image" when advertising concentrates on the image of the brand, it is called "branding".

One qualitative research technique often used is to ask people to imagine brands/products as people with human personalities, with questions like, "If Miss Marie Claire came into the room what would she be like?" or "What sort of personality does Mrs Ariel or Mr Jaguar have?", and so build up "copy" from the responses. Research can also contribute to decisions about the product itself and its packaging.

CASE STUDY

Developing the creative concept for *Marie Claire*

Marie Claire was launched in September 1988, and in 1989, three TV commercials were developed by its then advertising agency Howell Henry Chaldecott Lury (HHCL). Adam Lury, remembers them as "timeless commercials which are as relevant to today's audience as they were then".

At launch stage results from qualitative focus groups demonstrated that Marie Claire's target audience did not wish to be categorised into boxes labelled 'certain types of women'. They also questioned one of the several copy lines suggested – 'for women with a mind of their own' – saying that they did not like the implication that some women had no minds of their own. Clearly, the research showed that Marie Claire readers could not be summed up in two or three lines.

Later at a creative group meeting at the agency, the question was asked – 'Who is Marie Claire?' – which lead to defining both the woman who reads the magazine and the magazine itself as if they were one and the same. After long discussions with the then Editor, Glenda Bailey, who expressed the personality of Marie Claire in terms of who she was and, more importantly, who she wasn't, the creative team came up with a strong brand identity. The brand personality was conjured up by a series of adjectives which personified the readers' attitude of mind, rather than how the readers looked or what they did.

The launch commercial was first produced and was followed by two further ones with similar themes and were pre-tested amongst the target audience. In fact each one of them communicated quite clearly that the magazine and its readers were intelligent, fun, fashionable and stylish and each one portrayed that she was an interesting individual and interested in a number of different things.

Adam Lury, of Howell Henry Chaldecott Lury

The steady increase in circulation figures and the international success of the magazine shows that the branding formula has been a success.

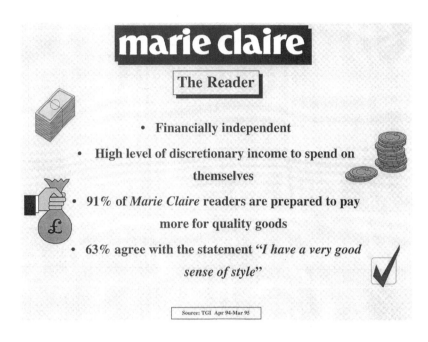

marie claire

The Reader

- **Financially independent**
- **High level of discretionary income to spend on themselves**
- **91% of *Marie Claire* readers are prepared to pay more for quality goods**
- **63% agree with the statement "*I have a very good sense of style*"**

Source: TGI Apr 94-Mar 95

marie claire

is <u>the</u> top selling

upmarket fashion glossy

in the UK with a

circulation of

452,521

Source: ABC Jul-Dec 1995

Fig 7.15 *Marie Claire* as an advertising medium. Some of the presentation materials used in their press pack. Courtesy: European Magazines Ltd.

Testing the advertising

Finished advertisements can be tested in more realistic situations, for example, a press advertisement can be pasted into a magazine or a TV commercial may be shown with others to test out how much of the advertisement people recalled.

Sometimes TV commercials are actually transmitted in one region of the country before they go out nationally to test their effectiveness. By doing this, and following it up with research, you can test whether the advertising has created a shift in attitude about the product, as well as measuring sales in that region.

Scheduling the campaign

Choosing a suitable media for the advertising can either be influenced by the needs of the product itself, for instance, it may be that TV's moving image and sound is the only effective way to promote the product's benefits. On the other hand, your research may have revealed that your target audience 'uses' one medium much more than another, so you may decide to focus on magazine advertising.

Timing is all important (the *when* in the communications mix plan) and you need to ask yourself about the availability of the product and decide whether you want the advertising to appear before the product is available, or on the day of the launch. If you want to advertise on the day the product becomes available, you will need to use newspapers, television and radio. If you decide to advertise a month ahead, you could consider magazines. For print media, you need to think about date of publication and for audio-visual products, you need to think about the day and time of day when the advertising is most likely to reach the target audience.

You also need to consider the length of time it takes to produce an advertisement — TV advertisements can take several weeks, while a radio ad can be ready for transmission in a matter of hours.

Frequency

Another factor which will affect the choice of advertising media is based on decisions around frequency of advertising. If the aim is for high repetition of the advertising message in a short period, then TV or radio or perhaps many of the national newspapers combined with magazines may prove to be the most effective media. If the widest possible coverage of the target audience is more desirable, then TV would be better. Often, a combination of coverage and repetition works best.

Today many advertising campaigns combine media using the characteristics of each one so that they complement one another and tell the *full* product story.

Which media?

■ TV is used to draw attention to the product and its pack while the print media provide a more detailed story about the product's benefits.

> ■ A TV commercial may draw attention to the product's print advertisements in which there is a special sales promotion offer that has to be sent away for.
>
> ■ TV may draw attention to a product's revamped sales packaging.

When mixing media groups, there should be common themes for consistency. For example, if there is a strong copy line, slogan or logo, then these should be used in all methods of communication, in all the material. It is more costly to produce mixed media, so it is important that each part is just one element of the full story and that the impact of the combined creative treatments, overall, is greater than the sum of each part.

Similar creative treatments should also be transferred to any other promotional material which is to be produced for the product, e.g., brochures, leaflets, videos, exhibitions, etc.

Producing drafts and treatments

One general point to remember is that whether advertisements are for audio-visual media or print, they should *emphasise the benefits to the consumer*, not the product features.

The typefaces or graphics selected may play a vital role in the process of communication. They may be the same as the brand's logo or in keeping with its image or be very easy to read. At the rough stage, if a typeface is an important ingredient to the overall creative design, then it should be researched to see its overall effect. Today, typesetting and graphics are usually generated on computer, which makes it much easier to experiment at an early stage of design development. The following points will help you focus your attention on advertising, but you should also read the relevant sections in Unit 2.

All of the production units explain the pre-production processes required of each media, with Unit 2 particularly focusing on this stage, where you will find some examples of radio scripts for advertisements.

Television   Roughs for a TV commercial are a sequence of drawings to represent still shots from the commercial. Storyboards combine the visual element (pictures) and audio (sound). Storyboards and animatics are the most frequently used method of conveying the treatment of the product in the advertisement. They are also effective ways of presenting the treatment to the client, and to audience research focus groups.

See storyboards, p. 283.

Print media   The process for print media is perhaps more of a difficult job because press advertisements have to grab people's attention without using sound or music. With press, the headline and initial paragraph have to be strong to catch the reader's eye, to make them stop and want to read more. The benefit to them should come right up front!

When writing copy for press advertisements, it is important to think of where the ads. are appearing and change the message to suit the different target groups. The length of the copy depends on the task in hand.

Photographs may be shot especially for the advertisement or existing photographs can be used which have been either bought in from a photographic library or are already owned by the product or company. When putting together roughs, it is enough to select suitable material from other publications to illustrate the type of picture required.

When developing rough ads for print media, the rough designs should include:

- the headline;
- the main feature picture and any others;
- the copy or words;
- the logo or product name;
- the positions of all these on the page (layout).

DID YOU KNOW

Press advertisements for many magazines will include photographs which have already been in past issues of the magazine. This utilises material which has already been paid for.

DID YOU KNOW

Cheaper paper absorbs ink far more than more expensive papers and means that detailed design work may be lost on the poor paper quality. So, when considering photographs or illustrations, you need to think about the paper quality to be used. There is no point producing intricate detail for an advertisement which is to appear in newspapers — it would not reproduce very well so the audience would not be able to see all of it.

Radio and posters Roughs for radio can be produced very inexpensively. You need a script, someone with a good voice for the voice-over and a tape recorder to record the advertising message. Roughs for the poster medium require a similar treatment to that of the press.

TASK

Take a media product you are developing or take an existing product which you are relaunching. List the possible advertising approaches. Present them to your group and ask them to score each approach against the following criteria:

■ relevance to product;

■ relevance to target audience;

■ content;

■ treatment;

■ resources required.

Discuss the outcome and the reasons behind each of your scores (1 = low; 5 = high).

7.4 PRESENT DRAFTS AND TREATMENTS FOR ADVERTISEMENTS

In the industry, client approval is obtained, in most cases, by a formal presentation. A good creative idea is not enough on its own if the client is to be convinced of the advertising approach. The idea has to be sold *before* any money is spent on producing the finished advertisement. 'Selling the idea' means designing a presentation which is in a form appropriate to:

- the drafts and treatments themselves;
- the audience from whom you need approval.

This may be nerve-racking, but it is essential, particularly if the creative ideas are very different and new. It may take the client a while to acclimatise to them. In this situation, a useful way is to get the overall idea approved first of all, and then leave the detail to a later meeting. Doing it this way also saves time and effort because if a client rejects the idea, then little time has been spent on developing it.

Presentations require pre-planning, selecting the most suitable and relevant way to put across the creative concepts — both in terms of equipment, the people who are to present, what is said and how it is said. What you say and the way in which you present the information will influence your audience response: you will either convince them or not, and everything from tone of voice, the words you choose, your speed of delivery, the quality of your presentation materials and even your own body language all make a difference.

Uppermost in your mind, when preparing a presentation, should be **audience** and **purpose.**

Checklist: A guide to better communication

Be brief	■ do not waffle, give only relevant details.
Be clear	■ do not frustrate the listener by going 'all round the houses'.
Be direct	■ use simple language and keep to the point.
Be concise	■ use positive rather than negative language;

Be polite	■ do not be aggressive, it can alienate.
Be assertive	■ use the right tone of voice to give emphasis to important points. This signals that they should be given priority and that a response is needed.
Use a logical order	■ briefly outline the order in the introduction so people know what to expect; ■ do not jump from one subject area to another — connect them.
Be enthusiastic	■ it is stimulating to watch and hear someone enjoying themselves

You should also bear these hints in mind:

■ use the client's name;
■ establish an empathy with them;
■ explain at the start what is going to happen;
■ listen to what the client has to say;
■ be up-front, admit and apologise for any mistakes made.

However, while clear and concise instructions are one thing, clear and concise understanding is another. It is, therefore, important to obtain feedback from the audience before taking any follow-up action.

Body language

Body language is a vital part of communication because it can influence the reactions of the audience. It can potentially communicate more about what you really mean than the words you are using.

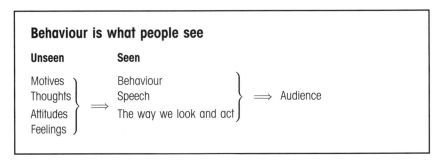

Behaviour is what people see

Unseen	Seen
Motives	Behaviour
Thoughts	Speech
Attitudes	The way we look and act
Feelings	

⟹ Audience

DID YOU KNOW

70% of communication is non-verbal.
Non-verbal communication is all forms of communication other than the actual words and their meaning, for instance:

- vocal pitch and emphasis;
- breathing;
- facial expression;
- eye contact;
- eye movement;

- speed of speech;
- posture and stance;
- clothing/dress;
- gestures/movements;
- status symbols.

Body language includes movements, postures, sitting/standing positions, use of arms, the way you shake hands, the way you walk, and so on. While some body language is conscious (e.g., a clenched fist raised as a threat), unconscious body language can be the most revealing: it is important to become aware of habits that could be distracting to an audience — do you play with your hair or jangle loose change in your pocket? Video rehearsals of presentations can cure you of irritating habits!

DID YOU KNOW

Body language: some common give-aways

- Raised shoulders show tenseness.

- Crossed arms and legs signal defensiveness.

- Walking around and not keeping in one spot may show restlessness or impatience.

- Hands behind the head signals a confident and superior person.

- A scowling face signals 'beware'!

How to keep your audience's attention

- Changing the speed with which you talk.
- Changing the tone of voice to give emphasis.
- Make sure that there are high points throughout the presentation.
- Use visual or audio-visual aids wherever possible. The spoken word backed up by visuals is more memorable than words alone.

The size of the audience can determine whether the presentation takes on a more informal tone. For instance, if there is only one person to present to, then a more informal (but not too casual) approach is better, with perhaps questions and answers taking place throughout the presentation — just like a conversation.

Oral presentations on their own are often difficult to follow. The use of visual or audio-visual aids to illustrate the content of the advertisements will definitely help make an impact. The quickest way to catch the audiences' interest is to *show* them what you are actually talking about.

CASE STUDY

Advice from an expert

Ian Fraser, Presentations Manager, IPC Magazines.

Modern technology — keep it in perspective! Bearing in mind all the technical wizardry which is currently available on the presentation scene, it is all too easy to make the very common mistake of denigrating tried and trusted methods of presentation in favour of an all-singing and all-dancing approach. Each and every presentation, however small, however big, should be carefully considered in isolation. Only after consideration of the presentation objectives, the location, the audience size and of course the budget (if any) should a decision be made regarding the use of audio-visual aids. For example, an overhead projector can be a totally suitable medium rather than a complex, expensive multi-media kit.

It is so much better to use a simple, reliable piece of equipment with which the presenter is familiar. Similarly, the quality of any presentation will always be enhanced by the use of good software, and that does not necessarily mean expensive. Dirty slides, grubby overhead acetates, poorly drawn flip chart sheets will alienate an audience very quickly.

A golden rule for any presenter is to take the trouble not only to rehearse with their audio-visual material, but also ensure that whatever equipment is being used is really up to scratch. In effect the ideal is to ensure that if something is not perfect with presentation, then it is an act of God, rather than an act of omission.

Deciding on the right approach

Different techniques can make for a more effective presentation, but the key is to find an appropriate method for your purpose. If you are considering using visual or audio-visual aids, you need to be careful that they support what is being said at the right time (not too early or too late), rather than compete for attention with the presenter.

You should think of a presentation as you would the creative treatment of factual material for a TV programme — you need high spots throughout to bring back the audience's attention and interest if it has waned. You need to grab them, gain interest and, ultimately, gain their approval.

Preparing visuals

Visual aids and audio-visuals can be very simple, perhaps using only a flip chart or some overhead transparencies (sometimes called 'acetates'), or could involve interactive multimedia presentation.

Visual aids

Display material, including product display
Flipchart
Overhead projector
Writing board
Magnetic and other display boards
Slides
Filmstrip
Video display of single images
Video display of computer output (graphics and text)

Source: Effective Audio Visual, Simpson Focal press 1996

(a)

Audio-visual

Super 8 mm movie
16 mm movie
35 mm movie
70 mm movie
Filmstrip with sound
Single slide with sound
Dissolve slide with sound
Multi-image slides with sound
Videotape/videodisc/displayed by monitors
Videotape/videodisc/displayed by projection
Multi-screen video
Computer output display linked to sound
Sound and light technique
Mixed or multi-media

Source: Effective Audio Visual, Simpson Focal Press 1996

(b)

Fig 7.16(a)–(b) The distinction between 'visual aids' and 'audio-visual' is that the former accompany a live presenter, whereas the latter uses recorded sound. Many presentations use a combination of both

Some general points to note are as follows:

- A visual should be a support, not a substitute for the presenter.
- Ensure visuals are legible — this means bold, appropriate letter size and uncluttered presentation.
- Never put more information than necessary on a visual to make a point.
- Do not show complicated diagrams, as this can distract the attention of the audience away from the presenter.
- Keep the number of words to a minimum.
- Do not show large amounts of text that allow the audience to read ahead of the presentation.
- Use graphs or pie charts rather than figures or tables.
- Use colour where possible to distinguish between sections of a diagram.
- Use a build-up sequence if the final chart is complex, or if different parts of the chart need to be explained separately.
- Ensure all visuals are the same format (all landscape or all portrait).
- Only use relevant images, and do not show them too early.

Source: Robert Simpson (1996), *Effective Audio-Visual*, Focal Press.

■ Remove images from the screen as soon as they have been discussed.

Flip charts

Flip charts are generally A2 size. You may wish to pre-prepare flip chart visuals, or you may be writing them live in the presentation. Whatever the case, you should not use letters less than 20 mm high for a maximum viewing distance of 8 metres. Obviously, if you are presenting in a large space, letters would need to be even bigger.

Fig 7.17 Flip chart

Overhead transparencies

Overhead transparencies are projected by overhead projectors (OHP). You can write directly on to the transparent film with special OHP marker pens. You can also very effectively create slides using simple word-processing and graphics computer applications. If you can print directly from a computer to a laser printer, you can get special photocopier/laser printer transparencies that can be loaded directly into the printer or photocopier.

■ If you want to show a page layout or storyboard, you can simply photocopy them on to transparency.
■ It makes good marketing sense to incorporate your company logo on to OHP slides.

Fig 7.18 Overhead projector

Information packs

You may also wish to supplement your presentation with an information pack which can be taken away by the audience. You may decide to reproduce your OHP slides and present them as a bound booklet, as in the Virgin Radio example on page 463.

Animatics

Animatics can be produced easily, so long as the original storyboard is clear and of high graphic quality. Using a video camera (on a rostrum if you have one, otherwise you will need to find an alternative method of getting the camera close-in enough to use the macro setting) shoot each frame of the storyboard for 30 seconds. This becomes your visual source tape. Record your voice-over/sound-track on another video tape which has control track, ensuring that you time it to the required 20 or 30 seconds. Then insert edit the visuals from the storyboard to match the sound-track. You might find that you use a selection of the storyboard for animatics, to get across the main ideas.

Presenting drafts and treatments to an audience

There is no set way to make a presentation, but if it is long or complex, or if different team members have taken responsibility

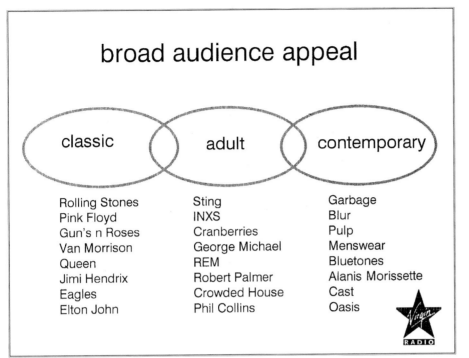

broad audience appeal

classic	adult	contemporary
Rolling Stones	Sting	Garbage
Pink Floyd	INXS	Blur
Gun's n Roses	Cranberries	Pulp
Van Morrison	George Michael	Menswear
Queen	REM	Bluetones
Jimi Hendrix	Robert Palmer	Alanis Morissette
Eagles	Crowded House	Cast
Elton John	Phil Collins	Oasis

Virgin Radio

★ 4.24 million listeners

★ 32.7 million listening hours

★ 86% of reach aged 15-44

★ 87% of listening aged 15-44

★ reach 9% of all adults

★ reach 17% of all men 15-44

★ reach 12% of all women 15-44

source : Rajar Qtr 4 1995

Fig 7.19

for different aspects of the presentation, then it is better not to have a single presenter.

CASE STUDY

Teamwork: An advertising agency view

Mike Turnbull, Managing Director of Incision.

I never thought I would trust my work to be presented by someone else if I were part of a creative team, unless I had every confidence in their ability to understand how the recommendation had been developed and to sell it and defend it when presenting it to a client. The responsibility has historically fallen on the account manager's shoulders to present creative work. Some are excellent presenters. Some are not. Just as some creative teams like to present their own work and some would rather be saved from that exposure.

Indeed some clients like to have the opportunity of discussing the creative work with the people that have written it whilst others feel they can express their views, and usually their criticisms, more confidently if they don't have to share them directly with the authors! Just as the creative brief is developed by the team, so is the work assessed by the team.

It is always a good idea if someone from the presentation team takes notes of the meeting to circulate afterwards to all those present so that everyone is in agreement about any revisions that are necessary. When taking notes we should consider four main headings for each subject matter discussed:

- *what: the item under discussion (e.g., print ad);*
- *how: the action decided upon (e.g., change illustration);*
- *who: responsibility for the action;*
- *when: deadline for the revision.*

If flip charts are used or any other visual aids, it is also a good idea for someone else – other than the presenter – to turn to charts over so that the presenter can concentrate on what they have to say.

It is also important to establish where the presentation is going to be held. You should if at all possible visit the presentation space to examine where the audience will sit, where the presenter will stand, and, if more than one presenter is presenting, where *they* will sit to ensure for a smooth handover from one person to another. Obviously, as with any other form of production, you should ensure that the correct equipment and facilities are available. You should certainly rehearse the presentation in full before doing it for real.

CASE STUDY
Being a good presenter

Ian Fraser, Presentations Manager, IPC Magazines.

Most presenters are normal people with normal feelings – that is they tend to hyper-ventilate when even thinking of presenting to a live audience. This shock to the average nervous system never actually goes away – but practice can keep it under some sort of control. Rehearse, rehearse, then rehearse again. Use a script, use cue cards or memorise it – but do it your way – whatever you feel comfortable with – ignore all the advice which says you have to do it this way or that way.

One of the great misconceptions is the suggestion that because you are only talking to a small group you don't need a voice reinforcement system [a microphone]. The quickest way to send the back rows of an audience to sleep is to ensure that they can't hear you!

A good presenter will always be early for their presentation taking the opportunity for a final rehearsal, equipment check, and so on. A good presenter learns the art of pacing a presentation; the most common fault is to go too fast and then get faster, and then gabble. If you think about it, all the great orators use measured tones.

Describe the product's key aspects

Creating the order of any presentation will make you focus on what needs to be covered. Start by writing an outline of the basic presentation format. This will give you a framework for the 'narrative' of the presentation. You could try the following:

Introduction

The opening will set the tone of the whole presentation. Introduce yourself and the other presenters. This all helps in getting to know each other better and starts to build up a relationship between you and the audience.

The introduction should state the broad aims of the presentation and tell the audience *why* they should listen, perhaps by indicating that the creative treatments will affect the brand, in a positive way:

'We're here today to talk to you about product X, and to show you a variety of different creative ideas and rough treatments for discussion. Treatments which emphasise the product benefits in a strong way.'

Outline of agenda

Give a broad idea of what is to come, briefly describing the structure and content of the presentation, such as:

'I'm going to tell you about the new product and the "thinking" behind the creative ideas. Then I'll hand over to the art director who will show you the rough creative treatments and why we think they would work, and then it's back to me to summarise. After that I'll put forward some recommendations of how we think we should progress, and then we can discuss them.'

People need to know what to expect in order to get interested. Outlining the presentation in this way helps to do just that, giving them landmarks to look out for. It also builds up some anticipation about what they will learn and allows them to pace themselves to stay with you until the end.

Background to the media product

Describe the **key aspects** of the product, the reasons for your **choice of medium**, its unique position and its **purpose** in the market-place, together with its advantages over similar products available. Include **target audience**, as well as the benefits the product can give to them. State the **rationale for advertising decisions** — why advertise and what the advertising should be achieving for the product; eg:

> 'The new product is a monthly magazine aimed at those people who enjoy gardening, but who also like to improve the outside of their homes using plants and tubs. It will be a "how to" publication and rely on photographs and illustrations, together with captions of how to do the different tasks. There is no other magazine on the market that offers this sort of editorial treatment. It will be aimed at all adults over 40 years old — both men and women. In order to build up sufficient interest in the product, it will be necessary to spend a large amount on advertising, to let people know that the new product is available.'

Main content

The creative idea together with the product's **content** and **treatment of material** will be the heart of the presentation, so it is important that this section is clearly understood.

Three approaches are discussed below.

1   Start with the rough content and treatments, together with the reasons why the particular creative approach was adopted. This makes an strong start, but the initial impact has to be maintained at intervals throughout the presentation.
2   Start by telling the audience how the different ideas were developed, revealing the different stages that the creative roughs went through. This gradually builds up an understanding of the whole picture. This makes the audience curious about the final treatment and then that becomes the focus of the whole presentation.
3   The final outcome of any advertising for any new product is to make people aware of it so that they 'use' it. So, for this approach, start with the 'punch line' by making a statement about the numbers of people who are likely to see and buy or view or listen to the product. This is a bold approach which may startle or intrigue the audience, but either way will entice them to want to know more.

Break down the content of the main part of the presentation into sections, which makes it easier to explain and easier for the audience to take in. For example, 'the idea behind this rough advertisement was ..., but after discussions among the creative team it was thought too similar to the competition for two reasons ... So this is how we progressed it. Here we have ...'

Justify the **rationale for any advertising decisions** (e.g., where you want to advertise, style, treatment, size of space, length of commercial). Research results should also be presented in this section to validate the creative treatments.

Ensure that people are listening. Show the product. You could hand-draw important points on a flip chart spontaneously or add hand-written points to existing acetates for the overhead projector, to accentuate certain areas. You could exhibit the different stages of creative treatment by placing all the development work around the room — but make sure that they are large enough for all the audience to see.

Recap each section and link each section

This helps to:

- reinforce the points;
- clarify the case;
- help the slow or inattentive person to catch up;
- ensure that everyone in the audience is ready to move on to the next part, together.

It is important to highlight in your script a purposeful link to the next section of the main content. This clearly signals that you are moving forward and developing the arguments. So, after giving the detail in a section and then recapping, you can then link to the next section:

"Now let us turn to the story board for the TV commercial ..."

Summarise the main content

Ideally, the summary should cover the major points, succinctly. A good method for the presenter to use is bullet points. These remind the audience of the main 'selling' points. The presenter can provide, additional information over each point. However, remember not to get carried away and repeat detail already covered.

Conclusion

This should be the high point of the presentation where everything is brought together. It should highlight the **content and treatment of material**, as well as the **Rationale for the advertising**. Show, once again, a few of the best visuals selecting the most graphic, dramatic and innovative examples. End on a positive note, by saying why the creative concept will work for the product.

Audience feedback

The tasks throughout the unit will also help you to build your portfolio.

As with all of the units, you should check carefully the **evidence indicators** in each element and ensure that you carry out the necessary tasks described in the performance criteria to produce the requirements.

Questions and discussion allows the audience to have their say. You need feedback so that you can find out why your advertising approach was liked or not by the client, and so that you can easily make revisions.

The evaluation of the presentation

Your presentation should be evaluated by your audience, in writing. It should be evaluated in terms of its 'fitness for purpose' — i.e., did it put across the drafts and treatments in a suitable and relevant way, bearing in mind the resources available and the audience to whom you were presenting. Was the product and its creative treatments suitable for the targeted audience? How well did the team perform?

EVIDENCE COLLECTION POINT

The following assignments provide a variety of approaches to collecting evidence for the assessment of Unit 7. You will find that most of the activities require that you undertake research activities, so you will also be able to collect evidence for Unit 6 at the same time. Studying the aspects of Unit 6 which focus on audience research for commercial purposes — i.e., targeting, locating a market, positioning a product within the market, and so on — and using the approaches described there alongside Unit 7 is the most efficient and relevant way of tackling this unit. You may wish to integrate this unit with practical work in any or all of Units 3, 4 and 5 — in other words, market your own products or something produced by others in your group. A good way to do this would be for students nearing the end of their first year of the course to pitch to second-year students undertaking major projects.

The **evidence indicator** suggests a formal written report. You may also wish to use this to structure a video, radio or print project on 'Marketing the Music Industry', in which case you could combine evidence for Element 7.1 with any of the practical units.

ASSIGNMENT 1

Marketing a band.

You are in the marketing team of a successful record label and you have recently signed up a new band. You are required to establish what potential the artist has in relation to TV, radio, the press and to develop the band's visual identity. You will also need to decide on the promotional techniques to sell it to the public.

■ Carry out some initial research into the role of marketing for the music business and produce a report describing the marketing activities undertaken. You will need to study the music press closely, as well as looking at the relationship between point-of-sale displays in record shops, merchandise (e.g., T-shirts, posters), music videos, and CD/cassette sleeves. You should also investigate radio airings and PR/publicity, for instance, appearances of music artists on children's television, on chat shows, fronting charity events, etc.

■ Devise a marketing plan for the band, which is based on market research. You will need to undertake qualitative and quantitative research, which you can use for assessment for Unit 6. Your marketing plan should be justified by the research and should cover product design, pricing, sales packaging, timing of the campaign and what forms of promotion and advertising you will use. The plan should also show how you will monitor its performance — you will check that the marketing will work.

You may wish, following the presentation, to use your market research as the basis for a project which involves the production of a music video, together with printed materials such as CD/cassette covers, posters, music reviews etc.

■ Develop an advertising approach for the band, which includes identifying what media you will use, as well as the treatment of the band image.

■ Produce drafts and treatments for the various elements of the campaign.

■ Produce a schedule for the campaign, which shows choice of media, timing and frequency of advertising.

■ Prepare and present a presentation of your rough drafts and treatments and evaluate the outcomes.

ASSIGNMENT 2

Marketing a radio station

You have recently gained a licence for a new independent commercial local radio station. You are due to go on air within the next two months and are looking to launch your station to advertisers, as your income is dependent on advertising revenue. Design a presentation and media pack to convince advertisers that your station will deliver a strong, targeted, sustainable audience.

■ Conduct research into the role of marketing in commercial radio, describing the importance of advertising, and other ways in which radio can be used to promote products. (Virgin, for instance, runs special weekend promotions based around a listener competition, in which the client gains substantial weekend coverage). You may find it useful to try and obtain a media pack from one or two of your local stations. Write up your findings as an illustrated report.

■ Draft a marketing plan for your station. How will you get listeners to listen? How will you guarantee audiences for advertisers?

8 INVESTIGATE OWNERSHIP AND CONTROL IN MEDIA INDUSTRIES

Media products are the result of particular industrial processes: they all require capital and investment, whether or not they are working within the mainstream; they are all subject to regulation, legislation and financial control; they all require systems of distribution and circulation. It has often been said of western societies that they are 'media saturated': the almost omnipresence of the media in the contemporary world, the emergence of increasingly sophisticated digital and satellite communication systems means that the remotest parts of the developing world are able to receive films and programmes, often generated by western producers, most notably the United States. This and the power and influence of the media make their industrial context an interesting and important area to study. Developments in digital and interactive technology further increase the importance of the media industries, as they provide not only new ways in which to distribute and consume media products, but whole new markets for new products.

In this unit, you will look at the principal media producers and their products; what type of organisations they are; ownership patterns; and how they generate and spend their income.

The evidence required for assessment in this unit takes the form of case studies and reports. Do not forget that these may take on various forms including, for instance, videos, radio items, printed booklets or even an interactive multi-media presentation, if your school or college has these facilities.

8.1 INVESTIGATE OWNERSHIP AND CONTROL IN MEDIA INDUSTRIES

How much can one company own?

The information about ownership contained in this unit could, of course, change as companies are taken over or go out of business and it is important that you also look regularly at other information sources such as the *Guardian Media Guide* to check on the current situation. The same can be said of regulation and control, and the multi-media industries in particular are changing at an incredibly rapid rate. You should also try to keep up with the trade press (*Broadcast, Campaign, Screen International*, etc.) and certainly read the *Guardian* Media pages published on Monday, and maybe the *Independent* Media pages, on Tuesdays. The *Guardian* 'On Line' section on Thursdays gives interesting coverage of the information technology world, and you can regularly find interactive multi-media featured here, as well as in specialist magazines like *Wired*.

Many media companies have interests across a range of sectors but the amount of ownership is controlled in the UK by the government. This has led some companies to look overseas to expand.

The diversification of ownership is partly driven by the twin gods of profit and influence, but also by the recognition that techno-logical change is blurring the edges between the various media. The *Guardian*, for example, transfers its content to CD-ROM and certain newspapers are also published on the internet.

It is the issue of undue influence that causes the government to regulate market share or 'share of the national voice'. Under the 1990 Broadcasting Act, newspaper companies with less than 20% national newspaper circulation could control radio and TV companies with up to a 15% share. Regional newspapers could not own local TV or radio licences if they controlled more than 30% of an area's newspaper circulation. The number of radio licences that a company could hold was limited to 35.

However, since the 1990 Broadcasting Act, there has been an increasing tendency to *deregulate*, relaxing some of these controls The most recent 1996 Broadcasting Act, which became law at the end of July 1996, and came into effect on 1 November 1996, removes most of the numerical limits on the holding of TV and radio licences. Instead of limiting the number of TV licences a company can hold, there is a ceiling of 15% total audience time. Total audience time is defined as the amount of time spent watching programmes broadcast or received in the UK as estimated by the ITC (Independent Television Commission). Cross media ownership of newspapers and certain broadcasters has to undergo a public interest test operated by the ITC and the Radio Authority. This test will be applied to regional and national Channel 3 services, Channel 5 national and local radio licences and national digital sound programme services. The test will assess the economic benefits of cross ownership and the effect on the operation of the broadcasting and newspaper. Issues around promoting plurality and diversity of views also form part of the criteria.

(*Source:* **Broadcast** *13 September 1996 — SJ Berwin/KPMG. Note:* **Broadcast** *has produced a very useful and detailed table summarising all of the changes in this issue*).

The global village

The advent of satellites means that western media owners can beam their signals (and ideas) into parts of the world where either the media is tightly controlled, or there is little production and distribution. You might like to consider whether this is entirely a good thing or not. Another thing to think about is whether media owners are motivated by profit or influence, or both.

Multi-national conglomerates

A multinational conglomerate is a company with many interests across national boundaries.

In terms of media ownership, multi-national conglomerates present the most powerful contributor to the idea of the global village, which is the idea that modern media can blur the identities of diverse cultures through an immediate and constant recipe of certain dominant ideas.

> *For some writers, globalisation is a process which results in 'sameness' or homogeneity on an increasingly word-wide basis. As Hebdidge has suggested in this context: 'The implication here is that we'll soon be able to watch* Dallas *or eat a Big Mac in any part of the inhabited world.' Put crudely, world culture and media have become relay stations for the most powerful multinational corporations and their forms of popular, profitable culture.*

Hebdidge (1989), 'After the Masses' *Marxism Today*, in. Tim O'Sullivan, Brian Dutton, Philip Rayner (1994), *Studying the Media*, Edward Arnold.

The most obvious multi-national conglomerate is Rupert Murdoch's News International. In addition to having the largest share of the UK national newspaper market (about 37%), it also owns book publishers Harper Collins and 40% of BSkyB. Then in the United States he owns Twentieth Century Fox, Fox TV, the *New York Post* among others; in Germany, nearly half of Vox satellite and terrestrial broadcasting; in Asia, it has a 99% holding in Star TV which is a satellite covering India, China, Japan, the Philippines, Thailand and Hong Kong; finally in Australia, 15% of Channel 7 TV together with numerous print groups and newspapers.

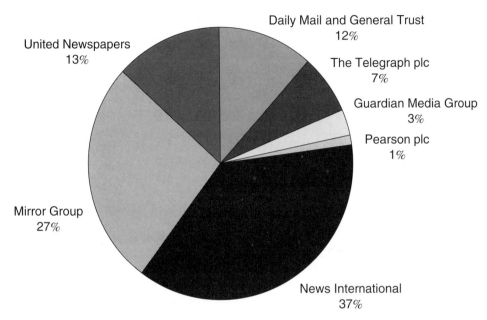

Market Shares of Media Corporations in the UK
Source: British Media Industry Group

Fig 8.1   Market Shares of Multi National Conglomerates: Source: British Media Group

Newspapers

National newspaper ownership

In terms of national newspaper ownership, Murdoch's News International owns the *Sun, The Times, News of the World,* and *The Sunday Times.* The next largest player is the Mirror Group with about 26% of the market. As well as owning the *Daily Mirror, Sunday Mirror, Daily Record* and the *People,* it holds a 43% stake in Newspaper Publishing, which publishes the *Independent* and the *Independent on Sunday.*

United News & Media, which publishes the *Daily Express, Sunday Express,* and Daily Mail & General Trust have roughly equal shares of the market at about 13%.

The *Daily Telegraph* and *Sunday Telegraph* are controlled by Conrad Black through a Canadian company and has 7% of the market, while the Guardian Media Group (*Guardian* and *Observer*) has 3%.

Pearson publishes the *Financial Times* and has only 1% of the national newspaper market but also owns the Longman Group of book publishers and the specialist magazine publishers Future Publishing. It has a stake in BSkyB, Thames Television, the new Channel 5, and also owns the fifth largest local newspaper group, Westminster Press.

Local newspaper ownership

Very few local newspapers are still owned locally and you will probably find that your local paper is actually owned by a large group. While many of the national newspaper owners have interests in local papers, the largest owner of local titles does not publish any nationals. Trinity International Holdings became the largest publisher of local papers by buying Thompson Regional Newspapers in 1995. Until 1985, Trinity published the *Liverpool Daily Post & Echo*, it then started to expand into London and the Home Counties with the purchase of the Argus newspaper group. It now has about 1,300 titles and a weekly circulation of 12,000,000.

The second largest regional publisher is Northcliffe Newspapers, which is part of the Daily Mail & General Trust. Northcliffe has only 60 titles but a healthy circulation of approximately 7,500,000.

Things change all the time as companies decide to dispose of parts of their empires so that they can be free to move into other areas. Government regulations that are dealt with in Element 8.2 restrict media ownership in certain areas. For example, the fourth largest publisher, Reed International, sold its regional newspapers to a management buy-out team called Newsquest.

In the middle of 1996, Emap startled the industry by offering its 43 paid-for newspapers and 28 free-sheets for sale. Emap actually started life as East Midlands Allied Press so it is particularly surprising that it has disposed of this part of its business. However, it is almost certain to expand its specialist business publishing and exhibitions promotion. It also wants to expand its share of the local radio market — it has interests in stations in London, Liverpool, Manchester, Preston, Leeds and Cardiff — and to move into television.

TASK

Look at your local newspaper (or newspapers) and discover who owns it. You should find this information in the paper (in small print at the foot of a page) or you can use *Benn's Media Guide* or the *Guardian Media Guide* to help you. Trace the ownership back until you reach the top, and then chart how your paper fits into the company's pattern of media ownership. For example, do they have other interests in the area that appear to be in competition?

Magazine publishing

Probably the area that has seen most expansion in recent years has been magazine publishing. From 1985 to 1995, the number of titles has increased by about 70%. There are now nearly 8,000 magazines published, two thirds of which are classed as 'business and professional' while the remaining third are consumer.

	Paid-for daily newspapers*			Paid-for weekly newspapers‡			Free weekly newspapers‡			Total:	paid-for and free	
	No. of titles	Circulation per issue '000	%	No. of titles	Circulation per issue '000	%	No. of titles	Distribution per issue '000	%	No. of titles	Circulation/distribution per week '000	%
TRN	11	929,882	16.0	18	538,525	7.2	37	2,347,001	7.1	66	8,464,818	11.3
of which: TVN	1	25,719	0.4	1	13,079	0.2	2	132,607	0.4	4	300,000	0.4
Northcliffe Newspapers	13	808,130	13.9	15	312,329	4.2	32	1,657,955	5.0	60	6,819,064	9.1
UPN	6	473,638	8.2	22	402,347	5.4	39	2,223,925	6.8	67	5,468,100	7.3
Reed	4	153,564	2.6	15	324,497	4.3	61	3,885,933	11.8	80	5,131,814	6.8
Westminster Press	8	427,016	7.4	19	382,473	5.1	35	1,796,406	5.5	62	4,740,975	6.3
Trinity‡	4	308,662	5.3	35	568,412	7.6	29	1,415,627	4.3	68	3,836,011	5.1
Midland Independent	3	319,632	5.5	2	149,535	2.0	24	1,519,718	4.6	29	3,587,045	4.8
GMEN	1	221,479	3.8	9	190,071	2.5	20	1,296,173	3.9	30	2,815,118	3.7
Midland News Association	2	317,855	5.5	4	42,929	0.6	18	646,092	2.0	24	2,596,151	3.5
Eastern Countries Newspapers	4	207,376	3.6	12	138,141	1.8	25	1,155,661	3.5	41	2,538,058	3.4
EMAP	3	114,474	2.0	36	534,122	7.1	31	1,253,196	3.8	70	2,474,162	3.3
Portsmouth & Sunderland Newspapers	4	195,482	3.4	7	106,624	1.4	15	792,412	2.4	26	2,071,928	2.8
Southern Newspapers	3	140,489	2.4	9	145,547	1.9	20	1,055,442	3.2	32	2,043,833	2.7
Bristol United Press	2	169,146	2.9	2	49,479	0.7	5	382,555	1.2	9	1,446,910	1.9
Johnston Press	–	–	–	27	405,769	5.4	25	976,731	3.0	52	1,382,500	1.8
Tindle Newspaper Group	2	98,467	1.7	10	116,414	1.6	21	658,748	2.0	33	1,365,964	1.8
Yellow Advertiser Newspaper Group	–	–	–	4	43,687	0.6	19	1,004,521	3.1	23	1,048,208	1.4
Yattendon Investment Trust	1	64,432	1.1	6	94,410	1.3	19	497,493	1.5	26	978,495	1.3
Southnews	–	–	–	9	147,131	2.0	17	741,044	2.3	26	888,175	1.2
The Adscene Group	–	–	–	7	77,241	1.0	9	573,425	1.7	16	650,666	0.9
Sub-total: largest 20 publishers (as above)	71	4,949,724	85.3	268	4,769,593	63.6	501	25,880,058	78.8	840	60,347,995	80.3
Others	16	854,648	14.7	199	2,724,190	36.4	154	6,981,538	21.2	369	14,833,616	19.7
Known total: all local and regional newspapers	87	5,804,372	100.0	467	7,493,783	100.0‡	655	32,861,596	100‡	1,209	75,181,611	100.0‡

*Does not include *Evening Standard*, an evening daily newspaper serving, primarily, the Greater London region (with an average circulation of 188,131 (January to June 1993).

†Includes local and regional Sunday newspapers. Also includes newspapers published more than once a week (but not daily) in different editions, but excludes newspapers published less frequently than one a week.

‡Figures do not sum to 100 due to rounding.

‡Includes data for Argus Newspapers (after deducting certain titles subsequently sold to Southnews) and Joseph Woodland & Sons Ltd.

Source: MMC, based on data for PressAd Services' data bank (as at 18 November 1993).

Figure 8.2 Top 20 publishers of local and regional newspapers in the UK (by circulation/distribution)

The advent of new technology like desk-top publishing means that magazines can make a profit on smaller circulations by cutting costs.

Magazines aimed at consumers are becoming increasingly specialist and based on niche markets that reflect readers' interests rather than age, gender or the other more traditional groupings. The business and professional or trade magazines have offered a specialist service to targeted groups for many years. However, whether your interest is in mountain bikes, diving, dentistry, China or family trees, you should be able to find a magazine to cover it.

There are a number of big names in magazine publishing. IPC Magazines (*TV Times, Woman's Own, Amateur Gardening, New Musical Express, Loaded, Marie Claire* and many more) is a wholly owned subsidiary of Reed Elsevier which is the largest magazine publisher. Emap is currently second placed with titles including *Angling Times, Kerrang!, Just 17, More, Big!* and *Practical Gardening.* Oddly the BBC, through a subsidiary BBC Worldwide Publishing is also a major magazine publisher with *Radio Times, Good Food, Gardeners World, Wildlife,* etc. It causes some resentment among other publishers that the BBC promotes its own magazines on air where no one else is allowed to advertise. Hence the need to include lines like. 'Other TV listings magazines are available,' in *Radio Times* adverts.

It is forecast that the expansion in magazines could well be a model for TV when perhaps 500 channels become available with the start of digital broadcasting. Perhaps 'narrowcasting' would be a better word but the television industry will also need to find ways to reduce its traditionally high costs without sacrificing too much quality.

Television

Television currently divides into three — terrestrial, satellite and cable. There will shortly be digital television to add to this list. Terrestrial is television delivered from a land-based transmitter and presently consists of two BBC channels and three independent channels. As television signals need to have 'line of sight' between the transmitter and your aerial at home, this means there are large numbers of transmitters especially in hilly areas.

Satellite channels are beamed from the service provider up to a satellite and then down to a dish aerial — these services can be coded so that only consumers who have paid a subscription can watch. The three main groups of satellites covering Britain are Astra, Eutelsat, and Intelsat.

Cable TV is delivered via cables like telephone lines (which can also provide telephone and other services). Obviously there has to be a cable outside your home before you can be connected to it. You must pay a subscription to receive cable services, many of which are the same as satellite.

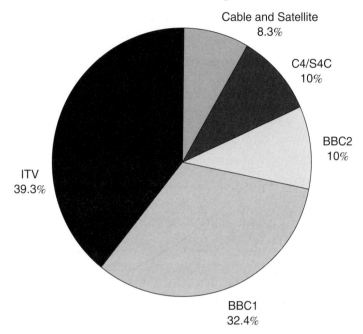

**Average TV Audience Share (%) of TV Channels.
Source: Screen Digest**

Cable and Satellite
8.3%

C4/S4C
10%

BBC2
10%

ITV
39.3%

BBC1
32.4%

Fig 8.3 Television Audience
Share

Digital television can be delivered terrestrially or from satellite and will hugely increase the number of channels that are available.

Terrestrial television

Terrestrial television divides into public service and commercial. The former is provided by the BBC on two channels and is paid for by the television licence fee. Each channel has a controller who commissions programmes from internal programme departments and at least 25% from independent producers. Each controller schedules the programmes to maximise audience while at the same time providing the distinctive mix required of a public service broadcaster.

However the Director General of the BBC, John Birt, has made a number of changes in the way that the BBC is organised. Firstly he introduced 'producer choice'. This basically means that a BBC producer can shop around for the best price for facilities to make a television or radio programme. As a consequence BBC technical departments have to tender for work in the same way as independent contractors. This has led to a growth of independent companies and freelancers, while the number of posts in the BBC has fallen by about 5,000.

As a logical extension of this process, the BBC has reorganised into two main business units called BBC Broadcasting and BBC

Production. The former will commission and schedule programmes for both TV and radio, while the latter will operate as a huge production company.

TV and radio news have also been combined and located at White City in west London. There is a major concern that BBC radio will become even more of a poor relation to television in the new set-up.

Ownership and the impact of the 1990 Broadcasting Act

The 1990 Broadcasting Act created the Independent Television Commission (ITC) which licenses and regulates all commercially financed television services in the UK. The Act also changed the way in which ITV companies applied for their franchises.

The companies now have to tender for their licences and state the amount that they are prepared to pay for a ten-year franchise. In the last franchise round, this amount varied tremendously and some companies are struggling to make the payments. The variations have little to do with size of area, more to do with market forces and a company's nerve in bidding low. For example, Tyne Tees pays £17 million a year, but Scottish Television only bid £2,000, Granada pays £9 million while Carlton pays over £43 million. There is no requirement for the ITC to accept the highest bidder if another bidder offers a 'proposed service that is substantially higher than the quality proposed by the highest bidder'.

One of the results of the new system has been new-style publisher/broadcasters like Carlton UK which commissions or acquires programmes from independent companies, working alongside more traditional producer/broadcasters like Granada, who also make and transmit programmes. One established company that was a victim of the system was Thames Television which lost the London weekday franchise. However, it still exists as an independent producer making programmes for both ITV and BBC.

ITV licences

The new Channel 3 licences came into force on 1 January 1993 and are valid for ten years. In London there are 2 licences, Carlton broadcasts on weekdays and LWT at the weekends. There is also a sixteenth company, GMTV, that provides breakfast programming.

Since the licences were advertised, the rules on ownership have been relaxed and some companies are now wholly or partly owned by another media group. For example, LWT is owned by Granada, which also has a 14% holding in Yorkshire-Tyne Tees TV Holdings and 20% of GMTV. Carlton Communications owns both Carlton and Central.

TASK

Build up a profile of your local Channel 3 broadcaster. Who owns it? Where do you fit into its broadcast area? How much local programming does it provide? Is your town covered effectively by news or by other programmes?

Networked programmes on ITV

Channel 3 is unusual in that while each region is serviced by a different company that each needs to keep shareholders and advertisers happy, it still needs a coherence to its scheduling. In general, each company transmits the same programmes at the same time especially during peak viewing hours. To manage this, the companies jointly own a Network Centre which commissions, purchases and schedules programmes. The Network Director in 1996, Marcus Plantin, had a budget of over £600 million to spend on programmes. This showed a large increase from 1995 when Channel 3 lost viewers and hence advertisers complained.

Company	Hours screened (h:min)
Anglia	151:45
Border	
Carlton	127
Central	184:40
Channel	51
Grampian	1
Granada	582
HTV	15:30
LWT	255
Meridian	45
STV	225
Tyne Tees	92:30
Westcountry	2:5
Yorkshire	204

Source: *The BFI Film and Television Handbook 1996*

Fig 8.4 ITV companies programme supply to the network

Independent Television News

The ITV companies also owned Independent Television News prior to the 1990 Broadcasting Bill. They were required to sell their controlling interest in order to allow competition from other news services. In effect there has been no change and ITN still supplies news to Channels 3 and 4.

In the UK, Channel 4 is an alternative commercial (advertising) channel that includes a distinct public service remit. Channel 4's remit was that it should appeal to tastes not catered for by ITV, encourage innovation and experiment and be distinctive. The channel is also required to act as a publisher of independent work rather than a producer.

Channel 4 also acts as a co-producer of films, *Four Weddings and a Funeral* and *The Madness of King George*, to mention but two.

In Wales, Sianel Pedwar Cymru (S4C) broadcasts about 30 hours a week of Welsh language programmes. About a third is supplied by the BBC with the rest coming from HTV and independent producers. The rest of the day is taken up with programmes in English that are often Channel 4 programmes. S4C is directly funded by the Treasury.

Channel 5

The Channel 5 franchise that was also subject to tender was won by Channel 5 Broadcasting with a bid of a little over £22 million. Channel 5 is also a publisher broadcaster, although it has made a commitment to using a more limited number of larger production companies to supply the programming. This company is owned by Pearson and MAI, and started broadcasting in March 1997 to at least part of the country. However, its allocated frequency interferes with video recorders and so all video recorders have had to be retuned before the start of transmissions.

Satellite television

Satellite broadcasting in the UK really started in 1989 when Rupert Murdoch launched Sky TV and paid for it with the profits from his newspapers. Ironically, when his papers were in trouble and needed to indulge in price cutting wars, satellite TV was able to bail them out.

In 1990 Sky TV merged (somewhat unequally) with British Satellite Broadcasting, which was struggling to compete. BSkyB was born and has gone from strength to strength. Over 3 million households now have a dish and BSkyB has about 4% of the total audience. Much of the increase has been due to BSkyB's exclusive sports coverage. The rate at which satellite television has been outbidding terrestrial television for sports rights caused the government to pass legislation safeguarding eight prime sporting events that must be available terrestrially. These include Wimbledon, the FA Cup Final and Test Matches played in England.

BSkyB also has a deal with the news agency Reuters to supply a 24-hour news service.

Other satellite services are available — MTV and the Asian TV Network are two examples — but they have a very small share of the market. Surprisingly the BBC is also a satellite broadcaster jointly with Thames Television. The UK Gold channel makes use of the extensive archives of both companies.

Year	Cable	No of subscribers	Satellite	No of subscribers
1986	12.2%	–	–	–
1987	13.3%	–	–	–
1988	14.3%	–	0.1%	–
1989	14.5%	–	2.3%	–
1990	16.6%	–	5.9%	–
1991	19.1%	–	7.9%	–
1992	21.5%	–	10.2%	–
1993	21.1%	–	12.1%	–
1994	22%	908 000	13.1%	3 960 000

Cable figures represents % take up in cabled areas.

Source: Screen Digest/*The BFI Film and Television Handbook 1996*

Fig 8.5 Cable and satellite penetration 1986–94

Channel Share (%)

Terrestrial Channels	65.6
Sky One	5.1
Sky News	1.1
Sky Sports	3.7
Movie Channel	2.8
Sky Movies	3.4
Sky Movies Gold	0.5
Sky Sports 2	0.4
Bravo	0.7
CMT	0.3
Discovery	1.0
Eurosport	0.8
MTV	1.0
Nickelodeon	1.4
Children's Channel	0.7
Family Channel	0.4
TNT/Cartoon Network	2.0
UK Gold	2.7
UK Living	0.5
VH-1	0.7
Others	2.6

Source: Screen Digest/BARB/*The BFI Film and Television Handbook 1996*

Fig 8.6 Viewing habits in cable and satellite homes 1994

Cable television

The ITC licenses cable operators and programme providers. The licence for the operators gives them the right to broadcast over a purpose-built network for 15 years. There are two figures that establish the effective coverage of cable. Firstly the number

Source: ITC, July 1996.

of houses that the cable passes, in other words the potential audience. In June 1996, this was 6.6 million homes. The other figure is the number of homes connected and this was 1.4 million connected to CATV, and 1.6 million connected to telephone.

While this is a comparatively small percentage, cable television is turning over somewhere in the region of £300 million a year and so is paying back some of the £10 billion that it cost to lay the cables in the first place. Subscribers pay a connection fee and then a monthly subscription, with an additional subscription for BSkyB programmes.

The system can carry up to 45 channels and can also provide a telephone line and interactive services like banking and shopping. There are some low-cost local services on offer — often this involves a journalist with a camcorder carrying out the whole operation, as demonstrated by the likes of Channel One for London. The Mirror Group's venture into cable has produced such 'gems' as topless darts. Leicester has a community channel; there's a home shopping channel; a Royal Opera Channel; an Arabic channel. The choice is wide and will increasingly meet the needs of niche markets as magazines have done.

Radio

As with television, the first main distinction to make with radio is between public service and commercial broadcasters; that is, between the BBC and independent radio. However, there are similarities as well as differences between the two.

Both sectors have national, regional, and local services. Each, albeit for different reasons, is interested to know and increase its listening figures.

BBC radio

In the UK, the BBC's national networks are somewhat unoriginally called Radio 1, Radio 2, Radio 3, Radio 4, and, just to change the pattern slightly, Radio 5 Live. Each has a distinctive style and aims at a particular audience.

Radio 1 is aimed at a young audience and relies largely on pop music to attract them. Radio 2, on the other hand, unashamedly goes for the opposite end of the age profile with older presenters, an increased amount of speech and a very different style of music. Its listeners are mainly drawn from socio-economic groups C2, D, and E, while Radio 3 and Radio 4 tend to attract ABC1s.

Terry Wogan, presenting his Radio 2 breakfast programme, makes a feature of the age of his audience. He runs a sort of 'club' for TOGs (Terry's Old Geezers or Girls) with a secret sign. They can leave messages for each other on the blackboard that can be seen over his shoulder (think about it!).

Radio 3 broadcasts mainly classical music in a very traditional way and consequently attracts an upmarket older audience. It also broadcasts some drama and talks. Radio 4 depends almost entirely on speech. A lot of this is news and current affairs, but there is also entertainment in the form of quizzes, drama, a soap opera (*The Archers*), and even alternative comedy.

Until 1995, Radio 5 Live broadcast educational programmes, and youth and children's programmes mixed with news and sport. Not unsurprisingly this led to problems both in terms of building an audience and keeping it loyal. For example, a football match going to extra time could lead to an educational programme being delayed or cancelled, while equally tennis fans tuning in early for Wimbledon would be expected to listen to the adventures of Wiggly Worm!

The decision was made to abandon children's broadcasting, move educational programmes to the middle of the night on Radio 3, and concentrate on news and sport. The resulting station is now regarded as being 'laddish' with an audience that is predominantly young and male.

BBC radio listeners

While this move to reposition a network was successful, the usual reaction when somebody in BBC management decides that the target audience for a network should be changed is one of outrage and/or a drop in the number of listeners. Recent examples of this have included the sacking of many of Radio 1's older DJs in an attempt to appeal to a younger audience. The effect was to alienate the older part of the audience who had grown up with Radio 1, and yet not attract younger listeners. The result was a large drop in audience figures (about 5 million). To turn this round the controller, Matthew Bannister, spent something like £2 million on an advertising campaign and a large amount to persuade Chris Evans to present the *Breakfast Show*.

Radio 4 listeners are notoriously conservative in their listening habits and any proposed small change causes an outcry. Many Radio 4 programmes have been running unchanged for 20 or 30 years so change happens slowly! An attempt to appeal to a more downmarket audience with a sequence programme called *Anderson's Country* was a complete flop, although it is interesting that its successor *The Afternoon Shift* is still fairly similar.

The BBC also provides two national services in Wales — the English language BBC Radio Wales and the Welsh language Radio Cymru. BBC Radio Northern Ireland is the corporation's national service in the Province.

The 1990 Broadcasting Act and radio ownership

The 1990 Broadcasting Act gave the Radio Authority the power to award three licences for national stations. Classic FM was the first and, as it name implies, it broadcasts light classical music, largely in competition with Radio 3. However, its less formal presentation and less heavy choice of music have widened the audience to which it appeals.

This was followed in 1993 by Virgin 1215 which broadcasts "enduring mainstream music for 20–45 year old adults". Despite only broadcasting on AM, the station was very successful at appealing to its target audience, and in April 1995 increased its reach via its sister station on 105.8 FM.

The final station, Talk Radio UK, was launched on an unsuspecting public in February 1995, and clearly the public was not ready for it! Talk Radio had a disastrous start. Its speech-based programming was designed to be downmarket and 'tabloid' in style and content. A diet of phone-ins and 'shock-jocks' has not produced the audience figures that were required and a whole series of changes have been made. The only things that the jocks produced in any number were complaints about their language and the way they handled sensitive issues. Indeed, one of the most outrageous lasted less than a month!

BBC local radio network

In England, the BBC claims that its local radio network now covers the whole country. However, in many cases this coverage has been achieved by adding further areas to existing stations and in some cases allowing them to opt-out for part of the day. For instance, Dorset FM opts out of Radio Devon and Somerset Sound from Radio Bristol.

Most of the BBC's established stations cover at least a county while recently some stations have been combined to cover several. Southern Counties Radio, for example, covers Surrey, Berkshire and Sussex. We could argue that this is no longer local radio in the sense that was intended when the stations were set up.

One of the first BBC stations was called Radio Brighton and it served the town and a small area around it. The station was renamed Radio Sussex and with the addition of a small studio in Eastbourne was expected to cover the whole county. Now it has been amalgamated into Southern Counties Radio with a main production base in Guildford.

TASK

How local might the people of Brighton feel this to be? What is the history of your BBC local radio station? Has something similar happened? Carry out a survey to find out how well local people feel served by the local radio station.

Fig 8.7(a)   Source: Virgin
Radio

	1 Week	4 Week
All Adults	892 000	1 426 000
Adults 20–44	683 000	1 074 000
Men 20–44	420 000	652 000
ABC 1 Adults	571 000	928 000

(source: RAJAR Qtr 41995/Virgin Radio)

Fig 8.7(b)   Virgin Radio's
audience level

Regional stations

As well as the three national stations mentioned, the 1990 Broad-casting Act allowed the Radio Authority to set up a number of regional stations as well as expanding the number of local stations.

These regional stations had to 'broaden the range of audience choice' and so none of them play straight pop. As a result their audience figures are not as large as they might otherwise be.

Century Radio broadcasts to the North East of England with a mixture of speech, easy listening and country music; Galaxy Radio covers the area around the Severn Estuary with classic and contemporary dance music; Heart FM transmits to the West Midlands with soft adult contemporary music; JFM 100.4 offers the North West of England jazz, blues, R&B and soul; and Scot FM gives Central Scotland speech and adult contemporary music.

Independent local radio stations are much more varied in the size of area that they cover. They range from stations that cover a single town (Boss FM covers Cheltenham; Wave covers Blackpool) through stations aimed at a particular audience (Viva is aimed at women in London; Sunrise FM serves the Asian community in Bradford; while London Turkish Radio serves the Turkish community) to stations that serve large areas (South Coast Radio covers most of Sussex and Hampshire). In London, some stations broadcast a particular style of music to make them distinctive (Kiss 100FM broadcasts dance music while Melody plays gentle tuneful music with very little chat from DJs).

Other restrictions on radio licences

There are other restrictions on who may hold a radio licence. UK local authorities (county or district councils), political bodies, and advertising agents cannot hold more than 5% of the shares of a company. If the areas overlap, a local newspaper may only own 20% of a radio station.

The BBC World Service

To add to the range of provision, the BBC has an international service called the World Service, which is transmitted in a range of languages appropriate to its audience. The English language service can be received in the UK as well as across the world. This service is the only one for which the BBC receives government money (from the Foreign Office).

Atlantic 252 — no UK regulation

Finally there is one station that is almost national (it covers the area to the north and west of a line running from Dorset to the Wash). It is extremely popular and broadcasts without a UK government licence or regulation from the Radio Authority. It is called Atlantic

252 and it beams a very powerful signal to the UK from the Irish Republic.

Public service broadcasting

BBC radio is run as a public service. It is funded from the TV licence fee. There is no separate radio licence anymore so if you do not have a television you get radio for nothing. However, radio has a very small slice of the cake compared to television — typically a local radio station's programme budget for a whole year would make about 40 minutes of modern TV drama.

Each radio network and local radio station is allocated a budget which is fixed for the year. It will receive this money regardless of how many listeners it has at, say, 6.30 on a Friday evening. BBC local radio can broadcast specialist programmes for a minority section of the community without worrying too much about how many people are listening. In fact in the off-peak evening hours, audiences can actually be increased by broadcasting specialist music programmes like jazz or country.

BBC networks often change tack completely between one programme and the next and do not worry too much when an audience tunes away or switches off for a while.

Commercial stations

In direct contrast to this, an independent station tries to build an audience and hold on to it for as long as possible. So whatever time of day or whatever day of the week you tune to the station, you should recognise its format and style.

This is important because the independent station's advertising rates depend on how many listeners it has at any given moment. The advertising rates and the number of adverts sold affects the station's income and this in turn affects profits. This is what independent radio is all about — making profits for shareholders.

Community Radio

There are a few community radio stations about run by groups of enthusiasts and staffed largely by volunteers. They serve a small area and, some would say, get nearest to the true ideals and original concepts of local radio.

The number of radio licences that a company can hold has increased as a result of legislation in 1995 from 20 to 35, while, in 1996, television companies can own radio stations provided there is no significant overlap in their coverage areas.

Although a licence may be issued to one group or company, if that company is then put on the stock market, then others can take it over, often against its wishes. As advertising revenue increased in 1994–95, so there were more take-overs, the biggest being Emap taking over Metro Radio and owning a majority share of Transworld Communications, and GWR paying over £20 million for the Chiltern Group. This means that at the start of 1996 there were only five major owners of independent local radio stations. These are Capital Radio, Emap Radio, GWR Group, Scottish Radio Holdings, Sunrise Radio Group.

Study the GWR Group. The take-over of the Chiltern Group gave GWR a problem. As Galaxy covered much of its existing area, it was not allowed to keep it and so had to sell it within a fixed period.

However, despite this we can see that from fairly small beginnings broadcasting to Wiltshire, GWR has grown to a large group with interests across much of England.

A major advantage of owning a large number of radio stations is that, as well as economies in administration by, for example, concentrating accounting services at one point, there can be economies in programming.

Many radio groups provide a sustaining service that is broadcast by all their stations in off-peak hours. Sometimes this is also sold to stations outside the group as well. An example of this was the Chiltern Group's Supergold service that could be heard on many stations across the country.

Modern technology means that a single DJ in a central studio can present a programme which still sounds local as, by pressing a single button, a local jingle or advertising package is played on each transmitter.

For a period during the 1980s, while the recession was at its worst and radio advertising revenue was extremely low, nearly all the programmes on Severn Sound in Gloucester were presented from a studio in Milton Keynes — only the adverts and a very few bulletin-board items were locally relevant and these were all played from computer-controlled 'cart machines' fired by a single button. The amount of local programming only increased again when the licences were nearly due for renewal or, perhaps, it was when the recession eased and advertising revenues increased.

TASK

As you can see you should be able to hear at least ten radio stations wherever you live in the country. Suppose you wanted to start a new radio station to serve your community. The Radio Authority says that you have to provide a service that broadens the range of audience choice. What kind of programming would you provide? What would your music policy be? Remember that there are people in your community who are of a different age to you.

- Research your current local radio stations and analyse their content and audience.

- Identify what is missing — you could use audience research skills from Unit 6 — and justify your choice of programming.

GWR GROUP
Based in Swindon

Beacon Wolverhampton	**Mid Anglia Radio**	**Chiltern Radio Network**
Brunel Classic Gold Bristol/Wiltshire		**Chiltern** Bedford/Luton
CN FM	**Hereward** Peterborough	**Chiltern Supergold** Bedford/Luton
Gem-AM Nottingham/Derby	**KL FM** Kings Lynn	**Galaxy** Severn Estuary
GWR FM/Classic Gold Bristol/Bath/Wiltshire		**Horizon** Milton Keynes
Isle of Wight		**Northants** Northamptonshire
Leicester Sound		**Northants Supergold** Northamptonshire
Mercia FM/Classic Gold Coventry/Warwickshire		**Servernsound /Supergold** Gloucester/Cheltenham
Ram FM Derby		
1332 Trent FM Nottingham		
2CR FM/Classic Gold Bournemouth		
210FM/Classic Gold Reading/Berkshire		
WABC Wolverhampton		

Fig 8.8   Source: The GWR Group

Where does the revenue come from?

The BBC

The BBC is funded largely through the licence fee that is fixed by the government. It does have a commercial arm which sells magazines, videos, cassettes, and books and also co-owns satellite rights. With a fixed income you would assume that the BBC would not be worried about viewing and listening figures. However, the view is that if its share of the audience fell sufficiently, then it would be impossible to justify the licence fee. Hence a future government might revise the way in which the BBC is funded. In the light of future expansion in the number of available channels, this could happen anyway.

£million	1984	1985	1986	1987	1988	1989	1990	1991	1992	1993	1994
Receipts (1)											
Film companies (2)	226	260	210	264	230	263	334	346	400	345	426
Television companies (3)	91	110	101	117	128	194	128	133	131	278	370
Total	**317**	**370**	**311**	**382**	**358**	**457**	**461**	**479**	**531**	**623**	**796**
Payments (4)											
Film companies	114	123	106	157	188	204	266	239	228	257	397
Television companies	90	86	99	130	121	186	207	233	254	251	296
Total	**204**	**209**	**205**	**287**	**309**	**390**	**473**	**472**	**482**	**508**	**693**
Receipts less payments											
Film companies	112	137	104	107	42	59	68	107	172	88	29
Television companies	1	24	2	-13	7	8	-79	-100	-123	27	74
Total net receipts	**113**	**161**	**106**	**94**	**49**	**67**	**-11**	**7**	**49**	**115**	**103**

1. Sums receivable from overseas residents
2. Includes transactions by film companies in respect of rights restricted to television
3. Includes transactions in respect of BBC sound broadcasting and independent Television News
4. Sums payable to overseas residents
Source: *BFI Film and Television Handbook, 1996.*

Fig 8.9 Overseas Transactions: Film and Television Material 1984–94

The press

Newspapers and magazines rely on advertising for a major part of their income. The cover price helps, but is not the most important, indeed many local newspapers are given away free and rely on advertising for their sole income.

TASK

Compare the content and quality of two of your local newspapers, one of which is paid for and one which is free. What conclusions can you draw about staffing and expenditure? Would people buy the free newspaper? Carry out a survey to find out if they would, how much they would pay and, if they would not buy it, what needs to be added/improved before they would.

Circulation figures

See the price wars case study on p. 423.

Circulation figures are clearly important to newspapers and magazines and the price wars during 1995–96, have been an attempt to increase the number of readers. *The Times* increased its sales as a result of this from 350,000 to about 670,000.

DID YOU KNOW

For some while, every guest staying in a Forte hotel received a free copy of the *Telegraph*. After Forte was taken over by Granada, guests suddenly started getting *The Times* delivered to their bedroom door. This is worth 20,000 copies on the circulation figure. Why the sudden change? Gerry Robinson, the Granada Chairman, is also Chairman of BSkyB. And who owns 40% of BSkyB?

Broadcasting ratings

Commercial radio and television also need to ensure that their figures are as high as possible in order to satisfy the requirements of advertisers. The advantage to the broadcasters is, of course, that the larger the audience, the more an advert costs.

Is it likely, then that you would see a specialist programme on Channel 3 between 8.00 and 10.00 in the evening? There was even a move at one point to move the main evening news later because it was in the way of programmes designed to attract peak viewing.

Sponsorship (Fig. 8.10)

ITV programmes can now be sponsored. This differs from advertising in that the sponsor has a credit at the beginning and end of the programme, and also at the start and finish of each advert break. Sponsors try to choose a programme that suits their business and will enable them to reach their target market.

For example, Heineken sponsors rugby coverage, the *Daily Mirror* has *Take Your Pick*, Beamish Stout sponsored *Inspector Morse* (despite the fact that he drinks real ale!). However, there can be problems if it is thought that a sponsor could be or is influencing programme content.

The Private Patients Plan (PPP) had to stop sponsoring *Peak Practice*, a series about a NHS doctors surgery because the risk of undue influence was felt to be too great.

TASK

See how many other sponsors you can list from other ITV programmes. What other sponsorship deals would be inappropriate for TV programmes?

The film industry

Even to refer to a British Film Industry is often greeted with the response '*what* British film industry?' Certainly since the advent of television, particularly since the mid-1950s, cinema admissions went down and the financing of film production in this country

For information on cinema
audiences see p. 375.

Vertical integration: when one
company owns more than one
stage in the process of
production, i.e., in the film
industry, studios, distribution
companies and cinemas.

Rufas Olins, *The Sunday Times,*
21 July 1996.

became an increasingly risky business. By the time the Thatcher government took office in 1979, various government funding mechanisms, including a number of tax concessions and the Eady Levy, which had channelled a proportion of box office revenue back to UK production, had been removed.

Whereas Hollywood has enjoyed the security of '**vertical integration**' for most of its output, the UK has had little institutional support — there have been no major production companies to speak of since the mid-1980s.

Major production companies, such as those in Hollywood, can spread their losses over a large number of films, so that the hits in effect pay for the flops. In the UK, there are no large production companies, so the whole industry is much more risky. The few 'medium-sized companies' that exist are, largely, subsidiaries of a larger group, like Working Title Films which made *Four Weddings and a Funeral* (Mike **Newell**, UK, 1994), which is owned by Polygram.

Small production companies are more common, which often consist of one or two enterprising producers striving hard to put together often just one film project at a time. Many small companies go out of business because UK films are rarely profitable on the scale of Hollywood, not so much because of their lack of talent or creativity, but because production is not on a scale that can mop up the flops.

However, 'among British film-makers and, increasingly in government and the City, there is a belief that Britain now has the wherewithal to offer America some competition.' From 24 films produced in the UK in 1981, the number rose in 1995 to 78. The UK continues to attract big US movies into production here, with *Mission Impossible* (USA, 1996) being shot at Pinewood.

Film financing in the UK

Patching together the money to make a film can be a complex and tiresome business. Sometimes feature films will have several dozen different financiers, each with different conditions and varying degrees of control over the final product. All financiers will be fighting to be first in line for profits. The most important funding sources for features are listed below.

Government sources

It is probably worth nothing that, unlike many other countries, rather than a department of culture, the UK government chooses to have a Department of National Heritage! Although the government managed to withdraw many of the favourable tax incentives for private investment in the film industry in the 1980s, it is gradually coming to recognise the economic importance of the film industry (although not particularly with hard cash). The Department of National Heritage provides funds for the National Film and Television School, the British Film Institute, British Screen Finance, the British Film Commission and the European Co-production Fund.

	1990	1991	1992	1993
National weather	Powergen	Powergen	Powergen	Powergen
World Cup	National Power			Panasonic
Local weather		Legal & General	L & G	L & G
Rumpole of the Bailey		Croft Port	Croft Port	
Inspector Morse		Beamish	Beamish	
Wish You Were Here		Barclaycard	Barclaycard	Barclaycard
Rugby World Cup		Sony		
Network Chart Show			Pope	Twix
Maigret			Kronenbourg	
European Championship				
Prime Suspect		Sega	Peugeot	Peugeot
Darling Buds of May			Tetley	Tetley
Poirot				AEG
Syrprise Surprise				BT
Premiere films				Diet Coke
Film season				Lynx
Taggart				Strathmore
Coltrane in a Cadillac				Coors
Fantastic Facts				Thomas Cook
Beats Per Minute				Max Dry Cider
British Lions Tour				Scottish Provident
Rugby World Cup 7's				Worthington Best Bitter
Travel UK				National Express
Pot of Gold				Daily Star
It's a Vet's Life				Pedigree
Annual totals	2	6	10	20

Figure 8.10 Sponsored TV programmes

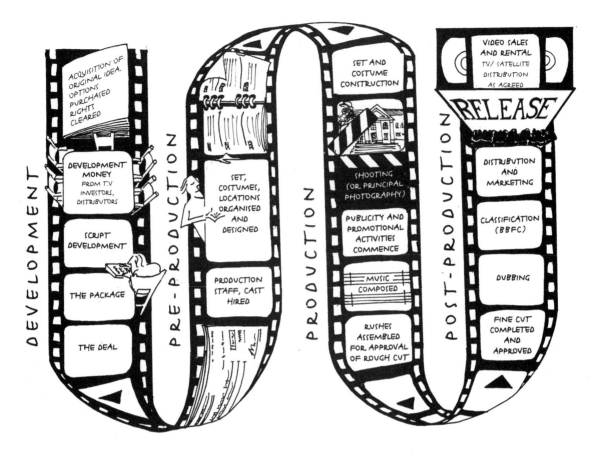

Fig 8.11 The Production Process

Television

While television can be seen to be one of the major sources of finance for UK film, its role is small compared to that of several European counterparts. Channel 4 contributed to over half of all UK films made in the 1980s, spending around 10% of its annual budget supporting new British Films. Usually, Channel 4 contributes to small and medium budget films, investing around £100,000 — £300,000 in return for favourable television rights. Sometimes the company underwrites the whole film and takes care of sales and marketing. Other companies like the BBC and Granada also back film production.

Feature films are increasingly important to television broadcasters, as was underlined in July 1996 with ITV's commitment to invest £100 million over the next five hears, joining the efforts of Channel 4 and the BBC.

Pre-sales

Theatrical pre-sales are the rights to films to show in cinemas, usually sold to distribution companies in different countries or 'territories'. Pre-sales are rarely in hard cash, but more often agreements with which a producer can take to a bank to back a loan. Usually banks will also need a completion guarantee, which means finding yet another backer who will supply 'completion bonds' and suck up yet another proportion of the potential income from the film. The banks will also require a fee for their services.

Satellite

There is little investment in film production from satellite companies, which tend to make deals with Hollywood concerning acquisition of product. BSkyB does invest with British Screen Finance in a limited number of UK productions in return for broadcast rights.

Foreign investment

After a fall-off of investment from the United States following various box-office disasters in the mid-1980s, it is beginning to look to UK shores again, particularly after successes like *Four Weddings and a Funeral.*

Europe

The European Co-production Fund, established in 1991, receives government funding of £2 million per year, to promote co-productions between UK and European producers.

Eurimages was established in 1988 as a Council of Europe initiative to support co-production between European partners of up to 20% of the total cost. Eurimages has contributed to several notable films, like Ken Loach's *Land and Freedom.*

The national lottery

The National Lottery is probably the most important new funding source for film production in the UK, accessible by producers with at least 50% of the money in place, and a guaranteed UK theatrical release (i.e., cinema screening). The Arts Council, which distributes lottery funding, estimates about £160 million available over the next few years for film production. While originally conceived as a support for features, a number of shorts have recently been successful in accessing lottery funding, potentially providing real opportunities for the development of new talent in the UK industry.

At the time of writing, approximately £18.6 million has gone into 35 films from the National Lottery.

Independent film and video funding

Independent film and video can be defined as those films and videos which do not have financial backing from the major commercial companies that dominate the market and are made outside the mainstream cinema and television industries. It includes a wide range of practices, from experimental and avant-garde work, to films which address issues of under-representation, to low-budget films by new, up-coming film-makers: — in short, the films are set apart from the priorities which drive the commercial and state-funded mainstream. The conditions under which they are produced, distributed and exhibited, however, make them 'dependent' on private and state patronage, on systematic

INDEPENDENT FILM MAKERS WIN NATIONAL LOTTERY

Projects by independent film makers Paul Bush, Emma Calder, Beryl Richards and John Hardwick are the first London Production Fund financed productions to receive financial support from the National Lottery through the Arts Council of England.

Paul Bush's THE ALBATROSS is an eleven minute animated film based on Coleridge's 'The Rime of the Ancient Mariner'. Taking inspiration from Gustave Dore's nineteenth century woodcuts, Paul Bush engraves directly into the film's emulsion to evoke the myths and metaphors of the sea. THE ALBATROSS received £23,000 towards a total budget of £78,000.

Emma Calder has developed a new watercolour technique for her six minute animated film, THE QUEEN'S MONASTERY. Inspired by Janacek's Sinfonietta, it explores themes of love, war and identity as a former acrobat is conscripted into the army and forced to leave his lover. THE QUEEN'S MONASTERY received £30,000 towards a budget of £68,969.

THE ALBATROSS and THE QUEEN'S MONASTERY are both co-funded by the Animation Unit at BBC Bristol.

Written and directed by Beryl Richards, produced by Natasha Dack, SEASON'S GREETINGS explores a village community thrown into frenzied activity as Christmas nears. A comedy portrait of trivia and village life. SEASON'S GREETINGS received £19,566 out of a budget of £39,132.

GLOTTIS follows 2 men in a supermarket at night. One has hiccoughs; the other tries to cure him. Over the 10 minute encounter, the men's relationship is exposed. Written/directed by John Hardwick, produced by Jane Harrison, GLOTTIS received £18,000 towards a budget of £36,000.

Fig 8.12 National Lottery Funding. Source: London Film and Video News — LFVDA Quarterly Newsletter

funding by organisations like the Regional Arts Boards, the Arts Councils, the British Film Institute and the newly emerging Media Development Agencies. Ironically, the increasing tendency is also to tie such funding to television slots, since broadcasters are often involved in regional production schemes.

The arts funding system is not insubstantial, with Department of National Heritage money channelled through the BFI, the Film Councils of Scotland, Wales and Northern Ireland, and the Arts Councils of England, Wales, Scotland and Northern Ireland to ten English Regional Arts Boards (RABs) which work with the national bodies to support and develop cultural activity in their regions.

To give a sense of scale, the Arts Council of England (ACE) has a turnover of around £200 million, of which about £45 million is passed on to the RABs. Somewhere between £1 million and £2 million of this ACE money is directed at the film and video activity of RABs outside London. In addition, about £2 million comes directly into artists' film and video activity.

Parallel to this RAB system is a small but growing network of Media Development Agencies such as the South West Media Development Agency is Bristol and the Moving Image Development Agency (MIDA) in Liverpool who secured European funding to establish the Merseyside Film Production Fund which offers 'top-up' finance to producers intending to shoot feature films in the Merseyside area. The London Film and Video Development Agency

CENTRAL GOVERNMENT

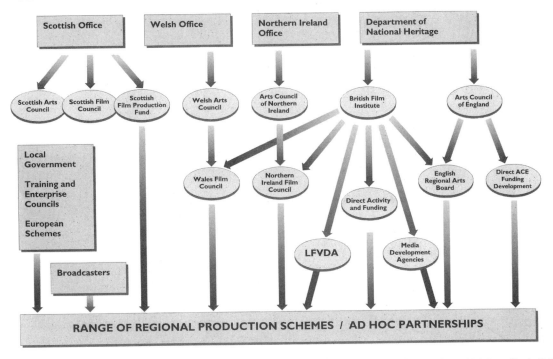

Fig 8.13 The structure of UK funding for independent film and video production. (Source: Steve McIntyre, *The Institutional and Funding Context of Artists' Film and Video, 11 O'Clock High Education Pack, ed. LFVDA T. Jenkins 1995) London Production Fund*

(LFVDA), with financial contributions from Carlton Television and Channel 4, runs the London Production Fund which supports innovative film and video production in London.

Film distribution

If in the financing of a film the rights have not been pre-sold, the producer will seek a distribution deal, which is essential if production costs are to be recouped and profit is to be made. Distribution companies deal with publicity and marketing of films, booking them with exhibitors (cinemas) and arranging for prints of the film to be struck. They also collect money from cinemas and pay it to the producers.

It is possible that a distributor will buy worldwide rights to a film, but for UK films, it is more usual that the distribution rights are sold to different distributors in each territory (see pre-sales) via the major markets such as the Cannes Film Festival, which is held in May every year.

Film exhibition

Cinema admissions hit an all-time low in the mid-1980s, but recently there has been a revival in cinema-going, with figures for

1994 topping 124 million — the highest for over 40 years. This is partly due to the development of multiplexes, offering several screens in one venue. (There are currently 1,800 screens operating in the UK.) However, because most multiplexes and the major distributors are owned by US studios, the opportunities for UK films to be screened are not necessarily improved, because of a 'blocking' system which effectively tempers competition.

CASE STUDY

Winchester Screen

Cinema attendance in the UK is now rising. Mainline Pictures has been a pathfinder in that revival. In 1970 it set a new direction for exhibitors with the successful launch of the Screen on the Green in Islington. Mainline practises adroit positioning in the market. Taking advantage of the gap between mainstream and art cinema, it showed the best popular films as well as accessible independent productions. Cinemas closed elsewhere, while Mainline achieved immediate profits. People responded to a policy that was radical not only in programming, but also in theatre design and marketing.

This approach has brought steady growth: Mainline now runs six Screen cinemas and a film distribution company. Its strategy is to deliver what the market needs, and to go for excellence in every area. The six Screens in and out of London are individually programmed for their local audience but all share the same standards of quality, including Dolby sound, luxurious seating, and widely admired interior design.

Mainline's most recent venture is Winchester Screen, which opened in February 1996'. It is part funded by the national lottery through the Arts Council of England.

Fig 8.14 Still from *I was Catherine the Great's Stable Boy* (Stephen Leshe', UK, 1995). It was co-funded by the London Production Fund and distributed with *Spanking the Monkey* (David O'Russell, USA, 1995)

The National Lottery has recently contributed to a number of independent cinema developments which mix programming of major US films and lower budget UK or art-house movies.

Distribution and exhibition of cultural independent film and video

Specialised distribution and exhibition of fine artists' film and video is undertaken by the London Film Makers' Co-op and London Electronic Arts (LEA), with the co-op housing over 1,600 films, ranging from landmarks of post-war North American and European avant-garde film-making through to an international range of work by contemporary film-makers. LEA is central in the distribution and exhibition of creative video and electronic media art, whilst Cinenova, formed in 1991 from a merger of London-based distributors Circles and Cinema of Women, distributes and promotes independent films and videos directed by women, with over 400 titles ranging from drama and documentary to animation and experimental work from women worldwide.

Most independent films, which do not conform to industry practices in terms of length or format (i.e., they are usually not available as 35 mm prints), cannot access screening in commercial cinemas. They are also usually uncertificated which is a requirement for commercial theatrical exhibition. Having said this, screening of theatrical shorts alongside commercial features has seen a recent revival.

(See British Board of Film Classification, p. 509.)

8.2 INVESTIGATE REGULATION OF MEDIA INDUSTRIES

The Independent Television Commission (ITC)

As has been mentioned earlier, the 1990 Broadcasting Act created the Independent Television Commission to replace the Independent Broadcasting Authority (IBA) which controlled both radio and television. The IBA was responsible for both regulation and the actual broadcasting of programmes. The ITC only licenses and regulates.

The regulatory function is carried out by issuing codes of practice for technical, content, advertising and sponsorship issues, and then monitoring programmes to ensure that they are complied with. The ITC is responsible to its Board of Members.

The BBC Charter

The BBC is 'regulated' by the terms of its Charter. One of the requirements — in fact the only thing that the BBC is *required* to broadcast — is a report of proceedings in Parliament each day. The BBC's management is ultimately responsible to the Board of Governors. They, like the ITC Board of Members, are appointed by the government. Do you still think that broadcasters are completely free of government control?

The Radio Authority (RA)

The radio functions of the IBA were given by the Broadcasting Act to the newly formed Radio Authority. This has three main tasks. Firstly, it researches frequencies and allocates them to new stations. This is a very complex task particularly in areas that are close to other countries. For example, WKR which broadcasts on two frequencies in Kent had to wait for its second one until after its launch date because the frequency negotiations with the French authorities were not complete.

The frequency and power of the transmitter are set by the Radio Authority for applicants for licences. They then have to find an appropriate transmitter site that has to be approved by the Authority. Changing any of these factors could result in interference with neighbouring stations.

The second task that the Radio Authority undertakes is awarding licences. Any group wishing to win a licence that has been advertised completes a very long form covering staffing, audience and local support, technical matters, and finance. Then they submit a number of copies to the Authority.

The application is judged on a number of factors including whether an applicant has carried out research in the local area to show that there will be a demand for their service. In general the applicant has to show that it will be extending choice for the listeners in the area and not simply providing another pop station.

However, the most important part of the allocation as far as the Radio Authority is concerned, is that the applicant should have a viable business plan and can afford the heavy start-up costs associated with a radio station. Radio stations are expensive to start and a licence is only awarded for eight years, so the company has to make its money back and make a profit in that time.

The Radio Authority's concern stems from the fact that it has awarded licences in the last few years to companies that have either never started to broadcast or that have very quickly closed.

It is, of course, possible to have your licence renewed at the end of the eight years and this is another task for the Radio Authority.

The Authority also deals with the awarding of national licences (Classic FM, Virgin 1215, Talk Radio UK) where there are two major differences. Firstly the Broadcasting Act specified what type of programming each of the national stations should have.

INR = Independent National Radio.

INR1 should concentrate wholly or mainly on the broadcasting of music which is not pop music.

INR2 should not duplicate INR1. INR3 has to be speech-based.

The other difference is that the prospective licence holders had to bid an amount of money that they were prepared to pay annually for the licence in the same way that television licences are allocated.

The fourth function of the Radio Authority is the regulation of stations through obligatory codes that cover programmes, advertising, sponsorship, and engineering. The programmes that a local station broadcast are covered by the promise of performance that was agreed between the licence holder and the Authority when the licence was awarded. The station is not allowed to change this without the Radio Authority's permission.

If you would like to know more about this, you can write to the Radio Authority at Holbrook House, 14 Great Queen Street, Holborn, London, WC2 5DG. It will send you on request a copy of its codes of practice and also the promise of performance for your independent local/regional stations.

Pirate broadcasting

There is one very important difference between print and broadcast media. Anyone can set up a newspaper or magazine to cover a particular geographical area or subject interest but you have to have a licence to broadcast legally. Pirate radio stations do exist but run the risk of very heavy fines and the confiscation of their equipment if they are caught.

Licences for cable operators

Cable companies also have to be licensed by the ITC which also regulates them but more loosely than terrestrial broadcasters. For example, there is no requirement for cable to broadcast anything remotely educational. The licences, like those for terrestrial television, were issued to the highest bidder who also had to be a 'fit and proper' person. The company needs two licences — one for the system and one for the programmes that it broadcasts.

The law

Defamation

The law on defamation is quite complex but everyone who works in the media needs at least a working knowledge of it. It is very easy for a guest on a live programme or phone-in to defame someone and the broadcast organisation can be held liable for publishing it.

Defamation divides into slander and libel and it is the latter that most concerns the media. Slander is spoken defamation, while libel is defamation that is written or permanently published. However, anything said on either live radio or television is classed as libel.

A journalist could slander an individual if he or she alleges someone has done something wrong to a third party or to the person directly. However, the most likely problem that a journalist faces is libel.

There is one sure-fire way to avoid being sued for libel — make sure that your story is true. This is the best possible defence and implies the need for proper research when you are writing your story. Should you be sued, you have to be able to prove that your story was true. If you are merely repeating someone else's rumour believing it to be true, then you have no defence.

The second main defence to libel is fair comment. For this to succeed you must be able to show that it was a comment on a matter of public interest. Your comment must be fair, based on true facts and not made with malice.

This is a very simplified view of defamation; if you need to know more, you could consult *Law and the Media* by Tom Crone (1995) published by Focal Press.

The final main defence is privilege. Put simply, this means that if you report accurately a statement that was made in privileged circumstances such as parliamentary or judicial proceedings, then you cannot be guilty of libel no matter how defamatory the original statement was.

The Official Secrets Act

The Official Secrets Act became law very hurriedly in 1911 and existed in that form until 1989. Prior to the new Act becoming law, there had been increasing problems with the original Act.

Section 2 of the 1911 Act meant that anybody who worked for a government department could not talk to anybody about any aspect of their work, however trivial. An extreme example was that a postman could not tell a member of the public where a dangerous dog lived if he was bitten as he did his rounds.

The new Act restricts the type of information to six categories and states that the person disclosing the information should know that it will harm the public interest.

There are three classes of person who could be prosecuted under the Act: people working in the security services, government employees who work with sensitive information, and people who publish information given to them by the previous two categories.

You may have heard about D-notices. These are letters issued by the government to let editors know that the publication of certain information would be against the national interest. A D-notice does not have the force of law and relies on the co-operation of newspapers and broadcasting organisations.

Copyright

Hughie **G**reen claimed that a TV station in New Zealand had infringed his copyright by broadcasting *Opportunity Knocks*. He lost because the courts held that, as the programme was not scripted, it was only the idea that had been copied.

Copyright exists to protect the interests of the creator of a piece of work. It is immaterial whether the work is a computer program, a song, a book, TV programme or a play. The Copyright, Designs and Patents Act 1988 is the relevant legislation.

You can copyright a piece of work that is original and that is created in a permanent form (a script, written music, a recording). You cannot copyright an idea.

The person whose skill and effort creates the work owns the copyright, and others may not copy the work. However, a journalist will probably find that a newspaper will claim the copyright for work that is done as a staff member.

The precise form of the work is as important as the content. Two newspapers could report the same story using the same facts and produce very similar stories. Provided one has not copied from the other, there is no breach of copyright.

In general, it is important to obtain permission to use copyright material. This will involve paying a fee to the author of the work. An exception is the use of music that can be used by the radio and television stations and a fee is paid afterwards.

In its simplest form, copyright protection in literary, dramatic, musical and artistic works applies for the life of the originator plus 70 years (not 50, as formerly). After the death of the originator, any money due goes to the heirs. As soon as this time has expired, the work is freely available for anybody to publish.

Industry codes of practice

The ethical framework of most of the media industries is linked to codes of practice, which are, in effect, self-regulation and professional standards designed to prevent irresponsible behaviour or unacceptable standards of production practice.

The Press Complaints Commission (PPC)

The Press Complaints Commission is responsible for the regulation of newspapers and magazines. It is paid for by the industry itself although there is a majority of independent members on the Commission to try to ensure impartiality.

The PCC was set up after the Calcutt Committee reported on privacy and related matters in 1990. The press was given one last chance to show that it could regulate itself and so the PCC was funded and set up its Code of Practice.

The PCC will normally only deal with complaints from someone who is involved in the story that is being complained about, and will judge the complaint against its Code of Practice. This covers issues like privacy, accuracy, harassment, discrimination, interviewing children, and payments for articles to those involved in crime.

The PCC does not deal with newspaper and magazine advertising. The Advertising Standards Authority monitors this but, in turn, does not deal with radio and television advertising.

The Advertising Standards Authority (ASA)

Like the PCC, the ASA has a Code of Practice. This states that 'All advertisements should be legal, decent, honest and truthful.' Complaints are evaluated by the Authority and if it feels there is a case to answer, it will send details of the complaint to the advertiser. The advertiser must satisfy the ASA that no breach of the code has taken place.

However, if the advert is found to breach the code, then the ASA can ask the advertiser to amend or withdraw the offending advert. Note that the ASA has no power to order the advertiser to do this. If it refuses to do so, then the media organisations that subscribe to the ASA will be told not to handle the advert.

The ASA publishes case reports of its findings every month and it is interesting to study these in conjunction with the adverts to see what is causing problems and why.

Fig 8.15 The ASA is called in after the Palace complains. *Daily Mail*, 24 July 1996

The Broadcasting Complaints Commission (BCC)

The Broadcasting Complaints Commission deals with complaints about unfair treatment in a programme or if someone's privacy has been infringed. All the Commission can do is order the broadcaster to transmit a summary of the complaint and the Commission's findings and also publish them in the press.

Total number of complaints received by the BSC in reports published in 1994: 2,285

Upheld complaints for Terrestrial Television Programmes

Violence: 27

includes:

Comic scenes of hanging in **M**urder **M**ost Horrid and Ain't **M**isbehavin';

ITN coverage of Cleveland schoolroom murder;

Clip from Farewell **M**y Concubine in Late Again

Violent scenes in:

Casualty

Eastenders

Knot's Landing

Glorification of guns in:

The Word

Men Only: In the Firing Line

Sex: 5

including:

Group sex scenes in The Buddha of Suburbia

Sex games depicted in Neighbours

Taste and Decency: 31

Most of these complaints were for swearing, such as Cutting Edge: **G**raham Taylor — The Impossible **J**ob.

Other complaints in this category included:

Use of holy names or blasphemy in:

Absolutely Fabulous

Newman and Baddiel in Pieces

Don't Forget Your Toothbrush

Use of drugs in Brookside

Treatment of the Bulger case in World in Action and Public Eye

Scenes thought to be frightening for children in The Paul Daniels **M**agic Show and in an advertisement for Tango.

Julian Clary joke at the *British Comedy Awards*

Source: BSC/BFI Film and Television Handbook 1996

Fig 8.16

The Broadcasting Standards Council (BSC)

The Broadcasting Standards Council deals with complaints about the way sex and violence are shown, and also matters of 'taste and decency'. This can include swearing, racial and religious offence, stereotyping, and the encouragement of smoking, the use of alcohol, or drug taking. A complaint must be made in writing within three weeks for a radio programme.

As with the BCC, the Council's only power is to have its findings broadcast and published. This is a more controversial body, however, because there is wide disagreement about what falls outside accepted taste and decency. What offends your parents may not offend you and vice versa.

The BSC's first Chairperson, Lord Rees-Mogg, was quite relaxed about standards and most broadcasters were quite happy. However, when Lady Howe became Chairperson, many more things were found to fall outside accepted standards.

The Programme Complaints Unit

The Programme Complaints Unit has been set up by the BBC but operates independently of it. It will investigate complaints about 'specific and serious injustice or inaccuracy, or a serious breach of accepted broadcasting standards'. If a complaint is upheld, then an on-air apology or correction will be broadcast as appropriate.

The Radio Authority (RA)

The Radio Authority deals with complaints about both programmes and adverts on independent radio. The ITC does the same for television. If the complaint is one that should be dealt with by the Broadcasting Complaints Commission, then the RA and ITC will pass it on. Otherwise they will deal with everything.

The Authority and the Commission have more teeth than the other bodies. They can require an apology or correction, prevent a repeat of a programme, impose a fine, or, for very serious matters, shorten or cancel a station's licence.

The British Board of Film Classification (BBFC)

The British Board of Film Classification differs in that it views films before the public sees them and can order cuts. If the Board decides that a film is suitable for distribution, it classifies the film according to the amount of sex and violence shown.

A local council may decide to alter the classification or ban the showing of a film in its area. This happens only rarely and the BBFC's decisions are accepted in the majority of cases. A film cannot get a theatrical release without BBFC classification.

Media Institutions

As well as the restraints on media production imposed by law and professional codes of practice, the way in which an organisation is structured, its philosophy, its ownership will all impact on the nature of the products being produced. The term of 'media institution' is often interchanged with 'media industry' and although it would be valid to study, for instance, a large company to explore it as an institution means that you would need to undertake some analysis and make some assessments as to how its structures and rules impact on the nature of the productions.

Branston and Stafford (1996),
The Media Students' Book,
Routledge.

CASE STUDY

A summary of Branston and Stafford's work on institutions is given below. **M**ost parts of our lives are in some way governed by institutions — for instance, the social institutions of marriage, the state institutions of education, the health service, the welfare state, etc. These provide enduring structures and rules by which we organise our lives.

Rather than thinking about individual organisations as 'institutions', it is probably more helpful to think about, say, 'public service broadcasting', which will extend beyond the BBC to incorporate some elements of Channel 4's remit. The press might be helpfully broken down into the quality press and the tabloid press.

A media institution must by definition display the following features:

■ *It must have a defined code of conduct and a set of values shared by all the practitioners in the institution (and understood generally by audiences).*
■ *It must include all the possible practitioners within its boundaries (there cannot be two separate institutions with identical features).*
■ *It must be staffed by recognised professionals, whose education and training will effectively exclude casual intruders as new staff.*
■ *It will set technical production standards (by default, if not by design) through the technology it uses.*
■ *It will define is own **formal** characteristics – genres, styles, formats, etc.*
■ *It must be recognised by its staff and its audiences as an institution.*

Regulation and press freedom

So how free do you think the press is in Britain? This section only just scrapes the surface of the main legal and ethical controls. Think about a war-time situation, the government virtually controls what broadcasters can say or show. Generally reporters in a war zone rely on the army or navy for protection and transport — the threat of withdrawal of facilities can be very effective.

DID YOU KNOW

For a long while, broadcasters were forbidden to use the voices of IRA supporters, including **G**erry Adams, the leader of the Irish political party Sinn Fein, to avoid giving them publicity. To get around this, the broadcasters simply used actors to speak the words. What effect do you think this had?

One of the provisions in the BBC's licence allows the government to take it over in the event of an emergency — could you envisage this situation? Would it be healthy? Should the provision be there?

8.3 INVESTIGATE THE DEVELOPMENT OF MEDIA INDUSTRIES

New technologies and professional practices

Many of the technological issues affecting the television, radio and music industries are similar. All are moving to digital broadcasting, using computers to help with editing, and have improved communications from the field using satellite links or phones. These new developments in technology affect the way in which material is gathered, recorded, transmitted and received.

Speed of the production process

Before computers were in use, the production of a newspaper involved a journalist bashing a story out on a typewriter, and then the sub-editor and editor would correct this with pencil marks. It might then be retyped for clarity. The copy would then be sent to a typesetter who would literally put metal letters in a frame (using a keyboard) which would be used to cast a plate.

Now a newspaper journalist will write a story on a computer — often on a laptop while still at an event. A story written in the office will go on to the main computer directly, while the story from outside will be filed via a modem and phone line. The sub-editor corrects the story on screen and sends the story to the appropriate page of the newspaper. When the newspaper is complete, it is likely to be transmitted electronically to a number of print works around the country so that a plate can be made photographically and the newspaper distributed more economically.

Satellite links enable a new generation of new technology to be used. A reporter in the field dictates the story on-the-spot and sends pictures from a video camera. The picture editor back at base will tell the reporter what shots are required and how they should be framed. The editor then uses a frame-grabber to find precisely the right picture. This is then stored on computer for future use.

Distribution of print products

A major cost of your daily newspaper is the paper on which it is printed so newspapers could well in a few years' time come to us in an electronic form. The *Guardian* already offers a CD-ROM version which many libraries have for reference purposes. It is almost feasible now for newspapers to be sent directly to your computer. You can access many newspapers and also magazines like the *Daily Telegraph, Vogue, GQ* and *Tatler* through the Internet already, and there are so called 'Webzines' on the World Wide Web.

These are normally free and are very cheap to set up. However, they often have a short life as the only income comes from persuading advertisers to take space on a page. The main advantage to an advertiser is that they not only know how many people access the page, but also who they are. The name and Internet address of a reader are automatically captured by the host computer.

Digital telephone networks

Some of the changes in radio are due to improvements in the phone network and the facilities that it offers. Most national radio stations now run successful phone-ins thanks to the availability of locally priced calls for listeners in any part of the UK (the 0345 service). A number of BBC networks now have helplines run in conjunction with programmes or special campaigns that use an 0800 (freecall) number. Equally many stations make money by having competitions for listeners on premium lines (0891) where the caller pays a high rate for the call and the provider of the service takes a percentage of the cost of the call. You will have noticed that in many cases the questions are ridiculously easy to encourage maximum participation.

With the improved quality of telephone lines, many more extended interviews are carried out with the interviewer in the studio and the interviewee at home or work. Reporters are able to file reports from the scene via the phone or by using improved quality digital mobile phones.

The increased coverage of the Gulf War and events in Bosnia is due to the advent of satellite telephones. These are still very expensive to buy and use but it does mean that the reporters are completely self-contained and independent. They can send a report back from the middle of the desert, under fire in a war zone or in the heart of the countryside. Even more importantly, they are no longer dependent on access to a telephone network in a hostile country with the possibility of interference or censorship.

ISDN: Integrated Services Digital Network

BT also offers lines called **ISDNs**, which operate in many ways like a phone line but with increased quality and capacity. This has changed the way in which outside broadcasts are made, particularly for local radio. Previously most local outside broadcasts would have used a radio link where this was possible or alternatively a landline would have been booked. A landline is expensive and is basically a line that connects two points and cannot be used for anything else. It is only possible to send one audio signal at a time and you can only send in one direction.

An ISDN is two-way and can handle more than one signal at a time. It can handle high-speed computer data as well as high-quality speech and music. This means that information can be sent to a computer screen for the presenter to use and also the output of the studio or talkback. Each ISDN is connected to the exchange like a telephone line and you can dial up another ISDN. This gives a cost saving as a radio station will only have two or three ISDNs which can then be connected to the AA for road reports, the football ground for live commentary or a remote studio in another part of the area.

ISDN and radio

Two examples of ISDN capability: not unsurprisingly, Radio Wales' sports programme on a Saturday afternoon is presented live from Cardiff Arms Park whenever Wales has a home rugby match. ISDN means that the presenter can have scores from football matches on a screen. He or she can hear information from the studio operators and can run a phone-in quiz. In fact, the programme is as easy to do from an outside location as in the studio.

Radio 4 has a long-running programme called *Any Questions* that tours the country and has a panel of, largely, politicians who answer the audience's questions on news issues. Its chairman, Jonathan Dimbleby, also presents a phone-in follow-up programme called *Any Answers* early on Saturday afternoon. He has an ISDN to his house and presents the programme from home. The producer is in the London studio and can choose phone calls, send information to a screen as to who is next, etc. Naturally Jonathan Dimbleby can hear the calls and also sounds as though he is in the studio.

Many independent stations that are owned by a group receive syndicated material and news bulletins via satellite. This is now the most reliable and cheapest way to link radio stations together.

The end of the 'rusty dial' syndrome

There are also changes in the way that radio is distributed and received that have a number of implications for broadcasters. The relatively simple development of radios for the home similar to those in cars that are pre-programmed means that it is easier to change from one station to another.

Traditionally the average listeners stayed tuned to their favourite stations, a few daring ones listened to a couple but it was so difficult (especially for elderly people) to find stations accurately that most people did not bother. Now it is simple to say, 'I don't like this music, let's see what radio X has got on.' One of the effects of this has been an even closer targeting of music and speech to the needs of the audience.

Radio Data Service (RDS)

The introduction of Radio Data Service (RDS) mainly on car radios means that there is a visual display of the station that is selected.

The radio will also retune to the strongest available signal for a given station as you travel from area to area. Local travel bulletins interrupt whatever you are listening to, including tapes, so that you can avoid the worst traffic jams.

Digital Audio Broadcasting (DAB)

The BBC is introducing Digital Audio Broadcasting (DAB) which currently requires a very expensive receiver. No doubt in time the price will fall as demand increases. Digital Audio Broadcasting has three main advantages: many more stations will fit into a given frequency bandwidth: the quality will be better, with less fading or interference; and it will be possible to send much more information alongside the radio programme.

The way in which radio programmes are produced is also being changed by new technology. Much of this is computer-based and relies on dealing with sound digitally rather than in an analogue format.

CASE STUDY
A day in the life of a digital news operation

A reporter collects material on minidisc or Digital Audio Tape (DAT), brings it back to the station, or sends it via a phone link or ISDN, and then puts it on to the hard disc of a computer. An editing programme on the computer allows the material to be edited, using fades or cuts as appropriate, mix extra effects or music and then save it to the station's main computer. The bulletin editor can then review the piece and include it in the running order for the bulletin. The reporter has also word-processed the necessary cue material that can also be used on screen or paper.

Meanwhile in the main studio (and the news presentation studio), there is very little equipment to be seen. There is only a microphone or two, some headphones, and two touch screens. These enable the presenter to call up material including CDs, adverts and jingles, and play at a touch of the screen. The microphone is turned on and off and its level set from the screen. Adverts and jingles are stored on disc in the central computer while the CDs are locked away and are accessed via CD jukeboxes. This has the added advantage that CDs do not go missing!

As we have seen the music policy of a station is vitally important. Indeed many stations believe it is too important to be left to the whims and tastes of DJs. The computer will programme the music and can be set so that the person in the studio cannot change the musical content at all — the computer's choice is the only thing on offer on the screen. The computer can also recalculate timings if things need to change and can then come up with an alternative piece of music to fit the time available.

In the same way, the news-reader plays inserts directly from the computer by touching a screen. The inserts will be available in a predetermined order so that there are no problems about finding and cueing up the next piece.

There are other advantages for the computerised station in terms of staffing. The computer will automatically log the playing of adverts and will generate accounts.

There are very few listeners to radio in the evening and overnight yet, to prevent listeners retuning, stations want to offer something. The low-cost solution is to get the computer to do the broadcasting. When the last human presenter goes home the computer is switched to automatic and takes over.

Often at weekends, there may only be one person on duty in a small station. What happens if a major news story breaks? The computer is put on automatic, the reporter goes off to cover the story with a minidisc and a tone pad. When it is appropriate the reporter phones the computer and keys in a given code. At the first appropriate moment, the computer plays a news flash jingle and fades up the phone for a live report. At the end of the report, the computer takes over again, adjusting its timings to take account of the next fixed point in its schedule.

A final staffing advantage is in engineering costs. Equipment with motors (tape machines, record decks) takes most maintenance. Computers are comparatively reliable and need virtually no servicing. On the other hand, a computer failure would be a disaster!

Broadcast News-gathering in the regions

Ron Neil, Head of BBC Regional Broadcasting Directorate, quoted in *Quiet Revolutionary*, by Jason Deans, *Broadcast*, 7 June 1996.

The whole of BBC regional broadcasting is looking to change its news-gathering operations, with more journalists deployed on the ground in news-gathering, in a role similar to local newspaper district reporters, with fewer employed in production back in the newsroom. Desk-top technology will enable us to address individual transmitters with customised and localised output. So listeners or viewers living only 10 or 15 miles apart can hear different news on the hour. Electronic news production system (ENPS), will enable a journalist in a remote part of the country to call up the same information, pictures, sound and archive as a someone working in Television Centre in London. The flip side to this for the regional journalists, however, is the accompanying 15% cut in the annual budget over a three-year period.

CDs

The extensive use of CDs in radio demonstrates how developments in the music industry have had wider effects. The way in which we listen to recorded music has changed radically. It is only about 45 years since the only way to listen to recorded music was with a very fragile record that was 10 or 12 inches in diameter and contained about three minutes of sound as it travelled at 78 revolutions per minute.

The introduction of EPs and LPs (extended play and long play) and later singles on vinyl was a major step forward. EPs were 7 inches in diameter and usually contained four tracks, while LPs and singles changed little in their format over the years.

The widespread introduction of the cassette meant for the first time it was possible to listen to music 'on the move'. The disadvantage for record producers was that illegal copying became a major problem.

The CD was a major step forward in terms of quality and ease of use. The digital recording of sound gives greatly increased clarity, less background noise, and the ability to find different tracks very easily. It is also possible to programme the order in which you listen to tracks on a CD, or to repeat the same one over and over again.

The need for better quality caused changes in the way that music is recorded and mastered. Strangely the new technology is often cheaper than the older technology that it is replacing. It then becomes more accessible and encourages smaller producers to produce discs and so gives bands an opportunity that might not otherwise have been available.

To take the computer influence back still further into the process, much of the music that we hear has been composed and played using computers. This means that some bands can never play live — who wants to sit and watch a computer all evening?

On the other hand, live music in pubs and clubs has probably increased as an individual or a duo can, with electronic backing mixed with live instruments, produce an acceptable sound. And that's not including karaoke!

Computers can sample and reproduce instruments. A composer can select instruments, mix tracks, lay down bass lines, harmonise, and play the finished product without ever leaving home. This is how most sound-tracks for television or adverts are made. However, there are many who would argue that live performance, with its subtleties and nuances, cannot be replaced by electronic reproduction. Indeed MTV capitalised on this through its 'unplugged' series of recordings of top artists, using acoustic rather than electric or electronic accompaniment.

Non-linear editing

[See p. 335.]

The ability to translate moving pictures into digital code — a set of numbers that a computer can understand — has already had an effect on production and will soon have an effect on distribution. The cost of hiring non-linear editing services is coming down every week, making programme-making increasingly cheaper. One effect, however, is that there is also no longer any need for an assistant editor which means that much of the craft of editing in recognising what 'works' and what does not will no longer be learnt 'on the job'.

Digital TV Transmission

Soon to come to the UK is the digital transmission of television. Terrestrially, this means that around 20 channels will be on offer. BSkyB has plans for over 500 to be delivered direct from satellite or by fibre-optic cable. But what will be transmitted — more of the same or something different — remains a question. One idea is that a film could be screened on a number of channels, with each starting at five-minute intervals so that you could virtually have video on demand.

David Elstein, former head of programming at BSkyB, (now head of Channel 5) writing in the *Guardian* in May 1996 had more ideas for the future, including designating a dedicated channel for each sport so that you could cut from one to the other when you want or indeed stay with your favourite throughout. Equally every football match in the country could be screened (on a pay-per-view basis) on a different channel.

In fiction, parallel channels could carry different interlinking versions of the same story and the viewer could choose to move from one to another to create their own unique drama — (a truly 'unclosed' text?).

Multi-media

Multi-media is one of the most rapidly growing serious industries in the UK (and beyond), with over 1,000 developers keen to find ways of developing new products. There are varied understandings of what multimedia actually is. The following provides a useful definition:

> *Multi-media can be understood to mean the combination of* **any two** *of the following elements mediated by a computer: images (still or moving); sound (including music); the written or spoken word; and lastly, in interactive multi-media, some form of determination by the audience or user.*

Lisa Haskel (1996), *Plugged In: Multimedia and the Arts in London,* London Arts Board.

The industry has an increasing global presence, with expanding markets in North America, Europe and the Far East. Sales of multimedia-related hard and software exceeded £7 billion in 1995. It is not surprising that the larger international media companies are investing heavily in developments. Training for producers in interactive multi-media is also a key priority of Europe's MEDIA II training strand, in an attempt to stimulate the creation of new markets and new productions in Europe.

Multi-media employers follow a largely similar pattern to the UK independent production sector, with large numbers of small organisations employing freelancers on short-term contracts, and a few larger companies, most of which are well-established media organisations seeking to use the medium to 'repurpose' existing products.

With the requirements of multi-media products to use the whole gamut of communication tools (moving image, audio, etc.), there is likely to be a more rosy future for multi-skilled people to work in the area of multi-media production.

Interactive television

Some cable operators currently run interactive services, such as Videotron's interactive channel which broadcasts three parallel signals simultaneously, enabling the viewer to select which signal to watch by a control panel — for example, if a concert is being

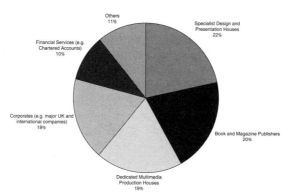

Fig 8.17 Types of Organisation employing multimedia staff. Source: Skillset

transmitted, viewers might have the choice of selecting between a close-up of the drummer, a long shot of the whole band and a close-up of the lead singer — in effect, vision mixing their own version of the performance. Recent research suggests that interactive television is likely to include a range of services, from home shopping to local services, to live sports, new movies, adult entertainment and specialist interests like theatre, travel and so on.

8.4 INVESTIGATE EMPLOYMENT IN THE UK MEDIA INDUSTRIES

The range of jobs in the media is vast and increasing with the advent of multi-media. In each sector some will be involved with making the product, others will distribute it, while yet shares will persuade us that we want it and companies that they should advertise. It is not possible to detail every type of work in this chapter and so, if there is a particular area that you are interested in, you will need to carry out further research. You will find many of the functions of the various media industries described in the various units (like roles within the production process, etc.). This unit will focus on some of the more general employment issues, and provide an insight into some of the jobs in the media through mini-interviews with people working in a selection of roles.

Origination of material — insights into the life of the writer and illustrator

Writers are responsible for producing the raw material of media products. In print and broadcast media, journalists will either be staff or freelance, undertaking commissions for one or a range of publications. Sometimes a journalist will offer material to publishers in the hope that they will be interested. In television, the BBC and those ITV companies which are still major producers employ journalists and staff writers, but most are freelance. New skills are rapidly developing in multi-media, where a non-linear approach to the construction of texts is required.

CASE STUDY

Helen Wright, writer

I left university in 1984 with a degree in Drama and English, and started working in film production. Over the next eight years, I assisted with the production and editing of pop promos, animation for commercials, model building, programme research and finally trained as a film editor and worked as an editor at the BBC. I also made an independent film on Super 8 with three friends.

In 1991, I started work on a 6 × 1-hour comedy drama series which I co-wrote with another woman. We produced a proposal and first episode on 'spec' (for no money), then the BBC commissioned the work in 1993 and we spent a year writing it. Since then we have been commissioned to write a film for BBC and a pilot for a long running series for ITV. We are currently submitting new ideas to broadcasters both together and independently, and have been commissioned to write a novel each.

There are two modes for a writer. One is thinking up and researching new ideas, and the other is actually writing scripts or manuscripts.

Typical day — research

9.30 am Visit the library and get books on chosen subject.

11 am. Read the newspapers — is anything pertinent to current work? (This also puts off having to do any actual work.) Also check the day's television listings. Are there any programmes which may help with research? Morning chat shows and imported American chat shows often cover controversial subjects and give useful insight into people. They are also riveting television.

Afternoon. Read books and use information to develop storylines and characters. (Try to keep away from the fridge, mending a bicycle puncture or re-arranging my sock drawer. Any job looks more attractive than actually getting down to work.)

Evening. Watch anything on telly which might be useful (I can persuade myself that anything is useful for research).

Typical day — writing

9.30 am–5.30 pm. Write. Nothing else counts as work. Get at least three pages written by the end of each day, and if I haven't done three pages by 5.30 pm, then work in the evening until they are done. If an insurmountable problem arises, than move on to a section I feel happy about writing or go back to square one — am I being truthful to the character? Is the scene necessary to push the plot forward?

Tips

Believe in what you write. **Perseverance** — it will take years to become an established writer. Never hand in anything you feel is less than brilliant and keep away from the fridge.

See interview with Eamon McCabe Unit 3

At the same time illustrations might be commissioned, perhaps photographs to illustrate the story which will go to a picture editor on a large newspaper. The picture editor will decide which photo to use and how to crop it or scale it to fit. A graphic artist might prepare maps or charts.

In magazines there will be an art department that is responsible for the 'look' of the product and who will commission illustrators when needed. The publisher of a book will also be using illustrators to produce cartoons or drawings. Printed materials, whether in book form, pamphlet or as part of an exhibition, will use a designer to give the product a look, and combine images, text and graphics effectively.

GLC — Greater London Council
GLA — Greater London Arts

CASE STUDY

Litza Jansz — illustrator

From childhood I always loved drawing and would take any opportunity to develop and exhibit my work. I would design posters for charity events, publicity for friends' gigs and cartoons for amateur magazines. When it came to deciding on a college course, I was split — I wanted to do an academic degree but I also wanted to develop my visual skills. Taking time out, I worked for an advertising agency as a 'girl Friday' and after showing them my portfolio (at the time I kept my pictures in a black bin bag!), they got me to design their in-house publicity.

My portfolio, by now, was building up and it proved invaluable in gaining me a place on the Communications Studies degree course at Goldsmiths College. The course suited me as it introduced me to film, video, photography, animation and graphics while making me think about and apply theories of ideology, politics and culture. While at college, I made crucial contacts with other like-minded colleagues and staff. At college you have an opportunity for people to see your work and the way you work, the way you think through ideas and relate to others.

It was the heady days of the early 1980s — the days of the **GLC**, **GLA**, early Channel 4 and feminist activism. Representation affected people's lived experiences and through representation we were all set to change the world.

I formed a production company (Pictures of Women) with colleagues from Goldsmiths and we were one of the first groups to be commissioned by Channel 4's "Eleventh Hour" to produce a series called *The Sexuality Series*. Through producing programmes, I developed skills in TV graphics and film animation, picking up practical skills from other women in the field. Working on independent production means long periods of time between presenting ideas and gaining commissions. In that time, I was able to continue illustrating and co-wrote and illustrated a feminist children's book which became the launch title for Pandora Press. Through this book I was commissioned to work on a sequel. The pictures I produced, although intended for a published book, also doubled as a storyboard for an animated film project developed by Channel 4.

As the TV work became more fraught, with the drop in commissions from Channel 4 and the lack of commitments to experimental/political work, I found myself focusing more on illustration and cartoons. I have recently been engaged in producing cartoons for books projects that interest me (like this one) and graphic novels. I currently work on the 'For Beginners Series' which are illustrated adults books which use cartoons and illustrations to make complex ideas on culture, history and society accessible and pleasurable. My background in using images to convey complex theoretical debates and my knowledge of media has helped me in my current work.

My career has not been linear — it's not a case of starting at the bottom and working to the top. My work life has been project-orientated where you develop the skills demanded by the project. Every time a project is rejected, I question my career and wish that I'd been a dentist or an accountant. The freelance life is extremely insecure. When a project comes to fruition it's more than a job, it gives you a voice in the world — it's a good feeling!

The important thing is to keep producing. Even if the project is not finally produced or published, the work you did is never wasted. It adds to your portfolio, it informs other projects and it helps to develop contacts. Producing work, paid or unpaid moves you forward.

Film and television

The television and film industries probably cover the widest range of different skills and trades. In production alone, there could be a need for animators, costume designers, graphic artists for visual effects, title sequences or captions, lighting designers, runners, editors, journalists, make-up artists, hairdressers, engineers, set constructors and prop makers, painters, special effects designers and writers.

The size of crew on a single camera shoot is becoming smaller. It is now normally a presenter/reporter/director, a sound operator and a camera operator. Some equipment does away with the need for a sound operator, and the reporter holds his or her own microphone. A crew of this size would normally service news. However, programmes like *The Bill* are mainly shot using a small single camera crew with a director.

Working in the studio involves a larger number of people, the director is in charge. It is important to note that the producer is mainly responsible for finance and administration to enable a programme to happen, the director deals with the content.

A lighting technician is needed and there will also be a vision supervisor who ensures that the technical quality of the picture is up to standard. The programme will often be recorded and then the director works with an editor to make the finished product. The whole process is dependent on engineers, who are responsible for the smooth technical operation of the production process.

CASE STUDY

Natasha Dack, Freelance Producer

I studied for a degree in Modern Languages at Edinburgh University, but spent most of my time there either watching films at the local cinema or stage-managing plays. I'd always wanted to work in the film industry but heard that it was incredibly difficult to get work unless you were related to someone already in the industry or were prepared to start at the bottom and work your way up. As the nearest any of my relatives has come to the film industry is an auntie who lives near Shepperton Studios, I had to go for the latter option, and spent the summer after graduating working as a runner for various commercials companies which mainly involved making cups of tea, picking up the director's dry-cleaning and taking the producer's dog for a walk. I then managed to get a job as a freelance commercials producer's assistant. A year and a half later, I was beginning to get fed up with working on commercials for shampoo and building societies, and looked for a job in drama production. After working as a production assistant on a Channel 4 film, I realised that what I really wanted to do was to produce films and work with people my age on the sort of films that I wanted to see, so I applied to the Royal College of Art Film School and got on to the producers course (they take on eight trainee producers, directors and designers, and two camera and sound trainees every two years).

Being at film school not only increased any practical knowledge of film-making but also provided me with the opportunity to make contacts with commissioning editors at

BBC and Channel 4, established film and television producers, script editors, agents and film exhibitors and distributors. I also learnt about the legal and business aspects involved. I got the chance to produce five short films which have won awards and been shown on television, at film festivals all over the world, and two of them were even shown in the cinema as shorts, supporting features. However, I think the most important thing I gained from my time at the RCA was self-confidence.

Since leaving the RCA a year ago, I've set up a small production company, Pomegranate Pictures, with another ex-RCA student producer. Our long-term aim is to produce a feature film, but for the time being we're concentrating on working with new writers and directors, developing drama scripts and ideas for documentaries. To date we've received funding from Channel 4, the Arts Council, the London Production Fund, North West Arts and the Lottery, and produced various short films, corporate videos and pop promos.

I see myself as a creative producer, which means that not only am I responsible for the financial side of things — raising money, doing deals and keeping the budget — but also that I have creative input into the film, from discussions about the script to decisions about locations, casting and key crew members. Ultimately when all these things have been decided upon it is my job to support the director and his/her vision of the film and to ensure that it gets made.

Obviously there will be a camera operator for each camera (except in a news studio where they may be remotely operated). The floor manager relays the director's instructions and comments (at times suitably edited!) to the people on the studio floor. There will usually be sound assistants on the floor and a supervisor in a control booth.

CASE STUDY

INTERVIEW

Alexandra Sage, Filmmaker/Consultant, specialism: sound

T.J.:   What inspired you to enter the field of sound?

A.S.:   I was working at the Arts Council of England on experimental and independent film and video and became fascinated by the fact that people paid little attention to the sound-track — it seemed to be a thoroughly neglected area. By sound, I don't solely mean music — it includes a whole range of sync sound and SFX as well. I really believe that developing a sophisticated sound-track is a relatively easy way of raising your production values. If a film has a rough sound-track, you get an impression of low quality and it's really easy to avoid, relatively simple and cheap. I thought I could have an effect by learning how to record and dub sound, and I think it makes a massive contribution to the impact of a production, working in parallel with the images.

That was one reason. The other reason was that I wanted to be able to work as part of a two-person crew (at the time, I wanted to make 'non-interventionist' documentaries and needed either camera or sound skills (in fact, the kinds of documentaries I want to make now are somewhere between the non-interventionist and more controlled style). Also, sound is one of the least "popular" skill areas (although the balance might have shifted a bit now), so you're likely to be able to work, whereas there is more competition for jobs if you are a camera operator or camera assistant. Most people I know in sound work regularly.

T.J.: You clearly didn't enter the field straight from school or college. Could you describe the steps you took to change career direction?

A.S.: At the Arts Council, I was working in a production management/administration position. Sometimes I worked on very low budget films doing very simple sound recording, so I had some basic skills. I then applied to the Northern Film School in Leeds to do sound. The NFS is run on the same lines as the National Film School, i.e., it recruits people according to the specialisms they want to follow and combine them as crews, to learn the skills on productions throughout the course. People who follow this route tend to be older — I was 27 at that time. I trained for a year and returned to London, spending a year in an almost full-time job at the Tate Gallery (this wasn't sound — it was to pay off debts) and doing bits of freelance sound recording. That strategy enabled me to begin to build up a network of contacts without making myself financially precarious — very important when you're a freelancer. I then went freelance and got myself a diary service.

A diary service is very important when you're freelance. It's slightly different from an agent. I pay mine about £58 per month and for that, she gets me work to fit in around the various contracts I'm working on. You have to prove your credibility to get a diary service — their reputation depends on you — so usually you need to get a recommendation from an established professional. This service got me most of my work last year.

T.J.: What aspects of sound do you like best?

A.S.: I've done lots of sound editing as well as recording. In sound recording I like working on documentaries, where the crew is quite close-knit and documentaries are observational rather than formal. *Who* you work with — obviously you have to be able to get on with anyone and everyone, and work as a team, but if you like the people too, that's a real bonus because you spend a huge amount of intensive (and intense) time when you're on a shoot.

I also record news features, like concerts at the Jazz Cafe, for instance — I like that kind of work too. In terms of editing, from a creative point of view, sound editing on drama is more challenging — there is more scope for 'surrealism' and manipulation, whereas documentaries usually require an accurate picture of what was actually there.

T.J.: What range of programmes do you work on?

A.S.: I haven't really done much drama. I've focused on documentary because I love the genre. I've done TV and factual programming/documentaries ranging from news to hour-long BBC programmes like *QED Horizon* and programmes for the World Service. I was dubbing editor on a Channel 4 series about the FBI. I also work on corporates.

T.J.: What would you say is a typical working pattern on a shoot?

A.S.: There isn't a typical working pattern — every situation is different. With *QED*, for example, it was shot over ten days. The schedule was put together at the last minutes, so I had to be very flexible. Working in this industry, you have to be able to rearrange your life at the drop of a hat. On that particular shoot, the hours were long, meeting at 7 am and finishing at 8 pm. You have a shot list for each day — interviews, or other shots linked with the story. Normally you meet and drive together to a location, film, then pack up and move on to the next location — there might be several in one day. It can get very pressurised and intensive. There is both lots of waiting around as shots are being prepared, then when you're actually recording, it must be done quickly. In one day, I might do two simple interviews, then a meeting in a large room with ten people talking, which demands a high level of skill. Your whole range of skills are called upon all the time and you need to deal with every situation efficiently.

T.J.: What would be your advice to aspiring sound recordists?

A.S.: You have to be able to understand technically the way equipment behaves and have a 'good ear'. You must be calm, organised and flexible. You meet many different people every day and the job can be very demanding, impacting on everything else in your life — family, friends, social life. If you are a creature of habit, you would hate this work. But most important of all: you have to love filmmaking.

BROADCAST ENGINEERING

'Get Trained in Engineering,' *Television Buyer* Supplement, April 1996.

... *whether placing healing hands on broken equipment or soothing technophobic nerves, engineers can reassure harassed production staff just with their very presence. For many engineers this is the appeal of the job, as well as the satisfaction of getting to grips with a range of broadcast systems — not only working out how systems function, but how to fix them and modify them to suit production requirements.*

The interest for most engineers is in problem-solving, otherwise you're an operator, says Joan Leese, Director of London-based training, maintenance and facilities company, Video Engineering & Training (VET). 'That can mean problem-solving in a mechanical way, in a systems way or in a digital environment where you really do need to understand computers fully.

Joan Leese came to engineering later in her working life, having started out as a social worker who used video and photography as a tool in youth and community work. The potential of the media caught her interest and she went on to a Communications and sociology degree at Goldsmiths College, University of London.

VET was set up in 1986 with support from the Greater London Council, Greater London Arts, Channel 4 and the British Film Institute to provide 'infrastructural support to the independent film and video sector to facilitate it to explore new and progressive social and artistic uses of the audio-visual media'. Since then it has been developing and delivering high quality training both for independent filmmakers and the industry.

CASE STUDY

Joan Leese, Director of Video Engineering and Training

One problem for me was that I couldn't actually recognise the skills that I already had because I had picked them up informally. I continued to do more community video work, but decided to try and develop my craft skills because I'm not really so much of an ideas person. The route I chose was technical, starting by doing City and Guilds 224 Part 1 (radio/TV services) on a day-release basis at a local college.

I was the only woman doing the City and Guilds course and most of the lads were on day-release from employment — they all had more practical experience: I was picking up a soldering iron for the first time! When I finished the course, I was offered a job as a lab technician at the college.

I realised that I needed to go further and follow a dedicated engineering training, but I'd already done a degree and needed to find a way to finance myself through another course. In fact, I was lucky, as the Greater London Council was still in existence and supported me with a grant. It also happened to be Women into Science and Engineering year, which helped my argument. I went to Ravensbourne College of Art and Design to do BTEC HND in Engineering for Broadcast Television.

At Ravensbourne I had a tricky time at interview, where I was asked to undertake a range of tasks that I would have found impossible without the foundation of the City and Guilds course. The interviewers tried to persuade me to do A level maths or physics for a year. I did not want to do this and — probably because I was a mature student — I was offered a place with the proviso that I would have to address my own shortcomings in my lack of maths background.

Ravensbourne was one of the hardest experiences I've ever put myself through. I also felt an enormous responsibility as a woman, not wanting to allow myself to fail. On the first day, I found myself in a classroom with loads of 18 year old boys: I was ten years older! Then a woman walked in, dressed in black leather and a pink Mohican and we ended up becoming very good friends!

Most people had done A level maths and physics, so I had to top up with Level three maths at college. I had to get private tuition to help me get levels 3 and 4, and work two nights a week to pay for it.

After graduation I was hired by the BBC as a direct entry engineer to news and current affairs at Television Centre in London. I was the first woman direct intake engineer — other women were taken on as trainees.

Part of my initiation was a six-week block at Engineering Residential Training at BBC Wood Norton — this was interesting, challenging . . . and very male.

I became a senior engineer at the BBC, and was acting supervisor when I left.

I left when Video Engineering and Training (VET) obtained funding from the British Film Institute to support women engineers in the independent film and video sector.

I was always committed to this area of work — I went the BBC route to get proper skills.

To do technical jobs in film and television, such as engineering, technical operations, systems maintenance, hardware and software design, although a media course would provide good hands-on experience of the production process, they don't tend to focus on the technical side, so it's necessary to look at additional study in maths and/or physics, and/or computer sciences and skill. There are many more operational and craft skills jobs which do not require so much technical expertise, but it's important to be able to cope with technological change and have technical confidence and the ability to be flexible around equipment.

As for qualities, engineers need to be good problem solvers, work to tight deadlines and under pressure; they need to be flexible, good team players and work in the background — there is no room for ego.

Working in radio

The main functions carried out in radio vary to some extent depending on whether the station or network is BBC or independent and also whether it is national or local.

In the BBC, as with many other organisations, there is an increasing trend towards flatter management structures. In local radio, each station is controlled by a managing editor who, in turn, is responsible to a regional head.

Below this level, there is now a single deputy who has responsibility for both news and programmes. Senior producers normally take control of a part of the week's output or for the news bulletins on a particular day. This has meant that most senior producers work for four long days often over the weekend.

Many presenters will be on freelance contracts and will have little or no responsibility for the content of their shows. Production assistants carry out routine work such as answering phones and editing of material.

In Independent local radio, each station or group of stations will be the responsibility of a Managing Director who will be responsible to a Board of Directors. Working with the Managing Director will be a Programme Controller who will have day-to-day responsibility for output.

CASE STUDY

Claire Cottam, Regional Radio Journalist

I decided I wanted to be a journalist from a very early age, but the opportunity didn't come along right away.

I took A levels in English and sociology and, rather than go on to university, got a job with a local building society I loathed it ... it was so boring! So I gave it up and travelled for a while.

I came back in 1990, in the midst of a recession, and took odd jobs, like bottling in the local Eldridge Pope Brewery, and meanwhile applied for the BBC Local Reporter's course (the only BBC non-degree entry course) but didn't get on it. Meanwhile, a new local radio station was starting up in Dorchester, **BBC Dorset FM**, and they really wanted to recruit local people, with local knowledge and contacts, but who could also show evidence of a longer term commitment to radio. I was in — very much a lucky break! — employed as a PA [Production Assistant]. I never thought I could present, though, but soon I was presenting a three-hour Saturday show.

Regional Radio Journalist Claire Cottam now works for BBC Radio Solent, broadcasting across much of the south coast from Dorset to Sussex.

You really need to be **multi-skilled** in radio: you need an eye and an ear for news — a 'news sense'; you need to be able to conduct an interview well; you need to be technically competent, or a fast learner; and you need to work with people and make yourself indispensable.

The BBC has given me a lot of on-the-job training, and have sent me on core skills courses at **G**rafton House in London, where you not only learn about media law and admin., but actually set up a working radio station, producing programmes with three qualified trainers hanging on your every word — far harder than any real broadcast!

One thing they teach you is that you should always feel you are talking to someone personally — it is a very personal medium — so when I'm presenting, I always try to convince myself that no one's listening except my mum — I'm just talking to her and nobody else!

Being under pressure is the best training you can get!

Bi-media is now the buzz word in all the regional centres, streamlining radio and television journalism — management love it! At Southampton there's a news room with radio studios on one side and television studios on the other, with correspondents in the middle planning, researching and writing for both media. At Bristol and Plymouth they're currently making the most radical changes, training staff into becoming both radio *and* television journalists.

Bi-media is clearly the future for regional broadcast journalism.

As independent stations play a higher proportion of music than BBC local stations, an important post is Head of Music, who will review new releases and determine a playlist often with the aid of a computer. A computer playlist is, of course, only as good as the selection of tracks that it has been given and also the rules that it uses to compile the list. Both selection and rules will be the responsibility of the Head of Music.

DJs may be allowed to play a small amount of music of their own choice (this varies from station to station), but the majority will be from the playlist in a predetermined order. They are unlikely to have assistance in answering phones especially on smaller stations.

An independent station has to sell advertising to survive. The adverts have to deliver for the advertiser. So two important departments are sales and commercial production. The station also has to market itself to both the public and potential advertisers and increasingly sponsors. Many stations now have sponsored weather forecasts or travel information.

Both types of stations employ journalists. A BBC station will have many more to service its speech-based output. Increasingly BBC journalists are trained to be bi-media (multi-skilled) and can therefore cover stories for both radio and television. Network radio and television increasingly see local radio stations as outposts to service their needs.

Employment Patterns in Radio

According to Skillset's radio survey carried out in 1993–94, there were about 3,800 people employed in the radio industry. Of these 2,200 work for the BBC and 1,600 in independent radio. The BBC has been working to reduce the number of people that it employs full time by the introduction of schemes like Producer Choice which works for radio in a similar way to television. The amount of programming for radio made by independent producers has also increased dramatically over the last few years although it still lags some way behind television.

The number of people working on continuing contracts (full-time permanent staff) is 2,600 while those on short-term freelance contracts is 1,200.

The workforce in radio is also shown to be comparatively young with two thirds being aged 34 or less. It is also noteworthy that about a quarter of all jobs were found through word of mouth or from friends or colleagues, especially in the independent sector. Also 19% started off in unpaid voluntary jobs with both the BBC and independent sectors.

Economies in staffing

The general trend in employment is a move to cut full-time numbers with a corresponding increase in short-term contracts or freelance work. The two main reasons for this happening are the change in the structure of the industry and technological advances.

Significant factors include the need for the BBC to reduce its full-time staff to appear more cost effective coupled with the requirement for 25% of television to be made by independent producers. The smaller independent companies cannot afford to have a camera operator sitting around just in case they need one. It is likely that the only full-time staff will be producers and administrators.

Another advantage of employing freelancers is that they, and not the employer, are responsible for sorting out tax and National Insurance. This saves on the employers' administrative time and also saves more money as there is no employer's contribution to National Insurance to pay.

The downside for the camera operator is, of course, that some weeks they may have no work or only work for one day. This can make it quite hard to pay the mortgage (and even harder to obtain one in the first place).

As part of its economies in staffing, the BBC is engaged in cutting the numbers of engineers that work in local radio. Many engineers now travel to cover a number of stations that in the past had two or three people of their own. There is an increasing market in freelance engineers.

Each BBC network is run by a controller and individual programme departments and independent producers will make offers to them. The internal programme departments are now often to be found in the regions to make better use of studio and other facilities. For example, religious programmes come from Manchester, natural history and science from Bristol, arts and education are still in London. The controller decides which offers will best meet his or her needs and commissions work in a similar way to television.

Network programmes are more highly staffed than local radio and will have much more technical and administrative and secretarial back-up.

The economics of new technology

A technological advance like non-linear editing can save a significant amount of time. A complex 30 minute programme is likely to take about ten days to edit on non-linear compared with about six weeks on film. In addition, the assistant editor is no longer needed.

Often the technology means that the skilled person needs to be employed for less time. For example, a graphic designer might simply do a few days to put together a concept that can then be carried through by less skilled operators using sophisticated software.

Working in Multi-media

Multi-media may well be where you use your production skills for a variety of products, which can include anything from interactive games, to educational products, point-of-sales advertising or visitor information at tourist attractions or museums.

Multi-media is all about team working — and the ability to understand the differing needs and backgrounds of colleagues. Computer literacy — and a serious interest in the constant developments in technology give a necessary 'core' of ability, but different jobs will all have specific requirements. Employers regularly complain that good staff are hard to find. There are several reasons for this, including the fact that many organisations want someone who will 'take over' an entire project that they themselves often barely understand. Many college leavers have found themselves swamped by complex projects. If you are to succeed in multi-media, it is worth considering methods of developing these sought after skills:

See Skillset 'Working in **M**ultimedia' for fuller description of job areas

- A broadly based understanding of both design and technology (and an ability to communicate with designers and techies!).

- Flexibility of movement between different software packages. Understanding which is the best 'tool for the job'!

- Social and interpersonal skills, including the ability to 'account manage' clients.

- Project management — planning organisational, financial skills and the ability to lead a team of disparate people.

CASE STUDY

Helen Doherty, Freelance Interactive Multi-media Producer

There are so many career routes into interactive multi-media that guidance which is too specific is unadvisable. The best recommendation is to try out as many skills areas as possible then specialise in what you enjoy and are best at. All key subjects areas are potential contributors: art, mathematics, music, computer science, media studies and more.

Be aware that one of the most important attributes you should have is the ability to work as part of a team which includes people of many disciplines and perspectives. Team work is so vital that I recommend anyone seeking a career in interactive multimedia to study how groups work.

Interactive multi-media is a new medium which draws on traditional media such as photography, video and audio as well as more abstract disciplines such as aesthetics. It is a new medium partly because of the transformations enabled by computer but mostly the difference lies in interactivity.

Films, for example, are linear, the action unfolds from beginning to end. Interactive multi-media is non-linear. The user can break into the time line through interaction to move or not as they choose at each opportunity. The scope of this apparently simple addition of interaction is so vast that people in the industry are still working on the implications. If you like problem solving and conceptual challenges then here is your opportunity to help shape this new medium.

Most people working in the interactive multi-media sector do not have specialist qualifications as it is such a new industry. I came to the field from a background in education, media production and business development and have an MA in Interactive Multi-media. At the time of writing there are a few qualifications and provision is dominated by the higher education sector. As schools and colleges begin to provide this subject, then qualifications in interactive multi-media will become necessary for career development.

In the meantime, read about and use interactive multi-media, try to make work at home or school/college. Remain curious about the future of this new medium whether it becomes your main career or a leisure interest.

Training

The amount of training that is available tends to be rather patchy despite the efforts of organisations such as Skillset, the Industry Training Organisation for Film, Video and Broadcasting, which conducts vital employment research, raises money for training (of freelancers in particular) and which is developing NVQ standards (now also for multi-media).

New Entrants

There is a limited range of industry-recognised new-entrant training schemes. Some are specialist like CYFLE which is for Welsh speakers or the Gaelic Television Training Trust which helps provide quality programmes for Gaelic speakers. ft2 (Film and Television Freelance Training) is a new entrant technical training scheme which has about 32 places per year while the National Film and Television School runs two courses a year. The British Animation Training Scheme offers day-release to enable animators to improve their skills and become assistant directors.

The BBC has a radio training department with its own budget that provides staff training. There are, however, needs identified in the survey for freelancers working for the BBC and in the independent sector. Journalistic skills are becoming increasingly important in the BBC and it is unlikely that anyone without them will progress far up the career ladder. Local radio is increasingly seen as 'on-the-job' training for television and has a very high staff turnover. The recent recruitment by Radio 5 Live of many young journalists has caused a shortage in both BBC and independent local radio. There may well be a promotion log jam in a few years' time when all these journalists are looking for their next career move.

Pre-Entry Training

The Skillset booklet *A Career in Broadcast, Film and Video* offers some useful advice as to questions to ask when selecting a further or higher education course.

Pre-entry training includes the GNVQ course that you are currently studying. There are A level courses in media and other related subjects, such as photography or film studies, offered by a number of exam boards. Many universities offer media courses — some are very theoretical while others are extremely practical. It is important

Siobhan McElaney, deputy editor, "Derry Journal", left, presenting the Domhnall MacDermott Memorial Cup to Peter Nerrigan, for the Best Media Studies student at the North West Institute for Further and Higher Education, and Mr. Colm McCarroll, managing director, presenting the "Derry Journal" Cup for Most Promising New student to Stephen Farren. Back, from left, are Carol Hippsley, Kate O'Halloran, course tutors, Tricia Jenkins, London Film and Video Development Agency, and Faustina Starrett, GNVQ Media co-ordinator. (7/6/C5)

Fig 8.18 Source: Derry Journal, 7 June 1996

to check what is actually being offered when you apply for higher education.

While it is generally recognised that the media industries are largely graduate-entrant, quality courses which develop strong local industry links can enable students to progress to industry schemes or even employment. Some of the interviews in this unit demonstrate this very fact.

The NCTJ and the NCTBJ offer journalist training that can be pre-entry or on a day-release basis. Satisfactory completion of one of their qualifications is often a requirement to work as a journalist.

The Newspaper Society takes a broad interest in local newspaper training and has been responsible for sponsoring a scheme for students known as the Newspaper in Education scheme which links schools and colleges with local newspapers.

No matter what pre-entry training you do at whatever level, there is no guarantee that this will find you employment and you should be suspicious if people try to tell you that a particular course will lead to a job.

National Vocational Qualifications

National Vocational Qualifications are *not* training courses, but national standards of competence which are, as much as possible, assessed on the job on real productions. While a number of further and higher education establishments offer NVQs in journalism, they will always have a very strong work experience element to enable trainees to be assessed in the workplace. In the film, video and broadcast industries, however, further and higher education courses cannot provide you with NVQs, although the underpinning knowledge and experience that you gain by doing a GNVQ or BTEC — or any kind of quality education or training — can be accredited to you towards your NVQ at a later date. Indeed, without the necessary experience to access one of the industry-recognised schemes or work on productions, you would not be in a position to register for a NVQ! Some of the more practically-based higher education courses are beginning to use the NVQ standards to inform their own curriculum and assessment.

Voluntary sector training providers

There is a range of organisations offering support, facilities at subsidised rates and training. Film and video workshops are often funded by a range of sources, including the Regional Arts Board or Media Development Agency. They often have a cultural remit, which involves providing access for traditionally under-represented groups, or for working innovatively and experimentally.

Find out about these through your Regional Arts Board, or through the Skillset/BFI database.

Most of these organisations provide short course training at subsidised rates; some are now working in partnership with further education to provide subsidised practically-based courses.

European funding is another way in which these training providers are able to offer targeted training with proper back-up for trainees — for instance, creche provision for women trainees.

If you are taking a media course or have recently completed one, it is a good idea to supplement your training with specialist skills, or take advantage of cheap equipment to produce your own material independently of a training course. Many workshops are now beginning to accredit their training, identifying exactly the level and value of the skills you will come out with. Increasingly, some are using NVQ standards to inform their technical training curriculum. You can also get yourself on to crew lists for productions being made at workshops, thereby enabling you to get to know a network of people at various levels of experience.

Employer organisations

The main employer organisations in the print industry include the Newspaper Publishers Association — a trade association for national newspaper publishers — and the Newspaper Society that has a similar function for local and regional publishers. The Periodical Publishers Association represents magazine publishers. All of these lobby on their members' behalf, arrange conferences and publish material of mutual interest.

The power of the unions in the print industry has diminished considerably in the last ten years. The National Union of Journalists (NUJ) is the main body representing journalists and you will find the chapel (union branch) is still quite a force to be reckoned with. There are a number of specialist associations — the Football Writers' Association or the Fleet Street Motoring Group — which provide a forum for their specialist concerns.

Employees in broadcast will be represented by the NUJ (journalists), Equity (actors) or BECTU, Broadcasting, Entertainment, Cinematograph and Theatre Union (non-performing staff). Each negotiates terms and conditions and pay rates for its members.

Independent television producers are represented by PACT (Producers Alliance for Cinema and TV) which produces a wide range of guidance and advice together with a regular magazine. Corporate video producers join together in the International Visual Communications Association which provides similar services.

The two main employer bodies in independent radio are Commercial Radio Companies Association (CRCA) and Independent Association of Radio Producers (IARP).

CRCA is an organisation that represents the interests of the companies that own and operate radio stations. They meet together to discuss common issues and are involved in negotiations with government and other bodies.

IARP is a group of independent producers that represents the interests of the growing number of producers who make programmes for the BBC and independent radio. It runs regular

BECTU
BROADCASTING
ENTERTAINMENT
CINEMATOGRAPH &
THEATRE UNION

STUDENT LINK-UP

A NEW
SERVICE WHICH PUTS
MEDIA AND ARTS STUDENTS
WHERE THEY WANT TO BE.
**IN TOUCH
WITH THE INDUSTRY.**

Fig 8.19   BECTU Student Link-Up is a new service for media and arts students on vocational cources in broadcasting, film and theatre. For £10 per year, students can receive the BECTU journal (10 months per year), *Stage, Screen and Radio*, and learn about highspots and hazards of careers in the cultural sector from people who are actually working. Contact: BECTU, 111 Wardour St, London W1E 6JZ

seminars and events for its members and provides help and support as well negotiating on general issues.

A freelance world — be prepared

As the industry continues to fragment, it is clear that freelance work will be the main employment model for media workers. Already, over 60% of people *beginning* their careers start out as freelancers. This means that you will need to have determination, staying power, the ability to work flexibly, at short notice and at anti-social hours. You will need to familiarise yourself with organising your own tax and insurance, and pension contributions. You will need to keep your own financial situation in order. You will need to find ways of seeking employment, which often means that, to start with, you may find yourself working for very low rates or for free to gain that all-too-important credit on a production.

The contributors to this book wish you the best of luck if you decide to pursue a career in the media!

BIBLIOGRAPHY

Alvarado, M. *et al* (1987) *Learning the Media*, Macmillan Education

Ang, I. (1986) *Watching Dallas: Soap Opera and the Melodramatic Imagination*, Methuen

Baehr, H and Ryan, M. (1984) *Shut up and Listen!* Comedia/Campaign for Press and Broadcasting Freedom

Barthes, Roland (1977) *Image-Music-Text* (essays selected and translated by Stephen Heath) Fontana/Collins

Branston, G. and Stafford, R. (1996) *The Media Student's Book*, Routledge

Brunsdon, C. and Morley D. (1979) *Everyday Television: Nationwide*, BFI

Connel, I. (1984) in *Television Mythologies: Stars, Shows and Signs* by L. Masterman (ed) Comedia/MK Media Press

Davis, A. (1988) *Magazine Journalism Today*, Butterworth-Heinemann

Dyer, R. (1979) *The Dumb Blond Stereotype*, BFI

Fiske, J. (1982) *Introduction to Communication Studies*, Methuen

Galtang J. and Ruge M. (1965) 'The structure of foreign news'. *Journal of International Peace Research*

Giles, V. and Hodgson, F. W. (1990) *Creative Newspaper Design*, Butterworth-Heinemann

Gordon, P. and Rosenberg, D. (1989) *Daily Facism*, Runnymede Trust

Hall, S. *et al* (eds) (1980) *Culture, Media, Language*, Hutchinson

Haske, L. (1996) *Plugged in: Multimedia and the Arts in London*, London Arts Board

Kent, R. (ed) (1994) *Measuring Media Audiences*, Routledge

Masterman, L. (ed) (1984) *Television Mythologies, Stars, Shows and Signs*, Comedia/MK Media Press

McQuail, D. (1969) *Towards a Sociology of Mass Communications*, Macmillan

Morley, D. (1986) *Family Television: Cultural Power and Domestic Leisure*, Comedia

Morley, D. (1980) *The Nationwide Audience*, BFI

O'Sullivan, T. *et al* (1983) *Key Concepts in Communication*, Methuen

O'Sullivan, T. *et al* (1994) *Studying the Media*, Edward Arnold

Root, J. (1986) *Open The Box*, Comedia

Skillset (1994) *Employment Patterns and Training Needs*, Skillset

Strinati D. and Wagg S. (eds) (1992) *Popular Media Culture*, Routledge

RELATED TITLES FROM FOCAL PRESS

Basics of ... Series
The Basics of Video Production
The Basics of Video Lighting
The Basics of Video Sound

Media Manual Series (a selection of titles)
16mm Film Cutting
Basic Betacam Camerawork
Basic TV Reporting
Continuity Handbook for Single Camera Shooting
Creating Special Effects for TV and Video
Effective TV Production
Grammar of the Edit
Grammar of the Shot
Lighting for Video
Local Radio Journalism
Multicamera Camerawork
Single Camera Video Production
Use of Microphones
Video Camera Techniques
Video Studio

Other titles
Audio Explained
Basic Photography
Broadcast Journalism
Broadcast Sound Technology
Directing the Documentary
Effective Audio Visual
Electronic Imaging for Photographers
Encyclopedia of Animation Techniques
Essential Director's Handbook
Essential Television Handbook
Film Directing: Shot by Shot
Film Production
Graphic Design for Television

International Dictionary of Broadcasting and Film
International Libel Handbook
Law and the Media
Modern Newspaper Practice
Photojournalism
Pinhole Photography
Practical Director
Production Management for Film and Video
Production Research
Radio Production
Sound and Recording: An Introduction
Sound Assistance
Starting Photography
Television News
TV Scenic Design
Video Editing
Video Production Handbook
Videojournalism

For a free Focal Press catalogue listing over 400 titles, or to obtain inspection copies of Focal Press books, contact Claire Johns, Customer Services Department, Butterworth-Heinemann, Linacre House Jordan Hill, Oxford OX2 8DP or telephone 01865 314080.

INDEX